Presidential Campaigns and Elections

PRESIDENTIAL CAMPAIGNS AND ELECTIONS

Issues and Images in the Media Age

Second Edition

MYRON A. LEVINE

Albion College

F.E. PEACOCK PUBLISHERS, INC   **Itasca, Illinois**

ILLUSTRATION CREDITS

Table 3.1, From Herbert F. Weisberg with David C. Kimball, "The 1992 Presidential Election: Party Identification and Beyond," paper presented at the 1993 American Political Science Meeting in Washington, D.C. Reprinted by permission of the author./Figure 3.2, Reprinted by permission of the publishers from THE DECLINE OF AMERICAN POLITICAL PARTIES: 1952–1980 (p. 97) by Martin P. Wattenberg. Cambridge, MA: Harvard University Press, Copyright © 1984, 1986, 1990, by the President and Fellows of Harvard College./Figure3.3, Reprinted from THE ELECTORAL ORIGINS OF DIVIDED GOVERNMENT (p. 11) by Gary C. Jacobson, 1990, by permission of Westview Press, Boulder, CO./Figure 4.1, From PRESIDENTIAL PRIMARIES AND NOMINATIONS (p. 118) by William Crotty and John S. Jackson, published in 1985 by Congressional Quarterly. Reprinted by permission of the author, John S. Jackson./Table 4.2, Copyright © 1974 from THE POLITICS OF REPRESENTATION (p. 32) by Denis G. Sullivan et al. Reprinted by permission of St. Martin's Press, Inc./Table 4.3, From PRESIDENTIAL PRIMARIES AND NOMINATIONS (p. 63) by William Crotty and John S. Jackson, published in 1985 by Congressional Quarterly. Reprinted by permission of the author, John S. Jackson./Table 4.4, From "Yes—The Nominating Process Is Representative," by John S. Jackson III, in Gary L. Rose, ed., CONTROVERSIAL ISSUES IN PRESIDENTIAL SELECTION. Copyright © 1991 by State University of New York Press. Reprinted by permission of the publisher./Table 4.5, From FINANCING THE 1988 ELECTION (p. 41) by Herbert E. Alexander and Monica Bauer. © Citizen's Research Foundation. Reprinted by permission./Figure 5.1, From Philip E. Converse, "The Nature of Belief Systems In Mass Publics," in David Apter, ed., IDEOLOGY AND DISCONTENT, published by Free Press in 1964. Reprinted by permission of the author./Table 5.1, From THE AMERICAN VOTER (p. 144) by Angus Campbell et al., published in 1964 by John Wiley and Sons. Reprinted by permission of the authors./Table 5.2, From VOTERS' CHOICE (p. 172) by Gerald Pomper, published in 1975 by Dodd, Mead. Reprinted by permission of the author./Table 5.3, From "From Confusion to Confusion: Issues and Voters, 1952–1972," *American Political Science Review* 71 (March 1977), pp. 31–43. Reprinted by permission of the American Political Science Association and the author./Table 5.4, From Philip E. Converse, "The Nature of Belief Systems In Mass Publics," in David Apter, ed., IDEOLOGY AND DISCONTENT, published by Free Press in 1964. Reprinted by permission of the author./Figure 5.2, Reprinted by permission of the publishers from THE CHANGING AMERICAN VOTER (p. 129) by Norman H. Nie, Sidney Verba, and John R. Petrocik. Cambridge, MA: Harvard University Press, Copyright © 1976 and 1979, by the President and Fellows of Harvard College./Figure 5.3, Reprinted by permission of the publishers from THE CHANGING AMERICAN VOTER (p. 165) by Norman H. Nie, Sidney Verba, and John R. Petrocik. Cambridge, MA: Harvard University Press, Copyright © 1976 and 1979, by the President and Fellows of Harvard College./Figure 5.4, Reprinted by permission of the publishers from THE CHANGING AMERICAN VOTER (p. 167) by Norman H. Nie, Sidney Verba, and John R. Petrocik. Cambridge, MA: Harvard University Press, Copyright © 1976 and 1979, by the President and Fellows of Harvard College./Table 5.5, From "Plus ça change..." by Philip E. Converse and Gregory B. Markus, *American Political Science Review* 73 (March 1979), pp. 40–41. Reprinted by permission of the American Political Science Association and the authors./Table 8.1, Reprinted from TRANSFORMATIONS OF THE AMERICAN PARTY SYSTEM, Second Edition (p. 289), by Everett Carll Ladd and Charles D. Hadley, with the permission of W. W. Norton & Company, Inc. Copyright © 1978, 1975 by W. W. Norton & Company, Inc./Table 8.2, From "The Majority Party Reunited? A Comparison of the 1972 and 1976 Elections," by Arthur H. Miller, in *Parties and Elections in an Anti-Party Age*, ed. Jeff Fishel (p. 129). Copyright © 1978 by Indiana University Press, Bloomington, Indiana. Reprinted by permission of the publisher./Table 8.3, From "The Majority Party Reunited? A Comparison of the 1972 and 1976 Elections," by Arthur H. Miller, in *Parties and Elections in an Anti-Party Age*, ed. Jeff Fishel (p.132). Copyright © 1978 by Indiana University Press, Bloomington, Indiana. Reprinted by permission of the publisher./Table 8.4, From "Public Opinion Trends," by Kathleen A. Frankovic (p. 100), in Gerald Pomper, ed., THE ELECTION OF 1980, Copyright © 1981 by Chatham House Publishers. Reprinted by permission of the publisher./Table 8.5, From "Public Opinion Trends," by Kathleen A. Frankovic (p. 114), in Gerald Pomper, ed., THE ELECTION OF 1980, Copyright © 1981 by the Chatham House publishers, Reprinted by permission of the publisher./Table 8.6 From "Political Attitudes During An Election Year: A Report on the 1980 NES Panel Study," by Gregory B. Markus, *American Political Science Review* 76 (Sept. 1982), p. 543. Reprinted by permission of the American Political Science Association and the author./Table 8.7 From "Political Attitudes During An Election Year: A Report on the 1980 NES Panel Study," by Gregory B. Markus, *American Political Science Review* 76 (Sept. 1982). Reprinted by permission of the American Political Science Association and the author./Table 8.8, From "Political Attitudes During an Election Year: A Report on the 1980 NES Panel Study," By Gregory B. Markus, *American Political Science Review* 76 (Sept. 1982). P. 544 Reprinted by permission of the American Political Science Association and the author./Figure 9.1, From "Public Opinion in 1984," by Scott Keeter (p. 94), in Gerald Pomper. ed., THE ELECTION OF 1984: REPORTS AND INTERPRETATIONS, Copyright © 1985 by Chatham House Publishers. Reprinted by permission of the publisher./Figure 9.2, From THE PERSONAL PRESIDENT: POWER INVESTED, PROMISE UNFULFILLED, by Theodore J. Lowi (p.18). Copyright © 1985 by publisher, Cornell University Press.Used by permission of the publisher, Cornell University Press./Table 11.1, From the "The 1992 Vote for President Clinton: Another Brittle Mandate?" by Everett Carll Ladd, *Political Science Quarterly* 108, 1 (1993), p. 3. Reprinted by permission of *Political Science Quarterly*.

Copyright ©1995, 1992 F.E. Peacock Publishers, Inc.
All rights reserved
Library of Congress Catalog Card No. 94–069683
ISBN 0–87581–394–1
Printed in the United States of America
Printing: 10 9 8 7 6 5 4 3 2 1
Year: 99 98 97 96 95

To my father, David Levine,
for his love, hard work, sacrifice,
and faith in the abilities of his children.

CONTENTS

FIGURES and TABLES

FIGURES

TABLES

POLITICAL ADS

PREFACE

Does American democracy work in the age of television? Can Americans use elections to hold their government accountable? Are Americans offered a choice at the polls based on manufactured personal images or one based on more substantive policy concerns?

This book is written in the tradition of V.O. Key: Voters are not fools. Issues count in presidential elections. While there is still great disagreement regarding the sophistication of the American voter and how, exactly, issues are incorporated in the voting decision, there is a virtual consensus in the more recent voting behavior literature that issues do influence presidential voting. However voters may vary in their sophistication, they are nonetheless capable of choosing presidential candidates they prefer on key issues.

Yet, despite the evidence, journalists, political pundits, and filmmakers often argue the exact opposite point of view—that elections fail as an instrument of democratic choice and accountability. Indeed, there is a strong belief, in the American popular culture, that issues do not count in the presidential race, that politics has been stolen from the people by a cadre of professional image-makers, pollsters, and spin doctors.

How can the existence of this popular belief be explained despite the volume of political science evidence to the contrary? In part, the failure lies with a political science literature that has become so methodologically complex that it is often understood only by persons narrowly trained in the field. Recent writing may point to the importance of issues in the presidential decision, but the evidence is so quantitative and dense that it has not permeated popular discussion. In this book I have sought to "translate" this evidence, to take the findings of complex voting studies and make them accessible to a broader public.

But this book does more than simply present a summary of voting studies which, in their statistics, fail to capture the dialogue, content, drama, and nuance of presidential elections. In studying American elections, it is important to look at individual races and analyze what candidates say, not just how voters respond. No analyst can fully assess the mix of issues, candidate images, and partisanship in the presidential race without first reviewing the specific events and dialogue of a particular election. In the later chapters of this book we will review recent presidential elections with special attention to the televised campaign—that part of the presidential campaign that most Americans see. We will analyze political advertisements for the content of their messages. (Transcriptions of many political spots are included in the text.) Such a review should help dispel the popular misperception that presidential campaigns are won solely by the actions of professional image wizards.

This book contains an in-depth look at contemporary presidential elections with a focus on political advertising, inasmuch as the advertising contains the messages that are presented to the American voter. While personal image-building remains an important part of the presidential campaign, issues, too, are an important part of the campaign dialogue. Political advertising is not as issueless or irrelevant as is commonly assumed. In fact, the issues are often in the ads, and frequently the most effective images in a presidential campaign are those that are issue-based, not personality-based. Presidential campaigns are won on substance as well as on images of a candidate's personal leadership abilities.

American presidential campaigns and voting behavior seldom meet the strictest tests for prospective issue voting. The major candidates rarely offer a clear choice of detailed, workable policy solutions on issues of importance to voters. Still, to note the imperfections of campaign dialogue is not to conclude that issues have been excluded from the presidential race. Far from it. Whatever the shortcomings of the televised campaign, voters are still presented with messages that allow them to distinguish meaningfully between the candidates.

In a presidential year, media messages regarding the presidential race are so pervasive that voters cannot help but learn something of substance about the candidates. Voters cannot totally shut out news reports and competing paid messages. Voters also possess a great deal of political information that they acquire through their daily lives. They know substantially more about the presidential race than they do about races for less visible offices.

Voters often cast their ballots retrospectively—on whether they want the incumbent party or president to continue in office or if they prefer a change. They can also distinguish differences in the broad, general policy directions offered by the major presidential candidates. Voters can discern the differences between the candidates on certain key or salient easy-to-understand (as opposed to more complex) issues. Video-literate Americans "reason" as they filter media messages. They understand the exaggerated nature of paid political claims. They also use their own personal experiences and their perception of national economic conditions to help them to evaluate the competing claims of presidential contenders.

In part, the decay of political parties and the post-1968 reforms in the presidential nominating process have allowed issues—as well as personal images—to play a new role in the presidential race. The presidential nominating process is no longer controlled by party leaders or "bosses." In the general election, a party's presidential nominee can no longer rely on party identification or strong political party organizations to turn out a winning vote in November. Instead, we have entered the era of the candidate-centered campaign where a presidential aspirant must forge his or her own relationship directly with voters. Oftentimes this is done through televised image-making, But the reformed nominating process has also given a new prominence to active interest groups and issue constituencies. In assembling a winning coalition, the presidential hopeful will often take a stance on issues to appeal to large blocks of voters.

While issues play a greater role in presidential elections than the critics of televised democracy admit, still, all is not well with the electoral process. The post-Watergate system of public funding was an attempt to remove the role of money from the presidential race. Under the reformed campaign finance rules, the nominees of the two major parties were to spend approximately the same amount in their pursuit of office; they would owe little to special interests. Voter choice was not to be contaminated by imbalances in campaign spending. Over the years, however, a variety of provisions or loopholes in the campaign finance laws have allowed private money to reenter the presidential race. The emergence of precandidacy campaign PACs (political action committees), "soft money," and independent spending by unaffiliated PACs are important and troubling features of the modern presidential campaign.

A second and more troubling problem concerns the nature of modern campaign discourse. While political attacks have always been a part of the American presidential campaign, in recent years negative advertising has reached new heights. In the shallow and bitter political exchanges that marred the 1994 midterm elections, perhaps the nastiest in American history, House and Senate candidates rarely discussed substantive issues or offered policy solutions. Instead, candidates simply promised that they were not part of the mess in Washington and attacked the personal qualities and private business dealings of their opponents. The vitriol of the U.S. Senate race in Virginia, where Democrat Chuck Robb and Republican Ollie North characterized each other as an immoral liar, was perhaps the worst in what was a bad year for quality campaign dialogue nationwide.

Yet, even in the midst of the mudslinging of 1994, substantive concerns were part of the voting decision and the GOP tidal wave that swept the nation. The Republicans won a majority in both houses of Congress (taking control of the House for the first time since the 1952 election!) by picking up 8 new Senate seats and 53 additional House seats (an astonishing accomplishment!). Immediately after the election, Senator Richard Shelby, of Alabama, reinforced the Republican trend by switching from the Democratic party, giving the GOP a 53–47 majority in the Senate. The Republicans also won 8 additional governorships in 1994, giving them control of the executive mansion in 31 of the 50 states.

Voters ousted the Democrats from power as they held the party accountable for failing to cope effectively with the problems posed by high taxes and unbalanced budgets. The deficit reduction and tax reforms that Bill Clinton had initiated during his first two years in office were not enough to satisfy voters who saw continued big-spending and big-government proclivities in his health plan and in his administration's approach to government in general. Clinton had campaigned for the presidency in 1992 as a "new Democrat," but by 1994 exit polls showed that many voters had come to see him as a continuation of the big-government, Democratic Washington establishment. Personal factors, too, were part of the 1994 vote, as Clinton continued to receive largely negative ratings from the public despite what had been a fairly prosperous and growing economy.

Although voters have expressed their disenchantment with negative advertising, it continues because it works; it influences voter decisions. The concluding chapter of this book will evaluate potential reform measures for dealing with the problem of negative advertising. Ads that distort an opponent's record or attack a candidate's personal qualities diminish democracy. However, not all negative ads are as bad as the critics complain. There are negative ads that contribute to the substance of campaign dialogue by presenting accurate information that allows voters to distinguish between the competing action orientations of the candidates on issues that voters deem to be of importance.

The final chapter of this book also reviews contemporary electoral trends, including the evidence on voter realignment and dealignment. The book concludes with a discussion as to just what strategies Republicans and Democrats can best follow in their pursuit of the White House if voters respond to substantive concerns more than is commonly believed.

The second edition of *Presidential Campaigns and Elections* has been thoroughly revised. Earlier chapters have been rewritten to include the newest research, as well as examples from the 1992 presidential campaign—an election that is discussed in great detail in Chapter 10. The chapter on the 1988 election has been fortified by the inclusion of voter studies that point to the importance of both retrospective evaluations and substantive concerns in determining the outcome of the Bush-Dukakis race. The second edition of this book also incorporates much of the perspective of Samuel Popkin's *The Reasoning Voter.*

Bill Clinton's election in 1992 helps to validate much of the argument presented in the first edition of the book. The Democrats lost presidential elections in the 1968–1988 period because they nominated candidates that many voters, especially middle-class voters, found unacceptable. Clinton won the presidency by reorienting the party to the concerns of working-class and middle-class voters, winning back those so-called Reagan Democrats who had defected from the party in previous elections. Yet, the preferences of this powerful swing group are unstable, and in the 1994 mid-term election many of these voters returned to the Republican banner. Exit polls also indicated that voters who backed Ross Perot in 1992 broke two-to-one in favor of the Republicans in 1994. By 1994, as noted above, Clinton had lost much of his "new Democrat" image. He also faced the unparalleled hostility of a group that can best be described as Clinton haters. This hostility permeated the public's attention in talk radio. It remains to be seen whether or not Clinton will be able to win reelection in 1996. Much depends on how the public evaluates both his personal qualities and his performance in office, as well as the personal qualities and substantive orientations of his Republican opponent.

The author wishes to thank: Glenn Perusek and Kim Tunnicliff for their continuing discussion of presidential politics; reviewers Emmett H. Buell, Jr. of Denison University, James E. Campbell of Louisiana State University, Thomas Holbrook of the University of Wisconsin-Milwaukee, and James Hutter of Iowa State University for their helpful comments on the first edition; Byron W. Dawes of Brigham Young University and James A. McCann of Purdue University for their reviews of this revision; Ruth Ann Boyd for her invaluable assistance; Albion College for the award of a sabbatical and grant assistance that helped with the completion of this manuscript; Leo Wiegman for his belief in my writing; John Beasley for his gentle but helpful editorial assistance; and, at F.E. Peacock Publishers, Jura Azvienis and Ted Peacock for their patience as well as their continued support.

Presidential Campaigns and Elections

CAMPAIGNING IN THE TELEVISION AGE

I n this book we seek to determine to what extent issues are incorporated into contemporary presidential campaigns. To what extent are presidential campaigns won on the basis of substantive issues as opposed to candidate-centered personal imagery?

There is much debate over the relative importance of issues and images. However, one long-term trend in voting behavior is very clear: Since the 1950s, the influence of party identification has declined. While partisanship still exerts an important influence on how many individuals evaluate presidential candidates, it no longer possesses the power it once had. More and more Americans profess to be political independents[1] and, to some extent, the introduction of television is responsible for this trend. Television allows voters to see candidates almost as if they were in their living rooms; viewers form political judgments for themselves free of the influence of party labels and partisan intermediaries.

But what is the relative role played by issues and images in the new media-dominated presidential contest? Much of the popular wisdom castigates the allegedly issueless nature of the modern media campaign. According to critics, candidates are packaged by professional pollsters, media merchants, and image consultants. Voters seldom are given meaningful information regarding the issue positions of the candidates. According to this critique, elections are fraudulent. Democracy fails as voters cast their ballots on the basis of manufactured personal imagery and fragments of incomplete, often misleading, issue information.

But issues play a greater role in the presidential race than this critical commentary suggests. Presidential campaigns in the television age are a curious combination of issue-based as well as personal-image advertising. While image advertising persists, presidential campaigns are far from issueless; voters learn during them. The paid advertisements in the presidential race do more than simply establish personal images of the candidates. Television advertising also helps voters to discern the competing issue dispositions of the candidates.

Behind-the-scenes media handlers do not control the outcome of the presidential race. The power of the professionals to manufacture images that will determine an election outcome is often greatly overstated. Voters are not merely blank slates. Rather, they possess various pieces of political information about such important matters as the state of the nation's economy and the incumbent president's performance in office—information that the image merchants, no matter how capable, find difficult to alter. The image merchants must work within the sharp confines of what voters already know and believe.

ISSUES AND IMAGES: A BRIEF LOOK AT THE 1992 ADS

Relatively brief 30- and 60-second spot ads can be used to build candidate images or to convey important pieces of substantive information to voters. A brief look at four ads from the 1992 presidential race—two from the beginning and two from the end of the long 1992 campaign season—will show that presidential advertising is neither entirely issue- nor image-oriented. In the age of the televised campaign, image spots coexist side by side with advertisements that convey more substantive messages regarding a candidate's policy dispositions and past performance in office.

In 1992, Democrat Paul Tsongas established his seriousness as a Democratic presidential contender by winning the critically important first-in-the-nation March primary in New Hampshire, which, of course, attracts great media attention. In 1992, the New Hampshire results helped separate the serious candidates from the also-rans in a crowded Democratic primary field.

As the people of New Hampshire were about to go to the polls and vote, public opinion soundings showed that Tsongas, the once unknown former senator from Massachusetts, had moved to the front of the pack. Tsongas had achieved this surprising show of strength by staying "on message" with his calls for extensive economic reform. Throughout the New Hampshire race, Tsongas pounded out the single message of the need for painful economic reform. In dealing with the economy, Tsongas declared, there was "no Santa Claus." He attacked the gimmickry of a middle-class tax cut embraced by his rivals: The nation could not afford a tax cut in the midst of mounting budget deficits.

But Tsongas's success was the result of image-building as well as issue position-taking. In one spot aired early in the New Hampshire race, the Tsongas campaign tried a piece of almost pure image-building quite different from the more substantive ads of the campaign. A second version of the spot was aired late in the New Hampshire race in an effort to both solidify Tsongas's image and build on the "bandwagon effect" generated by statewide polls that pointed to a likely Tsongas victory:

Paul Tsongas SWIMMER—NO LONGER ALONE ad

VIDEO: Shot of an empty, indoor swimming pool. A solitary figure approaches the end of the pool. Tsongas is clad only in a swimsuit. Camera pulls in for a slow-motion close-up as Tsongas dives into the pool and does a butterfly stroke.

AUDIO (Narrator): "Alone, he took on the president they said was unbeatable and sounded the economic alarm. He doesn't offer gimmicks, just straight, tough answers."

VIDEO: Quick cut to scenes of a window with an "Out of Business" sign taped to it, a worker on an industrial assembly line, and a close-up of fingers placing an electronics assembly into its place on a board.

AUDIO (Narrator): "On day one he'll declare an economic emergency, halt unfair bank foreclosures,

make business invest in jobs and quality, and create a strong recovery that lasts."

VIDEO: Return to the slow-motion close-up of Tsongas
doing the butterfly. Then a shot of Tsongas shaking
hands at a campaign stop, and another return to
Tsongas swimming the butterfly.

AUDIO (Narrator): "Now he's no longer alone. Paul
Tsongas. He'll take charge from the start."

VIDEO: As Tsongas continues to swim, the logo
"Tsongas: Democrat for President" appears on the
bottom of the screen

AUDIO (Narrator): "Paid for by the Tsongas Committee."

The ad communicates virtually nothing of substance, other
than to hint broadly as to Tsongas's seriousness on economic reform. Instead, the ad communicates Tsongas's personal qualities. Tsongas, the ad informs us, had the courage to declare for
the nomination when other Democrats were scared off by President Bush's 80 and 90 percent public approval ratings after the
United States's victory in the Gulf War. Tsongas's courage and
strength are visually represented in the ad and by the senator's
willingness to appear in public in skimpy Speedo swim trunks—
a true act of courage for most fiftyish politicians!

Of equal significance was the personal image-building that
the swimmer ad used to put to rest potentially damaging rumors
that Tsongas was still suffering from lymphoma, a form of cancer.
Voters will not cast their ballots for a candidate who is—or is
perceived as—physically incapable of handling the arduous du-
ties of the presidency. Tsongas had left the Senate, after being di-
agnosed as having lymphoma, in order to spend more time with
his family. But during the presidential campaign, the candidate
and his doctor declared that the Massachusetts senator had undergone treatment for only a most mild form of cancer and was
now quite well. What better way to put the rumors of Tsongas's ill
health to rest than by showing him to be vigorously active and
physically fit, capable of swimming achievements that his rivals
could not hope to match? In the original version of the Swimmer
ad, the narrator confronts the cancer story directly, declaring

that "guts and determination helped Paul Tsongas beat the odds and go on to beat cancer." The original Swimmer ad also had the additional benefit of attracting valuable unpaid news coverage (referred to as **free media**) to a campaign that was unable to make the media buys of its better-financed opponents. After the ad, news reporters followed Tsongas to record his daily morning swims.

Both versions of the Swimmer ad were successful; they helped to establish Tsongas's image and "inoculate" him on a potentially critical area of weakness—concerns about his health. Tsongas went on to win the New Hampshire primary, turning the Democratic contest into a two-man race between himself and second-place finisher Bill Clinton.

But the Swimmer ads raise very troubling questions about modern political advertising: They were deceptive. Tsongas was not enjoying the good health that the visual images imply. After the 1992 election was over, his cancer flared and the former presidential aspirant underwent renewed chemotherapy. At that time, Tsongas's physician admitted to having downplayed concerns regarding Tsongas's health during the course of the campaign. The Swimmer ads were part of a deception whereby voters were denied the information they needed in order to draw valid judgments as to the health and stamina of a potential president.

But are all spot ads as politically successful and manipulative as were the Swimmer spots? Two ads produced on behalf of George Bush show the limitations of televised image-building in a presidential race. These Bush ads could not effectively counter the substance of what voters already knew about the Bush record and the nation's economic condition.

Following is the transcript of the first ad that the Bush campaign aired in New Hampshire, after polls began to indicate that New Hampshire Republicans, feeling the pain of continued economic recession, would give an unexpectedly strong vote to the protest candidacy of Patrick Buchanan:

 George Bush PAIN ad

VIDEO: President Bush sits in an audience during his recent visit to New Hampshire. Slow-motion shot as the president turns to listen to an agitated young woman. Close-up of the woman.

AUDIO (Woman): "Mr. Bush. I have never seen it so bad where people have to lose their homes. People don't have jobs, they don't have..."

VIDEO: Shots of Bush in the audience listening, reaction shots of the audience. Shift to scenes of Bush talking with the people of New Hampshire.

AUDIO (Bush's voice in voice over): "You can give it to me straight because we've known each other a long time. A lot of you are hurting. I've seen the pain in people's eyes, from those who own struggling businesses to those who work in them."

VIDEO: Bush at a microphone speaks to a New Hampshire audience.

AUDIO (Bush): "This state has gone through hell, it's gone through an extraordinarily difficult time. I am determined to turn this state around."

VIDEO: Slow-motion of Bush walking off with the people of New Hampshire.

AUDIO (Announcer): "Paid for by the Bush-Quayle 1992 Primary Committee."

The ad sought to establish the president as a caring man who is familiar with New Hampshire and its people. But the ad fails; it is not convincing. The spot does not effectively dispel what voters know about the poor state of the economy or about the president's reluctance to undertake stronger government action to generate an economic recovery. The ad is not credible because it gives voters no specific evidence from which they can judge the seriousness of Bush's professed economic determination or the adequacy of his new economic proposals. The ad also does not dispel additional information that voters had, a fact that Patrick Buchanan hammered away at throughout the New Hampshire—that Bush, as president, broke his 1988 "No new taxes!" vow. Finally, the ad does not effectively counter the perceptions of New Hampshire voters that Bush was out of touch with conditions in their state. New Hampshire residents knew that Bush rarely visited the state; the events recorded in the commercial were from the president's first visit to the state in over a year. Buchanan ultimately won 37 percent of the state's Republican vote, embarrassing the president and exposing vulnerabilities that would continue to plague him throughout the general election.

Personal image-making also failed Bush in the final days of the fall general election. As polls showed George Bush well behind Bill Clinton, the Republican campaign stepped up its attacks against Clinton's record and credibility. But the advertising was not purely negative. One positive ad sought to refashion Bush's personal image:

George Bush WHAT I AM FIGHTING FOR ad

VIDEO: Close-up of letters and words appearing in green on a computer monitor, as if someone is typing them on a computer terminal: "The world is in transition." Switch to an extra close-up of George Bush as he would appear on a video monitor. Alternating close-ups of Bush and the words he utters as they appear in green on the computer monitor.

AUDIO (Bush): "The world is in transition. The defining challenge of the 1990s is to win the economic competition, to win the peace." (Throughout the ad, a musical fanfare and a pulsating beat accompany Bush's speech. The click of computer keys accompanies the letters as they appear on the monitor.)

VIDEO: Close-up of "to win the peace" as the words continue to be typed on the computer monitor.

AUDIO (Bush): "We must be a military superpower, an economic superpower, and an export superpower."

VIDEO: Quick cuts to pictures of a jet fighter taking off from an aircraft carrier, a metallurgical factory at work, the words "an export superpower" being written on the monitor, and a freighter at sea. Return to extra close-up of Bush. As the president speaks, continue to interpose pictures of Bush's words being printed on the video terminal.

AUDIO (Bush): "In this election, you'll hear two versions of how to do this. Theirs is to look inward. Ours is to look forward, to prepare our people to compete, to save and to invest so we can win. (Up musical fanfare.) Here's what I'm fighting for:

Open markets for American products. Lower government spending. Tax relief. Opportunities for small
business. Legal and health reform. Job training and
new schools built on competition ready for the 21st
century."

VIDEO: Quick shots of an automobile assembly line, the
Washington Monument and the Capitol, a 1040 tax form,
students working on a computer, a family lounging on
the grass, and a class of students reciting the
Pledge of Allegiance are all interspersed with continued close-ups of Bush and the president's words as
they appear on the video monitor.

AUDIO and VIDEO: After the words "21st century" appear on the screen, muffled booms and flashes accompany extra close-ups as the letters B-U-S-H
almost seem to be hammered out on the video screen,
spelling out "BUSH" to the accompanying sounds of
applause and cheers.

The ad, with its computer screen imagery, MTV-style quick
cuts, flashes, and sound booms, is meant to appeal especially to
young voters. Shown in extra close-up on a grainy video screen,
Bush almost takes on the persona of Max Headroom, the one-
time chief character in a hip television comedy. (Polls showed
that Bush had lost the edge that Ronald Reagan enjoyed among
younger voters; the young had cast a majority of their votes for
Reagan, the nation's oldest president, as Reagan-era growth held
out the promise of new job opportunities.) The ad was designed
to equate Bush with the promise of a vigorous, high-technology,
competitive American future; the Democrats, in contrast, are portrayed as the party of the past. "What I Am Fighting For" was designed to win back the young. But it couldn't. While the ad was
technically and visually impressive, image-making, no matter how
well done, could not offset what young voters already knew about
their own personal economic situation and the president's failure
to provide effective action as the recession plagued the nation.

In contrast to the technical proficiency of the Bush 21st Century ad is the purposeful, amateurish quality of an ad produced
by the Clinton campaign in the general election. The Remember? ad is brief but effective as it provides voters with a clear and
credible reason to vote for Clinton:

Bill Clinton REMEMBER? ad

VIDEO: Grainy blue screen (a close-up of a video
   screen?) with the question "Remember?"

AUDIO (Announcer): "Remember?"

VIDEO: Switch to a grainy video screen. President
   Bush speaks into the camera in what appears to be a
   clip from an old television ad. The words "November
   1988" are transcribed at the lower right.

AUDIO (Bush): "And if you elect me president, you
   will be better off four years from now than you are
   today." Throughout the ad, Bush's words are accompanied by an undertone of eerie music.

VIDEO: Bush's image is replaced by a screen that
   rolls up from the bottom, containing the following
   statement: "Average family income down $1,600 in
   two years." Smaller print in the lower right-hand
   corner reads: "Commerce Department Bureau of Census
   9/3/92."

AUDIO (Announcer): "Average family income down $1,600
   in two years."

VIDEO and AUDIO: Repeat of the grainy clip of Bush as
   he says "You will be better off four years from now
   than you are today."

VIDEO: New sign rolls up from the bottom of the
   screen: "Family health care costs up $1,800 in four
   years." Smaller print in the lower right-hand corner reads: "Health Insurance Association of America
   1988; KPMG Peat, Marwick 1992."

AUDIO (Announcer): "Family health care costs up
   $1,800 in just four years."

VIDEO and AUDIO: Repeat of the grainy Bush clip: "You
   will be better off four years from now."

VIDEO: New sign reads: "The second biggest tax increase in history." In smaller print at the lower
   right: "Congressional Budget Office Study 1/30/91;
   New York Times 8/7/92."

AUDIO (Announcer): "The second biggest tax increase in history."

VIDEO AND AUDIO: Repeat close-ups of the grainy clip of President Bush roll up from the bottom as if the horizontal hold on the television is broken. Repeat of Bush saying, "Well, if you elect me, you will be better off four years from now than you are today."

VIDEO: Two signs roll up from the bottom to reinforce the words as they are read by the announcer.

AUDIO (Announcer): "Well, it's four years later."
"How're you doing?"

The ad spurns personal image-building for an attack on the Bush record. Is the spot ad an issue ad? Not by the standards of prospective issue voting! Nowhere is there a hint as to what Bill Clinton will do if elected. Voters cannot judge the relative merits, costs, and workability of his economic proposals. The Remember? ad points to the limitations of spot ads as political discourse. No single 30- or 60-second televised ad can provide a full and informed public discussion of political issues.

But if the Remember? ad falls far short of perfection as a prospective-issue ad, neither can it be charged with being entirely issueless. The ad points to Bush's economic failure and broken tax promise. It also points to rising health care costs under Bush—a point which, by inference, underscores the need for Clinton's promised national health plan.

The Remember? ad, then, does provide valid pieces of information and reasons for voting for Clinton, or at least for voting against Bush. Citizens dissatisfied with Bush's performance in office have only one real alternative, to turn him out and try someone else. Except for the sizable 19 percent of the electorate that turned to Ross Perot, voters grievously dissatisfied with Bush's performance had no meaningful choice other than to vote for Clinton.

The ad urges voters to look not so much at candidate's promises for the future but at the president's past performance. In arguing that citizens should look backward at the past performance of the incumbent administration, the ad is urging a form of issue voting known as **retrospective voting**. As will be pointed out, retrospective voting is one of the major ways by which issues are incorporated in citizen's voting decisions.

The success of the Remember? ad also points to the importance of the economy to the outcome of recent presidential elections. As Samuel Popkin argues, voters learn politically relevant information from both their daily lives and the televised campaign.[2] Voters see how the economy affects them. They also see the economic stories that dominate the news. During economic lean times, voters will demand change; during boom times, they will reward the incumbent administration.

The Remember? ad proves effective as it attempts to mobilize voters on the basis of the substantive knowledge they already possess. The ad exploits voters' frustrations with both Bush's failure to bring about an economic recovery and his reversal of his 1988 "No new taxes" vow. It also taps into voters' frustrations with the rising costs of health care. The ad works because it seems reasonable on the basis of what voters already know. Bush's "What I Am Fighting For" spot, in contrast, fails as it attempts to construct an entirely new personal image of George Bush that is dissonant with voters' existing knowledge. Image-building must work within the confines of what the public already knows.

One minor but interesting aspect of the Remember? ad, and of a number of political spots produced in 1992, also deserves note. Ad writers included references to studies, newspaper articles, and other seemingly neutral authorities as a means of lending credence to the sometimes quite arguable claims advanced in the ads. Political advertisers in 1992 feared a possible backlash against negative campaigning. Especially after the mud-throwing of the 1988 Bush-Dukakis race, media tacticians feared that voters might tire of attack advertising. Adverse public reaction against a negative ad, though, could be minimized if the attacks contained in the ad appeared reasonable and were backed by seemingly reputable authority. At the same time the campaigns were able to uncover different sources to authenticate their often competing versions of the "facts" presented in the ads.

ISSUES, IMAGES, AND PARTISANSHIP: AN OVERVIEW OF THE BOOK

As we have just seen from our brief review of ads from the 1992 race, personal images and substantive issues both play a role in the contemporary presidential campaign. Partisanship, too, plays

a role in retrospective voting and holding a president accountable for his party's performance in office. In the general election, party labels also provide voters with cues that help to
structure perceptions and voters' choice.

The exact influence that issues, images, and partisanship
exert in presidential elections is still a matter of much debate.
The argument here will be that issues count, that they have
a greater influence on how Americans vote for president than
political commentators often allege. Presidential campaigns are
not image-making spectacles devoid of issues.

Yet, this argument can be made only by reviewing the extensive research that has sought to analyze the voting decision.
An examination of individual presidential elections will produce
clearer insight as to the role played by issues, candidate images,
and partisanship in any specific election.

Chapter 2 provides an overview of the complex system by
which Americans select their president. Americans first nominate their presidential candidates in a series of primaries and
caucuses. The chosen candidates then compete in the fall general election. Voter knowledge of the candidates and the issues
will vary greatly at the different stages of the presidential selection process.

Chapter 3 reviews the changing context of American presidential elections, focusing on the pervasiveness of television, the
rise of professionally mediated campaigns, and the growing independence of the American voter. The declining significance—
though far from the disappearance—of partisanship has allowed
both personal images and policy issues to play a greater role in
presidential voting.

Reforms in the presidential nominating system and campaign finance have also led to a new prominence of both issue
groups and professional image-makers in the age of the candidate-centered campaign. These changes and their impact are
discussed in Chapter 4.

Chapter 5 examines the evidence in the issue-voting debate.
For a long time political scientists were of the opinion that party
identification and candidates' personality factors were the most
important influences on voter choice. Issues appeared to have little, if any, influence on presidential elections. Even today, political
scientists continue to produce evidence of the lack of sophistication of the American voter. Yet, in recent years, political scientists
have begun to conceptualize the various ways by which voters incorporate substantive evaluations into their voting decisions.

This book emphasizes three variants of issue voting. Under **retrospective voting**, voters look at past performance when choosing a presidential candidate. In recent years, voters' retrospective evaluations have focused on the nation's economic well-being and the president's handling of foreign policy. Voters also engage in **directional voting**, whereby they make broad choices between the general policy directions or action orientations offered by the competing presidential candidates. Of course, voters do not vote on all possible issues, and not all issues lend themselves to issue voting. **Easy-issue voting** occurs as voters are generally more prone to vote on the basis of issues that are relatively simple and clear cut as opposed to issues that are conceptually difficult and complex. The argument presented here is sympathetic to Samuel Popkin's portrait of a **reasoning voter**, who knows how to read the mass media, relies on informational shortcuts, and uses the information gathered from both the media and daily life experiences in evaluating presidential candidates.[3]

The rest of the book is devoted to an examination of how Americans have chosen presidents, from Franklin Roosevelt to Bill Clinton. The relative importance of issues, personal images, and partisanship varies from election to election. Chapter 6 describes the New Deal political era, a time when partisanship may have been the dominant influence on the voting decision. But even here the relative impact of issues is still the subject of some debate. Chapter 6 also observes the role of television in its infancy, a role that has changed over time as both political elites and the public at large have grown more accustomed to television as an everyday part of their lives.

Chapter 7 describes the 1964–1972 period during which issues became a more prominent part of American elections. Voters perceived a fairly distinct directional choice between Democrats and Republicans in each of the presidential elections of this period. As will be argued beginning with Chapter 7, presidential advertising can be constructed on issue-based images as well as on more personal candidate-oriented images. When issue-based images are employed, the televised campaign helps voters to distinguish between the competing action orientations of presidential candidates.

Chapters 8 through 11 detail the 1976–1992 "retrospective era" during which voters' evaluations of the administration's performance on the economy and other matters were critical to the outcome of each election. Chapter 10 devotes special attention to the 1988 contest between George Bush and Michael Dukakis, an election in which Bush is often viewed as having made his comeback almost entirely as the result of the professionally crafted negative images that dominated the campaign's discourse. Yet, despite the numerous distortions contained in the attack ads, advertising in the 1988 race still helped voters to perceive a basic directional choice between the candidates, a choice that worked to the advantage of Republicans. Retrospective evaluations centering on peace and prosperity also mattered in 1988.

As Chapter 11 details, Bill Clinton won the 1992 election on the basis of the economic issue and voter dissatisfaction with George Bush's performance in office. Clinton's presentation of himself as a more moderate, pragmatic "new Democrat" was also a critical element in this success.

At times, personal images dominated press coverage of the 1992 elections. The press probed various allegations of Clinton's past misconduct, examining charges that he had engaged in extramarital affairs and reviewing in detail his efforts as a student to escape the draft. They also repeated without substantiation Ross Perot's charge that Bill Clinton, as the governor of a small state, lacked the necessary qualifications to be president. Had personal images been all that counted to voters in the 1992, it is doubtful that a badly tarnished Bill Clinton could have won the presidency. But issues and more substantive voter judgments, not personal image, determined the 1992 election outcome.

The concluding chapter of this book looks to the future. It discusses the problems—and virtues!—of negative advertising. It also seeks to identify those strategies that the Democratic and Republican parties can profitably adopt if they want to win elections in an age when issues count in the presidential process.

THE STAGES OF THE PRESIDENTIAL SELECTION PROCESS

The relative importance of issues, images, and partisanship varies with the different stages of the presidential selection process. In the earliest stages, a candidate who is unknown needs to establish both name recognition and the claim to personal leadership qualities. Only after voters become somewhat familiar with a candidate are they ready to learn more about where he or she stands on various issues.

A candidate needs to take a stand on various issues in order to gain an advantageous tactical position in a multicandidate field. Ambiguity on political issues can serve only as a temporary campaign strategy. While ambiguity offers the advantage of allowing voters to project their various policy views onto the candidate, this distortion of public perception is most severe during the early portion of the primary season. As the primary season progresses, the candidates are subjected to more critical press scrutiny, and the voters perceive more accurately where candidates stand on the issues.[1] More ideological candidates spurn ambiguity and from the very beginning use issues to mobilize select policy constituencies that play a disproportionate role in the presidential nominating process. This was the strategy that George McGovern used so successfully in 1972 as he rode anti-Vietnam war sentiment to the Democratic nomination.

In the general election, Republican and Democratic nominees rely on a combination of partisanship, personal images, and issues in their efforts to win votes. The nominees each seek to mobilize their party's cores of strength by portraying themselves as the inheritors of the party's best traditions. They seek to attract more independent voters through a combination of image-based and issue-based appeals that emphasize their leadership attributes, the virtues of their party philosophy and performance, and the disabilities of their opponent's record.

As a result of their long duration and multiple appeals, American presidential elections are a confusing spectacle. To simplify matters, the process can perhaps be best understood if divided into two grand parts: the nominating process and the general election.

The **nominating process** centers upon the intraparty battle through the late winter and spring, culminating at the parties' national nominating conventions. States use either caucuses or a primary to pick the delegates who will attend. A **caucus** is a precinct-level or other local meeting during which participants choose representatives to attend county, congressional district, or state conventions. The district or state convention then chooses delegates who will attend the party's national convention to select the presidential nominee. Caucuses and conventions often conduct other items of party business in addition to presidential selection. A **primary,** in contrast, is not a party meeting but almost a minielection, a day-long event during which voters go to the polls to vote directly for a candidate. The results of a state's primary determine, to a large extent, how many national convention delegates a state awards to each presidential aspirant.

At one time, participation in primaries and caucuses was restricted to party members. Over time, however, the proof of party membership has been relaxed to allow greater public participation. Although the exact rules differ from state to state, generally speaking, any person who is willing to declare himself or herself a party member can participate in a state's caucuses or primary.

The **national party convention** sets party rules, writes the party platform, and formally nominates the party's candidates for president and vice president. The national party conventions also mark the beginning of the interparty general election contest between the winning Democratic and Republican nominees. The victorious nominees use the media showcase provided by the convention to identify those issues and images that they hope will dominate the fall campaign. Quite often, excerpts from the nominees's speeches reappear as clips in the televised ads that appear throughout the remainder of the fall campaign. The **general election,** in which voters finally select who will be president, is held in November.

The meeting of the **Electoral College** in December for all intents and purposes is only a formality that ratifies the choice that the voters made on Election Day. The Electoral College was originally intended to give an elite group of better-educated citizens a free hand in the choice of a president. However, today, electors from each state no longer have the freedom to vote for their own personal choice. Exercise of independent judgment by the Electoral College would be seen as undermining the choice made by the people in a democracy. Electors today are virtually pledged to vote for whichever candidate wins the plurality of the popular vote cast in their state in November.

To assist in understanding the presidential election process, six distinct stages can be identified (see Table 2.1).

STAGE ONE: THE PRELIMINARY PERIOD

Two or more years before a presidential election, potential candidates begin raising the resources and political support necessary for a presidential race. Would-be candidates visit local party leaders and activists in an effort to gain their support. Better-known presidential aspirants speak at fundraising dinners for state and congressional candidates in order to win their gratitude and commitment.

No candidate can attempt a serious presidential campaign without first establishing a broad base of funding. Even in advance of declaring for the presidency, candidates set up exploratory committees and **precandidacy political action committees (precandidacy PACs)** to begin raising funds and garnering voter support. This fundraising enables a presidential candidate to pay for early campaign travel, public appearances, and other organizational efforts. As the actions are nominally undertaken by the PAC to assist a party's state and local candidates, they do not count against the strict ceilings on contributions and

Table 2.1   Overview of the Presidential Nomination and General Election

	Nomination Politics	
Stage	What the Candidate Does	What the Media Does
1. The Preliminary Period Begins 24 or more months before November general election	All potential Democratic and Republican candidates form exploratory committees and begin fundraising and issue development. Candidates attempt to secure the support of important political leaders and groups, especially in key primary and caucus states.	The press plays the part of the "Great Mentioner," speculating as to which candidates will enter the race and which are the true "heavyweights."
2. The Early Rounds January–February of election year	Iowa's party caucuses and New Hampshire's primary are the first tests of voter response to the candidates; candidates begin advertising blitzes in states with upcoming primaries.	Media focus heavy attention on the candidates who do well or better than expected.
3. The Long Haul March–May of election year	Serious contenders emerge in both parties as more states hold primaries or caucuses to select delegates to the upcoming national conventions. Super Tuesday and Super March are key events. In 1992, California and New York likely also become important states in a "front-loaded" primary system.	Media scrutinize all aspects of front-running candidates; attention turns away from weaker candidates, further depleting their ability to raise money and support. Media attention also shifts to delegate counts.
4. The Final Races May–June of election year	If the race within a party is close, the final states' primaries can be very decisive. Most often, races are decided before the final primaries.	Media begin comparisons of leading Democatic and Republican candidates and speculations on potential vice presidential nominees.
5. The National Party Conventions July of election year	In separate national conventions, the Democratic and Republican delegates chosen in preceding state races meet to cast ballots for the party's presidential nominee. The chosen nominee's first duty at the convention is selecting a vice presidential running mate to complete the party's ticket.	The conventions are media events carefully orchestrated to appeal to a national viewing audience. The media analysts scrutinize the acceptance speech, which usually contains some hints about the candidate's issues and positions as reflected in the party platform adoped at the convention.

Election Politics		
6. The General Election Campaigns August through national election day, first Tuesday after the first Monday in November	The two presidential tickets now tour the country in media-oriented stops. The official campaigns are paid by public funds. Both campaigns use "tracking polls" to adjust their message daily. Especially during the final days of the race, campaign resources are devoted to winning pivotal states in the Electoral College. Independent groups also sponsor ads, both negative and positive, on behalf of the candidates.	The media give scrutiny to each member of the ticket. More often than not, media coverage focuses on candidtates' gaffes and errors, on polling results, and on other "horserace" aspects of the race rather than on the details of the candidates' policy promises. The media bore in on the candidates' performances in televised debates.

spending set for the presidential campaign by federal law. Pre-candidacy presidential PACs enable candidates to circumvent virtually every provision of the Federal Election Campaign Act.[2] The presidential precandidacy PAC will even make campaign donations to favored congressional candidates in an effort to win their loyalty.

Early financial contributions and other indications of organizational strength are important to a presidential campaign for three reasons. First, early fundraising can be crucial to the success of a nationwide campaign. In 1984, Walter Mondale fended off a surprisingly strong challenge by Gary Hart for the Democratic nomination—to a great extent because the former vice president, not Hart, had the financial and organizational backing to run a national campaign. Hart concentrated his resources in New Hampshire and won that state's first-in-the-nation primary; but Mondale had the resources to come back in the southern and midwestern contests that followed. Similarly, in 1992, Bill Clinton survived his New Hampshire defeat by Paul Tsongas as a result of the superior financial and organizational strength of the Clinton effort, which allowed him to defeat Tsongas in the races that followed.

Second, early contributions that meet the eligibility requirements set by federal law help a candidate to qualify for federal matching funds. Federal matching funds multiply the impact of small-money contributions during the nominating season.

Third, early contributions and other shows of strength serve as evidence of a candidate's political viability. The press looks for indicators of a candidate's strength in sorting the more serious from the less serious presidential contenders. Bill Clinton helped establish his early credibility by garnering an edge in campaign contributions.

During this early campaign period, both front runners and long shots will pay frequent visits to Iowa and New Hampshire, sites of the two earliest selection contests. In 1993, a full three years before the 1996 election, the list of Republican presidential hopefuls to visit Iowa and New Hampshire included Robert Dole, Phil Gramm, Jack Kemp, Dick Cheney, Lynn Martin, and William Bennett.

Kansas Senator Bob Dole learned from his previous presidential efforts the importance of building a campaign organization in this precampaign period. Early in 1994, announcing that he had not yet decided whether he would enter the 1996 presidential race, Dole instructed his advisers to seek commitments from key fundraisers and Republican strategists around the country. His political action committee, Campaign America, paid for the Senator's travels around the country as he sought to assist Republican candidates for other offices. Campaign America also hired more than a half-dozen strategists in key primary states, including Iowa and New Hampshire. Dole had learned from his failed 1988 presidential bid, when George Bush locked up the support of key Republican activists and gained the party's presidential nomination, that delay only invites defeat: "If you wait until you decide to do it, you may be behind the curve. I've had that happen to me."[3]

During the preliminary stages of the presidential race, the press plays the role of what *Washington Post* columnist David Broder once called "the Great Mentioner." In deciding which candidates in a large field are prominently mentioned in the news, the press virtually tells the public which candidates merit their serious consideration. In screening potential presidential aspirants, the press has undertaken a job once performed by party "bosses."[4]

Candidates who are not mentioned prominently by the press need a good showing in an early political contest to break into the elite circle. Candidates stack state conventions with their supporters in an attempt to win otherwise meaningless **straw polls** and influence press and public perceptions. Well before the first 1992 primary was held, Bill Clinton used his victory in a nonbinding straw poll at the Florida state convention to move to the front of the "six pack" of Democratic presidential aspirants (Clinton, Paul Tsongas, Bob Kerrey, Jerry Brown, Tom Harkin, and Doug Wilder).

During much of the preliminary stages of the race, potential contenders refrain from officially announcing their candidacies. The public is treated to the spectacle of candidates who are vigorously campaigning for the White House but who yet refuse to formally declare their candidacy. As Edward "Ted" Kennedy found out much to his chagrin in 1980, one who moves toward official candidacy receives more intensive scrutiny from the press. As Kennedy prepared to announce, the press raised new questions of his preparedness for the presidency and revived old questions regarding the senator's actions in the automobile-related death of Mary Jo Kopechne at Chappaquiddick in 1969. Kennedy's campaign quickly lost momentum.

STAGE TWO: THE EARLY ROUNDS

Because they signal the start of the road to the White House, the first-in-the-nation Iowa caucuses and the New Hampshire primary have attracted media coverage grossly disproportionate to the small number of national party convention delegates that are actually chosen in these states.

The news media has recognized the unfairness posed by the exaggerated significance given these two relatively small states. News organizations have drawn up plans for more balanced coverage of the entire primary season. However, for the most part, the media goes where the candidates go. While news organizations have at times restrained their coverage of the Iowa caucuses, the media has not been able to curb its appetite for the news that is being made in New Hampshire.

In 1992, the Iowa caucuses received very little media coverage, as there was no real contest in Iowa. Patrick Buchanan decided to take on President Bush in New Hampshire, not Iowa; and the Democratic field conceded Iowa caucuses to the state's "native son" Senator Tom Harkin.

Candidates who are short on resources concentrate their efforts in Iowa and New Hampshire, hoping that a good showing will bring new publicity and financial contributions, resources that can be used in the races that immediately follow. Front-running candidates need a good showing in these states in order to maintain momentum.

Campaigning in Iowa and New Hampshire is dominated by an intense **retail politics**, where candidates attend coffee-klatches and meet small groups of voters. A candidate may even stay in the homes of local supporters. In 1992, Paul Tsongas spent 70 days and Bill Clinton spent 43 days campaigning in New Hampshire; Bob Kerrey, Tom Harkin, and Jerry Brown spent 57, 52, 40 days there, respectively.[5] Much of the highly interpersonal campaign activity of retail politics is done in the absence of national media coverage. Such intense interpersonal campaigning has a clear political payoff; one study of the Iowa caucuses showed that a large number of supporters had met the candidate, attended one of his campaign rallies, or had been visited or phoned by a representative of the campaign.[6]

Once the initial nominating contests approach, though, one-on-one retail politics is no longer enough. The emphasis of presidential campaigns switches to the **wholesale politics** of mass-media, especially televised, campaigning. Those who can afford it will blitz strategic early caucus and primary states with television ads. Positive ads are used to build the image of a candidate's leadership credentials in the eyes of the voters. Negative ads are also deployed to diminish a front-runner's political standing.

The early primaries serve to winnow the presidential field, setting the table for the nominating races that follow. Gary Hart in 1984 and Paul Tsongas in 1992 both used victories in New Hampshire to catapult into the Democratic race. In contrast, candidates who do poorly in the initial contests have trouble raising money and support and soon drop out of serious contention.

"Winning" or "losing" early races sometimes has less to do with the actual vote cast than with the media's interpretations of the results. In 1972, Maine Senator Edmund Muskie won 46 percent of the vote in New Hampshire; South Dakotan George McGovern finished second with 37 percent. But according to the press's general interpretations at the time, Muskie, the front-runner, "lost" New Hampshire because he had done less well than expected in a state neighboring his home. Similarly, in 1992, Bill Clinton won the battle of the media interpretation of New Hampshire despite the fact that Tsongas beat him by a vote of 33 percent to 25 percent. In a skillful political move that helped to determine the story line of the New Hampshire results, the media-savvy Clinton campaign took to television as soon as an early indication of the results were in. Clinton proclaimed himself "the Comeback Kid" and described his second-place showing as a great victory, given the extensive media coverage of his alleged past marital infidelities and his student attempts to sidestep the draft.

STAGE THREE: THE LONG HAUL

As the experiences of Gary Hart and Paul Tsongas show, an early victory does not guarantee the party's presidential nomination. The nomination is won by amassing delegates over a course of fifty or so primaries and caucuses. A candidate must demonstrate staying power, and this is where fundraising and organizational work during the preliminary stages of the presidential race can provide an important advantage.

The **frontloading** of the system, whereby more and more states have scheduled primaries and caucuses in the early part of the nominating season, has placed an additional premium on campaign resources and organization. Some of the frontloading of the primary season is the result of the creation of **Super Tuesday.** Southerners and other more conservative and centrist elements in the Democratic party sought to create an event that would afford the South a greater voice in the selection of the Democratic presidential nominee. As a result, Florida, Georgia, and Alabama agreed to hold their nominating contests on the same date early in March, just two weeks after the New Hampshire primary. They were the southern centerpiece of Super Tuesday, a day on which nine states held presidential primaries and caucuses. They hoped that the selection of a large block of delegates on a single day would attract media attention and prove to be the decisive event in the selection of the Democratic presidential nominee.

But Super Tuesday initially did not work to strengthen the South's influence in presidential selection. In 1984, Gary Hart and the more liberal Mondale split the southern states on Super Tuesday, and the presidential race moved on to other states. By 1988, Super Tuesday became even more super with twenty states conducting their Democratic presidential selection contests on a single day! Arkansas, Kentucky, Louisiana, Mississippi, Oklahoma, Tennessee, Texas, and Virginia joined their neighbors in holding simultaneous primaries in an effort to increase the importance of the South in presidential selection. But the South's potentially decisive influence was diluted when states from other regions in the country also decided to hold their delegate selection contests on that very day. Liberal Democrat Michael Dukakis escaped the Super Tuesday trap in 1988 with a strategy that emphasized a "four-corners" offense; Dukakis offset his weaknesses in the South as a whole by winning more liberal constituencies in Rhode Island, Massachusetts, and Maryland in the Northeast; Florida in the Southeast; Texas in the Southwest; and

Washington in the Pacific northwest. Only in 1992 did Super Tuesday at last work as originally envisioned, giving a decisive victory to native southerner Bill Clinton and putting him back on track toward the nomination.

After Super Tuesday, the incessant weekly battles of state caucuses and primaries continue. As the primary season goes on, losing candidates launch more negative attacks in an effort to get back in the race. Front-runners also go negative in an effort to deliver a death blow to continually nagging opponents. In 1992, Clinton, Tsongas, and Jerry Brown all exchanged bitter words and charges as the primaries entered the industrial states of Illinois and Michigan. In patriotic Georgia, campaign ads on behalf of President Bush attacked Patrick Buchanan for having failed to support the Gulf War. In automobile-industrial Michigan, one ad attacked Buchanan for driving a foreign car.

The press's coverage also changes as the primary season progresses and different candidates are placed under the microscope of press scrutiny. Gary Hart in 1984 and Paul Tsongas and Ross Perot in 1992 were all candidates who initially enjoyed favorable media coverage; they were portrayed as heroic figures taking on the political establishment. But when Hart and Tsongas were elevated to serious contention by their New Hampshire victories, and Perot continued to receive strong poll ratings establishing his credentials as a bona fide presidential candidate, the tone of press coverage changed, and each campaign was subjected to more critical scrutiny.

The terrain for the 1996 nominating race has been altered by the decisions of California, New York, and Ohio to move their primaries to an earlier point on the nominating season calendar. California's traditional early June primary was the last major race in the primary season. But Californians had come to resent the fact that their state, the most populous in the nation, had been bypassed in recent years inasmuch as the presidential nominations in both parties were usually decided by the time the process reached California. In an effort to regain political prominence, California voted to reschedule its 1996 primary for March 26, just two weeks after Super Tuesday and only one week after a "Midwest primary" in the populous states of Ohio, Illinois, and Michigan. New York, not wishing to be eclipsed, leapfrogged in front of California, moving its 1996 primary to the first Thursday in March—just two days after Junior Tuesday (the date of the Colorado, Georgia, and Maryland primaries and a number of state caucuses) and five days before Super Tuesday.

The earlier scheduling of these big-state primaries exacerbates the problems posed by the frontloaded nominating process. The resulting, more compact nominating schedule reshapes the presidential race in ways that are yet to be fully anticipated. **Super March**, in effect, becomes a close approximation of a national primary in terms of the financial, organizational, and travel requirements placed on presidential candidates, who seemingly must campaign everywhere at the same time. As somewhere around 80 percent of the delegates to the Democratic National Convention may well be chosen by the end of March, the creation of a Super March may serve to increase even further the importance of money and media in the presidential race, advantages enjoyed by front-runners. Alternatively, a "hot" dark horse (or outside) candidate might be able to ride the momentum from an early primary victory to a series of additional important victories in a closely spaced primary schedule. Moreover, the abbreviated primary season runs the danger of short-circuiting voter learning. If a presidential candidate suddenly catches fire, the media has only a brief period of time to probe his or her past record and issue positions before a new set of primaries takes place. Voters will not have the time to form second judgments as they learn more about the candidates.

The new prominence of the California primary may be a factor in Ross Perot's decision whether or not to run for president in 1996. Should he decide to enter the race as a Republican, not an independent, California offers Perot a substantial opportunity. Coming so soon after Texas, another bastion of 1992 Perot support, California could offer him the chance to win both a sizable number of presidential delegates and considerable momentum. If Republican party officials do not modify the winner-take-all rules for the California primary, Perot can conceivably win the entire California delegation—and with it nearly 20 percent of the delegates necessary to win the Republican nomination—by capturing a plurality of the vote in a multi-candidate California field.

STAGE FOUR: THE FINAL RACES

If the race is close, the battle for the nomination can come down to the final primaries. In 1964, Barry Goldwater, may have clinched the Republican nomination with his closing primary victory over Nelson Rockefeller in California. In 1972, George

McGovern's win in California was essential to his winning the Democratic nomination.

However, in recent years, as we have said, the final state races have not always been that decisive to the nomination. Instead, the more usual pattern is for one candidate to build a clear lead with delegates won in the early and midprimary season states. Opposing candidates, suffering a loss of momentum and financing, drop out or offer only token opposition; many of their delegates switch to support the front-runner. The leading candidate then wins enough support in the nominating season's remaining contests to secure the nomination.

As a result of reforms in the presidential nominating rules, the vast number of delegates selected throughout the nominating season are bound or otherwise committed to a presidential candidate. There is little prospect that a "free" national party convention will abandon the party's leading vote getter for a candidate who shows unexpected strength in the final nominating contests. The total number of delegates committed to a candidate, not the momentum gained in the final contests of the campaign, is the key to winning a party's presidential nomination.

The new dates of the California and Ohio primaries have the potential of changing the nature of the nominating endgame. Should no candidate jump to a clear and insurmountable delegate lead after California, the few big-state races that remain in April and May assume new importance. With California and Ohio no longer competitors for the national spotlight on the last major date in the primary season, the New Jersey primary or some other late contest may assume national importance should a nominating race go down to the wire.

STAGE FIVE: THE NATIONAL PARTY CONVENTIONS

The role of national party conventions has changed greatly over time. Earlier in the century, party conventions acted as independent vehicles at which party leaders gathered to choose a presidential nominee. Today, however, the free selection of a presidential nominee by party elites would be considered an undermining of democracy, a devaluation of the people's ballots cast in the caucuses and primaries.[7] The decline of party organizations and the reform of presidential selection rules guarantee that national party conventions can no longer play the roles they once did.[8] As we have said, national party conventions are no longer assemblies where party leaders choose a presidential nominee; instead, national conventions affirm the choice made by voters during the nominating season.

The national conventions also give some hints as to the political orientations and style of a candidate and his or her supporters. Party platforms are candidate-centered; they are to a very great extent written under the direction of the party's winning presidential team.[9] Will the new nominee compromise on certain policy planks in an effort to promote party unity? Or will the winning candidate and his or her supporters insist on maintaining their ideological purity? The party's platform and the nominee's televised acceptance speech both reveal the action orientations and themes likely to dominate the fall campaign.

The selection of the vice presidential nominee is almost always made by the party's presidential nominee. Presidential candidates say they look for a person who is most capable of assuming the presidency should circumstance dictate. They also look for a running mate who can balance or otherwise add politically to the ticket. In 1988, George Bush chose Dan Quayle, whose youth and vote-winning ability among women were seen as political assets. Michael Dukakis chose Texan Lloyd Bentsen as his running mate with the hope that he could pull Texas into the Democratic column. In 1992, Bill Clinton chose Tennessee Senator Al Gore for a number of reasons: Two southerners on the Democratic ticket could break the Republican presidential hold on the South. Gore's reputation as an environmentalist also soothed some of the party's more liberal wing, who were suspicious of Clinton's progressive credentials. Also, as both Gore and Clinton were in their forties, the selection of Gore helped affirm the image that this was a new generation of Democrats committed to the future and to change.

The national convention has increasingly become a televised spectacle that provides a candidate's media handlers one more opportunity to craft a carefully sculpted message for the viewing public.[10] Campaign managers attempt to orchestrate the convention for public consumption, promoting the virtues of the party's nominee. In recent conventions, the presidential candidate has been introduced by a film, a retrospective piece designed chiefly for the viewing audience at home, not the delegates on the convention floor. The video, decor, and music of the 1992 Democratic convention were all designed to make Clinton-Gore appear as the ticket of the young, the ticket of the future. Al Gore's introduction to the convention was accompanied by the beat of Paul Simon's "You Can Call Me Al." At the convention's close, Clinton and Gore, their families, and their supporters waved to the audience, accompanied by the refrains of Fleetwood Mac's "Don't Stop Thinking About Tomorrow." A "video wall" set behind the rostrum reinforced campaign themes. The well-scripted and harmonious Democratic convention stood in sharp contrast to the Republican convention, marred by the more hostile rhetoric of Patrick Buchanan and Patrick Robertson as they attempted to steer the GOP further to the Right. In 1992 it was the Republicans, not the Democrats, whose nomination process was marred by an intraparty insurgency that continued all the way through the national convention.

STAGE SIX: THE GENERAL ELECTION CAMPAIGNS

Traditionally, candidates pause after the summer conventions and recoup after the exhaustion of the nominating race. Nowadays, however, there is little pause; the fall campaign begins well in advance of the traditional Labor Day kickoff. Political strategists have come to recognize the importance of establishing and reinforcing campaign themes during this summer lull period. It was during this time that George Bush continued to hit at the symbolic themes that turned around the 1988 election. The inspired postconvention Clinton-Gore bus trip through the upper Midwest went a long way to solidify the ticket's support among crucial traditionally Democratic constituencies.

The fall campaign is increasingly geared to television. Often campaign stops do little more than serve as backdrops for free media televised messages—news clips that will reach the viewing audience at home. The 1992 race showed the emergence of new forms of free media, new competitors to the usual television news and political talk shows. Candidates chatted with talk show hosts and entertainers, bypassing professional news interrogators. Candidates also fielded questions directly from citizens via live telephone calls. Independent candidate Ross Perot seemingly owned CNN's Larry King Show as he mulled his entry, withdrawal, and reentry into the presidential arena. Bill Clinton appeared on Arsenio Hall, MTV, and various cable stations and early morning talk shows. George Bush, unwilling to give up the advantage of appearing presidential, was late in taking advantage of the opportunity provided by these unorthodox media venues. In the last week of the campaign, Bush at long last relented and appeared on MTV, looking quite uncomfortable as he was interviewed by their 24-year-old news anchor.

Presidential debates have become an increasingly commonplace, almost institutionalized part of the general election campaign. Presidential candidates usually declare their willingness to debate, but the meetings are not easily arranged because each camp's advisers seek to negotiate debate terms that will be to their candidate's advantage. Predictably, the candidate who trails in the polls will challenge an opponent to a series of televised encounters, hoping that the results will lead citizens to change their voting intentions. The leading candidate often will seek to limit the number of debates or otherwise insist on a format that will afford a strategic advantage or minimize the chance of making a politically damaging gaffe. In 1992, George Bush, trailing badly in the polls, agreed to a three-debate series that included, at the insistence of the Clinton camp, a more informal session conducted in a Phil Donahue–type setting. While the president sat stiffly on his stool, a more relaxed Bill Clinton moved about freely and easily while talking to the studio audience.

Presidential candidates entail a mix of paid advertising and free media. Despite the new prominence of negative advertising, presidential campaigning is not predominantly negative. Presidential advertisers feel that the public must have someone to vote for, not just someone to vote against. As a result, positive ads establish a candidate's personal warmth and presidential stature. Ads that stress positive images can also help compensate for weaknesses in a candidate's record. The paid advertising in a presidential race includes upbeat "bio" (biography) and image ads as well as more negative attack ads that are used when the situation requires. Presidential campaigns almost always finish with a positive, upbeat message. The 1992 Bush campaign, with its desperate closing attacks on Clinton, was an exception to this rule. While the Bush campaign relied on fear-arousal messages, a majority of the ads of both the Clinton and Bush campaigns alike emphasized criticism of the opponent. The 1992 presidential ad campaign may have been the most negative in history.[11]

THE POST-RACE: THE ELECTORAL COLLEGE

Largely, the Electoral College is an antiquated institution. Technically, Americans do not vote directly for the president;

instead they vote for electors who meet in December to choose the president. But, as already noted, electors do not act as an independent voice in presidential selection—as the founders of this nation had intended. Except for the problem caused by an occasional faithless elector who does vote independently, the Electoral College merely affirms the popular vote winner in each state in November. It is the November election, not the Electoral College, that decides who wins the presidency.

The fall campaign schedule is dictated to some extent by the unique demands of the Electoral College. Political campaign strategists gear their schedules to producing the majority of Electoral College votes required to win the presidency. They use tracking polls to find out how they are doing in each state and, especially in the closing days of the campaign, concentrate their efforts in those winnable states whose votes are needed to produce an Electoral College majority. Under the Electoral College's **unit rule**, the entire electoral vote of a state is cast as a single block on behalf of whichever candidate wins the popular vote plurality in that state. Thus, it is important for a presidential candidate to win middle-sized and large states, even if such states are carried by very small margins of victory.

The workings of the Electoral College are seldom understood, and there are constant calls for its reform or abolition.[12] Potentially troubling is the prospect of a "wrong winner" where a second-place finisher in terms of the popular vote garners enough votes in key states to emerge as the Electoral College winner. Such a wrong-winner outcome would impoverish the presidency, ensure deadlock, and possibly even lead to a constitutional crisis. In 1824, a deadlocked Electoral College threw the election into the House of Representatives, where John Adams emerged victorious despite having received fewer popular votes than Andrew Jackson in a multicandidate presidential field. In the disputed election of 1876, Rutherford B. Hayes became president despite finishing in second place to Samuel Tilden's 50.9 percent of the popular vote.

One relatively minor reform can eliminate the potential problem posed by the faithless elector; it would automatically cast an elector's ballot for whomever carried the state in November. More extensive reform calls, though, center around three different plans: the district plan, the proportional plan, and direct popular election.

Under the **district plan**, the unit rule in the Electoral College is abolished and electors are awarded to the candidate who wins a district; two additional electors are awarded to the winner of a state. In recent years, this reform plan has lost support inasmuch as it represents a radical shift of power to small and more conservative states. More importantly, the district plan does not guard against the nightmare scenario of a wrong Electoral College winner. In fact, it would act to produce such unmitigated disasters. Had the district plan been in place for the 1960 election, the popular vote loser, Richard Nixon, would have beaten John Kennedy. If the district plan had been used in 1968, third-party candidate George Wallace's vote in the South would have prevented both Nixon and Humphrey from receiving an electoral vote majority and would have thrown the election into the House of Representatives.

The **proportional plan** would award a presidential candidate the exact proportion of a state's electors justified by his or her share of the popular vote received in November. Like the district plan, the proportional plan abolishes the unit rule and thereby gives increased power to small states at the expense of reducing the critical importance of big states to an Electoral College victory. The plan also seemingly encourages multipartyism.

The **direct popular election plan** is the most simple and commonly suggested reform alternative. Under this plan, voters would cast their ballots directly; whoever won the most votes would be president. The direct election plan is an appeal to populist democracy. It is the only reform plan that guarantees against the wrong-winner scenario.

But the direct election plan, too, suffers from problems. In order to prevent the possibility that a fringe or extremist candidate might emerge from a multicandidate field as president as a result of his ability to mobilize a hard core of support, a second or run-off election between the top two candidates would be required if the leading candidate in the first election was unable to win a required percentage of the popular vote. A run-off election would be expensive and television-oriented; it would further exhaust the candidate finalists and the nation.

A second objection is that the direct election plan might help undermine a president's governing power. In his early days in office, a president is often powerful only to the extent that he or she is acting as the agent of a voter's mandate. The Electoral College's unit rule usually acts to give winning presidents a greater electoral vote victory than that which would seemingly be justified by the popular vote. As the margins of victory under the direct election plan will likely be less than they are under the Electoral College, a victorious president under direct election is denied the appearance of a landslide victory or popular mandate that can help him govern.

The direct election plan might also have the effect of reducing the political importance enjoyed by racial minorities and other constituencies in large states under the unreformed Electoral College. Under a system of direct election, presidential candidates do not necessarily have to appeal to the big two-party states. Instead, they could orient their campaigns toward small and mid-sized states that can generate large margins of support on election day. Tennessee, Alabama, and Arizona can potentially provide greater popular vote margins in the presidential race than more closely divided electorates in New York, New Jersey, Ohio, California, and Texas. Under the present Electoral College arrangements, presidential candidates must appeal to voters of Hispanic origin in such critical states as Florida, Texas, and California. Hispanic voters would enjoy no such privileged position of influence under direct election. Moreover, Jewish voters who live in critical Electoral College states would find their influenced diminished by direct election.

Given the deficiencies of the reform alternatives and the impossibility of predicting the full range of effects that will result from reform, many political scientists argue that the Electoral College has worked pretty well over the years and should be maintained as is: "If it isn't broke, don't fix it."[13] Others argue that the Electoral College is a ticking time bomb that needs to be reformed now and replaced with a direct election plan that protects the legitimacy of the presidency by guaranteeing against the election of a wrong winner as president.

SUMMARY

The presidential selection system has become an extended, drawn-out process that fatigues candidates and voters alike. The media is a prominent part of the process. Presidential aspirants can no longer win the nomination by relying solely on the endorsement of party regulars and the support of key activists. Retail politics is no longer enough. Instead, candidates have to use both paid media and free media in their wholesale politics efforts to reach potential voters. Even the role of the national party convention has changed in this media-intensive age; it now functions less as a genuine forum in which party leaders select the party's presidential nominee and more as an event staged for television. During the general election, media appeals are crucially important as candidates seek to win votes from an electorate that is no longer strongly attached to political parties. The role of the mass media, especially television, and the rise of voter independence are the subjects of Chapter 4.

THE CHANGED SETTING OF PRESIDENTIAL ELECTIONS: MEDIA WIZARDRY AND PARTISAN DEALIGNMENT

3

A changed political environment has given rise to the professionally mediated, televised campaign. Presidential campaigns are no longer dominated by decisions made in the back room by political party bosses. The rise of new image merchants, the rise of voter independence, the decline of political parties, and changes in the presidential nominating rules and campaign finance laws have all acted to alter the nature of the presidential race. In this chapter we take a look at the rise of the new image merchants and voter independence. Chapter 4 will recount the impact of reforms in the nominating system and campaign finance rules.

According to conventional wisdom, candidates avoid most issues, perhaps the most important issues of the day, as there are no easy, winning answers to difficult policy questions. Candidates find it difficult to communicate effective and coherent strategies to complex policy problems. They also fear that a strong stand on an important policy issue will offend large blocks of voters. Consequently, candidates give vague promises and commitments, rather than present voters with well-reasoned and realistic solutions to the problems that grip the nation. They also rely on professionally crafted, personal imagery, rather than detailed issue positions, to win elections.

But are issues as irrelevant to the presidential race as the conventional wisdom assumes? Is it the professional image merchants who determine who will be president? In this chapter we detail the rise of the professional image merchants and determine to what extent the power they are said to possess may be overstated. The changed environment of the presidential race, including the new voter independence, has created room for campaign appeals based on issues as well as on images. In the race for the presidency, issues play a much larger role than is commonly believed.

THE RISE OF IMAGE-MERCHANDISING

New cadres of public relations, fundraising, and advertising personnel occupy prominent positions in the modern presidential campaign. To a large extent, public opinion pollsters, media consultants, computerization experts, direct-mail specialists, and other practitioners of new campaign technologies have displaced an older generation of party politicians from positions of authority in campaign hierarchies.

As Joe McGinniss claimed in *The Selling of the President 1968*, his study of the Nixon campaign, professional image merchants package and sell candidates to the public in 30- and 60-second spot ads, much as a laundry soap or sports car is marketed.[1] Television is a visual medium that encourages viewers to judge candidates on the basis of their personal image, much as if the candidate were the host of a late-night television show. Media consultants advise candidates on what to say and how to behave on live television; speech coaches work to make a candidate's speech pacing and hand gestures more effective; and image consultants even advise prospective presidents how to dress for the camera: The dark-blue suit and red tie have almost become the official uniform of the presidential candidate appearing on television.

The presidential campaign often appears to be a battle of **sound bites,** in which candidates attempt to utter the slogan or witticism that will shape the next day's news coverage. A campaign's **spin doctors** further attempt to influence news reporters to put a favorable interpretation or "twist" on the day's events.

Paid advertising often promotes a candidate's personal qualities and leadership abilities and offers only brief hints as to policy concerns and commitments. Clearly, the 30- and 60-second spot ads rarely provide sufficient details by which voters can judge the feasibility and desirability of a candidate's policy promises.

The modern media campaign has become increasingly sophisticated. Presidential campaigns do not seek to present a single image of a candidate to the entire nation. Instead, campaign consultants use computer analyses of voter demographics in order to determine how a candidate will be marketed to different segments of the polity. Satellite hook-ups allow the candidate to "appear" before various groups of voters around the country, with messages tailored to each audience.

A sophisticated campaign can emphasize different themes and concerns when appealing to Hispanic as opposed to Anglo voters. Such concerns are marketed through commercials aired only in predominantly Hispanic communities. More specialized messages are placed in Spanish-language newspapers and on Spanish-speaking television and radio. Polling and other marketing tools allow the campaign to tailor a speech or advertisement to voters of Mexican, Cuban, and Puerto Rican ancestry, as Hispanic citizens do not necessarily share the same concerns.

Public relations specialists organize **focus groups** comprised of members of key voting groups, both to test potential media ads and to uncover potential "hot-button" issues that a campaign can exploit. Campaign consultants use **dial testing** to record a focus group's reaction to each different part of a potential campaign commercial. Public opinion experts take in-depth **base polls** that identify potential campaign issues and themes. Briefer daily **tracking polls** conducted over the telephone monitor a campaign's progress nad permit a campaign manager to fine-tune political strategy. Advertising specialists possess the capacity to manufacture new spot advertisements and deliver them to television and radio stations virtually overnight, enabling a candidate to respond quickly to an unexpected turn of events or to answer charges made by an opponent.

HOW DOMINANT ARE THE CAMPAIGN WIZARDS?

Journalists who cover the presidential race contribute to the perception that presidential elections are determined by behind-the-scenes manipulations of brilliant campaign strategists.

Formerly, news reporters told of the machinations of party professionals. Now they describe the technological wizardry of the new image merchants.

To a great extent this tradition of reporting has its roots in the works of Theodore White, whose landmark book, *The Making of the President 1960,* captured the drive, energy, and tactical mechinations of John F. Kennedy and his staff as the campaign maneuvered to victory in the spring primaries, the national party convention, and the fall election.[2] White wrote similar epics that detailed the strategic elements of the 1964 and 1968 contests. His style of reporting was quickly emulated by other campaign chroniclers, including McGinniss in his enormously popular *The Selling of the President 1968.*

Efforts to capture and expose the inner workings of the modern political campaign have not been confined to the written word. Television and the movies, too, have set out to reveal the nature of the modern campaign. Just one year after Clinton's victory, *The War Room,* a documentary shown in big-city theaters and released on videotape nationwide, replayed the behind-the-scenes actions of Clinton strategists James Carville and George Stephanopoulos as they dealt with the press, prepared new campaign ads, and generally dictated campaign strategy.

There is perhaps no more searing Hollywood indictment of the conduct of contemporary American elections than Jeremy Larner's 1972 movie, *The Candidate.* Robert Redford plays a young idealist, the public-interest advocate J. J. McKay, who is recruited by a professional campaign consultant to run for the United States Senate. (The unnamed state is clearly California.) In his search for victory, McKay loses both his ideals and his morality. Following the advice of his campaign consultants, he retreats from the clear stands on issues he took earlier in the campaign. His commercials are all personal-image puffery. In his public appearances, he utters stock phrases from a set campaign speech. After he wins, McKay asks his campaign manager, "What do we do now?" McKay has become a politician; he stands for nothing and can no longer act without his handlers and a script.

The movie forcefully portrays the techniques of the new campaign consultants. The campaign is geared to television. Media consultants test alternative spot ads and gauge the candidate's progress in tracking polls. McKay's handlers change the candidate's schedule at the last minute to take advantage of new media opportunities. On the command of one of his advisers,

McKay even switches neckties before participating in a televised debate.

The movie also shows the torture-trail aspects of election-eering in major state and national races. In what is essentially a **tarmac campaign,** the candidate, near exhaustion, repeatedly makes brief speeches at sites near airports as he seeks to appear in as many media markets as possible in a single day. Of course, in presidential campaigns that begin in earnest two or more years before the actual election, the rigors of the campaign trail can serve to weed out potential candidates. In 1976, former Vice President Walter Mondale dropped out of the presidential race as he could no longer tolerate a life of fundraisers, "rubber-chicken" dinners, and empty hotel rooms away from his home and the people he loved. New York Governor Mario Cuomo may have chosen to forgo the 1988 and 1992 presidential races for similar reasons.

For all their accuracy in describing the conduct of modern elections, however, movies like *The War Room* and *The Candidate* glorify and exaggerate the power of the new campaign elite. Media consultants and spin doctors do not possess the power at-tributed to them. A candidate listens to consultants when their expertise is deemed to be of value; but ultimately it is the candi-date, not the handlers, who decides what happens in a cam-paign. While it is a poor candidate who will attempt to be his or her own campaign manager, it is still the candidate who hires and fires top campaign staff and sets the parameters that delim-it their action. A candidate who defers to advice on how to dress for television may not so easily give in to requests to alter entrenched patterns of behavior or compromise deeply held convictions.

Candidates habitually ignore the advice of their consultants. Walter Mondale refused to restyle his hair in a way that his han-dlers thought would enhance his appeal to younger voters. Michael Dukakis resisted consultants' advice to respond to the Willie Horton ad by bringing in his own family history to dra-matize his concern about crime. The ad charged Dukakis with being opposed to the death penalty but supporting a policy that allowed furloughs to convicted murderers. Horton, a first-de-gree murderer, had received ten weekend passes from prison, "fled, kidnapped a young couple, stabbing the man and repeat-edly raping his girlfriend." But Dukakis would not exploit his family's personal tragedies for political gain. Only late in the campaign, with his presidential effort in dire straits, did Dukakis reluctantly tell the nation how his father had been robbed at gunpoint and how his brother had been killed by a hit-and-run driver.[3] In 1992 President Bush similarly resisted the admonition of trusted advisers to make an early and vigorous campaign effort in New Hampshire in light of the Patrick Buchanan insurgency; Bush would not shift from his "governing mode" to a "campaign mode."

The point of *The Candidate* most worth debating is its portrayal of the American election process as devoid of issue content. McKay wins on the basis of his dynamic image, good looks, and vacuous slogan "McKay. The Better Way." Hollywood has found an easy theme: American democracy does not work; the election process has been stolen by the professional image merchants. Similarly, *The War Room*, in its focus on the actions of Carville, Stephanopoulos, and others of the Clinton campaign elite, slights the events and issues outside the war room that may have been crucial to determining the outcome of the 1992 primaries and general election.

Imagemaking and the actions of spin doctors and campaign strategists are very real and important parts of the modern media campaign. But, in presidential elections, issues play a larger role in voters' decisions than a critique like *The Candidate* and the focus of *The War Room* would lead us to believe. Numerous studies have pointed to the rise of a new type of independent voter who is capable of taking issues and performance evaluations into account when going to the polls.[4] Voters learn from the media. The most persuasive advertising in recent presidential elections is not the sort of issueless ads scorned in *The Candidate* but ads that fuse together images and issues, using powerful symbols that enable voters to discern the different general policy orientations of the candidates.

GEORGE BUSH'S RISE AND FALL: THE RESULT OF IMAGES OR ISSUES?

The 1988 race for the presidency, perhaps more than any other contemporary presidential election, was reviled as a contest in which television imagery determined the outcome. Well into the presidential race, George Bush, then vice president, trailed Democratic challenger Michael Dukakis, the governor of Massachusetts, by 17 points in the polls. Bush campaign advisers—campaign manager Lee Atwater, media adviser Roger Ailes, pollster Bob Teeter, chief of staff Craig Fuller, and long-time friend Nicholas Brady—urged the vice president to get more aggressive. They and other Republican consultants tested potential campaign themes and issues before focus groups of **Reagan Democrats**—those nominally Democratic swing voters who had voted for Reagan and whose support Bush needed to win the election.

The Republican convention and fall campaign developed those themes identified by the focus group discussions. At the Republican national convention, Bush declared, in Clint Eastwood fashion: "Read my lips; no new taxes!" The focus group results also showed that voters reacted negatively to information indicating that Dukakis as governor had failed to mandate that all teachers lead their classes in reciting the Pledge of Allegiance; Bush closed his national convention speech by reciting the Pledge. In addition, the Republicans hit hard at Dukakis's alleged record on crime. The Bush campaign charged Dukakis with having run a "revolving door" prison program as governor. An advertisement sponsored by an independent PAC went even further, showing the picture of Willie Horton, a black man, who had escaped and committed heinous crimes while on furlough from a Massachusetts prison. The Bush ads derided Dukakis's leadership of "Taxachusetts." They further charged Dukakis with being soft on national defense and being responsible for the pollution of Boston Harbor. The Bush presidential effort stuck faithfully to its prechosen "theme of the day" and "theme of the week," carefully coordinating all public appearances and campaign statements to maximize the effective presentation of a predetermined message. These themes helped Bush to win the election.

But the Bush campaign, so successful in 1988, faltered badly in 1992. Some observers attribute the reversal to the loss of Lee Atwater, perhaps the most aggressive strategist of the 1988 campaign, who had died of brain cancer. Had he lived, according to these observers, the Bush campaign would have quickly dispatched the intraparty challenge posed by Patrick Buchanan and struck more boldly at Bill Clinton's liabilities.

But there is an alternative explanation for the reversal of George Bush's political fortunes between 1988 and 1992. Message, not message discipline, was the basis of George Bush's election in 1988 and his defeat in 1992.

In 1988, Bush had a message that voters were willing to hear. The rhetoric and paid advertising of the Republican campaign allowed voters to distinguish the competing value orientations and policy dispositions of the Republican and Democratic nominees.[5] Bush emphasized themes on crime and taxation that the voters found persuasive. As Jean Bethke Elshtain observes, voters and candidates jointly determine the issues that dominate a presidential race.

> Issues are what actually take root as preoccupations and themes. Thus, whether the symbolic meaning of the Pledge of Allegiance **is** an issue becomes an issue; the outcome of the 1988 election turned partly on who had best made his case. Voters and candidates are co-constructors of issues. Candidates speak and act in response to their perceptions of the concerns of the electorate.[6]

But, by 1992, the economy and the entire political environment had changed. As the nation was suffering a prolonged recession, Bush's attacks on the ills of Democratic party liberalism fell on deaf ears. Instead, voters were motivated by their dissatisfaction with the president's unwillingness to initiate more aggressive recovery efforts. They also remembered that Bush raised taxes despite his 1988 campaign vow. It was now Bill Clinton, with his promise of economic change, who had the message that voters wanted to hear. Even the most brilliantly orchestrated Republican campaign could not alter the Bush record. Nor, given the state of the economy and the constant stream of media reports focused on the recession, could even an aggressive campaign have easily switched voters' attention to issues other than the economy. Issues and performance, not poor campaign mechanics, lost the election for Bush in 1992.

TRENDS IN PARTISANSHIP

Increased Independence (or Merely Submerged Partisanship?)

The rise of voter independence over the past decades would appear to be one of the clearest trends in American politics. The surveys of the National Election Studies taken since the 1950s reveal the declining hold of political parties on the American electorate, although the decline has leveled off in recent years (see Table 3.1). In 1988, for the first time, the number of voters who identified themselves in surveys as independents exceeded the number of self-identified Democrats.

Table 3.1   Party Identification, 1952–1992 (percent)

	1952	1956	1960	1964	1968	1972	1976	1980	1984	1988	1992
Democrats	47.2	43.6	45.3	51.7	45.4	40.4	39.7	40.8	37.0	35.2	35.4
Independents	22.6	23.4	22.8	22.8	29.1	34.7	36.1	34.5	34.2	35.7	38.0
Republicans	27.2	29.1	29.4	24.5	24.2	23.4	23.2	22.4	27.1	27.5	25.7
Democratic plurality	20.0	14.5	15.9	27.2	21.2	17.0	16.5	18.4	9.9	7.7	9.7
Democrats plus											
Democratic leaners	56.8	49.9	51.6	61.0	55.2	51.5	51.5	52.3	47.8	47.0	49.3
Pure Independents	5.8	8.8	9.8	7.8	10.5	13.1	14.6	12.9	11.0	10.6	11.5
Republicans plus											
Republican leaners	34.3	37.4	36.1	30.2	32.9	33.9	32.9	32.6	39.5	40.8	38.3
Democratic plurality	22.5	12.5	15.5	31.1	22.3	17.6	18.6	19.7	8.3	6.2	11.0

Source: Herbert F. Weisberg, with David C. Kimball, "The 1992 Presidential Election: Party Identification and Beyond," paper presented at the Annual Meeting of the American Political Science Association, Washington, DC, September 1993.

But even here there is some scholarly debate. At least one important study argues that most journalists and political scientists have overstated the rise of voter independence.[7] According to these authors, a submerged partisanship lies just below the surface of most voters' declared independence. The study asserts that when asked, the clear majority of self-proclaimed independents admit to having partisan leanings, and that there is little difference between being an independent and a weak partisan. The number of true or "pure" independents is much less than is commonly assumed, only about one-third of the number of voters who claim to be independent.

It is true that many nominal independents are in fact submerged partisans. But trends in self-identified partisanship are only one of a number of indicators that point to increased voter independence. Many avowed partisans profess allegiance to a party but cast their votes as if they were "behavioral independents."[8] **Switchers** vote for the presidential candidate of one party in one election and the candidate of another party in the next election. **Ticket splitters** fail to cast a straight party ballot in a single election; instead they vote for candidates of different parties for different offices. Figure 3.1 documents the rise of ticket splitting.

Who are these ticket splitters, these new independents? According to Walter DeVries and V. Lance Tarrance, the ticket splitter tends to be better educated, professional, suburban, and of high or middle income. The ticket splitter is also inclined to be both politically active and an avid consumer of the mass media,

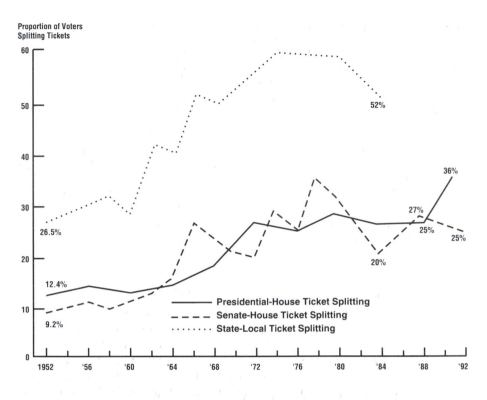

Figure 3.1   Ticket splitting, 1952–1992

Source: Michael M. Gant and Norman R. Luttbeg, *American Electoral Behavior* (Itasca, IL: F.E. Peacock, 1991), p. 37; Martin P. Wattenberg, *The Decline of American Political Parties, 1952–1992* (Cambridge, MA: Harvard Press, 1994).

a person who decides how to vote on the basis of what he or she has learned about the candidates in an election.[9]

The ticket splitter described by DeVries and Tarrance is a far cry from the self-identified independent observed in one of the most influential voting studies in political science, the classic *The American Voter.* Using survey data from the 1950s, the authors found respondents who identified themselves as independent apparently only because they did not care enough to follow political campaigns or identify with parties. Independents were the least educated, least interested, and least participant citizens.[10] The increased number of ticket splitters, in contrast, represents a new force in American politics, the rise of a more informed and aware independent voter.

But even here, some analysts disagree. The authors of *The Myth of the Independent Voter* doubt the emergence of such a new force in American politics. Not only are the ranks of genuine or pure independent voters much smaller than is commonly assumed, "pure" independents continue to rank at the bottom in terms of their education and their interest, information, and participation in politics. Pure independents are the least ideological and least issue-oriented of citizens; they are no different from the independents characterized by *The American Voter* in the 1950s. The apparent civic virtue of the new independents is the result of a large number of better-educated citizens who vote as if they were partisans but still claim to be independent.[11]

As we shall see throughout this book, there is no consensus as to the nature of the American voter. Different studies and different methodologies have led to different conclusions. While some political scientists point to the rise of issues in presidential elections, others emphasize the continued importance of imagemaking and partisanship.

Still, the overwhelming evidence points to continued **dealignment,** the move away from political party attachments. The rise of voter independence continued in 1992.[12] The Perot phenomenon was part of that independence. In 1992, self-proclaimed independents rose to a post-1940s high of 38 percent of the electorate; party identification had even less influence than usual on the presidential vote.[13]

Changes in the Partisan Balance and Voter Turnout

As Table 3.1 also reveals, the partisan advantage enjoyed by the Democrats over the Republicans has narrowed considerably since the New Deal, when the Democrats became the majority party. But by the 1980s, fewer voters saw the relevance of political parties formed along the cleavage lines of the New Deal era. Public approval of Reagan's performance as president led new voters to the Republican party.[14] The Democratic advantage of twenty or so points in party identification in 1952 was reduced to just seven points by 1988.

The Democratic partisan advantage in 1988 virtually disappears when differential rates of voter turnout are considered. Republican voters tend to be better educated, of higher income, and of nonminority status—all factors associated with higher rates of voting.[15] As a result, the Democrats enjoyed only a very narrow 47.2-to-46.1 percent advantage among persons who said that they voted in 1988.[16]

In 1992, however, the Democrats regained much of their partisan edge. When party "leaners" are included in the number of party identifiers, the Democrats enjoyed an eleven-point advantage over the Republicans in 1992, and talk of a Republican presidential era faded. George Bush's victory in the Gulf War brought few new converts to the Republican party. Instead, as the economic recession continued, voters professed a renewed allegiance to the Democrats. Party identification was not fixed but instead "oscillated" in response to political events and the public mood.[17]

The Republican sweep in the 1994 mid-term elections underscored the transitory nature of partisanship. The gains in partisanship that the Democrats had made in 1992 did little to prevent, just two short years later, a Republican takeover of the House and Senate and a clear majority of state governorships.

The 1992 election also saw a 5 percentage point increase in voter turnout, a sharp reversal of the declining turnout rates in presidential elections since 1960. Still, the turnout rate of 55.2 percent is low compared to the participation rates in other Western democracies where voting rules make it easier for citizens to register and vote.[18]

The number of marginal voters attracted to the candidacy of Ross Perot likely accounts for some, but not all, of the increase in turnout, especially as his candidacy prompted otherwise disinterested citizens to come out and vote.[19] Turnout rose in 1992 also because the candidate choice was more attractive and voters sensed more important stakes as compared to 1988.[20] As Ruy Teixeira has theorized, increased turnout is also possible if voters are "reconnected" to politics.[21] The presidential candidates' appearances on Larry King and popular talk shows were part of a process in 1992 that seemingly brought politics to the voters, reconnecting Americans to the political process.

However, heightened voter turnout, alone, does not account for Bill Clinton's victory in 1992. Increased electoral participation does not aid Democratic candidates to the extent commonly believed. George Bush would still have beaten Michael Dukakis in 1988 even if blacks, Hispanics, and poor whites had all voted at a rate approximating that of better-off whites.[22] Nonvoters are more heterogeneous, and less Democratic, than is commonly assumed. Even the full mobilization of nonvoters produces only a relatively minor impact on the outcome of the presidential race.[23] Issues and voter conversion, not enhanced voter turnout, were the decisive factors in Clinton's victory.[24]

Causes of the New Voter Independence

The move away from political parties in this country has been of long duration. As Walter Dean Burnham has observed, the "onward march of party decomposition" has been happening since the turn of the century. It was briefly interrupted during the New Deal, when the Democratic party became the Depression-era advocate of Americans in need. According to Burnham, voters have come to see parties and elections as increasingly irrelevant.[25]

What other reasons underlie the general decline of parties and rise of the new independence? They can be summarized as follows:

Education.   Voters are better educated today; they can decide how to vote without depending on a party label for guidance. Yet, as Martin Wattenberg notes, the rise in education alone does not explain the new independence. Independence has increased even among voters of low education.[26] Increased education also does not produce "pure" independence. Highly educated voters who identify themselves as "independent" often tend to be hidden partisans; the attraction of genuine voter independence is greatest among the least educated.[27]

The Pervasiveness of Television.   Americans report that they get most of their information from television, and viewers cannot help but learn something about presidential candidates. Even viewers who do not watch news programs will see paid spot ads and hear references to the election on celebrity talk shows. Inundated with political messages from television and other media, citizens fashion their own views regarding issues and candidates without having to rely on party labels.

Candidate-Centered Campaigns.   Political party organizations have decayed as agents of mass voter mobilization. Reforms in the presidential selection process have only further acted to reinforce the perception that party organizations are irrelevant. Both the financial and nominating rules were reformed in the late 1960s and 1970s to create a more open and fair presidential selection process, and those changes helped free presidential candidates from dependence on party leaders. As a result, political party leaders no longer screen presidential hopefuls; instead, presidential aspirants are self-selected. Candidate-centered organizations have displaced political parties as the most important

portant vehicles in presidential campaigns. Presidential aspirants put together their own personal fundraising and vote-getting organizations beginning before the spring primaries. The party's nominee essentially dictates the party platform and the fall campaign themes.[28] The nominee's loyal advisers, not senior party officials, determine general election strategy. In a presidential year, the national political party becomes little more than an adjunct to the candidate-centered campaign.

Changing Media Coverage.   The way the mass media covers elections, too, reinforces the public's perception of the decreased relevance of political parties. Newspapers, magazines, and television have all adapted to the rise of candidate-centered campaigns. Election stories have increasingly focused on the candidate, to the exclusion of mentioning partisan philosophy or even political party ties. Martin Wattenberg has examined the presidential campaign coverage of two newspapers (the *Chicago*

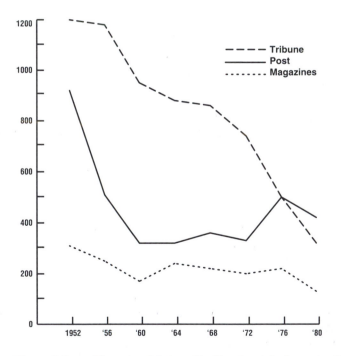

Figure 3.2   The role of the media: Number of substantive linkages between parties and candidates in news stories, 1952–1980

Source: Martin P. Wattenberg, *The Decline of American Political Parties, 1952–1988* (Cambridge, MA: Harvard Press, 1990), p. 97.

Tribune and the *Washington Post*) and three weekly news-magazines (*Newsweek, Time,* and *U.S. News and World Report*). His analysis clearly shows that news stories no longer prominently link presidential candidates to their political parties (see Figure 3.2).[29]

The Fading Relevance of the New Deal Party Alignment. The basic division between the Democratic and Republican parties was forged during the New Deal era. The Democrats stood for a more activist approach to government and a fairer distribution of America's industrial wealth. The Republicans, in contrast, stood for a less interventionist, more laissez-faire approach to government. Given the vast social insecurity that existed at the time, people wanted the protection of government programs. The Democrats became the majority party.

But in the postindustrial age that followed, new issues emerged that divided Americans from their New Deal partisan loyalties.[30] As New Deal programs such as Social Security were institutionalized, Americans took them for granted. Further, Americans were unwilling to see their taxes raised to pay for the extension of benefit programs, especially to beneficiaries seen as undeserving. New public concerns over inflation, limiting the cost of government, and social issues often proved more salient than New Deal era causes. The racial issue was especially divisive in shattering the Democratic electoral coalition.[31]

The 1994 election of Republican majorities in the House (for the first time since 1952) and Senate was the culmination of the public's rejection of the big-government Democratic approach to problem solving.

For many Americans, neither the Democratic nor the Republican party represents their views across the broad range of issues. Large numbers of Americans find the Democratic party acceptable on basic economic protection and health care, but too liberal on welfarism and affirmative action, and too soft on national defense. Other Americans approve of the generally conservative Republican approach to taxing and spending, yet consider the Republicans to be too supportive of the rich and too conservative on personal morality issues and environmental protection. These voters, the new behavioral independents, vote in a presidential race in response to candidate, issue, and performance evaluations. The unexpectedly large vote for Ross Perot in 1992 may be indicative of voters' frustrations with the two major parties as organized around the cleavage lines of the New Deal era and apparently unable to deal with the problem posed by runaway budget deficits.

Generational Replacement. Younger citizens are among the most independent in the nation. They are also the age group least likely to vote. In part, younger citizens have yet to build up the habit of voting, which reinforces party identification. The electorate as a whole becomes more independent as the New Deal generation of partisans dies off and is replaced by a generation of more independent voters.

According to Paul Allen Beck, today's younger voters have not been well-socialized into the affiliations of the New Deal era. More senior voters who lived through the New Deal era see a meaningful choice between Democrats and Republicans. Their children, in turn, were socialized at the dinner table about the virtues of one political party over another. They learned from their parents just who were the good guys and bad guys of American politics. Today's younger voters, in contrast, have not been taught with equal passion the importance of partisanship. Unless a partisan realignment occurs that will raise the salience of new issues and generate a new and meaningful sense of the importance of parties, younger voters are likely to continue to be independent.[32]

Yet, some political scientists argue that the **dealignment,** or move away from parties, of younger voters is often overstated. Martin Wattenberg observes that the decline of partisan attachments is evident among voting groups of all ages.[33] Also, even though young voters profess to being politically independent, few are altogether without partisan affinities; "independent" younger voters have a partisan preference.[34] A "life-cycle" of partisanship may be reemerging; as young independents mature, they tend to become hidden partisans with a firmer sense of partisan preference. If the independence of the younger voters continues to fade with age, dealignment may have already peaked.[35]

Consequences of the New Independence

The rise of voter independence has led to a **two-tier system** of American elections—a system of split results where the outcome of presidential races is separated from the outcome of congressional races (see Figure 3.3).[36] In recent years, Republicans have

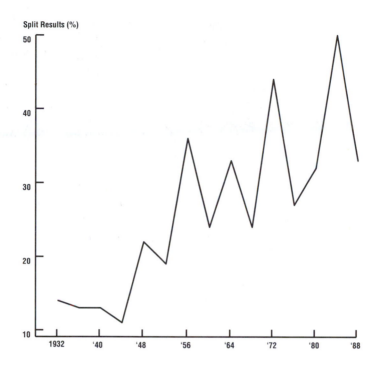

Figure 3.3　　District-level split results of House and presidential elections, 1932–1988

Source: Gary C. Jacobson, *The Electoral Origins of Divided Government* (Boulder, CO: Westview Press, 1990), p. 11.

done much better in presidential elections than in races for Congress; Republicans won five of the seven White House elections from 1968 to 1992, a period in which the Democrats generally maintained control of Congress—resulting quite often in **divided government.** In 1994, a new twist on divided government emerged, as the Republicans won control of Congress while the Democrats and Bill Clinton commanded the presidency.

In 1994, this two-tiered electoral system has emerged as the Republicans enjoyed advantages in the presidential race while the Democrats enjoyed advantages in the congressional races. Salient issues of the day and voter evaluations of candidates and their past performance records have dominated the presidential voting decision. Republicans successfully exploited broad symbolic issues—the social issue in 1968 and 1972, and the issues of big government and tax relief in the 1980s—to win the presidency.

But in races for Congress, until 1994 Democrats were able to use the advantages afforded by partisanship and incumbency to maintain control of the House of Representatives. While the national economy and presidential popularity do exert an influence on congressional races,[37] elections for the House and other, lower-visibility offices seldom turn on broad national issues and performance evaluations. Instead, name recognition, constituency service, the perquisites of incumbency, the prevailing partisan balance of a district, and unique local issues are all more important forces in congressional elections. Many Democratic incumbents also face challengers who lack the political experience, organizational support, and funding base to make a truly serious race for Congress.[38] In the 1994 mid-term elections, however, a new wave of anti-Washington outrage muted the advantages of incumbency, and the Democrats were turned out of office.

In recent years neither political party has been able to establish dominant control over the Senate. The margin of Democratic control in the Senate is more narrow than in the House; and in 1980, Republicans briefly regained control of the Senate for the first time since 1953. Senate races are more visible than House races. Moreover, statewide senatorial districts are larger and more heterogeneous than House districts; constituent service, homestyle, and the careful gerrymandering of district boundaries cannot be used to afford Senators the same measure of political safety that House members enjoy. Hence, a political shock of seismic proportions was registered in 1994 when Republicans picked up enough seats to win the House as well as the Senate.

Voter independence produces divided government and a behavioral reinforcement of the separation of powers that often leads to frustration and deadlock.[39] Even when the president and Congress are of the same party, there is no assurance that the two, elected independent of each other, will cooperate in solving the nation's problems.[40]

Some observers fear that a new age of **rootless politics** or voter volatility is emerging as citizens' votes are no longer secured by the moorings of party identification.[41] The result can be political instability. Voter confidence in government shrinks as the nation ineffectively lurches back and forth from one policy direction to another, as one party is replaced by an opposing party. The 1992 to 1994 swing in voting from Democrat to Republican underscores this instability of partisan attachments.

A rootless electorate, not anchored by partisanship, may also succumb to demagogic candidate appeals. The dangers of rootless politics, however, are overstated if many voters who claim to be independents are, in fact, hidden partisans.[42]

Ross Perot's amazing showing in 1992, where he received approximately one of every five votes cast in the general election, would seem to indicate that voter independence has opened the door to third-party politics. The 1994 mid-term election results also point to the continued strength of antigovernment sentiment.

Yet, the ground for a third-party ascendancy may not be as fertile as the Perot vote would seem to indicate. There is no single, unified block of independents that a third-party candidate can easily mobilize. Rather, the ranks of the independents embrace diverse groups of citizens with quite disparate political attitudes. It is difficult to imagine a political platform behind which this diverse group of voters could be rallied.[43] Perot's calls for budget reduction and "reform" were vague, and his supporters did not agree to the specifics of any budget-cutting plan. Perot's showing in 1992 was more a protest vote than an indication of the potential for a third party committed to an alternative political philosophy. As a protest candidate, Perot is likely to see less support when economic times are good and voters are satisfied with a president's performance.

SUMMARY

In the age of the candidate-centered campaign, a new elite of pollsters, image merchandisers, and other professionals has displaced political party leaders from the prominent roles they once played in American presidential elections. The power of political party organizations to mobilize the vote of an increasingly independent electorate has also declined. While the power of the new image wizards can easily be overstated, the important role they play in the modern campaign cannot be denied. As we shall see in the next chapter, reforms in the nominating and finance rules have also helped contribute to the emergence of candidate-centered presidential campaign organizations.

THE NOMINATING SYSTEM AND CAMPAIGN FINANCE REFORM: THE RULES OF THE GAME

4

Beginning in the 1960s and 1970s, great reforms were made in the rules governing the presidential nominating system and the means by which presidential campaigns are financed. The cumulative impact of these rules changes has been to open the process to new participants. No longer do the favored candidates of state party leaders and local party "bosses" enjoy a great competitive edge in the presidential selection process. Instead, new candidacies have emerged. Presidential candidates must directly appeal to voters, not just to party leaders. As the influence of party leaders declined, with the introduction of a more open nominating system, both personal images and issues began to play a heightened role in the selection of presidential candidates.

THE REFORMED PRESIDENTIAL NOMINATING PROCESS

As we discussed in Chapter 2, currently, presidential nominations are won during the primary and caucus season. National party conventions merely affirm the voters' choice in the primaries, which was not always the case.

For more than a hundred years, a national convention of state and local party officials actually selected the party's presidential nominee. Presidential hopefuls generally did not even need to campaign in primaries, which were relatively few in number; instead, they politicked for support among party leaders. Beginning in the mid-1950s, presidential primaries assumed new importance as a way by which a candidate could demonstrate political viability to party leaders. In 1960, John Kennedy won the Wisconsin and West Virginia primaries and thereby demonstrated that his relative youth and Catholicism posed no insurmountable barriers to his electability.[1] Rule changes introduced as a result of the social turmoil of the 1960s would soon make winning the primaries the only effective route to a party's presidential nomination.

The Turbulent 60s: Prelude to Reform

The shape of the presidential nominating process was changed forever as a result of the tumult that surrounded the 1968 Democratic convention in Chicago. In 1968, a Democratic party badly divided over the Vietnam war gave its presidential nomination to Hubert Humphrey. Humphrey had not won a single primary that year; he had not even entered the primaries. The vast majority of the Democratic convention delegates were chosen not by voters in primaries but by party leaders in meetings or caucuses that were closed to the public. A prominent Democrat of long standing and Lyndon Johnson's loyal vice president, Humphrey was able to use his ties to the Democratic party establishment to win the nomination.

Antiwar Democrats claimed that the presidential selection system was unfair and undemocratic, and the 1968 convention turned into a riot as police and antiwar activists clashed in the streets of Chicago and angry exchanges marred the proceedings. All the ill events were duly recorded on television. The Democrats went down to a narrow defeat; Republican Richard Nixon became president.

Reforms were needed to bring the Democratic party together in order to avoid a repeat disastrous performance in the next election. It was widely recognized that the existing procedures for nominating the president were undemocratic and in need of change.

Four years previously, party rules changes had focused on civil rights. At the party's 1964 convention, a slate from the Mississippi Freedom Democratic Party challenged the seating of the all-white regular Mississippi delegation. In a compromise, the convention voted to seat two of the Freedom Democrats and treat the rest as "honored guests." The convention also passed resolutions banning discrimination in the delegate selection process and asserting the party's right to require compliance. The national party convention was no longer a place where state political leaders assembled once every four years. The national party had begun to expand its control over the delegate selection process, control that it would assert more strongly after the events of 1968.[2]

Nominating Reform: McGovern-Fraser and Succeeding Rules Changes

The initial post-1968 Democratic party rules changes were popularly referred to as the **McGovern-Fraser reforms**, after South Dakota Senator George McGovern and Minnesota Representative Donald Fraser who cochaired the party's commission on reform. In succeeding years, other party commissions would add to and refine the basic rules changes adopted under McGovern-Fraser.

Under the old delegate selection system, state and local party leaders often chose national convention delegates in caucuses and conventions that barred the participation of all but a few loyal party regulars. In some states, these delegate selection meetings took place well in advance of the presidential calendar year, before the major contenders for the nomination were known.

The McGovern-Fraser reforms emphasized the values of timeliness, openness, and demographic representativeness. The new rules sought to increase the public's involvement in presidential selection. The reforms required that the public be given adequate advance notice of any meetings involved in delegate selection and that the process of delegate selection take place in the same calendar year as the presidential convention. All persons who declared themselves to be Democrats were entitled to participate in these meetings.

The new rules also required that delegates to the national convention be picked in such a way as to ensure the fair representation of minorities, women, and youth. These were the constituencies that had been severely underrepresented in past party conventions dominated by aging white, male party leaders. The McGovern-Fraser rules changes here were greatly criticized for constituting population quotas. They were later modified by the party's Mikulski Commission, which set out strict requirements for affirmative action but explicitly barred the use of quotas. In the early 1980s, though, the Democrats did adopt one quota: The Winograd Commission mandated the equal division of convention delegates by gender.

The rules changes succeeded in increasing the representation of women and African-Americans at the Democratic National Convention. Women comprised only 13 percent of the prereform 1968 convention delegates; they were 48 percent of the 1988 convention. African-Americans were 5 percent of the delegates at the 1968 convention; they were 22 percent in 1988. Gains made by youth proved more ephemeral as the requirements for youth representation were later relaxed. In 1972, the first convention of the reform era, 22 percent of Democratic convention delegates were under the age of 30. But by 1988 the figure for youth representation fell back to just 4 percent, the prereform level.[3]

States could meet the party's various new delegate selection rules by reforming their caucus and convention processes or by switching to a primary in which all Democrats could vote. As Table 4.1 shows, states immediately began to switch to primaries. States that chose to create a Democratic presidential primary often chose to have a Republican primary as well. Beginning in 1972, the majority of convention delegates in both parties were chosen in primaries. No longer could a candidate hope to win a first-ballot convention victory, as Humphrey had in 1968, without entering and winning state primaries. Party leaders lost their control over the nomination; the presidential race became more open to outsiders.

As a result of the McGovern-Fraser rules changes, the number of Democratic officeholders who attended the party's national conventions dropped sharply. Party leaders who supported losing presidential contenders during the primary season were no longer entitled to a seat at the convention. Many leaders would not even consider running for convention delegate under the new reformed rules; elected officeholders did not wish to alienate constituents loyal to other presidential hopefuls. With the eclipse of party leaders, more issue-oriented and ideological activists began to play a greater role at the national convention.[4]

Table 4.1   Proliferation of Primaries and the Growing Importance of Presidential Primaries to National Convention Votes, 1968–1984

	Democrats			Republicans		
year	no. of primaries	no. of delegate votes	% of all votes	no. of primaries	no. of delegate votes	% of all votes
1968	17	983	37.5	16	458	34.3
1972	23	1,862	60.5	22	710	52.7
1976	29	2,183	72.6	28[a]	1,533	67.9
1980	35	2,378	71.8	34[b]	1,516	76.0
1984	25[c]	2,431	62.1	30[c]	1,551	71.0

[a]Does not include Vermont, which held a nonbinding preference primary but chose delegates by caucus/convention.

[b]Includes Puerto Rico and DC. Does not include Vermont.

[c]Includes Puerto Rico and DC. Does not include five states that held nonbinding primaries but chose delegates by caucus/convention.

Source: William Crotty and John S. Jackson III, *Presidential Primaries and Nominations* (Washington, DC: CQ Press, 1985), p. 63.

Critics of the McGovern-Fraser rules charged that reform had gone too far in excluding party leaders, including top elected officials, from any role in selecting the party's presidential nominee.[5] Elected officials represent important constituencies. Party professionals also are some of the party's most capable and seasoned campaigners. Critics argued that the inclusion of party leaders was necessary in order to add a voice of reason and balance to a party convention that had become vulnerable to capture by issue activists and party outsiders.

The Winograd Commission sought to increase the voice of party leaders at the convention. An add-on of up to 10 percent in additional convention seats was set aside for party leaders for 1980. Four years later, the Hunt Commission increased the number of **superdelegates**—officeholders and party leaders entitled to attend the national convention on the basis of their position—to 566, or 14.4 percent of the convention total. But in 1988, Jesse Jackson sharply complained that the award of superdelegates discriminated against his candidacy, that he did not receive the fair share of delegates merited by the popular vote he won. In response to Jackson's complaint, the Democratic party's Fairness Commission reduced the number of superdelegates from 644 in 1988 to about 250 for the 1992 convention.

The Republicans were less aggressive in the pursuit of delegate selection reform. A more homogeneous party, they were less torn apart than the Democrats by the Vietnam War and by the social polarizations of the 1960s and 1970s. Further, having won five of the six presidential elections from 1968 to 1988, the Republicans saw no great urgency to reform a candidate nominating system that, from their point of view, was working so well.

Yet, the new spirit of openness in the Democratic party generated pressures for the Republicans to revise their rules to make their conventions more open to participation by rank-and-file party members.[6] The Republican party relied on more informal efforts to achieve diversity. Their efforts increased the participation of women at the GOP national convention, but, overall, Republicans did not achieve the demographic representativeness of the Democratic convention. From 1968 to 1988, the presence of women at the Republican convention doubled, increasing from 16 to 33 percent of the convention's delegates. But in 1988, African-Americans still accounted for only 4 percent of Republican National Convention delegates.[7]

The manner by which Republicans allocate convention delegates is also quite different from the Democrats. The Republicans were less willing than Democrats to insist on modified **proportional representation (PR)** rules in an effort to represent more fairly the diverse candidate and policy factions at the national convention.[8] Under PR, each candidate receives a number of delegates from a state roughly in proportion to the votes received in the state's caucuses or primary. A candidate who loses a state's nominating contest but whose vote was above a certain minimum threshold still wins delegates to the convention.

In the Democratic party, PR rules have allowed divisive primary season battles to drag on and on; even when victorious in major states, the winning candidate receives only a portion of the state's delegate total, rather than the entire block of state delegates which would put him in the clear lead and help wrap up the nomination. PR also permits divisiveness at the national convention, where the party's nominee faces a convention with many delegates committed to the candidacy and policies of rivals.

While a number of Republican states have turned to some form of proportional representation, Republican rules permit a greater variety of delegate selection plans than allowed by the Democratic party. In 1988, 13 states, including California, Florida, Ohio, and Texas, still chose their Republican convention delegates under winner-take-all rules, where the candidate who wins the plurality of votes in a state primary is given the entire state delegation to the national convention. Other Republican states have variations of winner-take-all rules that reward winning candidates at the expense of less successful challengers.

The Republican party's refusal to adopt strict PR rules worked to George Bush's advantage in the Republican nominating contests in 1992. State Republican parties loyal to President Bush kept the threshold required for winning national convention delegates high, often as high as forty percentage points. As a result, even though Patrick Buchanan scored well in the primaries against Bush, often receiving a fourth or more of the vote in early races, his vote usually fell below the requirement that was set for a candidate to win any delegates to the national convention. Despite his early strong showing, only 78 delegates at the 1992 GOP National Convention cast ballots for Buchanan; 1,846 voted for Bush. Democratic party rules, with their stronger emphasis on proportional representation, would not have permitted such extensive discrimination against a party faction.

Questions of Democracy, Policy Representativeness, and Ideological Polarization

The Democratic party's reforms assured a more open delegate selection process and produced national conventions that were a better demographic mirror of rank-and-file Democrats. But were the rules truly democratic? According to critics, the reformed nominating process in both parties produced presidential conventions vulnerable to ideological factions and issue activists whose views are more extreme than those of the average American or party member. Openness and demographic representativeness are no guarantee of policy representativeness. The democratic nature of national party conventions is still very much a matter of debate.

The unrepresentative nature of the 1972 Democratic convention, the first conducted in compliance with most of the reformed nominating rules, is evident when the policy views of convention delegates are compared with those of rank-and-file Democrats. One study, conducted by Denis Sullivan and his associates, reveals a serious difference of policy views between convention delegates and the rank and file.[9] Democratic convention delegates were more liberal than the party's mass base on school busing, amnesty for draft evaders, and proposals to establish a guaranteed annual income (see Table 4.2). Jeane Kirkpatrick's more extensive study confirms the view that the national convention was out of touch with party followers. Kirkpatrick showed that 1972 Democratic convention delegates were vastly more liberal than rank-and-file Democrats when it came to such issues as

Table 4.2   Differences between Delegates and Democratic Rank and File on Issue Opinions, 1972

	delegates	rank and file
Busing		
Favor busing with no qualifications	25%	30%
Favor busing if only means to racial balance and educational equality	54	not available
Oppose	21	70
Amnesty		
Favor without punishment	46	31
Favor with punishment	36	not available
Oppose	18	69
Guaranteed Annual Income		
Favor	74	43
Oppose	26	57

Source. Denis G. Sullivan, et al., *The Politics of Representation: The Democratic Convention, 1972* (New York: St. Martin's Press, 1974), p. 32.

welfare policy, school busing, crime control, and attitudes toward both the military and political demonstrators.[10] The convention was so unrepresentative of the American people that its nominee, George McGovern, was rejected in November by a landslide margin.

How could the 1972 convention be so unrepresentative of the party's base? According to Kirkpatrick, the reformed delegate selection rules helped to facilitate the seizure of the party by a "new presidential elite," a new breed of issue activists loyal only to their candidate and their cause-of-the moment.[11] Dedicated to stopping the war in Vietnam, McGovern's issue-intense followers packed the open caucuses and district conventions while more moderate Democrats remained at home.[12] McGovern's followers were even able to stack caucuses and conventions in such conservative states as Oklahoma and Virginia.

Open caucuses are vulnerable, then, to capture by a candidate with an intensely motivated group of supporters. In 1988, Jesse Jackson won the Democratic presidential caucuses in Michigan, a low-turnout event, as the result of relatively high voter turnouts in poor and black sections of Detroit and other cities. The lack of representativeness was a matter of policy views, not social class. While better educated, higher-status voters usually are overrepresented in low-turnout elections, such was not the case in Michigan in 1988.

Not all political scientists accept the view that the open presidential selection system is as biased as Kirkpatrick and other critics charge. Thomas Marshall, for instance, has examined the 1972 caucuses in Minnesota. While he found the overrepresentation of upper-status groups in the caucuses, he did not find the policy views of caucus participants to be greatly out of line with those of party supporters.[13] Similar claims can be made for Iowa; while participants in that state's important caucuses are more affluent and better educated than Iowans generally, the caucuses have not been dominated by fringe candidates and zealots. While the Reverend Pat Robertson found strong support in the Iowa Republican caucuses in 1988, over the years the list of Democratic and Republican winners in the Iowa caucuses—Edmund Muskie, Jimmy Carter, Gerald Ford, George Bush, Walter Mondale, Richard Gephardt, and Robert Dole—is a list of political moderates.[14]

Representativeness appears to be less of a problem for primaries than for caucuses. With turnouts larger than those associated with caucuses, primaries are less prone to capture by unrepresentative bands of candidate and issue activists. Herbert Kritzer found Democratic primary voters in 1972 to be fairly representative of Democrats as a whole.[15] A study by William Crotty and John Jackson of voting in the 1980 primaries essentially reinforces Kritzer's conclusions. While ideologically extreme voters were active in primaries, the issue preferences of primary voters did not differ very much from those of nonvoters.[16]

The reforms of the nominating system are not entirely to blame for the unrepresentative nature of national party conventions. As Herbert McClosky demonstrated in his classic study of the prereform Democratic and Republican conventions of 1956, national convention delegates generally tend to be more to the extreme than rank-and-file party members. National party delegates, like other political elites, are more interested in politics and aware of issues than is the average citizen.[17]

The more extreme nature of the 1972 convention was also a result of the anti–Vietnam War insurgency that captured the Democratic party. McGovern rode antiwar sentiment to the nomination. As Crotty and Jackson observe, once the Vietnam issue passed, Democratic national conventions lost some of their extreme left-wing flavor. Democratic conventions in succeeding years have been less liberal than the 1972 convention (see Table 4.3).

Yet, as both Tables 4.3 and 4.4 show, the problem of policy representativeness remains; delegates to these national conventions

Table 4.3   Self-Identified Ideology of National Convention Delegates, Party Members, and Mass Public, 1972–1980

self-identified ideology	1972		1976		1980		party members (1980)		mass public (1980)
	D	**R**	**D**	**R**	**D**	**R**	**D**	**R**	
Liberal	79%	10%	40%	3%	46%	2%	21%	13%	19%
Moderate	13	35	47	45	42	36	44	40	49
Conservative	8	57	8	48	6	58	26	41	31

Source: William Crotty and John S. Jackson III, *Presidential Primaries and Nominations* (Washington, DC: CQ Press, 1985), p. 118.

are still more liberal than both rank-and-file Democrats and the general public. Warren Miller and M. Kent Jennings, too, found that delegates at the 1976 and 1980 convention were more liberal than Democratic followers. Yet these delegates showed a new willingness to compromise and a concern for winning, as compared to their McGovernite predecessors.[18] Even issue-oriented activists want a candidate with a chance of winning in November.[19] Evidence from 1984 and 1988 continues to show Democratic conventions more liberal than both registered party members and the general public.[20]

As Table 4.4 shows, Republican as well as Democratic National Conventions have been ideologically out of line with party followers and the mass public. Delegates to Republican conventions

Table 4.4   Philosophical Position of the 1988 Republican and Democratic Delegates vs. the Mass Public

	1988 Republican Delegates	Republican Identifiers	American Public in 1988
Liberal	0%	11%	20%
Moderate	36	44	48
Conservative	59	40	32

	1988 Democratic Delegates	Democratic Identifiers	American Public in 1988
Liberal	43%	26%	20%
Moderate	43	42	48
Conservative	5	28	32

Source: John S. Jackson III, "Yes—The Nominating Process Is Representative," in *Controversial Issues in Presidential Selection*, ed. Gary L. Rose (Albany, NY: State University of New York Press, 1991), pp. 31–32.

are more conservative than either convention identifiers or the public at large.

Nominating system reforms, in summary, opened the way to new candidacies and increased the ideological polarization of the national conventions. Democratic conventions are to the left, and Republican conventions are to the right, of a more moderate rank-and-file party membership and a general public located closer to the political center. With elected officials playing a less prominent role, party conventions were free to move off to ideological extremes.[21]

Democratic and Republican conventions are populated by delegates of competing ideologies who offer two different visions of America. As Crotty and Jackson argue in their review of the nominating and convention system:

> It is no longer accurate, if it ever was, to say the parties are alike as Tweedledum and Tweedledee. In fact, the parties may now offer more systematic philosophical differences at the elite level than ever before in their history.[22]

National convention elites are prone to nominate candidates who offer voters a choice on the issues.[23]

The Triumph of Ideological and Issue Interests

Intraparty battles among ideological factions and issue-interest groups often continue after the nomination has been settled. The candidacies of Ted Kennedy, Jesse Jackson, and Jerry Brown continued long after it was clear that they had lost the Democratic nomination. Yet, these candidates and their supporters pushed on as they championed progressive policies to meet the needs of forgotten Americans. Similarly, in the Republican party, George Bush in 1992 continued to suffer harping criticism from Patrick Buchanan long after it was obvious that Bush would easily win renomination. Buchanan and his supporters were seeking to keep the Republican party loyal to conservative traditions.

Intraparty battles that continue after the nomination has been sewn up are more about issues and ideology than the nomination itself. Intraparty factions even fight over a platform that is not binding on the presidential nominee or any party candidate. Their goal is to publicize an issue, educate the American public, and influence policy makers outside the convention.[24] Advocates of women's rights, civil rights, and gay rights are only some of the more notable groups that have attempted to advance their policies at Democratic conventions. Evangelical Christians and advocates of right-to-life and "family values" similarly have attempted to pull Republican conventions away from the political center.[25]

Teachers are an organized interest that has gained prominence under the openness of the reformed convention rules. The National Education Association (NEA), the largest organization of public school teachers in the United States, was a vital part of Jimmy Carter's successful drive to the 1976 Democratic nomination. The NEA supported Carter largely as a result of his promise to create a cabinet-level Department of Education. Similarly, NEA members comprised a large part of the vote that gave Carter his initial victory in the Iowa caucuses. In localities across the nation, the members of the NEA *were* the Carter campaign! The importance of the NEA to Carter's victory was also quite apparent at the 1976 national convention, where 302 delegates were members of the NEA, a number larger than any state delegation except California. The 269 NEA members committed to Carter formed his largest single block of convention delegates and comprised 16 percent of the total needed to win the nomination.[26]

As party leaders can no longer provide the delegates that candidates need for the nomination, presidential hopefuls have little alternative but to mobilize the support of outside constituencies. Issue promises given to specific groups are a part of the presidential nominating process.

FINANCE REFORM

Public reaction to the financial improprieties associated with Watergate reinvigorated efforts to establish a new system for funding presidential elections. A new system involving public (or taxpayer) funding was set up in an effort to limit the potentially corrupting influence of private money, equalize spending between the major parties in the general election, and increase public accountability through more strict requirements for disclosure of campaign contributions and spending. Public funding succeeded in enabling outsiders and new-issue candidacies to enter the presidential race. Over the years, however, presidential campaign organizations and private interests alike have found ways to circumvent the intent and provisions of campaign funding rules. Private money has found its way back into the presidential race.

How the FECA Works

The Federal Election Campaign Act (FECA) amendments of 1974 (hereafter referred to as the Act) provide a very complex set of rules for the financing of presidential elections. Put most simply, the Act seeks to limit the potential of private money in the presidential race. The Act provides for full taxpayer funding of the major-party national conventions and fall presidential campaigns, the partial public funding of primary campaigns, and the imposition of certain limits on donations and on spending by candidates who choose to accept public funds. The amount of funds given to a third-party presidential candidate depends on the vote that the candidate receives on election day.

In effect, presidential candidates choose to give up their right to freely solicit and spend money in exchange for taxpayers' assistance in financing their candidacies. Presidential candidates almost universally choose to accept public funds. For many candidates, government funds represent more than the candidate can hope to raise on his or her own. Other candidates accept public funding and its accompanying restrictions because they do not wish to be branded as the captive of "special interests."

Since the introduction of the new public financing rules, only two presidential candidates have refused to accept public funding; both had access to rich sources of private money. In 1980, Texan John Connally thought that he could rely on his access to oil money and other wealthy contributors in his bid for the Republican nomination. He was mistaken and won only one delegate. Similarly, in 1992, multibillionaire Ross Perot spurned public funding as he did not wish to abide by the accompanying spending limits. According to one estimate, Perot put almost $60 million of his own money into the race.[27] While this amount is roughly equivalent to the total public funds that Bush and Clinton each received for their party convention and fall campaign, the sum greatly exceeds the amount that the Perot campaign would have been permitted to spend under the third-party provisions of the FECA.

To receive matching funds during the primaries, a candidate must raise a total of $100,000 in donations from individuals, of which $5,000 must be raised in each of twenty or more states. The government matches only the first $250 of each individual contribution; no match is given to money received from political action committees (PACs). The purpose of the Act is to have candidates seek a broad base of support from individuals and small-money donors rather than rely on big contributors. A candidate who fails to win 20 percent of more of the vote in each of two consecutive primaries loses his or her eligibility for matching funds. Eligibility can later be restored if the candidate receives 20 percent of the vote in a primary contest.

The donation and spending limits imposed by the Act are similarly complex. No individual can give more than $1,000 to a candidate's primary and general election campaigns. Nor can an individual's donations in any year exceed a maximum of $25,000 to all federal candidates. A PAC can give a candidate donations up to a ceiling of $5,000. Each candidate is subject to limitations placed on overall spending and on spending in each primary and caucus state.

The state-by-state spending limits imposed during the primary season proved particularly difficult to enforce. Candidates found ways to evade the spending limits in key early contests such as Iowa and New Hampshire. Campaigns shifted expenses to other states—for instance, renting cars in neighboring states for staff use in Iowa and New Hampshire. Some campaigns charged much of the media costs of the New Hampshire race against the spending ceilings allowed for Massachusetts, inasmuch as the commercials originated from television stations located in New Hampshire's neighbor to the south. Campaigns also face no real penalty for breaking the state spending ceilings; any Federal Election Commission–ordered fine will be imposed well after the election is over.

As a result of these evasions, the Federal Election Commission in 1991 relaxed its interpretation of the state-by-state spending rules, in effect legitimizing a number of the practices that campaigns and their lawyers had used to circumvent the state spending restrictions.[28] Some political experts argue that as the state spending ceilings are unenforceable and serve no real purpose, they should be repealed.[29]

The Return of Big Money into the Presidential Race

The FECA initially succeeded in reducing the impact of private money in the presidential race. But the 1980s saw the reintroduction of substantial sums of private money into presidential elections.[30] In reviewing the financing of the 1992 election, one analyst concluded that "the large contributions removed from American elections in 1974 returned full-blown in 1992."[31]

The Act is filled with loopholes. The various members of a family can each give $1,000 to a presidential candidate. While each PAC is limited to $5,000 in the donations it gives to a candidate, affected interests in a policy area may form multiple PACs, and, within certain limitations, each may contribute up to the allowable ceiling.

Both PACs and industry executives also attempt to evade contribution limits through a practice known as **bundling,** where an interest-group representative gathers the maximum donations permitted from a number of individuals and presents the checks to a candidate in a single package.[32] While bundled money technically is a collection of individual donations, candidates know just whose interests are represented by the large sums that are collected. In recent years, campaign finance directors have been complicit in identifying potentially affected interests and soliciting bundles of donations through intermediaries.

Private money has also reentered the presidential race as a consequence of the 1976 United States Supreme Court decision *Buckley v. Valeo.* The *Buckley* decision overturned part of the FECA amendments, ruling that some of the spending limitations imposed on independent organizations amounted to an undue restriction on free speech.[33] Individuals and PACs possess the free-speech right to spend money to advocate the election of the candidate of their choice. These **independent expenditures** cannot be counted against a candidate's allowable spending ceiling so long as the actions of the independent committee are not coordinated with those of the official campaign. Some critics, however, doubt that such expenditures are truly independent because spending by PACs and a candidate's authorized campaign can be coordinated in subtle ways.

In 1988, the pattern of escalating independent expenditures suddenly reversed. While independent expenditures declined from 1984 to 1988, independent expenditures made on behalf of presidential candidates still totaled an estimated $14.3 million.[34] One explanation for the drop is that private interests increasingly took advantage of other newfound means to funnel money into the presidential race and did not have to rely on the creation of independent PACs.

Precandidacy candidate PACs provide another vehicle for the reentry of unregulated money into the presidential race. In advance of making a formal announcement for the presidency, a candidate travels around the country as the spokesperson for a PAC as it aids friendly Senate, House, and state and local candidates.

The precandidacy PAC pays for the travel and organizational expenses of the early parts of a presidential campaign, expenses that are not later charged against the candidate's permissible spending ceiling, as the precandidacy PAC is seen to be an independent entity, not part of the official campaign.

Technically speaking, these multicandidate PACs are created to raise money for a party's candidates running for state, national, and local offices. But as the spending records of these committees demonstrate, precandidacy PACs are in reality little more than "shadow" extensions of the presidential campaign. In 1988, George Bush's Fund for the Future of America raised over $11 million but contributed less than $850,000 to the congressional candidates that the committee was ostensibly to assist.[35]

Thus, precandidacy PACs enable campaigns to raise and spend money not otherwise allowed under federal law. The precandidacy PAC taps individual donations beyond the $1,000 limit imposed by law; as the precandidacy PAC and the candidate's later campaign are considered separate entities, contributors can give to the precandidacy PAC and still give the maximum to the official campaign. Precandidacy PACs also escape some of strict finance disclosure rules that govern campaigns. According to Anthony Corrado, a precandidacy PAC possesses a "nearly unfettered ability to solicit funds and virtually unlimited fundraising potential."[36]

Precandidacy PACs unbalance the funding of the presidential race by allowing well-known frontrunners like Reagan, Mondale, and Bush to get an early financial and organizational head start. For instance, in 1986, two years in advance of the presidential election, the Fund for the Future of America had *already* raised over $9 million on behalf of George Bush.[37]

But PAC spending is not the only vehicle by which "big money" has reentered the presidential arena. In recent years, large donations have been given under the general rubric of **soft money** that is not subject to the same strict federal rules governing a campaign's "hard money." Under soft money, donations are directed to state and local party organizations whose efforts are then coordinated with that of the presidential campaign. Soft money is a result of the 1979 FECA amendments that sought to strengthen political parties and grassroots democracy by favoring contributions to state and local party organizations. No limitations were placed on the amounts that state and local parties could spend to register voters, print literature and sample ballots, pay for bumper stickers and yard signs, and organize get-out-the-vote drives. Only a portion, at most, of the costs incurred would be allocated as presidential expenditures.

According to campaign finance expert Herbert Alexander, the most notable financial phenomenon in the 1988 race was the competitive and high-profile search for soft money.[38] In 1980 and 1984 the Republicans had far outstripped the Democrats in raising soft money. But in 1988, Dukakis's campaign operatives aggressively sought to mine sources of soft money in order to change the funding gap that had worked to the disadvantage of the Democratic candidates. The Democrats steered potential contributors who had "maxed out" or could not otherwise give to presidential campaigns to make large donations to state and local party organizations. The Dukakis campaign that year even put two key operatives in each state on the official campaign payroll to help direct state party activities; as a result, money nominally in state party coffers was effectively controlled by the presidential campaign, not by the state party chairs.[39] The 1988 Democratic efforts were successful, and the party narrowly surpassed the Republicans in terms of soft money: $23 million for the Dukakis campaign as compared to $22 million for the Bush effort. Republicans in 1988 claimed 267 contributors of $100,000 or more; Democrats reported 130.[40]

In 1992, both parties escalated their efforts to mine sources of soft money, raising a combined total of $66 million in soft money for the 1992 election, an increase of nearly 50 percent over 1988.[41] Democrats organized a drive for "trustees" who gave the party $100,000 or more. The Bush campaign continued its Team 100, contributors of $100,000 or more. Those belonging to Team 100 received special briefings from the administration and even accompanied members of the administration on overseas travel.[42] A number of Team 100 donors from 1988 received nominations as ambassadors to foreign nations, an apparent return to the pre-Watergate practice of rewarding big financial donors.[43] A Common Cause study revealed that eight $100,000 soft money donations were given to the Bush-Quayle team by individuals linked to the savings and loans industry, which was then undergoing a multibillion dollar governmental bailout.[44] Big money was clearly back in the presidential race.

An Assessment of Campaign Finance Reform

The rules governing the public funding of the race for the presidency have had a number of inadvertent impacts. First, public funding has helped lead to an earlier start to the presidential campaign as candidates undertake the formidable task of scouring the country in search for early contributions that will qualify them for matching funds. As Frank Sorauf details:

> Lining up a fund-raising wizard thus becomes the major early decision for a budding president. The need is far more than brokering— it is for metabrokering, since a wizard in essence functions as a broker of the brokers, the person with access to the intermediaries whose ability to raise money is locally or regionally based.[45]

Second, the FECA has led to a centralization of authority in campaigns in order to comply with the various accounting requirements, limits, and deadlines of the finance laws. The result has been to limit the initiatives of state organizations.[46]

Third, the FECA did not anticipate the group revolution and the tremendous growth of PACs and may even have contributed to the heightened role that PACs play in the presidential race. While public funding did succeed in reducing the influence of individual big donors (or "fat cats"), the spending limits set under the Act are unrealistically low for a national campaign and led candidates and their allies to search for various means that will allow them to spend beyond the sum provided by public funds. In recent years, presidential candidates themselves and party committees have both been actively involved in the recruitment of soft money, incurring obligations to large contributors. "Interested money" has returned to the presidential race.[47]

A brief overview of how contemporary presidential campaigns are financed reveals the different streams by which money enters into the presidential race. According to Herbert Alexander, it is useful to think of the presidential general election campaign as three parallel campaigns conducted simultaneously.[48] The official **limited campaign** or **controlled campaign** is mostly subsidized by federal funds; spending is legally restricted. The second entails the **unlimited campaigns** or soft-money operations of state and local party committees and various PACs; it has no legal spending limits. Although it lies partly outside the control of the candidate and his or her organization, the activities of the second campaign frequently are coordinated with those of the first. Finally, there is a third campaign of PAC **independent spending** which is undertaken without consulting the candidate or his or her campaign representatives.

The relative size of these three campaigns can be seen by looking at figures from 1988 (see Table 4.5). The official campaigns of

Table 4.5 Sources of Funds, Major Party Presidential Candidates, 1988 General Election (in millions)

Sources of Funds		Bush	Dukakis
Limited campaign			
(Candidate controlled)	Federal grant	$46.1	$46.1
	National Party	8.3	8.3
Unlimited campaign			
(Candidate may coordinate)	State and local party	22.0[a]	23.0
	Labor[b]	5.0	25.0
	Corporate/association[b]	1.5	1.0
	Compliance	4.0	2.5
Independent of candidate	Independent expenditures[c]	6.8	.6
Total		$93.7	$106.5

[a] Includes money raised by the national party committee and channeled to state and local party committees.

[b] Includes internal communication costs (both those in excess of $2,000, which are reported as required by law, and those of $2,000 or less, which are not required to be reported), registration and voter turnout expenditures, overhead, and other related costs.

[c] Does not include amounts spent to oppose the candidates: $2.7 million against Dukakis, $77,325 against Bush, and $63,103 against Quayle.

Source: Herbert E. Alexander and Monica Bauer, *Financing the 1988 Election* (Boulder, CO: Westview Press, 1991), p. 41.

the Democratic and Republican nominees, funded by taxpayer money, were equal in terms of spending. Campaign spending by the two national party organizations was also equal, a reversal of past years when the Republicans enjoyed a clear lead. There was also little Democratic-Republican difference in the area of soft-money, spending technically controlled by state and local party organizations. Democrats had greatly increased their soft-money spending as a result of aggressive fundraising solicitation by Dukakis campaign operatives. Republicans continued to enjoy clear advantages in PAC spending, especially spending by business-related and conservative ideological PACs. Democrats countered with an enormous edge in spending by labor organizations. Organized labor also provided personnel for phone banks and get-out-the-vote drives. Figures for the 1992 race show only a marginal difference from 1988.[49]

The existence of three parallel campaigns illustrates the difficulty of regulating money in the presidential arena. Numerous openings for private money exist under the provisions of federal law and court decisions emphasizing free-speech rights.[50] The escalating large sums of money in the presidential race indicate that efforts to rein in presidential spending have not been effective. The Act has been successful in allowing the public to see the source of a campaign's money. But even here the rise of pre-candidacy PACs has compromised public disclosure. Also, despite the promise inherent in public funding, candidates must continue to devote considerable time to fundraising.

The Act, though, has enjoyed one clear area of success. By helping to pay for the costs of a presidential race, public funding has aided the candidacy of outsiders. Jimmy Carter could not have easily made his successful presidential bid were it not for public funds. Party outsiders, fueled in part by public funding, help bring new issues into the presidential arena. Jesse Jackson, Pat Robertson, and Patrick Buchanan are all candidates who were not the favorite of party leaders but who were able to spread their message widely as a result of public funds. The 1980 third-party candidacy of John Anderson was also aided by the promise of public funds—funds that he received by winning 5 percent of the vote on election day. In 1976, Ellen McCormack, running solely to publicize right-to-life's opposition to abortion, received over $244,000 in public funds. In 1992, fringe party candidate Lenora Fulani received $1.9 million in federal funds.[51]

Campaign finance reform and the resulting loopholes and court interpretations have led to a prominent role for PACs in the presidential race. Activities by PACs, especially independent ideological ones, can bring up issues that presidential candidates find too politically troublesome to push. The 1992 election also saw the rise of women-oriented PACs and donor groups, although the most famous women's donor group, EMILY's List (Early Money Is Like Yeast), chose to concentrate its effort on aiding women in congressional races and for the most part avoided the presidential contest.

PACs introduce issues. Critics, however, object that PACs frame issues in irresponsible ways. In 1988, the more controversial Willie Horton spot was aired not by the Bush campaign but by a California-based PAC, the Committee for the Presidency.

SUMMARY

The United States has entered an era of candidate-centered campaigns. Political party leaders no longer play the role they once did in selecting presidential nominees and in running presidential campaigns. Nor do presidential candidates depend on the pull of party loyalty to win votes in the fall election. Instead, each presidential hopeful is supported by a personal campaign organization. Each candidate uses the mass media to appeal directly to an electorate that has become increasingly independent. Changes in presidential nominating rules and finance laws have also served to diminish the power of party leaders and to give new voice to more issue-oriented constituencies and candidates.

Reforms in the nominating process, in particular, have opened the door to new issue groups. Presidential contenders appeal to organized constituencies for support. Delegates to recent Democratic and Republican conventions are more ideological than both the general public and rank-and-file party members. Democratic conventions tend to be more liberal than the public; Republican conventions more conservative. They offer voters a choice. PACs and soft money represent still other vehicles by which issue groups and interested money have reentered presidential politics.

Studies of voting behavior completed in the 1940s and 1950s refuted any idea that Americans were issue-oriented. But in the wake of the civil rights movement, urban riots, and the Vietnam War, issue activists in the 1960s and early 1970s seized control of the nominating process and presented voters with candidates who offered clearer choices. Issues became part of presidential elections.

Yet, as we shall see in the next chapter, this revisionist portrait of American presidential elections is not universally accepted. While a number of studies observed the increased issue orientation of American voters, studies by other political scientists pointed out that Americans failed to meet the requisites of issue voting. Chapter 5 examines the continuing debate.

THE
DEBATE
OVER
ISSUE VOTING

5

Numerous academic studies have attempted to determine what role issues have played in American elections. A number of studies point to a prominent role played by issues; other studies point to the continuing influence of partisanship and candidate personal images. While no consensus exists, there is a greater recognition of the role played by issues today than there was a decade or two ago.[1]

The debate over issue voting has been framed largely by the standards set down in *The American Voter*, the University of Michigan Survey Research Center's highly influential portrait of voting behavior in the 1952 and 1956 elections.[2] *The American Voter* followed a decade of research on voting behavior by a group of Columbia University sociologists. These two studies revealed new and unflattering insights into the nature of voting in the United States.

SOCIAL SCIENCE DISCOVERS THE AMERICAN VOTER

Not until the late New Deal era were social scientists able to perfect public opinion and survey research instruments that provided for in-depth studies of the American electorate. In the initial studies done in the 1940s, sociologists interviewed and reinterviewed panels of voters in a single community. Although a limited national survey was undertaken in 1948, it was not until the 1950s that political scientists at the University of Michigan were able to complete a series of national surveys with questions directed at gaining better insight into why Americans voted as they did.

Largely, the findings of these studies came as quite a surprise. They dispelled any notion that Americans behaved as classic democratic citizens. *The People's Choice*, which looked at voting behavior in the 1940 election in Erie County, Ohio, found that most Americans did not listen to the promises of the competing candidates before deciding how to vote. Newspaper and radio coverage of the campaign had little effect on the voting decision.[3] Instead, most Americans decided whom to vote for before the campaign even began, before the parties chose their candidates at the national nominating conventions! Voters knew whether they approved of Franklin Roosevelt for a third term or if they wanted a change. Voters were also influenced by their membership in different social groups. Protestant and higher status groups were more likely to vote Republican; Catholics and lower status groups were more likely to vote Democratic.

Bernard Berelson, Paul Lazarsfeld, and William McPhee gave a similar disparaging portrait of Americans in *Voting*, their study of Elmira, New York, during the 1948 presidential election.[4] These researchers found that political preferences are highly self-maintaining, that even voters who admit some dissatisfaction with their party's performance tend to return to their normal party preference as the campaign progresses.

According to Berelson and his colleagues, voters have a psychological need for conformity. Citizens, though, are often subject to the cross-pressure of competing opinions because of their involvement in heterogeneous work and social groups. These citizens are likely to resolve the conflict by lessening their interest in politics and abstaining from voting. They are able to maintain their working and social relationships only by coming to believe that political questions are of no great importance.

The Elmira study was potentially troubling for a country that saw itself as a model democracy. As most voters exhibit long-lasting partisan loyalties, it is the least interested and least informed voters who switch from one party's candidate to the other's and thereby decide the outcome of elections: "Since the bulk of each party's votes move only sluggishly if at all, the short-term change that 'decides' a close election is disproportionately located among those closer to the border line of disinterest."[5] Berelson continues, "The classic 'independent voter' of high interest but low partisanship is a deviant case."[6]

How can American democracy survive if the polity fails to meet the requirements of an alert electorate? Berelson can only offer an **elitist theory of democracy** where he argues that the political system is actually helped by the passivity of so many of its citizens. Continuity and stability in the political system are provided by the many Americans who show enduring party allegiances. Their moderation further helps to mute the intensity of political conflict. Those persons least committed to democratic norms of compromise and respect for the rights of others fortunately are the least likely to participate. The mass base for fanatical and extremist movements is thereby removed from American politics. Passivity and apathy further afford political leaders room for pluralist bargaining and compromise: "The apathetic segment of America probably has helped to hold the system together and cushioned the shock of disagreement, adjustment, and change."[7]

The group theory of politics advanced by the sociologists would soon be found wanting. The political scientists at the University of Michigan would cast it aside in favor of a different theory, one that emphasized the primacy of psychologically based party identification.

THE AMERICAN VOTER MODEL

The Prevalence of Partisanship

The American Voter included results from the 1948 election study but focused on the more extensive data collected during the Eisenhower elections of 1952 and 1956. The second great volume of University of Michigan research, *Elections and the Political Order,* studied voting behavior during the 1960 election and essentially reinforced the interpretations advanced in the earlier work.[8]

The American Voter painted a portrait of an electorate where the partisan decisions of individuals are "profoundly affected by...psychological forces."[9] The great majority of Americans had some sense of affiliation with one party or the other, the roots of which were to be found in social psychology, not in rational decision making. Individuals did not choose their party affiliations after carefully weighing the competing issue positions of the two major parties. Rather, identification with party was formed quite early in life, before individuals even had the ability to understand politics and issues. There was a close correspondence between the party affiliation of voters and their parents. Party identification was transmitted from parent to child and remained relatively immutable over time.

Party identification served "as a supplier of cues" by which individuals evaluated candidates and political events.[10] Republican and Democratic partisans tended to judge their party's candidate favorably even when they knew little about him other than his party label. If necessary, a voter would even distort his perception of events to be consonant with his partisanship:

> Identification with a party raises a perceptual screen through which the individual tends to see what is favorable to his partisan orientation. The stronger the party bond, the more exaggerated the process of selection and perceptual distortion will be.[11]

Republican identifiers who favored the government provision of health care for the elderly were likely to believe that Eisenhower supported such a program, even though Ike had actually opposed such an initiative as the beginning of socialized medicine.

The Relative Unimportance of Issues

The American Voter found that citizens were for the most part unfamiliar with and disinterested in issues. The public's understanding of issues was poorly developed. For instance, the Democratic party chose to make the antilabor Taft-Hartley Act a major point of attack in its 1948 campaign; yet "almost seven out of every ten adult Americans saw the curtain fall on the presidential election of 1948 without knowing whether Taft-Hartley was the name of a hero or a villain."[12]

Most voters had no strong opinions on key issues of the day. Even when they did, voters could not discern differences between the parties on the issues. The public paid scant attention to politics and the campaign debate. Issue discussion was for the most part confined to political leaders and a thin top strata of the electorate.[13]

The authors of *The American Voter* specified three conditions that had to be fulfilled before an issue could be considered to have influenced an individual's voting decision[14]:

1. "The issue must be cognized in some form." The voter must be familiar with what the government is doing on an issue and have an opinion on the matter.
2. "It must arouse some minimal intensity of feeling." Unless a voter cares about an issue, it cannot influence the voting decision. Issues that arouse only mild sentiments are not politically important.
3. "It must be accompanied by some perception that one party represents the person's own position better than do the other parties." The voter must be able to see a difference between the parties on the issue and discern which party better represents his or her point of view.

In a survey of citizens' beliefs on sixteen issues, *The American Voter* found that only 22 to 36 percent of the electorate in 1956 were able to meet these three minimal conditions on any specific issue. Yet, even these numbers overstated the extent of issue voting: "[T]hey represent no more than a maximum pool within which the specified issues might have conceivable effect."[15] A voter might have an opinion, care about an issue, and see a difference between the parties on the matter, but still find that other factors outweighed the policy issue in determining the voting decision.

Self-described independents were the least informed and aware of all voters. These citizens seemingly classified themselves as independents only because they did not care at all about politics.

The Lack of Voter Sophistication

Voters lacked strong opinions on many questions but still answered pollsters' questions anyway. Philip Converse labeled these responses, which did not indicate strong convictions or well-thought-out beliefs, **nonattitudes.**[16] Voters' opinions on policy questions were quite unstable and varied greatly over time. When posed the same question at different points in time, a respondent would often give different answers.

Converse's evidence is presented in Figure 5.1. A panel of voters interviewed in 1958 was revisited in 1960. The numbers presented on the chart are rank-order correlation (tau-beta) coefficients. If all persons interviewed had exactly the same opinions on an issue in 1960 that they had in 1958, the correlation coefficient for that issue would be 1.00. Roughly put, the greater the stability of opinions over time, the higher the correlation coefficients; the greater the apparent opinion change, the lower the coefficients.

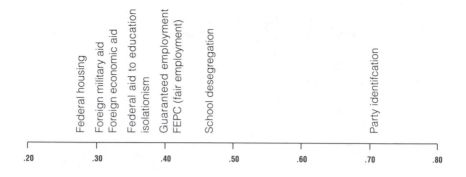

Figure 5.1   Temporal stability of different belief elements for individuals, 1958–1960

Source: Philip E. Converse, "The Nature of Belief Systems in Mass Publics," *Ideology and Discontent,* ed. David Apter (New York: Free Press, 1964).

As Figure 5.1 indicates, the public's opinion on most issues showed very little stability; opinions varied widely over the course of only two years. It was almost as if the public had no serious opinions on policy questions. Only on the issue of school de-segregation did attitudes remain fairly consistent over time. Con-verse explains that this in itself does not indicate sophisticated thinking; rather, voters simply held strong attitudes toward a so-cial group, African-Americans, that ordered their opinions.

The strong .78 correlation over time for party identification stands out in marked contrast to the low longitudinal correla-tions for the various issues. Citizens were consistent in their par-tisanship over time. Apparently, party identification was more central than issues to the belief systems of the mass public.

The lack of voter sophistication was also apparent in citizens' answers to open-ended questions about what they liked and dis-liked about the parties and the candidates. *The American Voter* team attempted to explore the extent of **ideology** in voters—the degree to which voters were consistent in their opinions and able to understand the general liberal and conservative choices pre-sented to them by the candidates. As Table 5.1 shows, very few Americans—only 3½ percent of the electorate—had full-blown ideology. Only 15 percent of the electorate can be seen to possess an ideology, even defined in the broadest of terms.

For most American voters the terms *liberal* and *conservative* lacked clear meaning. Voters could not understand the choice offered by the two competing parties, one offering a more con-servative and the other a more liberal policy direction.

Table 5.1   Levels of Ideological Thinking and the American Voter,
1956

	proportion of total sample	proportion of voters
Ideology		
Ideology	2½%	3½%
Near-ideology	9	12
Group Benefits		
Perception of conflict	14	16
Single-group interest	17	18
Shallow group benefit responses	11	11
Nature of the Times	24	22
No Issue Content		
Party orientation	4	3½
Candidate orientation	9	7
No content	5	3
Unclassified	4½	4
	100%	100%

Source: Angus Campbell et al., *The American Voter*, abridged ed. (New York: John Wiley & Sons, 1964), p. 144.

Only in the area of domestic policy did the authors find some apparent structure or consistency of beliefs. But in-depth discussion revealed that voters could not explain their issue preferences with any sort of sophistication. Instead, what was apparent was merely "ideology by proxy," where group interest and personal self-interest gave some order to the voter's responses.[17] Voters cast ballots for the party of labor and the little man, or for the party of small business, or for the party of the farmer, or for the party of the South. A fifth of the electorate voted on the basis of "The 'Goodness' and 'Badness' of the Times"; in bad times they voted to oust the incumbent administration. Nearly 20 percent of the electorate was unable to give any issue-based reason whatsoever in answering questions about candidates and parties. Among this group were voters whose responses showed strong candidate and partisan orientations but no issue content whatsoever:

> (Like about Democrats?) I'm a Democrat. (Is there anything you like about the Democratic Party?) I don't know.

> (Dislike about Democrats?) I'm a Democrat, that's all I know. My husband's dead now—he was a Democrat. (Is there anything you don't like about the party?) I don't know.

> (Like about Republicans?) I don't know.

(Dislike about Republicans?) I don't know.

(Like about Stevenson?) Stevenson is a good Democrat. (Is there anything else about him that might make you want to vote for him?) No, nothing.

(Dislike about Stevenson?) I don't know. (Is there anything about him that might make you want to vote against him?) No.

(Like about Eisenhower?) I don't know. (Is there anything about Eisenhower that might make you want to vote for him?) I don't know.

(Dislike about Eisenhower?) I don't know. (Is there anything about him that might make you want to vote against him?) No.[18]

According to the Michigan studies, Eisenhower won the 1952 election on the basis of his strong personal appeal. The public's personal endorsement of Ike proved especially strong in his 1956 reelection. In 1952 the Republicans also gained the public's favor in the area of governmental management, responding to allegations of corruption and irregularities in the Truman administration. The short-term factors of Eisenhower's personal appeal and allegations of Democratic corruption overshadowed the advantages that the Democrats retained in domestic policy and group-related attitudes. These long-term partisan ties would help produce a Kennedy victory in 1960.

ARE THE VOTERS FOOLS?

The American Voter was a seminal work that widely influenced a generation of voting studies and the perspectives of informed observers of American politics. Yet its portrayal of the relative unimportance of issues in presidential voting did not go unchallenged. Harvard political scientist V. O. Key, Jr., reviewed Gallup poll data from the New Deal era and argued that

> voters are not fools...[I]n the large the electorate behaves about as rationally and responsibly as we should expect, given the clarity of the alternatives presented to it and the character of the information available to it. In American presidential campaigns of recent decades the portrait of the American electorate that develops from the data is not one of an electorate straitjacketed by social determinants or moved by subconscious urges triggered by devilishly skillful propagandists. It is rather one of an electorate moved by concern about central and relevant questions of public policy, of governmental performance, and of executive personality.[19]

Key accepted the Michigan Survey Research Center's finding that partisanship was a major influence on voting behavior. Yet Key did not find voters to be as anchored in place by party identification as *The American Voter* had reported them to be. Rather substantial interparty movement by voters takes place between elections even during periods of seeming electoral stability:

> Such evidence as can be mustered suggests that the popular majority does not hold together like a ball of sticky popcorn. Rather, no sooner has a popular majority been constructed than it begins to crumble …[T]o govern is to antagonize not only opponents but also at least some supporters; as the loyalty of one group is nourished, another group may be repelled. A series of maintaining elections occurs only in consequence of a complex process of interaction between government and populace in which old friends are sustained, old enemies are converted into new friends, old friends become even bitter opponents, and new voters are attracted to the cause—all in proper proportions to produce repeatedly for the dominant party its apparently stable and continuing majority.[20]

Key divided the electorate into **standpatters**—those voters who remained with the same party in two consecutive elections—and **switchers**—those voters who moved from one party to another in two consecutive elections. Key found that both groups of voters were basically where they should be on the basis of the issues. Those who stayed with their party did so as they approved of their party's record and promises. Those who were dissatisfied switched: "party switchers move towards the party whose standpatters they resemble in their policy views."[21] Switchers, whose movement decides the outcome of elections, were not the "repulsive type of 'independent'" described by *The American Voter.*[22] Switchers were as informed and educated as standpatters.

Key found that the Democratic party majority was based on voter approval of Democratic activist New Deal policies.[23] Even in the then-solidly Democratic South, loyalty to the Democratic party was not a simple reflection of partisan attachments handed down since the Civil War. As the poorest region in the nation, people in the South were the beneficiaries of the many Democratic economic and social welfare programs.[24]

The 1952 and 1956 elections were not simply personal endorsements of Eisenhower; rather, voters rejected the performance of the Truman administration on "Communism, Corruption, Korea." Charges of Communist penetration into the government in Washington, China's entry into and prolongation of the Korean War, and the allegations of corruption in Truman's kitchen cabinet were all important influences on the vote in 1952. According to Key, voters "ousted from power a political party of whose performance they did not approve."[25] In 1956, voters endorsed Eisenhower's first-term performance; the war in Korea had been brought to an end, and there was a general level of citizen satisfaction with things both at home and abroad. Kennedy's narrow 1960 victory represented a vote for change—a rejection of America's sluggishness during the late Eisenhower era.[26]

Issues, Key argued, were important to presidential voting even during the decade that provided the data for the generalizations made by *The American Voter.* Democracy in the United States was not endangered.

But Key's corrective was not universally acclaimed. Political scientists who accepted *The American Voter*'s viewpoint on the uninformed voter questioned the validity of Key's use of recall data. Voters had been asked why they voted as they did in previous elections, yielding the risk of selective memory and projection in their answers. Standpatters and switchers could have cast their ballots on any number of grounds but still justified their votes to the interviewer by claiming satisfaction or dissatisfaction with their party's performance and policies.[27] Furthermore, Key had not attempted to discover whether citizens met the issue-voting criteria set forth in *The American Voter.* He did not demonstrate that voters saw the party they voted for to be in agreement with them on the issues or that voters cared enough about the issues for which Key claimed they voted.[28]

THE DEBATE OVER ISSUE SALIENCE

David RePass was another political scientist who objected to the Michigan school's portrait of a voting decision "not rich with specific issue content."[29] RePass found that different voters were concerned with different issues. *The American Voter's* methodology was flawed. It had asked respondents to agree or disagree with a series of closed-ended, preformulated policy statements. According to RePass, *The American Voter* concluded that issues had little influence on the voting decision only because voters were asked their opinions on policy questions that mattered little to them.

When respondents are given the opportunity to identify for themselves which issues are of greatest importance, the results are much different. RePass analyzed voter responses to a new set of questions in the 1964 national survey, which allowed respondents to indicate how important they considered a particular issue to be. RePass found that voters were able to perceive differences between the parties on issues they considered salient. More important, voters' opinions on salient issues were closely linked to party identification and the presidential voting decision.

Defenders of the Michigan model point out that positions on salient issues explain the voting decisions of very few citizens.[30] They further point to the limited political significance of highly individualized issue concerns. In 1964, no single issue was considered salient by more than 12 percent of the respondents.[31] If each voter casts a ballot on the basis of a concern for a different issue, then election results cannot constitute a set of instructions or mandate for any specific policy change. For elections to constitute meaningful instruments of policy control, voters must be able to choose between the general liberal and conservative alternatives offered by the two major parties. Voters who cannot understand the liberal-conservative dialogue do not comprehend the basic programmatic choices before them in a presidental election.

IS THERE A CHANGING AMERICAN VOTER?

Many of the generalizations drawn from the first generation of University of Michigan studies are clearly time-bound, a factor not always made clear in the period's writings on voting behavior:

> The findings, and particularly the overall conclusions, of *The American Voter* were not presented as the results of a given era, but as relatively long-term truths about the characteristic quality and behavior of the United States electorate. The possibilities of change were hardly discussed, and the brief consideration of such possibilities was only in the context of unexpected catastrophes such as civil war or a major depression.[32]

A new generation of Americans was soon to come of voting age. They did not inherit the partisan orientations of their parents to the extent that voters had in the 1950s. The transference of party affiliation from parents to children, so much a part of the psychological model provided by *The American Voter* model, was greatly weakened in the 1970s and 1980s.[33] These younger and more educated voters would become part of a new rootless "no majority" electorate.[34] Unencumbered by strong party identification, these voters would be free to respond to new political cues—racial issues, social issues, and a changed economy marked at times by high rates of both stagnation and inflation.

The American Voter paradigm was challenged by a new set of works that purported to show that voting behavior became more issue-oriented and ideological as a result of the changed nature of the times. RePass's study of voting in 1964 concluded that issues were important, as Barry Goldwater and Lyndon Johnson presented Americans a distinct choice on specific policy matters. A number of major longitudinal studies also concluded that the nature of voting in the United States had changed.

Gerald Pomper: The Times Have Changed

Gerald Pomper found the increased influence of issues on party identification. He saw the new prominence of issues as the result of the "national metamorphosis" that occurred in the 1960s and 1970s.[35] According to Pomper, *The American Voter*'s conclusion as to the low ideological awareness of voters "may have resulted from the generally low level of ideological stimulation" during the Eisenhower years.[36] But television was soon to bring the turbulence associated with the black revolution, the Vietnam War, and the changing social mores into voters' homes. As politics became more pressing and relevant, Americans developed more coherent belief systems.[37] Pomper further theorized that, especially among the young, "The brutality of Vietnam, the cruelties of racism, the corruption of a president, the separatism of the youth culture have stimulated new loyalties and new attitudes."[38]

In 1956, as *The American Voter* had reported, issue preferences were only very mildly related to party identification. But starting in the mid-1960s, Pomper found that Democratic and Republican identified partisans were increasingly differentiated by their views on domestic policy.[39] By 1968, the parties had also developed much clearer identities. During the 1950s, a great many voters failed to perceive the Democrats as the liberal party. By 1964 and 1968 voters in all partisanship categories correctly saw the Democrats as the liberal alternative (see Table 5.2).

What explains the increase in voter awareness and partisan distinctiveness? According to Pomper:

> The most important electoral event of this period appears to be the 1964 presidential campaign. Senator Barry Goldwater consciously sought to clarify and widen the ideological differences between the parties. The evidence presented here indicates that he accomplished

Table 5.2 Consensus on Positions of Parties on Policy Issues, by Party Identification*

| | consensus on party positions | | | | | | | | | |
| | education, taxation | | | | | medical care | | | | |
group	1956	1960	1964	1968	1972	1956	1960	1964	1968	1972
Strong Democrat	90.5	95.2	96.5	94.1	64.6	93.9	95.8	98.2	98.8	84.0
Weak Democrat	88.5	90.5	93.6	82.6	71.4	84.6	90.4	95.8	88.7	80.6
Independent	66.3	74.6	83.8	64.3	76.1	76.4	87.7	93.5	82.7	90.5
Weak Republican	37.2	60.9	55.8	58.7	77.7	64.3	52.2	77.6	85.0	88.5
Strong Republican	31.6	47.9	55.0	41.2	83.1	57.8	51.3	79.8	63.6	89.7

| | fair employment, minority aid | | | | | school integration, busing | | | | |
group	1956	1960	1964	1968	1972	1956	1960	1964	1968	1972
Strong Democrat	64.6	83.5	96.9	97.3	78.5	39.1	34.7	96.2	95.3	65.6
Weak Democrat	63.6	65.5	93.9	88.3	81.3	51.5	42.5	90.3	87.1	64.6
Independent	49.4	53.4	89.5	75.6	72.4	45.8	46.4	91.8	83.4	68.0
Weak Republican	23.6	18.3	81.0	70.2	79.6	45.1	49.3	83.9	75.4	86.0
Strong Republican	6.0	17.2	67.6	56.4	88.5	59.4	48.5	71.3	69.5	94.0

| | job guarantee | | | | | foreign aid, defense, spending | | | | |
group	1956	1960	1964	1968	1972	1956	1960	1964	1968	1972
Strong Democrat	85.5	98.8	98.8	97.0	83.1	57.1	80.9	98.1	93.0	76.4
Weak Democrat	71.8	93.3	93.9	88.5	80.1	53.0	60.2	94.2	89.2	84.6
Independent	61.9	82.3	89.3	71.4	83.0	54.5	46.8	88.1	83.1	84.4
Weak Republican	60.0	67.3	72.5	69.4	91.4	46.2	13.0	67.8	81.5	86.1
Strong Republican	47.0	32.3	63.8	53.9	83.0	29.3	21.4	70.8	61.6	81.0

*Cell entries are percentages of voters that select Democrats as liberal among those voters who perceive party differences.

Source: Gerald Pomper, *Voters' Choice* (New York: Dodd, Mead, 1975), p. 172.

his goal, although this did not benefit the Republican party. Voters, previously unable to see differences between the parties, learned the lesson of "a choice, not an echo." They accepted the senator's characterization of the Republicans as conservative and the Democrats as liberal, and, on the specific issues involved, they preferred the liberal alternative.[40]

But according to Michael Margolis, Pomper's work does not necessarily document an increase in issue voting. Pomper's evidence pointing to the increased association between party identification and voters' issue preferences actually shows little about issue voting. It does not demonstrate that voters cared about specific issues, knew what the government was doing in these policy areas, or saw any differences between the parties on these issues.[41]

Even where Pomper does try to show that voters met some of the conditions of issue voting, Margolis is still critical. The problem is that Pomper's percentages in Table 5.2 are based not on the entire sample but on only those voters who perceive party differences. When Margolis recalculates Pomper's data for the entire sample (Table 5.3), increased voter awareness and recognition of party differences was not as strong as Pomper suggested.[42]

Do Voters Think Ideologically?

Pomper's findings were reinforced by those of a major research effort published under a title, *The Changing American Voter,* that indicated its quite different view of the electorate than the earlier University of Michigan studies. The most important of *The Changing American Voter*'s findings showed a dramatically sharp increase in ideological thinking beginning in 1964.[43] The American voter had changed over time.

The new findings represented a dramatic clash with those of the earlier era reported by Philip Converse.[44] As we have already seen, Converse found voter opinions to be so loosely held that he labeled them "nonattitudes." Converse further found that belief systems in the mass public were not well structured or well ordered. Voters did not hold consistent liberal or conservative opinions. Instead, a citizen who was a liberal on one issue was almost as likely to be a conservative as a liberal on another. Voters generally did not recognize the underlying philosophy or ideological dimension to link their opinion on one issue to their opinion on another.

Converse's original findings are reported in Table 5.4. The low correlation coefficients for the mass public (the cross-section sample) indicate the lack of issue constraint or ideological thinking. Had liberals on one issue been liberals on another, and had conservatives on one issue been conservative on another, the correlation coefficients for each pair of issues would have been much greater. Foreign policy attitudes are not at all linked in conservative-liberal terms with opinions on domestic matters.

It is not that ideological thinking is impossible. Converse contrasted the scores of the mass public with the much higher scores reported for a sample of congressional candidates (again, see Table 5.4). Political elites, but not the mass public, show evidence of consistent, ideological thinking.

Converse further found that only for the political elite was there a strong relationship between domestic policy attitudes

Table 5.3 Issues and Party Positions, 1956–1968

	aid to education				medical care			
	1956[a]	1960	1964	1968	1956[a]	1960	1964	1968
Democrats Favor	17%	32%	37%	31%	15%	35%	55%	46%
Republicans Favor	13	10	8	11	11	8	3	5
No Difference	28	34	25	30[b]	22	31	15	21
Don't Know	10	13	12	9	11	18	9	10
DK Gov't Policy	23	c	c	c	29	c	c	c
No Opinion or No Interest on Issue	10	11	18	19	12	9	16	16
N	1749	1898	1563	1553	1749	1905	1559	1541

	fair employment				school integration			
	1956	1960	1964	1968	1956	1960	1964	1968
Democrats Favor	13%	18%	47%	41%	18%	15%	43%	42%
Republicans Favor	15	17	6	9	16	11	5	7
No Difference	29	44	25	31	30	46	28	32
Don't Know	10	11	9	7	11	14	12	7
DK Gov't Policy	19	c	c	c	13	c	c	c
No Opinion or No Interest on Issue	13	11	13	12	12	15	13	11
N	1742	1910	1553	1550	1740	1913	1568	1542

	job guarantee				foreign aid			
	1956	1960	1964	1968	1956	1960	1964	1968
Democrats Favor	19%	39%	46%	42%	12%	14%	39%	31%
Republicans Favor	14	9	6	10	16	15	5	6
No Difference	25	27	23	27	29	46	36	42
Don't Know	8	15	10	10	10	13	10	8
DK Gov't Policy	23	c	c	c	16	c	c	c
No Opinion or No Interest on Issue	10	10	15	11	16	12	11	13
N	1750	1893	1564	1541	1748	1900	1560	1553

[a]In 1956 question of Aid to Education and Medical Care referred to which party was closer to the respondent's own position.

[b]Includes 1% who said Wallace favored aid.

[c]No question on whether R had information about government policy was asked after 1956.

Source: Michael Margolis, "From Confusion to Confusion: Issues and Voters, 1952–1972," *American Political Science Review* 71 (March 1977), pp. 31–43

and political party preference. For the general public the correlation is quite weak. Voters do not select a party on the basis of their policy views.

Given the starting point provided by Converse's research, the changes over time reported by *The Changing American Voter* are all the more startling (see Figure 5.2). Beginning in 1968 we find a

Table 5.4   Constraint between Specific Issue Beliefs for an Elite Sample and a Cross-Section Sample, 1958*

	domestic (%)				foreign (%)			
	employ-ment	educa-tion	housing	FEPC	econo-mic	military†	isolation-ism	party preference
Congressional Candidates								
Employment	—	.62	.59	.35	.26	.06	.17	.68
Aid to education		—	.61	.53	.50	.06	.35	.55
Federal housing			—	.47	.41	−.03	.30	.68
FEPC				—	.47	.11	.23	.34
Economic aid					—	.19	.59	.25
Military aid						—	.32	−.18
Isolationism							—	.05
Party preference								—
Cross-Section Sample								
Employment	—	.45	.08	.34	−.04	.10	−.22	.20
Aid to education		—	.12	.29	.06	.14	−.17	.16
Federal housing			—	.08	−.06	.02	.07	.18
FEPC				—	.24	.13	.01	−.04
Economic aid					—	.16	.33	−.07
Solders abroad†						—	.21	.12
Isolationism							—	−.03
Party preference								—

*Entries are tau-gamma coefficients, a statistic proposed by Leo A. Goodman and William H. Kruskal in "Measures of Association for Cross Classification," *Journal of the American Statistical Associations*, 49 (Dec. 1954), No. 268, 749. The coefficient was chosen because of its sensitivity to constraint of the scaler as well as the correlational type.

†For this category, the cross-section sample was asked a question about keeping American soldiers abroad, rather than about military aid in general.

Source: Philip E. Converse. "The Nature of Belief Systems in Mass Publics," *Ideology and Discontent*, ed. David E. Apter (New York: Free Press, 1964), p. 228.

sharp and relatively lasting increase in attitude consistency scores. The attitudinal consistency scores for the mass public in the late 1960s and early 1970s even surpass those of the 1958 sample of congressional candidates. Like Pomper, *The Changing American Voter* authors find the explanation for the increased coherence of mass belief systems in the changed social and political context of American elections.

The Changing American Voter also found increased issue voting. By 1972, the linkage between policy attitudes and the vote approached that of party identification and the vote (see Figure 5.3). Voters' answers to open-ended questions exhibited more

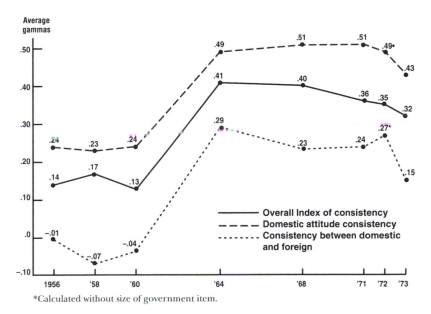

Figure 5.2   Changes in attitude consistency, 1956–1973

Source: Norman H. Nie, Sidney Verba, and John R. Petrocik, *The Changing American Voter* (*Cambridge, MA.: Harvard Press, 1976*), *p. 129*

frequent references to issues, nearly equaling the number of mentions of candidates' personal attributes (see Figure 5.4). References to partisanship fell dramatically.

But the conclusions of *The Changing American Voter* have been hotly debated. Between 1960 and 1964 the Survey Research Center rewrote many questions to rid their surveys of the hidden bias of an acquiescent response set resulting from their old format, which depended on one-sided questions. Critics of *The Changing American Voter* charge that much of the increase in correlation scores is an artifact of changes in question wording, not an indicator of genuine voter behavioral change. They further charge that in collapsing respondents' answers from a five-point scale to a three-point scale, Norman Nie and his colleagues, the authors of *The Changing American Voter*, inadvertently committed another methodological error that caused the rank-order correlation coefficients to increase in size.[45]

Could changes in question wording be responsible for most of the correlation coefficient increases reported by Nie? John L. Sullivan and his colleagues reported that they obtained a similar change in scores in a split-sample study where they submitted

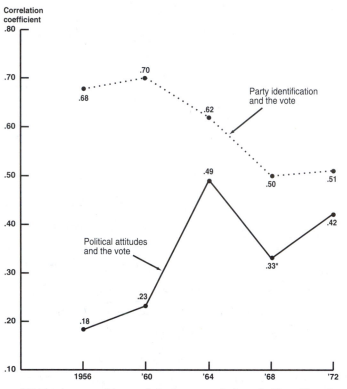

*Weighted average of the correlation between attitudes and a Nixon/Humphrey choice, a Nixon/Wallace choice, and a Humphrey/Wallace choice.

Figure 5.3   Pearson correlations between party identification and the presidential vote and between the summary measure of political beliefs and the presidential vote, 1956–1972

Source: Nie et al., *The Changing American Voter*, p. 165.

the old-format questionnaire to one-half of the sample and the new-format questionnaire to the other half.[46] Differences in question wording did produce differences in scores.

Norman Nie and James Rabjohn respond that the changes in political attitudes over time are real and are not simply an artifact of question wording. They report the increased consistency of citizens' responses to a set of questions, known as the Stouffer tolerance items, that were asked in both the mid-1950s and early 1970s and were uncontaminated by a change in format. The average association between questions increased in all but one of the thirty-six pairs.[47] Nie's critics respond, however, that the Stouffer items were intended to form a unidimensional scale and do not pose a

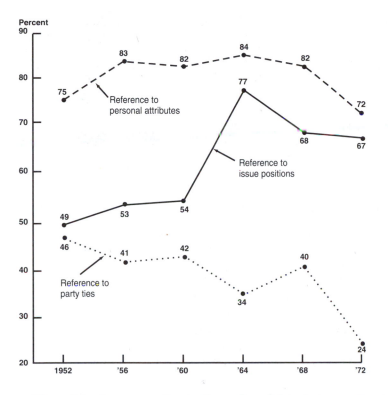

Figure 5.4   Frequency of evaluations of candidates in terms of party ties, personal attributes, and issue positions, 1952–1972.
Source: Nie et al., *The Changing American Voter*, p. 167.

valid test of the consistency of the public's beliefs across a broad set of domestic and foreign policy questions.[48]

The Center for Political Studies (formerly the Survey Research Center) repeatedly interviewed a panel of voters throughout the 1972 to 1976 period. The results from this panel study also challenge the notion of a changing American voter. The 1970s sample showed no increased attitudinal stability compared with the 1950s sample studied by Converse in his famous nonattitude study (see Table 5.5). Voter attitudes in the 1970s were no more stable than those of the earlier era.[49]

POLITICAL SCIENCE UNCOVERS THE ROLE OF ISSUES

The debate on voter ideology continues. But voters do not have to think ideologically or sophisticatedly to vote on the basis of issues.

Table 5.5   Attitudinal Stability over Time; the
1950s and 1970s Compared

	1956–60	1972–76
Government job guarantee	.457	.493
School desegregation	.397	.410
U.S. stay home	.347	.309
Foreign aid	.292	.264

Source: Philip E. Converse and Gregory B. Markus, "Plus ça change
…: The New CPS Election Study Panel," *American Political Science Review*
73 (March 1979): pp. 40–41.

Citizens can vote on the basis of isolated opinions or more frag-
mentary belief systems. They can also vote on the basis of results,
on evaluations of past performance, if not on the basis of future
policy promises.

While no consensus exists among political scientists as to the
degree of ideological or sophisticated thinking of the American
voter, there is a greater consensus that issues do play a role in
contemporary presidential voting. We now believe that election
results cannot be adequately explained without at least some reference to issues. Issues influence presidential elections, but in a
manner quite different from that suggested by *The American Voter*
in its criteria for issue voting.

The Survey Research Center/Center for Political Studies initially did not recognize the influence of issues; their data showed
that issues were not a major factor in presidential voting. But
V. O. Key's challenge forced the Center to respond. By 1968 the
Center admitted that the voter was capable of voting in response
to issues. Their data pointed to the fact that in the 1968 election
supporters of third-party candidate George Wallace, governor of
Alabama, were issue voters. But overall, according to the Center's
major report, issues had little to do with the voter choice between
Nixon and Humphrey. Voters could not discern clear differences
in the policy positions of the major-party candidates, even on the
question of the Vietnam War.[50] By 1972, however, the Center's
data would point to a great change: issues approached partisanship in influencing the choice between McGovern and Nixon.[51]

Yet the conclusions of the Center's interpretation of voting
in 1968 are somewhat incongruous. One of the least sophisticated segments of the American public, Wallace voters, is reported to engage in issue voting while more educated voters are

seen to be enslaved by partisan identification![52] How can this be? Two possible explanations come to mind.

The first is that voting choices congruent with party identification are influenced by issues, but in a manner that is not easily detected by the Center's methods. It is relatively easy to spot the influence of issues when policy concerns lead an individual to vote against his or her usual party. It is more difficult to discern the influence of issues independent of partisanship when policy positions reinforce a voter's traditional party loyalty.

The American Voter portrayed political party affiliation as psychologically determined and highly fixed. Once handed down from the parent to the child, it remained stable over the citizen's life. Yet, more recent studies of political behavior have begun to refute this picture of immobile, psychologically determined party identification. Recent findings show that voters' partisan affiliations do change over time, as they are greatly influenced by adult political experiences including policy attitudes.[53] The partisan balance of the electorate fluctuates with changes in presidential approval and voters' evaluations of the nation's economic well-being.[54] Party identification is not psychologically fixed but, instead, reflects issues and performance evaluations.[55] As Morris P. Fiorina put it, "Controversies about issue voting versus party identification miss the point: the 'issues' are *in* party identification."[56]

The second explanation is that voters do not have to be sophisticated to vote in response to issues. Wallace voters were moved by protest and racial backlash concerns. According to Edward Carmines and James Stimson, Wallace voters were responding to "easy" issues.[57] There was nothing complex about the Wallace voters' concerns about the Vietnam War, social change, and law-and-order. It was easy for these voters to have clear-cut opinions on victory through strength and the undesirability of school desegregation or street demonstrations. More complex and difficult issues, however, are less likely to become the basis for the mass public's voting decision.

Citizens, then, do not have to think in an ideological or sophisticated fashion to vote in response to issues. Indeed, voters do not even need to be able to explain the meanings of liberalism and conservatism. Instead, voters need only to perceive and be able to vote on a basic choice before them. For some voters that choice might be along liberal-conservative lines. For other citizens the voting choice might be based on an alternative ideological dimension or a key or salient issue. Still others might cast their ballots on the basis of their degree of satisfaction or dissatisfaction with the times, to choose to continue or change the direction of current policies in Washington. Many voters who fail to meet *The American Voter* criteria for issue voting still know why they voted as they did. As Fiorina explains, a voter

> need not spend his life watching "Meet the Press" and reading *The New York Times*. He can look at the evening news and observe the coffins being unloaded from Air Force transports, the increasing price of a basket of groceries between this month and last, and the police arresting demonstrators of one stripe or another. What does it matter if this voter is not familiar with the nuances of current government policies or is not aware of the precise alternatives offered by the opposition? He is not the professional policy formulator. He has not devoted a career to pursuit of public office nor sought such office on the basis of his competency to govern. Perhaps he can't "cognize the issue in some form," but can go to the polls and indicate whether or not he likes the way those who can "cognize the issue" are in fact doing so.[58]

The criteria for issue voting set down in *The American Voter* are increasingly irrelevant. "Perhaps," as Fiorina criticizes, "we find the electorate wanting because our tests are wanting."[59] Political scientists should begin to identify the various ways that issues influence presidential voting.

THREE COMMON VARIANTS OF ISSUE VOTING

More recent writings in political science have observed the prominent role played by issues in presidential elections. These writings have attempted to explain just how issues influence the voter's choice—why some issues have a greater effect on elections than do other issues. Three different variants of issue voting are particularly noteworthy: retrospective voting, directional voting, and voting in response to easy and hard issues.

Retrospective Voting

Relatively few Americans engage in prospective issue voting by comparing the policy promises of the two major parties and their candidates across a broad range of issues. Instead, policy concerns in presidential elections are often reflected in **retrospective issue voting** as opposed to prospective voting. Fiorina describes the thought calculus of citizens engaged in retrospective voting:

[T]hey typically have one comparatively hard bit of data: they know what life has been like during the incumbent's administration. They need *not* know the precise economic or foreign policies of the incumbent administration in order to see or feel the *results* of those policies. And is it not reasonable to base voting decisions on results as well as on intentions? In order to ascertain whether the incumbents have performed poorly or well, citizens need only calculate the changes in their own welfare.[60]

Citizens who vote retrospectively look not so much at a candidate's policy promises for future action as they look back at the recent past. If citizens are satisfied with the performance of the incumbent administration, they can vote to continue its tenure in office; if dissatisfied, they can vote for a change.

It can be argued that voting on the basis of retrospective evaluations provides a more reliable basis for voting than does voting in response to a candidate's promises. Candidates for office are too willing to promise citizens anything, no matter how unrealistic or unattainable, in order to get their votes. A party's past record also gives a fairly reliable indication as to the future actions a candidate might undertake.[61]

According to a number of studies, economic issues have played a prominent role in voters' decisions in statehouse and congressional as well as presidential elections. Whether citizens are voting in response to their own pocketbook or to their perceptions of the overall economic well-being of the country is still a matter of some debate.[62]

Retrospective evaluations have been evident in a number of presidential elections. In 1968 the electorate voted to reject a Democratic administration incapable of handling campus demonstrations, ghetto riots, and rising welfarism. The outcome of the extremely close race of 1976 was influenced by the public's dissatisfaction with Watergate and President Ford's pardon of Richard Nixon.[63]

Retrospective evaluations based on the economy have determined more recent presidential elections. In 1980 Jimmy Carter was ousted from office primarily because of his inability to handle the twin issues of recession and inflation.[64] Carter's standing in the polls was amazingly low even before the intrusion of the Iranian hostage crisis. By 1984, the nation's economy had rebounded and the United States was at peace. As a result, the 1984 race was essentially a retrospective endorsement of Ronald Reagan's first four years in office. Even the 1988 George Bush-Michael Dukakis race was influenced by retrospective evaluations as citizens cast their ballots to continue the long period of economic prosperity of the Reagan-Bush administration. Had the country in 1988 been in the midst of an economic downturn or suffering from high rates of inflation, both the rhetoric and the outcome of the election would likely have been quite different than they were. In 1992, both the economy and the election outcome *were* quite different. Tired of the prolonged recession, voters demanded more aggressive action and ousted the incumbent Republican administration.

Directional Voting

Retrospective voting is, in effect, a vote for a choice of direction, to continue or change present policies in Washington. Voters indeed have only one basic choice in a presidential election, a choice of direction, but that choice is not always a retrospective one.

Under **directional voting**, citizens need only to be able to discern a diffuse preference between the competing symbolic themes and broad policy alternatives represented by the two major-party candidates.[65] They do not need to possess great knowledge or well-thought-out opinions on a large number of specific issues. Instead, voters need only to discover which of the two general directions presented before them they prefer. Do they want to continue the general direction offered by the present administration or do they prefer an alternative? Do they prefer the general policy directions advocated by the Republicans or the general policy directions advocated by the Democrats?

Under directional voting, voters do not have to meet the rigid criteria traditionally used to gauge issue voting. A directional voter does not necessarily possess precise issue or ideological preferences. Nor does the directional voter need to discern the exact issue positions of the candidates in order to determine which presidential contender is closest to him on the issues. Instead, a directional voter need only determine which candidate is generally on "his side" or "her side" of the issues.[66]

Symbolism plays an important role in directional voting. As George Rabinowitz and Stuart Elaine Macdonald explain, "The key tenet of symbolic politics is that for issues (or other political cues) to have impact, they must evoke emotions and sentiments rather than simple objective appraisal of information."[67] In 1968, "law and order" and "welfare" were particularly powerful symbols; "middle America" voted for Nixon's more conservative approach to welfare and social issues as contrasted with the more liberal course of direction represented by the Democrats. In 1988, the Republicans found a particularly potent and visceral symbol in Willie Horton and Michael Dukakis's "revolving door" furlough program.

As Rabinowitz and Macdonald further explain, directional voting is likely to be quite strong in an election when one side fails to take a stand on a symbolically powerful issue:

> The most meaningful policy guidance that results directly from election outcomes occurs when a majority exists for a policy, but that majority is either not obvious to politicians or is not courted by one of the parties for ideological reasons. Under such conditions the election will tend to be won by the candidate espousing the majority direction.[68]

This observation helps to explain the outcome of the 1988 election. George Bush seized the Willie Horton issue. Michael Dukakis failed to respond quickly and strongly; he did not believe that the furlough question could dominate a presidential election. Dukakis was reluctant to compromise his progressive beliefs on penal reform. Furthermore, he also was not willing to take a strong law-and-order stance that could be perceived as racist. Bush courted the national majority on the issue and won; Dukakis did not declare his clear support for law and order until it was too late.

If voters are looking for a candidate who is on the "right side" of an issue, there is no clear advantage for a candidate to occupy the political center. Nor can a candidate afford to obfuscate important issues. Instead, a presidential contender will declare strong issue positions capable of convincing voters that he or she will move policy in their preferred direction. A candidate can win more votes by being on the "right side" of an issue—the side preferred by most voters—than by being at the mid-point of public opinion.

Still, it is oftentimes electorally advantageous for a candidate to avoid extreme policy positions. To maintain credibility, a candidate must advocate solutions that appear reasonable, solutions that fall within a "region of acceptability."[69] Also, as the electorate contains both proximity issue voters—voters who support the candidate closest to them on issues—and directional voters—voters who look for a candidate on "their side"—a candidate who stakes out extreme policy positions risks losing the votes from people at the center. Presidential candidates can be expected to stake out strong policy positions, but positions that are nonetheless still more toward the center than the extremes of voter sentiment.[70]

Easy and Hard Issues

Not all issues are capable of moving the American electorate. As the theory of directional voting indicates, issues that can be portrayed with emotive symbolism are more likely to evoke voter response than those that cannot be similarly portrayed. Symbolism plays an important role in another theory of issue voting, that advanced by Edward G. Carmines and James A. Stimson.

According to Carmines and Stimson, there are essentially two different types of issues, each capable of evoking a response from a different group of voters.[71] **Hard issues** present voters with complex and difficult-to-understand policy alternatives. Voters must use intellect and reason in sorting out the policy alternatives on hard issues. Well-educated, better informed, and more active voters—in short, more sophisticated citizens—are more likely to respond to hard issues.

Easy issues, on the other hand, evoke what Carmines and Stimson call "gut responses." Easy issues tend to be symbolic; they can be understood simplistically. They are also likely to be of long duration on the political agenda. As the easy-issue voter need not approach politics with any intellectual sophistication— the easy-issue voter only needs to know if he or she is for or against a particular matter—easy-issue voting in presidential elections is likely fairly commonplace.

The difference between easy and hard issues explains why race and crime were factors in the 1968 election but the Vietnam War was not. As Carmines and Stimson observe, the typical voter sees racial desegregation as a simple issue. White middle America did not want school busing or the quickened pace of racial integration, policy positions associated with the Democrats in 1968. Similarly, middle Americans did not want to understand the social roots of criminal behavior, urban unrest, or campus protests; they wanted law and order. These were easy issues, and in 1968 white middle America knew what it wanted and voted for it. The Vietnam War, in contrast, presented a more complex matter. In 1968 both candidates promised the goal of peace, but neither would state clearly how that goal was to be reached. Further, many voters could not themselves discern what road provided the best route to peace—accelerated bombing or a bombing halt, increased troop commitments or unilateral troop withdrawals, escalation of the military effort or de-escalation to promote peace talks. Vietnam was a hard issue, one that was too difficult to guide less informed, less sophisticated voters in casting their ballots.[72]

Similarly, in 1988, easy issues, not hard issues, were again factors in the presidential vote. The Willie Horton/furlough, the Pledge of Allegiance, and no-new-taxes matters were easy issues that evoked a gut response from many citizens. Voters knew where they stood. Opinions on the tax issue were also quite compartmentalized; voters could declare their strong opposition to new taxes without first resolving the question of how to solve the nation's budget deficit. The deficit itself, much to the Democrats' chagrin, was not an important influence on voting in 1988. Few citizens could discern a workable and desirable solution to the deficit problem. Nor could they discern desirable solutions to such intricate problems as coping with the foreign trade imbalance or the savings and loan crisis.

Race is an easy issue—a fact that helps explain its evolution and staying power in contemporary elections.[73] Race continued to be an important electoral factor as the United States entered the 1990s. The new race issue, at least for the early 1990s, was quotas and affirmative action. In North Carolina, conservative Republican Senator Jesse Helms withstood a challenge from Harvey Gantt, the black Mayor of Charlotte, in part with the help of an ad that appealed to white resentment of affirmative action programs. The ad showed the hands of a white worker crumbling a rejection notice in frustration as the audio announces that the worker was turned down despite the fact that he was the best qualified applicant for the job. Likewise, in Alabama incumbent Republican Governor Guy Hunt rode the affirmative action issue to reelection. In California, Pete Wilson gained a narrow victory in the gubernatorial race after Democrat Dianne Feinstein intimated that she would impose virtual racial quotas on hiring by the state government.

THE REASONING VOTER

Citizens "reason" before arriving at their presidential voting decision. According to Samuel Popkin, voters have learned how to "read" the media and incorporate learning from their daily life experiences into the voting decision.[74] A **reasoning voter** does not need to be a policy expert; he or she does not even need to follow public affairs closely. In fact, it would be irrational for a person to devote too much time to following politics when there is so little payoff for a person who becomes a more informed voter.[75] Instead, the voter relies on informational and psychological shortcuts in reading political events. The voter also uses his or her daily life experiences to filter televised messages and determine their relative significance.

Voters do not absorb all the political information to which they are exposed; nor do they use all the information they acquire. Nonetheless, voters acquire information, especially information that is contained in the forms of symbols and psychological "scripts" or scenarios that can be easily understood.[76] Most people also find that it is easier to understand personal information about a candidate than to deal with abstract political data. Voters will observe a candidate's personal behavior and develop a political narrative; they "assess political character from personal character."[77] Recently acquired, easy-to-absorb information can take on more importance than hard-to-assimilate information acquired in the past; new information can drive out the old as the voters learn during a political campaign.[78]

Popkin uses the term **low-information rationality**—or **"gut" reasoning**—to describe the kind of practical thinking by which voters rely on rules and shortcuts as they gather information from daily life experiences, the media, and political campaigns.[79] A voter whose own job prospects have shrunk or whose neighbors have been laid off as the result of a plant closure quickly sees the political significance of news stories about the nation's poor economy. Another voter may be incensed by new information that right-to-life concerns have led the Bush administration to issue regulations that interfere with fetal tissue research. Televised messages present the voter with information; they also help the voter identify which politicians are to blame for specific actions. Broadcast messages also help to identify just which party deserves credit for policies and actions that the voter approves.

Voters are both video-literate and politically literate. They do not uncritically accept everything they see on television or hear from a candidate. Instead, they evaluate information. Viewers are quite accustomed to discounting the exaggerated claims made in television commercials and political campaigns. They also know that information disseminated in paid political spots generally is more partisan and less trustworthy than the information received from the evening news.

Political messages must also strike a responsive chord with voters or they are screened out. In 1988, Bush's revolving-door-parole attack on Dukakis resonated with voters' anxieties about crime. Televised news programs, popular entertainment crime shows, and people's own personal experiences with crime had primed them for Bush's message. The attack seemed reasonable, and Dukakis's legalistic response unpersuasive, in the context of what voters already knew. But in 1992, the same electorate was not persuaded by the Bush campaign's attacks on Bill Clinton's lack of trustworthiness, his liberalness, and his record as governor of Arkansas. They saw such charges as irrelevant to their number-one concern—curing the nation's economy. Television news continued to focus on the economic recession. Viewers also discounted the Bush attacks as half-truths; they had competing information from news stories and Democratic advertisements that highlighted more positive aspects of the Clinton record. Voters knew that the true story was more complex than the caricature presented by the Republican assault.

As noted above, voters rely on symbols, stories, and other shortcuts that allow them to process and understand political information. A seemingly isolated event can stand for so much more as voters interpret the event by fitting it into a larger scenario. Popkin tells the story of classic campaign blunders: Campaigning in San Antonio, President Ford neglects to husk a tamale before attempting to eat it; in New York, George McGovern asks for a glass of milk to accompany a kosher hot dog.[80] Critics may charge that such anecdotes and gaffes should be irrelevant to the choosing of a president. But Popkin argues that such incidents contain political information. While tamale shucking is not the best test of a candidate's policy stands, "neither is it merely symbolism, devoid of content and without meaning for the political process."[81] It is reasonable for members of an ethnic group to conclude that a candidate who knows so little about their eating customs or dietary customs is also likely to be a candidate who has little familiarity with the community's leaders and the community's sensibilities and issue concerns.

Voters in New Hampshire in 1992 did not need to read George Bush's speeches explaining his economic policy and the dangers of overheating the economy. They heard his statements that the programs for recovery were already in place and that prosperity was just around the corner. They reasoned from these statements and his refusal to visit and campaign in New Hampshire (until just before the primary) that Bush was a president who was out of touch with the state's current economic conditions and the people's economic miseries.

One personal misstep by the president inadvertently delivered the same troubling message to voters across the nation. At a grocers' convention, Bush was mesmerized by an exhibit containing a computerized-scan checkout register. Reporters detailed Bush's wonder as he tested a machine that shoppers encounter daily at their local supermarket. Here was visual evidence that this president was not in touch with the everyday lives of Americans; voters could conclude that he was insulated and, despite his protestations, did not feel their pain. In contrast, Bill Clinton, in a televised interview, correctly estimated the price of bread and other household essentials; here was a candidate who was not insulated from the people's economic situation. Voters could reasonably look at both of these incidents and the two candidates' statements on the economy throughout the campaign and conclude that Clinton, not Bush, was going to be the president more likely to initiate a new and more vigorous economic policy.

Similarly, when Bill Clinton, wearing shades, played his saxophone on "Arsenio Hall," the event was more than mere personal image building. As Edwin Diamond and his colleagues observe, "The appearance seemed like a photo-op but actually was information-rich, making generational and racial points simultaneously.[82]

SUMMARY: THE IMPORTANCE OF ISSUES

In recent years, political scientists have begun to identify the various ways by which issues influence voting decisions in presidential elections. Relatively few voters live up to the model of the ideal democratic citizen who examines the prospective promises of each candidate before voting. Few meet the strictest tests of issue voting. Instead, voters retrospectively evaluate the health of the economy, the performance of the incumbent administration, and the general records of the two major parties. Voters are also capable of choosing between the broad, general policy directions offered by competing parties and candidates. Citizens also vote on issues they find to be of great salience. And easy issues, not hard issues, are more likely to influence the mass public's voting decision.

Of course, not all citizens are issue voters. Many persons continue to vote in response to their party affiliation or a candidate's personal image and qualities. Partisanship and personal images continue to be important influences on American voting behavior. The relative importance of issues, images, and partisanship varies with the context of the specific presidential election and the candidates. But the influence of issues in the presidential race is more and more evident. In summing up nearly half a century of research on voting behavior, Richard Niemi and Herbert Weisberg observe the emergence of a near-consensus in the political science profession as to the importance of issues as part of the presidential voting decision:

> In any case, whether stated in terms of easy issues, retrospective voting, or economic determinants, there is much greater emphasis on the role of issues in voting today than there was a few decades ago. Indeed, we think that the role of issues is one controversy that has been largely settled. Few political scientists would now characterize the electorate as always issueless or as chronically unequipped to deal with issues (whether due to intelligence or interest). Particular campaigns may be more or less issue-oriented, and some campaigns and some voters stress issues more than others. But there is no doubt that issues often play an important role in elections, especially in salient campaigns, such as for the presidency.[83]

In the following chapters we trace the changing balance between partisanship, candidate personal images, and issues in presidential elections. In each election, especially those since the mid-1960s, issue-based and performance evaluations played a role in the election outcome.

THE NEW DEAL ERA

6

We commonly think of the United States as having a more or less class-based party system. The Democrats represent a broad-based coalition of diverse ethnic and working-class constituencies against a Republican party dominated by business groups and upper-status interests.

Yet, this commonplace view provides an accurate picture of the political party alignment only at one point in time—the New Deal era. As we shall see, class-based cleavages did not dominate presidential voting prior to the 1930s. The importance of class-based patterns and partisanship to the presidential vote has also weakened over time.

As we saw in Chapter 5, the first high-quality insights into American voting behavior were gained from studies of presidential elections during the 1940s and 1950s. These studies pointed to the importance of partisanship and presidential candidates' personal images to the voting decision. Few voters were concerned with issues. The findings of these studies helped shape the thinking of political science for the next two decades and longer.[1]

Yet, even at the time, these conclusions were not universally accepted. V. O. Key, Jr., prepared a major work challenging the conclusions of these studies. According to Key, voters were not fools. Instead, substantive evaluations were a part of their voting decision. Many Americans cast their ballots in light of their retrospective evaluations of the performance of the incumbent administration.[2]

The accepted "truths" regarding American voting behavior are quite ephemeral. The American voter changes over time. We start by looking at voter attachments during the System of 1896, the party alignment that preceded the New Deal era.

THE SYSTEM OF 1896

In the early twentieth century, the key voting cleavages in the United States were along regional or sectional lines, not social class lines. Largely, voting behavior during the early part of the century was shaped by the election of 1896. This election is often described as a **critical election** as that year's campaign generated perceptions and loyalties that seemingly influenced presidential elections for the next three decades.[3] William Jennings Bryan, the 1896 Democratic presidential candidate, left the party with the taint of rural populism. It was an association that was not popular in a nation that was speedily becoming industrialized and urbanized.

Bryan appealed to farmers in the South and West who faced difficult times as a result of the Depression of 1893. These farmers resented the power of corporate elites. They further resented the alien cultures of immigrants who resided in the cities of the Northeast and the Midwest. An eloquent orator, Bryan promised to end the gold standard to inflate currency and thereby ease the repayment of their debts: "You shall not crucify mankind upon a cross of gold!" According to Bryan, it was clearly city folk who owed their existence to people in the country: "The great cities rest upon our broad and fertile prairies."

As Walter Dean Burnham describes:

> Bryan's appeal at base was essentially Jacksonian—a call for a return to the simpler and more virtuous economic and political arrangements which he identified with that bygone era. Such nostalgia could evoke a positive response among the native-stock rural elements whose political style and economic expectations had been shaped in the far-away past. But it could hardly seem a realistic political choice for the ethnically pluralist urban populations, large numbers of whom found such nostalgia meaningless since it related to nothing in their past or current experience.[4]

Bryanism was an appeal to the virtues of small-town and rural America that offered little to citizens of the big cities of the Northeast. Samuel Lubell observed that Bryan's "revivalist oratory might inflame the Bible belt—but in the city he was a repellent, even comic figure."[5] The nativist elements of Bryan's support only further alienated voters of immigrant stock. Bryan's fundamentalist following saw themselves, native Protestants, as virtuous; they too often viewed immigrants and Catholics as threatening intruders and the source of "demon rum," filth, disease, sloth, crime, and corruption.

Bryan's agrarian appeal cast the Democrats "in the role of reactionaries" who opposed change.[6] In contrast, Republican presidential candidate William McKinley promised a "full dinner pail," a new era of industrial growth that would provide prosperity for all Americans. Both factory workers and owners alike responded to this Republican appeal. Faced with a choice between Bryan's rejectionism and Republican industrialization, the urban masses voted Republican. The Democratic party was virtually wiped out by the reaction against Bryanism in large areas of the Northeast and the Middle West.[7] In the 1890s "the Republican party alone retained some relevance to the urban setting."[8]

After 1896 the United States was essentially a country divided politically by region. The Republicans gained dominance in national politics because of their popularity in the more populous Northeast. The Democrats dominated the South. White voters in the South also continued to vote solidly Democratic because of their memories of the Civil War and the harsh reconstruction efforts pushed by Radical Republicans. Agrarian protest movements would continue to rise in the West. Republican control over the presidency for the next twenty-six years was interrupted only as a consequence of Theodore Roosevelt's Bull Moose Party revolt, which divided the normal Republican vote. As a result, Democrat Woodrow Wilson won the presidential election in 1912 and was reelected four years later.

THE CHANGING SOCIAL FABRIC

An electoral system that ignored class issues could not last long in a nation that had to deal with the problems posed by a new industrial order. The Republican party could not represent the interests of factory owners while meeting the demands of workers who sought unionization, hours and wage legislation, safe working conditions, and social security. These workers would have to turn to an opposition party not allied with corporate owners—the Democrats.

The Democratic party was bitterly divided by a schism between its agrarian wing and a northern wing of big city voters and political machine leaders. The 1924 Democratic convention lasted 103 ballots. New York Governor Alfred E. Smith, an Irish Catholic and a "wet" on the issue of Prohibition, fought William Gibbs McAdoo, a Protestant and an antialcohol "dry" who also had the support of the Ku Klux Klan. Given the cultural and sectional cleavages that divided the party, neither candidate could gain the two-thirds vote then necessary for the nomination under the party's rules. The convention finally and unhappily settled on a compromise candidate, John W. Davis.

Four years later, Smith gained the nomination, setting off a virtual "Al Smith Revolution" as cities with large foreign-born populations were drawn into the Democratic column.[9] Smith had grown up on the streets of the East Side of New York City; he spoke with a New Yorker's nasal twang. He was the first Catholic to gain a major party nomination for the presidency. Smith's nomination sent a message to America's new arrivals, particularly to Catholics, in the Northeast: the national Democratic party was their party; it was no longer the party of Bryan.

Smith lost the 1928 race badly, as the nation was not yet ready to vote for a Catholic for president. The normally solid Democratic South was split by Smith's religion. The Republican candidate, Herbert Hoover, gained unprecedented victories in five states in the rim or outer South. Only in the Deep South, with its Democratic loyalty rooted in its Negrophobia, did white voters swallow their compunctions and vote Democratic.

In 1928, the Democrats lost the battle but began to win the war. The Irish, Italians, and other new-stock citizens voted for Smith in large numbers. They were the beginnings of a soon-to-be Democratic majority, a majority that would be cemented in place as a result of the Great Depression and voter endorsement of Franklin Delano Roosevelt's New Deal recovery programs.[10] The nation's Republican majority was about to give way to a new Democratic era.

THE NEW DEAL REALIGNMENT

The Great Depression and Roosevelt's New Deal response ushered in a new voting alignment that gave shape to the modern voting era—an era that is only now undergoing great change. Roosevelt was swept into office in 1932 as voters blamed the Republicans for the Depression. The Democrats derisively campaigned against Hoovervilles, the tent cities that had sprung up across America. For the next thirty years the Democrats would attempt to campaign against the ghost of Herbert Hoover. They would portray the Republicans as the party of the Depression. The Democrats, in contrast, would promise that "happy days are here again."

The Democrats won office in 1932 simply by blaming the Republicans for the nation's economic collapse. They promised economic recovery and relief, but were not yet wedded to activist government intervention in the economy and the provision of social welfare programs. The 1932 Democratic platform even went along with the prevailing economic philosophy of controlling government spending to ensure a balanced budget and enhanced business confidence.

Once in office, however, Democrat Franklin Delano Roosevelt switched to a more activist government response to the problems of the Depression. By 1935 the Democrats had initiated a number of programs that promised much needed benefits to huge numbers of Americans, including native-stock voters, members of more established immigrant groups, and more recent foreign-stock voters alike. The Works Progress Administration provided work relief for thousands. The National Labor Relations Act (also called the Wagner Act after the Democratic senator from New York who authored it) protected labor's right to organize and forced employers to bargain collectively with unions. The Social Security Act provided cash assistance to the elderly, the unemployed, and the disabled. A soak-the-rich tax bill in 1935 also clearly established the Democrats as the party of the working man fighting against the party of the upper class.

The result was that by 1936, working class, native-stock voters were added to the Democratic party's immigrant base, virtually completing the nation's **realignment** from a Republican to a Democratic era. Black citizens, among the nation's most deprived groups, were also gradually moving away from the party of Lincoln and shifting their loyalty to the party that was promising them much-needed material assistance in their lives. By 1936, the Democrats had assembled a coalition of labor, new-stock ethnic groups, southern whites, and a growing black vote to become the new national majority party.

The new class pattern to voting helps explain the sudden demise of the *Literary Digest* **poll** in 1936. The *Literary Digest,* a popular magazine, had accurately predicted the outcome of a number of presidential elections. In 1936, the *Digest* became the laughing stock of the nation when it predicted that the Republican, Alfred Landon, would win the presidency by nearly twenty points. As it turned out, Roosevelt won reelection by a landslide, taking 523 of the 531 electoral votes and 60 percent of the popular vote. The magazine lost credibility and soon went out of business.

What had gone wrong? The *Digest* had failed to poll a representative sample of American voters. Instead the *Digest* had its subscribers fill out and mail back sample ballots to the magazine. The magazine also used phone books, automobile registrations, and lists of club memberships in its polling effort which, not so coincidentally, was aimed at gaining the magazine new subscribers. Over 2 million ballots were returned. Yet, despite its large size, the sample was unscientific. During the Depression, only financially better-off citizens were likely to subscribe to magazines or own automobiles and telephones. The magazine had inadvertently overrepresented upper-status citizens, who were likely to vote Republican, and failed to contact a representative number of working-class and unemployed citizens, who were now likely to vote for Roosevelt.

The **New Deal realignment** took place over a series of elections. Voters did not convert at once to new Democratic loyalties. In 1932, the Democrats gained the crossover vote of Republicans disaffected because of the nation's distressed economic conditions. However, it appears that not as many voters changed their party identification as was once believed. The growth of the new Democratic majority was not simply the result of converting former Republican voters. The new Democratic majority also was forged by winning the loyalty of younger and newer voters, voters who had not built strong Republican identifications over the years and were free to respond to the new political cues created by Roosevelt's New Deal.[11]

Gerald Gamm reports in his study of Boston during this era that only Jewish voters in general seemed to convert from Republican to Democratic loyalties. Jews were attracted to the liberalism of the New Deal Democratic party, a liberalism that matched the teachings of their faith. Changes in the partisan attachments of Italians and black voters, in contrast, were much more gradual. While there were some conversions, it appears that the entrance of new voters explains much of the new

Democratic partisanship of these groups. Generational replacement provides a particularly strong explanation of the changed partisan affiliation of black voters. Older blacks committed to the party of Lincoln were dying off and were replaced by younger blacks more responsive to the economic and social programs now being offered by the national Democratic party.[12]

Generational replacement, then, helps explain much of the dynamic for change in the electorate. Older voters die off and are replaced by newer voters less restrained by the older loyalties and habits. In the 1960s and 1970s, change would emerge again as new voters not well-socialized into the New Deal loyalties would come of voting age.[13]

But as social change continued, new strains would emerge in the Democratic coalition. One immediate problem for the Democratic party was that of race. The party could not harmoniously accommodate blacks, southern whites, and northern liberals. In 1948, this fissure would begin to divide the Democrats. Hubert Humphrey, then mayor of Minneapolis and the darling of white liberals, had pushed through a civil rights resolution at that year's Democratic national convention. A number of southern whites bolted, forming their own party, the **Dixiecrats**, or States' Rights party. Its candidate for the presidency, South Carolina Governor Strom Thurmond (later to be a U.S. senator), carried four Deep South states, taking thirty-nine electoral votes. Faced with this revolt, the incumbent President Harry Truman squeaked to a somewhat unexpected and narrow victory, garnering 52 percent of the vote. The Dixiecrat revolt was a precursor as to how the Democratic New Deal coalition would begin to unravel over the years as memories of the Depression were forgotten and new racial and social matters displaced older economic concerns in the minds of the voters. As we shall see, a new invention, television, was also about to become a strong influence on voters.

THE 1950S: THE INFANCY OF TELEVISION

Television first became a factor in presidential elections in 1952. At that time approximately four of every ten American households owned a television set. That year saw the first televised broadcast of national party conventions. Dwight David Eisenhower's use of spot ads would begin to change the character of presidential elections.

At first, politicians schooled in the old ways of campaigning were unable to recognize the power inherent in the new communications medium. In 1948, President Truman still campaigned by a cross-country, whistle-stop train tour. His Republican opponent, Thomas E. Dewey, spurned as "undignified" the suggestion that he run television spots in key states in the closing days of his campaign. Had Dewey heeded this advice, he might well have been elected.[14]

In 1952, the Democrats ineptly responded to the opportunities presented by the new medium. Their national convention was so loosely run that Adlai Stevenson delivered his acceptance speech at 2:10 A.M., a time when most Americans had already gone to bed. During the fall campaign, the party bought time in thirty-minute blocks during which it aired lengthy campaign speeches that bored viewing audiences. The speeches were also aired late in the evening to reduce the costs of air time, so the Democrats missed much of their potential audience.[15] Stevenson's campaign headquarters also initially rejected an offer of free time from NBC for a televised presidential debate, despite the fact that the Democratic candidate, less well known than Eisenhower and trailing in the polls, needed the opportunity provided by the debate. Eisenhower's camp astutely rejected the offer knowing that it had more to lose in a televised showdown.[16]

The Democrats provided for the local broadcast of one of Truman's speeches. Technically, Truman was the first presidential candidate to use paid television advertising. Still, it was Dwight Eisenhower who, in 1952, demonstrated that television could be used as an effective presidential campaign tool.

Eisenhower opened his campaign with a simulcast on sixty-five NBC television stations and 165 radio stations. Radio was still essential for ensuring blanket coverage as less than half of the households in America then had television.[17] The Republicans also brought in the Madison Avenue advertising firm of BBD&O to help prepare their advertising campaign. Rather than buy huge blocks of time in the late evening or pay to preempt popular primetime shows, BBD&O and the party's strategists hit on the idea of presenting Eisenhower's image to the public in short spot ads, twenty seconds or so in length, to be aired during commercial time between television programs.

Eisenhower ran on the highly personalized slogan of "I Like Ike!" and he was sold to the public on the basis of his personal merits—a World War II hero and a citizen-leader who was above the normal political fray. As the campaign's advertising strategy was based on a personalization of the product, both Eisenhower and his vice-presidential running mate, Richard Nixon, were marketed to television viewers "so that the warmth of their personalities can be felt."[18] A Republican memorandum outlined the basic technique of this strategy:

> The spots themselves would be the height of simplicity. People . . . would ask the General a question . . . . The General's answer would be his complete comprehension of the problem and his determination to do something about it when elected. Thus he inspires loyalty without prematurely committing himself to any strait-jacketing answer.[19]

By today's standards, the Eisenhower spot ads seem quite amateurish and lacking in production values. Yet at the time they proved quite effective. Eisenhower was brought to a studio where a camera crew filmed his answers to a number of questions. In an early bit of television editing, Eisenhower's remarks were juxtaposed as answers to questions posed at different times by a group of everyday Americans. One typical Eisenhower ad was as follows:

EISENHOWER ANSWERS AMERICA ad

VIDEO: Sign reads EISENHOWER ANSWERS AMERICA next to
    a picture of Ike.

AUDIO (Announcer): "Eisenhower answers America."

AUDIO AND VIDEO (Elderly woman asks): "You know what things
    cost today? High prices are just driving me crazy!"

Switch to Eisenhower: "Yes. My {wife} Mamie gets
    after me about the high cost of living. It's anoth-
    er reason why I say it's time for a change, time to
    get back to an honest dollar and an honest dollar's
    work."

In his most famous pronouncement of the campaign, Ike promised to go to Korea, if elected, to bring the war there to an end. He did not, however, supply any hint as to what steps he would take to bring the war to a conclusion. Ike's election eve hour-long simulcast presented him as a man of the people. The program concluded with Ike and Mamie cutting a victory cake.[20]

Television also proved critical in rescuing Richard Nixon on the ticket after press stories reported allegations that the vice-presidential nominee had illegally pocketed money from an expense fund raised by his backers. The sums of money involved seem rather paltry by today's standards, but in the 1950s it was a major scandal. In the wake of the charges, Nixon's presence on the Republican ticket was an embarrassment to Eisenhower, who had campaigned vigorously against "the mess in Washington," including charges of corruption in the Truman administration. Eisenhower was ready to dump his running mate from the ticket unless Nixon could persuasively present his case to the American public. This Nixon did in his famous "Checkers" speech.

Nixon met with his advisers and decided to respond in a half-hour paid broadcast.[21] The broadcast drew what at the time was the largest televised audience ever for any campaign speech. It was produced by BBD&O and the Kudner advertising agency. Nixon spoke directly into the camera. He claimed never to have taken any money from the fund for his personal use and never to have profited personally from politics. Nixon talked about how he was not a rich man, how as a boy he had worked in the family grocery store. He had also worked his way through college. Nixon went on to say that "probably the best thing that ever happened to me happened" when "I married Pat." Pat, continued Nixon, "doesn't have a mink coat. But she does have a respectable Republican cloth coat, and I always tell her that she would look good in anything." The only gift Nixon acknowledged receiving was a dog:

> A man down in Texas heard Pat on the radio mention the fact that our two youngsters would like to have a dog, and believe it or not, the day before we left on this campaign trip we got a message from Union Station in Baltimore, saying they had a package for us. We went down to get it. You know what it was? It was a little cocker spaniel dog, in a crate that he had sent all the way from Texas—black and white, spotted, and our little girl Tricia, the six-year old, named it Checkers. And you know, the kids, like all kids, loved the dog, and I just want to say this right now, that regardless of what they say about it, we are going to keep it.

The camera focused on Pat at appropriate moments.

At the end of the broadcast, Nixon asked viewers to wire or write the Republican National Committee stating their feelings about his remaining on the ticket. The response was overwhelming; the public had been moved by the Richard Nixon story. The next day, Nixon flew to meet General Eisenhower in

Wheeling, West Virginia. Eisenhower met him and responded by putting his arms around Nixon, saying, "You're my boy."

By today's standards, the Checkers speech was a maudlin exercise. The entire scandal had been reduced to the imagery of his wife's cloth coat and a little girl's love for a puppy. One wonders if such a speech could so easily dispel the public's doubts today. In 1952, in the infancy of television, the American public had not yet built any great familiarity with the televised presentation of an orchestrated event.

Television had enhanced the personalization of politics. Viewers could see the candidates up close and judge them on whether or not they appeared to be warm, caring, and trustworthy human beings. Where radio focused on a candidate's words, television focused on a candidate's visual appearance. Candidates were now increasingly judged as individuals, as television performers, not as the purveyors of a political party's platform on issues.

Eisenhower's 1952 and 1956 victories are regarded by political scientists as **deviating elections** in the New Deal era. The Republicans won the presidency without converting new voters to Republicanism. Partisan affiliations established during the New Deal era remained unchanged despite Ike's victories. The Republicans won because of a short-term factor, Ike's personal appeal as a war hero and a citizen-leader above politics. Eisenhower did make substantial inroads in the South as whites in that region showed increasing dissatisfaction with the national Democratic party's progressive racial attitudes. Great ideological issues were seemingly absent from the 1952 and 1956 contests.[22]

Yet, were issues really *that* absent in 1952? More recent analyses have tended to point to the importance of substantive considerations, especially foreign policy, to the vote in 1952. Eisenhower and the Republicans chose to contest the 1952 election to a very great extent on foreign policy grounds. In the final days of the contest, Eisenhower campaigned almost exclusively on foreign policy.

By this account, the vote in 1952 turned on retrospective performance and policy evaluations. Americans held Truman and the Democrats responsible for "losing" China to the Communists and for getting the United States involved in a stalemated and costly war with Red China in Korea. Assessments of foreign policy performance were so important in 1952 that, according to one analysis of public opinion, they "not only influenced many individual votes, they also appeared to shift the balance of the election to a significant degree."[23]

General Eisenhower won because he was able to tie voter perceptions of his personal competence to the salient issue of the day—the war in Korea. The vote for Eisenhower in 1952 was no simple personal vote; instead, voters related Eisenhower's potential leadership qualities as president to the handling of a very important issue. Voters judged the General to be more capable than Truman of being able to bring the war to an honorable conclusion. As Samuel Popkin has observed, retrospective assessments in elections such as 1952 emphasize candidates' (especially an incumbent's) competence not just simple issue proximity.[24] Voters in 1952 did not choose which of the two presidential candidates offered a plan for Korea that was more to their liking. Instead, the Korean entanglement provided voters a reason to reject the performance of the Democratic administration and to search for the alternative leadership qualities offered by Eisenhower.

Domestic issue concerns were also important in 1952. Had Eisenhower been a more extreme conservative, voters who were worried about continued support for New Deal programs would likely have been less willing to vote for him. But the salience of issues changes when voters acquire new information over the course of a campaign. In 1952, voters who perceived a large difference between Democrats and Republicans on support for New Deal programs may have grown less concerned as the campaign progressed and they learned that Eisenhower had never been associated with the more virulent Republican attacks on Social Security and labor unions.[25]

1960: KENNEDY'S IMAGE PROBLEM AND THE GREAT DEBATES

By 1960, nearly all American households had a television set. The 1960 presidential race was the closest in American history; John Kennedy won the presidency by gaining just a hair over 50 percent of the two-party vote. Television was an important influence on the outcome of the election. Yet, in a race so close, image creation on television was only one of a large number of factors that can be said to have made the difference.

Kennedy confronted two major problems in his race for the presidency. First was his relative youth and inexperience. Kennedy was the somewhat unknown forty-two-year-old junior Democratic senator from Massachusetts. In the general election he was up against the Republican vice president of the United

States, Richard Nixon, a man whom Americans saw as being much more experienced in the critical arena of foreign affairs.

Second was Kennedy's religion; Kennedy was a Roman Catholic, and Al Smith had lost badly in 1928. Was America in 1960 ready to elect a Catholic? Although the presidential candidates themselves refrained from making religion an issue, ugly charges regarding Kennedy's religion and virulent anti-Catholic literature circulated among various groups in the population. Would a Catholic president subordinate his policy decisions to those of the church and Pope?

In 1960, only sixteen states used primaries to select their delegates to the national party conventions. In most states, delegates were chosen in closed caucuses dominated by state party leaders and other party loyalists. Candidates for the presidency did not need to enter or win a large number of state primaries. Instead, presidential candidates strategically picked which races they would contest, avoiding as much as possible those states where a possible setback could do critical damage to their presidential effort.

Kennedy needed key primary victories to show party leaders that his youth and religion were not insurmountable handicaps in his search for the presidency. Kennedy beat Hubert Humphrey in the Wisconsin primary, but the Wisconsin results were fairly close and did not prove that Kennedy could win in overwhelmingly Protestant America. Kennedy won by capturing the votes of Wisconsin's sizable Catholic population; he lost the state's Protestant areas.

West Virginia became the decisive showdown between Kennedy and Humphrey. Humphrey made a critical strategic mistake, that of choosing to meet Kennedy's challenge in this overwhelmingly Protestant state. West Virginia was significant in 1960, even though no presidential delegates were chosen in the state's primary. Kennedy used his victory in West Virginia to demonstrate to party leaders and national convention delegates that he could win even in Protestant-dominated areas of the country.

Kennedy met the question of his religion head-on in West Virginia. In a statewide paid television broadcast and in paid commercials Kennedy explained that his religious faith would not in any way affect his handling of the presidency. "Now," as Kennedy said in one of the ads, "you cannot tell me the day I was born it was said I could never run for president because I wouldn't meet my oath of office."[26]

The West Virginia primary underscored the critical role played by money in elections in the television age. Humphrey lacked the funds to effectively counter Kennedy's ads. A half-hour, election-eve telethon broadcast by Humphrey further illustrated the dangers that could result if a campaign lacked the necessary funds or otherwise failed to take the proper steps to control how a candidate's image would be presented to television viewers. Phone calls from the viewing audience were not screened. Humphrey actually fielded questions live from West Virginia's citizens. On the phone, a woman with a high-pitched West Virginia accent repeatedly berated Humphrey to "git out" of West Virginia. Humphrey was rattled. It was not quite the image that the campaign had hoped to get across.

As the media provided the public with additional information about Kennedy in addition to that concerning his religion, the initially hostile reaction of many Protestants was muted.[27] Still, a number of Protestants could not bring themselves to vote for a Catholic. Many Republican Catholics, on the other hand, now found themselves voting Democratic for one of their own.

Because of his religious affiliation, Kennedy lost about a million and a half votes more than he gained. Yet, in a curious way, his religion may have helped him win the White House. One study of 1960 concluded that "roughly one out of five Protestant Democrats or Protestant Independents who would otherwise have voted Democratic bolted because of the religious issue."[28] But many of the votes that Kennedy lost due to his religion were in the Protestant South. Although Kennedy lost Florida, Kentucky, Tennessee, and Virginia, defections from the Democratic banner in other southern states only cut into the normally sizable margins of victory usually enjoyed by a Democratic presidential candidate.

Catholic voters, in contrast, were concentrated in large two-party industrial states, key battlegrounds in winning the Electoral College in a close race. Kennedy won Illinois by a mere 9,000 popular votes; he won New Jersey by a similarly slim 22,000-vote margin. The greater-than-normal Democratic totals that Kennedy ran up among Catholics may well have accounted for his margin of victory in these two pivotal states. Overall, it appears that Kennedy's Catholicism helped him win Connecticut, New York, New Jersey, Pennsylvania, Illinois, and New Mexico and their combined total of 132 electoral votes, more than offsetting the 110 electoral votes he lost from the more Protestant states that would otherwise have gone Democratic had it not been for his religion.

Race may have played a role similar to religion in 1960. Martin Luther King, Jr., had been jailed and sentenced to hard labor in Georgia because of his role in a civil rights demonstration. As the presidential campaign drew to a close, Kennedy placed a phone call to King's wife, Coretta, to offer his assistance. Also, his brother, Robert Kennedy, intervened to help get King released on bail. The phone call alienated a number of white southerners, but it was widely hailed in the black community. The incident may have helped Kennedy to win Illinois and other key electoral states where black voters made up a sizable portion of the electorate.

In the fall campaign, television ads sought to enhance Kennedy's name recognition. One entirely issueless spot had a chorus repeatedly sing "Kennedy, Kennedy, Ken-ne-dy" as viewers were presented with a rapidly changing montage of campaign signs with the candidate's name. Other ads played up the image of Kennedy as a family man (prominently featuring his attractive and telegenic wife, Jackie), the brilliant author of the Pulitzer-prize-winning *Profiles in Courage,* and the heroic skipper of PT-109—a man who swam five miles to help rescue his shipmates.[29] In other ads Kennedy reviewed the Democratic party's achievements. He talked directly into the camera as if to underscore his maturity and seriousness. The Kennedy media campaign was designed to assuage voters' doubts about his youth and leadership abilities. It was almost as if Kennedy had directly responded to the line from the popular song at the time that said "Johnny, you're too young to run for president."

In the Republican ads, Nixon, too, often talked straight into the camera. These ads underscored the achievements of the Eisenhower years and Nixon's experience in foreign policy. The Republican campaign also trumpeted Nixon's "kitchen debate" with Nikita Khrushchev. Nixon made a major strategic mistake, however, by promising to campaign in all fifty states. In the closing days of the campaign he was still scrambling to fulfill his fifty-state pledge instead of concentrating on appearances in media markets in key swing states.

Without doubt the most prominent campaign events of 1960 were the Great Debates. Kennedy, as the lesser-known candidate, needed the publicity the debates would generate. His performance in the debates could also assuage the doubts of wavering Democrats.

Kennedy and his advisers understood that television is essentially a visual medium. They believed that Kennedy's performance in the first debate would be crucial in establishing the public's perception of their candidate. Kennedy was tanned (he used sunlamps) and rested. He switched to a dark-blue business suit and light-blue shirt to show up more favorably against the studio background. He was coached to deliver his answers to reporters' questions by peering directly into the camera and looking at the voter back home, not at the questioner or at Nixon.

Kennedy emphasized the need to get America "moving again" after the lethargic Eisenhower years. His own energetic performance seemed to indicate that he was the candidate capable of moving America forward with vigor. Kennedy rattled off a series of statistics that made him look knowledgeable, informed, and presidential; the presidency was not too large a job for him. In later debates he would even seize the vulnerable position of Quemoy and Matsu, two obscure islands off the coast of China, both to show his command of foreign policy and to attack the weakness of America's international position during the Eisenhower era. (After the debates were over, the fate of the islands was rarely discussed again.) Kennedy also attacked the Republicans for having allowed the United States to be caught on the wrong end of the missile gap.

In contrast, Nixon approached the first encounter much as he would any ordinary debate. He did not tailor his strategy to television. When the moderator asked him for a response to one of Kennedy's early statements, Nixon declined, in effect throwing away a very valuable ninety seconds of air time when the viewing audience's attention was at its peak. He also declined to draw sharp differences between Kennedy and himself.

In the first debate, Nixon focused on the content of what he said, not on his appearance. An infected knee was causing him pain. He had spent the morning in a contentious appearance before a labor union assembly and he was not rested. He wore a gray suit that did not show up well on television against the studio background. He refused CBS's offer to have professionally applied make-up for television. Instead, Nixon had a member of his own staff quickly apply pancake make-up, which did not effectively conceal his facial stubble. However, the mythology that has evolved around the debate greatly overemphasizes the extent to which Nixon's five o'clock shadow was apparent on television and an influence on viewer's reactions. It also exaggerates the degree to which Nixon visibly sweated under the studio's lights.

Polls showed that people who listened to the first debate over radio tended to judge Nixon as the winner. Kennedy, in contrast, did not try to win debating points. Instead, he sought to use the debates to fashion an image that would be presented to the television viewers across America. He would use the panel's questions as starting points from which he could launch into campaign statements that he had rehearsed with his advisers.

Media theorist Marshall McLuhan refers to how visual images dominated viewer reaction to the debates. Kennedy, he said, presented "an image closer to the TV hero . . . something like the shy young Sheriff" while Nixon "resembled more the railway lawyer who signs leases that are not in the interests of the folks in the little town."[30] Yet, McLuhan's assessment, part of the general mythology surrounding the Great Debates, is too severe. As we look at the tapes of the debate today, Nixon does not appear to do nearly as badly as this commentary would have us believe. But, in the first debate he does look *somewhat* less energetic, in-command, and presidential than does Kennedy.

Nixon, frustrated with the public's response to the first debate, adapted his performance to television for the three remaining exchanges. In the second debate, the temperature of the studio was kept very cool to minimize Nixon's sweating. He also had a professional apply his television make-up.

Nixon did better; but by then it was too late. Kennedy's first debate performance had dispelled Democrats' doubts. His campaign picked up momentum. With the age and religion issues somewhat mitigated by Kennedy's performance, normally Democratic voters could now more easily cast ballots for their party's candidate.

There was relatively little voter learning about substance and policy issues as a result of the 1960 debates. Candidates focused on presentation and performance, not informed issue discussion.[31] Even if viewers discovered, as a result of the debates, the existence of islands named Quemoy and Matsu, they learned too little to make an informed judgment as to what should be American policy regarding the defense of the islands.

The debates proved important as Kennedy's performance removed the qualms that potential Democratic voters had regarding their candidate. Voters who were leaning Democrat were now more likely to vote Democratic. In effect, the debates helped to crystallize the voting decision. But voters may well have moved in these directions as the campaign progressed even had there been no debates.[32]

Very few voters switched from Nixon to Kennedy because of the debates. Public opinion polls revealed no substantial change in voter preferences even after the first meeting, a debate Kennedy was generally acknowledged to have "won." **Selective perception** was at work; Democrats saw the things they wanted to see in Kennedy, and Republicans saw what they wanted to see in Nixon. Each side tended to believe that its candidate won the encounter.

Despite the closeness of the popular vote outcome, 1960 was essentially a **maintaining election** in the New Deal alignment. Kennedy won by gaining the votes of those constituency groups that over the past two-and-a-half decades had usually voted Democratic. Other than some defections in the Protestant South, the Democratic New Deal coalition for the most part remained intact in 1960. Partisanship and personal image were the keys to the outcome of the 1960 election.

SUMMARY

The presidential elections of the late–New Deal era provided the evidence for the University of Michigan Survey Research Center's model of voting. According to *The American Voter* and succeeding studies, party identification was the most important factor in explaining why people cast their ballots as they did. The personal images of candidates also influenced voters, especially less aware and more independent voters. Issues had little to do with the voting decision. Voters were, for the most part, unfamiliar with and disinterested in issues.

According to *The American Voter,* the Democrats were the nation's majority party because of group-related attitudes formed during the New Deal era. Yet, Republican Dwight David Eisenhower was able to win the 1952 and 1956 elections because of the strong personal evaluations of him by the American public. The public's personal endorsement of Ike was especially strong in 1956. The Republicans also gained the public's favor in the area of government management.

Still, even during Eisenhower's eight years in the White House, the Democrats retained their advantage among the voters in the areas of domestic policy and group-related attitudes. The Republicans continued to be viewed as the party of Depression and the rich; the Democrats, in contrast, were the party of prosperity and the workingman.

In 1960, with Eisenhower out of the race and his popularity no longer a factor, long-term, group-related attitudes reasserted themselves and carried the Democrats to a narrow victory. Kennedy's debate performance helped reassure wavering Democrats who had doubts related to his inexperience and religion. Partisanship, group-related attitudes, and personal image—not issues—were again the determining factors in a presidential election.

But V. O. Key, Jr., and others have disputed this view that issues had little to do with voting during the New Deal era. According to Key, any explanation of Democratic popularity during the New Deal era that failed to draw reference to policy considerations was absurd: "It became ridiculous immediately if one contemplates what the fate of Franklin Delano Roosevelt would have been had he from 1933 to 1936 stood for those policies which were urged upon the country by the reactionaries of the day."[33] The passage of the Social Security Act was a particularly important factor in building the Democratic majority in 1936.

Key and other political scientists have come to view the 1952 and 1956 presidential elections as more than a mere personal vote for Eisenhower. Eisenhower's victories were also the result of retrospective evaluations by the electorate. In 1952, voters rejected the performance of the incumbent Democratic administration on the issues of Korea, corruption, and communism. China's entry in the Korean War had exacerbated the difficulties of that conflict. As the war dragged on, voter anxieties climbed. Newspaper stories charged Truman's kitchen cabinet with scandal and corruption. Senator Joseph McCarthy and others blamed the Truman administration for the fall of China to the Communists. McCarthy bandied about charges of Communist penetration into the government in Washington. The simplest explanation of the outcome of the 1952 election is that voters "ousted from power a political party of whose performance they did not approve."[34]

By 1956 the Korean War was quite over. Citizens were generally satisfied with the order of things both at home and abroad. Voters gave their approval to Eisenhower and his apparent competence and problem-solving abilities. Voter appraisal was performance-related; it was not simply a response to personal qualities of the president irrelevant to performance in office.[35]

Even the 1960 election can be seen to have been influenced by performance evaluations. Kennedy's promise of "vigor" was more than simple image-merchandising; it was a rejection of America's sluggishness during the late Eisenhower era. Kennedy promised to get the country moving again. He would restart the economy. He would alter the missile gap. Republican Richard Nixon, the incumbent vice-president, bore the brunt of voter retrospective evaluations.[36]

The overall picture painted by *The American Voter* is that of an electorate in the 1950s and the beginning of the 1960s not very absorbed in the discussion of issues. Citizens had little understanding of ideology and the major alternatives before them. Partisanship and personal imagery were the dominant influences on the voting decision. Yet, as we have also seen, this portrait of the American electorate, once so dominant, has come under challenge. Critics of *The American Voter* have charged that issues and performance evaluations may have played a larger role in the New Deal elections than is commonly credited.

Any generalization regarding voter behavior is time-bound. As we saw at the beginning of this chapter, American voting loyalties changed significantly as the nation industrialized. The New Deal alignment replaced the System of 1896.

It is indeed quite likely that interpretations of American voting behavior based on survey data taken in the 1950s are equally time-bound. The United States was about to pass from the quiescent 1950s to the turbulent 1960s and early 1970s. Would voting behavior change? To the extent that *The American Voter* provided an accurate portrait of American voting behavior in the 1950s, would that portrait continue to be accurate in later years?

THE RISE OF ISSUES IN PRESIDENTIAL ELECTIONS: 1964–1972

7

The 1960s and early 1970s would be much different from the 1950s. The civil rights movement, inner-city riots, school busing, the war in Vietnam, the rise of the counterculture, and the "war at home" on college campuses would intrude on the lives of all Americans. Politics was no longer remote and distant. Beginning with the 1964 election, the presidential dialogue became increasingly concerned with issues, and the voters responded in kind. Issues as well as candidate images and partisanship determined the outcome of elections during this period.

THE 1964 LANDSLIDE DEFEAT OF BARRY GOLDWATER

Barry Goldwater was a different kind of candidate. A man of strong conservative convictions, he was unwilling to compromise or moderate his beliefs to win office. He ran on issues, offering voters "a choice, not an echo." His campaign slogan, "In your heart, you know he's right," pointed not only to the purity of his beliefs but also to the conservative ideological underpinnings of his candidacy. In his acceptance speech at the Republican convention, Goldwater reaffirmed his commitment to principles and his disdain for unprincipled compromise. He proclaimed that "extremism in the defense of liberty is no vice!" and that "moderation in the pursuit of justice is no virtue!" Goldwater would be tagged as an extremist; it was an image problem that plagued him throughout the fall election.

In 1964, most national convention delegates were still chosen by party activists—not in primaries but in closed party caucuses and state conventions. These party activists tended to be more ideological than the public at large—a factor that greatly worked to Goldwater's advantage.

Goldwater's chief rival for the Republican nomination was New York Governor Nelson Rockefeller. The fight between Goldwater and Rockefeller was essentially a battle between the GOP's conservative and more moderate wings for control of the party. In a close contest, Goldwater rode the fervency of conservative party activists to victory.

Rockefeller was dogged in the race by a serious image problem. He had divorced his first wife to marry his second, Happy, who, in order to marry Rocky, had divorced her first husband, leaving two children behind. In the early 1960s, such behavior was considered almost scandalous. Rockefeller image consultant Gene Wyckoff created a series of new commercials that focused on the governor's personal qualities. Wyckoff sought to develop a fresh image for Rocky and thereby overcome the divorce stain.[1] But days before the crucial California showdown, Happy gave birth to Nelson, Jr. The event was widely reported in news stories and reminded voters of Rockefeller's marital record; it resuscitated the morality issue. Goldwater's last-minute ads in the state not-so-subtly featured pictures of a harmonious, intact Goldwater family.[2] Goldwater won California by just one half of a percentage point.

Goldwaterites controlled the Republican National Convention, easily turning back the last-minute candidacy of Pennsylvania Governor William Scranton, who attempted to rally the party's moderates. But even in victory, Goldwater spurned the compromises that would have helped unite the party. He refused to accept three platform planks offered by the moderates. The first would give the president, not military field commanders, ultimate control over the use of nuclear weapons; the second would strengthen the party's commitment to civil rights; and the third condemned extremist groups such as the Ku Klux Klan and the John Birch Society. Goldwater backers believed that the purity of issue beliefs and political style were more important than concerns for winning in November.[3] Goldwater chose an unknown, conservative congressman, William Miller of New York, as his running mate. Miller added little to the ticket.

Goldwater alienated moderate voters and lost the November election to Lyndon Johnson by a landslide. Goldwater carried only five states—his native Arizona and four Deep South states (Louisiana, Mississippi, Alabama, and Georgia) where his conservative philosophy and states' rights emphasis, which would have retarded progress on civil rights, appealed to voters.

Lyndon Johnson had the advantage of inheriting a Democratic party that was fairly well unified in the wake of the Kennedy assassination. To further unite the party and help its more liberal wing overcome its suspicions of Johnson's Texas roots, Johnson chose Hubert Humphrey of Minnesota as his vice-presidential running mate.

The Democrats took advantage of Goldwater's many extreme policy statements to make Goldwater *the* issue of 1964. The Democrats made political capital out of Goldwater's proposal that Social Security be made voluntary, a move that the Democrats said would threaten the financial integrity of the Social Security system. One Democratic ad showed a Social Security card being ripped in half while the announcer informed viewers that "[E]ven his running mate William Miller admits that Senator Goldwater's voluntary plan would destroy your Social Security." Social Security was an overwhelmingly popular program, and the voters did not want it tampered with.

The Democrats also portrayed Goldwater as a reactionary on civil rights. In April 1963, Martin Luther King was jailed in Birmingham, Alabama. As the violence in the South continued, Johnson took to the airwaves in support of much-needed civil rights guarantees. Nowadays it is difficult to remember the astonishment and awe felt at the time the President of the United States—and a Texan at that!—repeated the words of Reverend King: "We shall overcome!" It was an action that had great emotional power and helped cement the loyalties of African-Americans to the Democratic party. Johnson and the Democratic party pushed through the landmark Civil Rights Act of 1964—an Act supported by African-Americans and most northern whites. Goldwater voted against the Act, a fact the Democrats used throughout the campaign. The national Democratic party's support of civil rights, though, did have one cost; it alienated many white southerners, especially in the Deep South.

Overall, the Democratic strategy was to turn Goldwater's rhetoric against him, to use the Republican's own words as evidence that he lacked the sense of balance and proportion to be president. The Democratic ads zeroed in on Goldwater's extremism:

EASTERN SEABOARD ad

VIDEO:A wood model of the United States is floating in a pool of water. The blade of a saw appears and cuts through Ohio and then down through the United States.

AUDIO (Announcer): "In a *Saturday Evening Post* article dated August 31, 1963, Barry Goldwater said, 'Sometimes I think this country would be better off if we could just saw off the eastern seaboard and let it float out to sea.' Can a man who makes statements like this be expected to serve all the people justly and fairly?"

AUDIO AND VIDEO: Saw cuts through the model. Sound of a crashing splash as the eastern seaboard is cut loose and floats out to sea.

The "Eastern Seaboard" ad was also specifically designed to push northeastern "Rockefeller Republicans" disenchanted with Goldwater toward voting for Johnson.

The most severe Democratic attacks against Goldwater concerned the Republican's allegedly relaxed attitude toward the use of nuclear weapons. The "Daisy Girl" ad is perhaps the most famous political spot in history. Although Goldwater's name is not mentioned in the ad, there is no doubt against whom the attack is directed:

DAISY GIRL ad

VIDEO: A young girl picks petals from a daisy and begins to count.

AUDIO (Little girl): "One, two, three, four, five, seven, six, six, eight, eight, nine, nine."

AUDIO: (Technician's voice in background begins a countdown as if for the launch of a rocket): "Ten, nine, eight, seven, six, five, four, three, two, one, zero."

VIDEO: Freeze frame of the girl's face. Move in to a close-up of her face. Camera continues to move in and look into her eye which serves as a screen against which we see the mushroom-cloud blast of an atomic bomb explosion.

AUDIO: Sounds of the blast.

AUDIO (Voice of Lyndon Johnson): "These are the stakes: to make a world in which all God's children can live, or go into the dark. We must either love each other or we must die."

VIDEO (Closing sign): VOTE FOR PRESIDENT JOHNSON ON NOVEMBER 3

AUDIO (Announcer): "Vote for President Johnson on November 3. The stakes are too high for you to stay home."

The attack was so hard-hitting that Republicans cried foul and demanded that the ad be withdrawn. In fact, the "Daisy Girl" ad was shown only once, on CBS's *Monday Night at the Movies*. The spot was too hot for the Democrats to repeatedly use as it risked drawing an adverse public reaction against mudslinging. Yet, the free media continued to convey the message in the ad for the Democrats. The national news networks aired the spot in their coverage of the controversy surrounding the ad. Print commentators, too, wrote about the spot and questioned whether or not Goldwater had demonstrated sufficient responsibility on the use of nuclear weapons. Daisy Girl had accomplished its mission; it probed a weak spot in Goldwater's record and kept the question of Goldwater-and-the-bomb before the American public.

The Democrats hammered away on the nuclear weapons issue in other fear-arousing commercials.[4] One ad, aired only a few days after Daisy Girl, featured a little girl eating an ice cream cone while the narrator informed viewers about the dangers of strontium 90, cesium 137, and radiation poisoning. The narrator pointedly reminded viewers that Barry Goldwater voted against the nuclear test ban treaty. It, too, like Daisy Girl, was aired only once. Still another Democratic commercial featured the visual of a flashing red light on the White House hot line while the announcer cautions, "This particular phone only rings in a serious crisis. Leave it in the hands of a man who has proven himself responsible."

Goldwater complained of the demagoguery in the Democratic ads. He claimed that his position on the use of nuclear weapons had been distorted, that he never proposed that battlefield control of nuclear weapons be given to NATO commanders but only to the single NATO commander, who for years already possessed such authority.[5]

Yet, despite these protestations, the nuclear weapons issue was a legitimate one. Goldwater had indicated a greater willingness to use nuclear weapons than had Johnson. Goldwater refused to rule out the use of tactical nuclear weapons in Vietnam. His off-the-cuff remark that he would "lob one into the men's room of the Kremlin" only heightened the public's fears of putting Barry's finger on the button.

Johnson, in his second term, did in fact prove reliable when it came to the use of nuclear arms. He escalated the war in Vietnam but did not introduce nuclear weapons into the conflict. Even when faced with the prospects of losing both the war and his hold on the presidency, Johnson did not resort to the use of nuclear weapons, even low-yield tactical or field devices. On the nuclear weapons issue, voters saw a meaningful difference between Johnson, the more moderate incumbent, and Goldwater, the hard-line challenger.

The Republicans tried to seize the offensive on the issue of military preparedness, arguing that the United States was not vigilant enough in the face of an aggressive Communist menace:

KHRUSHCHEV ad

VIDEO (Film clip of Soviet leader Nikita Khrushchev making a thumping speech. As he points his finger, his words are translated across the bottom of the screen): "WE WILL BURY YOU."

AUDIO: Khrushchev's speech in Russian.

VIDEO: Shift to a classroom in the United States where a group of students is being led in reciting the Pledge of Allegiance by their teacher.

AUDIO: "One nation, under God . . . "

VIDEO (Shift back to Khrushchev's thumping speech; he continues to point his finger. The translation reads): "YOUR CHILDREN WILL BE COMMUNIST."

AUDIO: Khrushchev's speech in Russian.

VIDEO: Shift back to the American classroom as the Pledge of Allegiance continues.

AUDIO: Children reciting the Pledge.

VIDEO: Goldwater appears on camera and speaks directly to the audience.

AUDIO (Goldwater): "I want American kids to grow up as Americans, and they will if we have the guts to make our intentions clear—so clear that they don't need translation or interpretation, just respect for a country prepared as no country in all history ever was."

VIDEO (Closing sign) Voice of an announcer reads the words:

"IN YOUR HEART YOU KNOW HE'S RIGHT.
VOTE FOR BARRY GOLDWATER."

In another commercial Goldwater attacked the Democrats for having allowed the Communists to gain control of Cuba.

But the Republicans could not gain the initiative. Goldwater's more flamboyant statements had already dictated the course of the 1964 election. The Republicans were on the defensive; they had to try to dispel the public's perception of Goldwater as a dangerous extremist. A number of Goldwater's commercials even featured the candidate talking calmly and directly to the viewing audience as if to demonstrate that he was a calm, thoughtful, and responsible leader, not the dangerous monster the Democrats had made him out to be.[6]

As we saw in Chapter 5, a number of analyses of voting behavior have observed the importance of issues in the 1964 presidential election. David RePass reported that citizens in 1964 cast their ballots in response to salient issues.[7] Norman H. Nie, Sidney Verba, and John R. Petrocik in *The Changing American Voter* report sharp increases in voter ideology beginning in 1964. They also report that at that time domestic policy and cold war attitudes were both increasingly linked to the voters' choice.[8] Furthermore, that ideology was related to the vote in 1964 is evident in that defections to Johnson were concentrated among liberal and moderate, not conservative, Republicans. An amazing 63 percent of Republicans who called themselves liberal crossed party lines and voted Democratic for President in 1964![9]

Perhaps the strongest statement regarding the role of issues in 1964 comes from political scientist Gerald Pomper, who sees the Goldwater candidacy as crucial in clarifying the public's perceptions of the differences between the parties. After reviewing attitudes and voting behavior during the years from 1956 to 1972, Pomper concludes:

> The most important electoral event of this period appears to be the 1964 presidential campaign. Senator Barry Goldwater consciously sought to clarify and widen the ideological differences between the parties. The evidence presented here indicates that he accomplished his goal, although this did not benefit the Republican party. Voters, previously unable to see differences between the parties, learned the lesson of "a choice, not an echo." They accepted the senator's characterization of the Republicans as conservative and the Democrats as liberal, and, on the specific issues involved, they preferred the liberal alternative."[10]

But not all voting studies have pointed to the clear-cut importance of issues in 1964. As we saw in Chapter 5, a number of political scientists dispute the methods and findings of both *The Changing American Voter* and the Pomper studies. Furthermore, Donald Stokes' highly influential study using data from the University of Michigan's Survey Research Center concluded that personal factors were more important than issues and partisanship in the 1964 election.[11]

Yet the Survey Research Center's major report on the election finds that "the mass public had some sense that 'important differences' between the two major parties were heightened in 1964."[12] The Center goes on:

> Throughout, the data suggest that Johnson was carried along to an image nearly as positive as Eisenhower's best, less by personal characteristics than by the policies with which he was associated (many of them identified by respondents as continuations from the Kennedy Administration). For Goldwater, if anything, the reverse was true.[13]

The candidates' images as perceived by the public were not the result of idiosyncratic personal evaluations. Rather, they were largely the product of the policies with which each was associated. Johnson was viewed positively despite the public's negative perception of him personally as wheeler-dealer. Likewise, Goldwater was viewed negatively despite the high marks given to him for his personal "integrity" and "sincerity."[14] Voter assessments of the personal attributes of the candidates reflected concerns relevant to presidential performance. They were not mere affective responses to a candidate's smile, charisma, or personal appearance.[15]

In 1964 the public's perception of candidate images largely reflected the candidates' competing positions on the issues. Campaign advertising helped to mold and heighten the public's awareness of the differences between the candidates.

While Goldwater lost the 1964 election by a landslide, his candidacy had two long-term effects that proved advantageous to the Republicans in the future. First, the Goldwater campaign showed that substantial sums of money could be raised through **direct mail**. The campaign maintained a list of highly motivated donors, variously estimated between 221,000 and 410,000, who gave an average donation of $14 to Goldwater. This list was used as the basis for future Republican fundraising efforts and helped give the GOP its initial edge in the direct-mail field.[16]

Second, Goldwater's candidacy effectively realigned the support of the South in presidential elections. The Republicans, the more conservative of the major parties, were becoming the voice of the white South in presidential elections. The third-party candidacy of Alabama Governor George Wallace would complicate matters somewhat in 1968, but the new Republican appeal in presidential elections would be clearly apparent soon thereafter. This new base of support for the Republican party would help produce Republican victories in five of the six presidential elections during the 1968-1988 period. The era of the solid Democratic South was long gone. In fact, the Democrats would lose the votes of a majority of white southerners even in the first two post-Goldwater elections, 1976 and 1980, in which they nominated a native southerner, Jimmy Carter.

IMAGES, PARTISANSHIP, AND ISSUES IN 1968

The 1968 election was the end of an era. The nominating rules changes enacted in response to the riotous 1968 Democratic convention would soon reshape presidential politics, paving the way for even greater influence by new issue-oriented elites and candidate-centered campaign organizations.

But all that would come later. In 1968, Richard Nixon and Hubert Humphrey both won their parties' nominations the old-fashioned way, by establishing ties to the elected officeholders and party officials who at that time dominated the selection of delegates to the national party conventions.

Personal images and candidate styles were important factors in the 1968 primaries. But contrary to the conventional wisdom, issues—not simply personal imagery—proved decisive to the outcome of the general election.

The Republican Race: The Unmaking of George Romney

After the Goldwater debacle in 1964, the Republican party was in disarray. Goldwater was discredited. Rockefeller could not command the respect of conservative Republican activists. Into the breach stepped Richard Nixon. In 1966, alone, former Vice-President Nixon traveled 30,000 miles and visited eighty-two congressional districts to raise money for Republican candidates; he also maintained control of a fund that he could use to distribute money to candidates of his choosing.[17] Nixon did yeoman's work for the party and earned the debts and gratitude of Republican officials nationwide. He would cash in on these IOUs in his 1968 race for the Republican nomination.

Another early front-runner for the Republican nomination was Michigan Governor George Romney, the former chairman of the board at American Motors. Romney's candidacy was propelled to a great extent by rising public dissatisfaction with the United States' prolonged involvement in Vietnam. The all-out Tet, or Lunar New Year, offensive by the Viet Cong in January 1968 had convinced Americans that no end to the war was in sight.[18] Although Romney did not take a crystal-clear position against the war, he was the first major presidential candidate to lean to the "dove" side and express grave reservations concerning the war effort.

But Romney's candidacy was all but destroyed when, in response to an interviewer's query, he explained his earlier position in support of the Vietnam War by observing that he had been the victim of Pentagon brainwashing:

> Well, you know when I came back from Vietnam, I just had the greatest brainwashing that anybody can get when you go over to Vietnam. Not only by the Generals, but also by the diplomatic corps over there, and they do a very thorough job. And since returning from Vietnam, I've gone into the history of Vietnam, all the way back into World War II and before. And, as a result, I have changed my mind . . . . I no longer believe that it was necessary for us to get involved in South Vietnam to stop Communist aggression.[19]

The substance of Romney's remarks is not that extraordinary. Romney was merely describing the process that the American military used to sell touring VIPs on the U.S. war effort in Vietnam. Like millions of other Americans, Romney had come to question a war effort he initially supported.

But the press focused on questions of Romney's personal abilities, not on the substantive basis of his comments, in the furor that surrounded his remarks. Press reports focused almost solely on Romney's unfortunate spur-of-the-moment use of the word *brainwashing*. *The New York Times* account of the interview ran under the title "Romney Asserts He Underwent 'Brainwashing' on Vietnam Trip."[20] **Pack journalism** guaranteed that the networks and the rest of the press would follow the *Times*' lead and pick up this "big" story. Romney's presidential image was destroyed. In the eyes of the public, a man who could be so easily brainwashed lacked the strength and judgment to be president.

Why did the press so unmercifully tear apart Romney's credibility and stature? In part, Romney was the subject of undue media scrutiny as he was the only active candidate then on the campaign trail. The press placed him under their microscope and found him shallow, ill-prepared, and wanting. As media commentator and reporter Timothy Crouse observes, "The press likes to demonstrate its power by destroying lightweights, and pack journalism is never more doughty than when the pack has tacitly agreed that a candidate is a joke."[21] Romney also suffered from the attention he received as the race's early front-runner. The media searches for dramatic news; and the fall of a front-runner is dramatic news—even if the press has to shake the wire under the candidate in order to see him fall.

Of course, Romney's withdrawal did not mark the end of the Republican nominating contest. After a great deal of hesitation, Nelson Rockefeller belatedly entered the Republican race on April 30. But by then it was far too late; the deadline for entering most delegate selection contests had already passed, and Nixon was well on the way to garnering a majority of GOP convention delegates. Rockefeller was also hurt by his much-publicized vacillation. The public would not vote for a man who did not seem to know if he really wanted to be president. Even newly elected governor of California Ronald Reagan's last-minute entrance into the race could not deny Nixon the votes he needed for the nomination.

Nixon sought to balance the ticket by reaching out to the Rockefeller wing of the party; he selected Maryland governor Spiro Agnew as his running mate. Agnew had the reputation of being a moderate. Largely, this reputation had less to do with Agnew's policy positions and more to do with the fact that he had won a substantial portion of Maryland's black vote in his 1966 contest against a Democrat who opposed fair housing laws and campaigned on the not-so-subtle racist slogan: "Your Home Is Your Castle, Defend It!" Agnew's misstatements and gaffes (such as his blooper, "When you see one slum, you've seen them all") made him the object of ridicule during the fall campaign.

The Unmaking of President Johnson and the Democratic Race

On the Democratic side, President Lyndon Johnson was looking forward to what he assumed to be certain renomination and likely reelection. Peace activists, however, were searching for a candidate to challenge Johnson in the primaries. They approached New York Senator Robert Kennedy and others who spurned their invitations because they saw an intraparty battle with Johnson as doomed to failure. Only Eugene McCarthy, the relatively unknown junior senator from Minnesota, took up the quixotic quest. McCarthy saw the Vietnam War as immoral. He also was not your usual politician. A former English professor, he would often take time out during the campaign, wandering from his advisers to read poetry.

The McCarthy campaign, too, was quite new and different. The campaign sent a virtual army of student volunteers, motivated by their antiwar convictions, to go house-to-house in New Hampshire to explain the McCarthy candidacy to the voters. "Clean for Gene" was the motto of these grassroots canvassers.

Johnson underrated the seriousness of the McCarthy challenge. He decided to stay out of the New Hampshire race. He would be the president who remained above the political fray. As a consequence, his name did not even appear on the ballot in New Hampshire, and a write-in campaign had to be organized by supporters on his behalf.

The results from the Granite State were stunning, McCarthy did much better than anyone had expected. In the nonbinding presidential preference portion of the ballot, Johnson won with 50 percent of the vote. But the fact that Johnson, running only as a write-in, had beat McCarthy meant little. It is the press, not the raw-vote totals, that determines who is the winner and the loser of a nominating race. The press virtually declared that McCarthy, in garnering an amazing 42 percent of the vote against a sitting president, was the winner.

A strategic error by the president's advisers also helped to shape the press's perception of a McCarthy victory. The Johnson camp had allowed too many local candidates to run for national convention delegate on the second part of the ballot. The result was the Johnson vote was split so many ways that McCarthy won almost all of the New Hampshire delegates.[22] McCarthy had won a great media-declared victory. Johnson suddenly was in political trouble.

The McCarthy miracle in New Hampshire cannot be interpreted as a public mandate to de-escalate the war in Vietnam. Certainly the war issue motivated the great portion of the army of grassroots volunteers who canvassed the state for McCarthy. But not all voters who cast their ballots for McCarthy were doves. According to a survey conducted by the University of Michigan Survey Research Center, nearly 60 percent of McCarthy's votes came not from doves advocating withdrawal from Vietnam but from persons who wanted the Johnson administration to push a *harder* line against Hanoi! As the only real alternative to Johnson on the ballot, McCarthy was the sole vehicle through which these more hawkish Democrats could register their protest against Johnson's handling of the war.[23]

Robert Kennedy entered the presidential race just four days after the surprising New Hampshire results. Kennedy, it can be argued, was more electable than McCarthy. He was better known, he had charisma, and he was acceptable to mainstream party leaders such as Chicago Mayor Richard J. Daley.

But it was a matter of personal image and style that divided the peace movement. McCarthy's supporters argued that their man had shown guts. McCarthy, they argued, had earned the right to the presidential nomination by taking on and slaying the presidential dragon in New Hampshire. Bobby, in contrast, was seen only as a Johnny-come-lately who presumed to be the successor to the throne only after McCarthy's victory made Johnson's weakness apparent. McCarthy's supporters vilified Kennedy as ruthless. They further charged that Kennedy was late in opposing the Vietnam War.

Kennedy was also unacceptable to many McCarthy supporters, as his candidacy did not represent a challenge to old-style politics. The McCarthy movement was more than just an antiwar campaign, it was also a populist effort that sought to change the established way of doing things—to open up party affairs and take party decision making out of the back rooms. McCarthy's campaign posters captured the spirit of this challenge. They showed a picture of the wind blowing through the candidate's white hair over the slogan "Like a Breath of Fresh Air."

After New Hampshire, the McCarthy campaign picked up momentum. President Johnson's campaign polls showed that McCarthy was certain to win the Wisconsin primary by a large margin. Rather than face such ignominy, Johnson withdrew from the presidential race. In his unprecedented televised address, the president said that he was withdrawing to facilitate peace talks with the North Vietnamese. No one would be able to interpret any new American peace initiatives as a cynical effort by the president to revive his sagging political fortunes back home.

With Johnson out of the race, the way was cleared for Vice President Hubert Humphrey to enter. The deadline for entering most primaries had already passed, and Humphrey chose not to enter or actively contest the few still open to him. Instead he would rely on Johnson's support and his own ties to party officials to garner the number of delegates necessary for the nomination.

The remainder of the primaries became essentially a two-candidate affair. Kennedy won the Indiana and Nebraska races but lost Oregon to McCarthy, thereby ending the Kennedy family record of thirty straight primary and election victories. Kennedy recovered to win the tough slugfest in California by four points. But after delivering his victory speech at the Ambassador Hotel, he was assassinated as he exited through the kitchen.

There is a widely held myth that had Kennedy not been shot he would have gone on to win the nomination. Of course, no one can say for sure what would have happened had Kennedy lived. But, in all likelihood, the nomination would still have gone to Humphrey, not Kennedy.

Even the most optimistic estimates of delegates in the Kennedy camp showed his coming up short of the nomination. The Kennedy people planned to conduct a guerrilla operation to persuade delegates committed to other candidates to switch to Kennedy. Kennedy was to campaign in major media markets. Scenes of enthusiastic crowds swarming him were to convince convention delegates that he was a winner. The Kennedy campaign also planned intensive advertising in those markets in an effort to produce poll results that would show him to have the best chance of leading the party to victory in November.[24]

But such a strategy was a long shot. Delegates committed to Humphrey were not likely to be easily swayed by poll results. Furthermore, poll results may not have unambiguously indicated

Kennedy to be the stronger candidate. At the time of Kennedy's murder, polls showed Humphrey, not Kennedy, to be the preferred candidate.[25] Also, it would have been difficult for Kennedy to unite the badly divided peace forces. The animosities between the Kennedy and McCarthy camps, already quite deep, were only heightened by the bruising battle in California. In the wake of Kennedy's death, his delegates would not merge ranks with the McCarthy forces. It was not McCarthy who got their votes but South Dakota Senator George McGovern, who entered the race at the convention in an attempt to rally Kennedy delegates.

Issues were important in the primary season to the extent that they motivated the grassroots, antiwar McCarthy organization and divided the party at its Chicago convention. Yet, as our summary of the 1968 nominating race has shown, questions of the candidates' personal qualities and styles, not issues, dominated the 1968 nominating season. George Romney was destroyed and Nelson Rockefeller was severely handicapped, as the public saw these candidates to be lacking desirable leadership attributes. Bobby Kennedy possessed charisma and turned on the crowds, but he was hindered by public perceptions of his being ruthless. Questions of personal style further divided the McCarthy and Kennedy camps. Kennedy was seen as a politician; McCarthy was anti-politics. McCarthy gained the support of advocates of a "new politics." The television images generated from the tumultuous convention at Chicago only served to further divide an already badly divided Democratic party.

The Selling of the President?

According to Joe McGinniss's *The Selling of the President 1968,* the 1968 election was a triumph of personal imagemaking. Richard Nixon was repackaged and sold to the American public much like a package of detergent, a brand of cigarettes, or any commercial product. According to McGinniss, "the citizen does not so much vote for a candidate as make a psychological purchase of him."[26] Issues have nothing to do with the selling of a politician: "On television it matters less that he (the candidate) does not have ideas. His personality is what the viewers want to share."[27]

As McGinniss portrays the campaign, the Nixon media team, under the guidance of creative director Harry Treleavan, developed a new image for Nixon. They sold Nixon as a warm, sincere, informal, humorous, spontaneous, and compassionate person. The old embittered Nixon, whom the voters had seen and rejected for the presidency in 1960 and two years later for governor of California, was to be deeply buried.

A series of paid one-hour television programs utilizing the **man-in-the-arena** format were a central element in constructing the new Nixon image. These shows were produced by Roger Ailes, then the twenty-eight-year-old executive producer of the Mike Douglas Show. Nixon answered questions live from a panel of citizen interviewers. The programs had suspense. Television viewers felt a rush of sympathy for Nixon as he fended off one attack after another. Nixon looked vulnerable and human. He also appeared informed, in-charge, and presidential.

To viewers at home, Nixon appeared to risk all in live television. In fact, Nixon risked very little as the setting was controlled in ways not readily apparent to television viewers. A relaxed conversational tone was established as Nixon exchanged opening pleasantries with University of Oklahoma football coach Bud Wilkinson. The panel of questioners was screened to exclude persons likely to ask tough questions. The studio audience was stacked with persons recruited by local Republican clubs. During the warm-up directly preceding the show the audience was instructed to applaud Nixon's answers and swarm the candidate at the program's conclusion to show their affection. The applause of the studio audience cued viewers at home that Nixon's answers, no matter how general, were winners.

The Republican media campaign also utilized still photography in many of its forty- and sixty-second commercials that attempted to associate Nixon with a series of quickly flashing positive images of America:

> The flashing pictures would be carefully selected to create the impression that somehow Nixon represented competence, respect for tradition, serenity, faith that the American people were better than people anywhere else, and that all these problems others shouted about meant nothing in a land blessed with the tallest buildings, strongest armies, biggest factories, cutest children, and rosiest sunsets in the world. Even better: through association with the pictures, Richard Nixon could *become* these very things.[28]

The ads further associated the incumbent Democratic administration with such problems as the Vietnam War, crime, unemployment, central city slums, urban and rural decay, rioting, and public disorder.

Nixon took no explicit stand on the Vietnam War. He blamed the Democrats for mishandling the conflict and promised to bring the war to an "honorable" end. He did not indicate if he would do so through hawkish escalation or dovish de-escalation of the United States's military involvement:

 VIETNAM ad

VIDEO: Fast-paced scenes of a helicopter assault in Vietnam. Wounded Americans and Vietnamese. Montage of facial close-ups of American servicemen and Vietnamese natives with questioning, anxious, perplexed attitude.

AUDIO (Voice of Richard Nixon): "Never has so much military, economic, and diplomatic power been used as ineffectively as in Vietnam. And if after all of this time and all of this sacrifice and all of this support there is still no end in sight, then I say the time has come for the American people to turn to new leadership not tied to the policies and mistakes of the past."

VIDEO: Proud faces of Vietnamese peasants. Close-up of the word LOVE scrawled on the helmet of an American G.I.; camera pulls back to reveal his face.

AUDIO (Nixon): "I pledge to you: we will have an honorable end to the war in Vietnam."

McGinniss, though, is guilty of overstating the power of the Nixon advertising effort. The Gallup poll showed Nixon with a lead of 16 points in mid-August and 15 points in late September. The Harris poll put the Nixon lead at 6 to 8 points during this same time period. Yet, running against a severely underfunded and divided Democratic party, Nixon wound up winning the November election by less than one percentage point. How can the disappearance of a 15-point lead in such a contest be seen as evidence of the success of the Nixon advertising effort? Of course, it cannot.

McGinniss's mistake is that he omits consideration of other factors that influenced the voting decision in 1968. Party identification was a strong determinant of voting behavior in 1968. Blue-collar Democrats were pulled back into the party as a result of the party's traditions of economic, social welfare, and trade union protections. Antiwar Democrats, too, found that they liked the Democratic record in such areas as civil rights, expanding support for education, aid to cities, and the war on poverty. As election day approached, they found it increasingly difficult to cast a ballot for Nixon, a longtime object of liberal scorn. Humphrey tried to make it easy for antiwar Democrats to return to the party. In a September 30 nationally broadcast speech from Salt Lake City, Utah, he promised a bombing halt as a risk for peace. Richard M. Scammon and Ben J. Wattenberg sum up the influence that partisanship had on Humphrey's rebound:

> Essentially, it was this pattern of party voting that enabled Humphrey to make his stretch run such a powerful one. He and his supporters raised the old banner of the Democratic Party, and most of the people who had saluted it in the past found they could not easily abandon it or the political overview that it had for so long represented.[29]

The statistical work of the Survey Research Center confirms the dominant influence of partisanship on the Nixon and Humphrey vote: "It is *party* that towers over all other predictors, and the central 1968 issues tend to give rather diminutive relationships."[30]

But why did Nixon win? Issues played a greater role in the election than McGinniss's theory and the Survey Research Center's data analysis would seemingly indicate. According to Scammon and Wattenberg the **social issue**—America's concerns over crime, riots, civil disorder, too-fast racial integration, welfarism, and a changed social fabric as seen in the challenge of hippies, drugs, and the counterculture—was at the base of the Nixon vote in 1968. Nixon was the "man in the middle" who stood between excessive Democratic liberalism and the extreme racial reactionism of third-party presidential candidate Alabama Governor George Wallace.[31] Nixon stood for the centrist course of action preferred by white, middle America, the portion of the electorate that the news media popularly referred to as the **Silent Majority.**[32]

Nixon's ads effectively tapped voter resentment on social issues, especially on crime and welfare. Nixon campaigned on the slogan of "Law and Order." He retrospectively attacked the inability of the Democratic administration to deal with rising crime rates and public demonstrations; citizens who did not like the Democratic record could vote for a change. Nixon also offered voters a clear policy direction. He was no soft-headed liberal who preached that society must understand the reasons underlying crime, violent dissent, and urban riots:

ORDER ad

VIDEO: Rapidly moving sequence of rioting. Crowds taunting police authorities. Flaming apartment house. Police patrolling deserted streets in aftermath of violence.

AUDIO: Sound effects of rioting.

AUDIO (Voice of Richard Nixon): "It is time for some honest talk about the problem of order in the United States."

VIDEO: Perplexed faces of Americans. Sequences of people moving through battered streets and by destroyed shops and homes. Eloquent faces of Americans who have lived through such experiences, climaxed by a single shot of charred crossbeams framing a riot ruin. In the center of the picture is a battered machine on which can still be seen in red letters the word CHANGE.

AUDIO (Nixon): "Dissent is a necessary ingredient of change. But in a system of government that provides for peaceful change there is no cause that justifies resort to violence. There is no cause that justifies rule by mob instead of by reason."

VIDEO (Closing titles): THIS TIME VOTE LIKE YOUR
WHOLE WORLD DEPENDED ON IT.
NIXON.

CRIME ad

VIDEO: A lonely policeman at a call box. Move suddenly to a series of shots of explosive criminal actions with police response—ending on image of a bullet-shattered automobile window. Pan upon a row of weapons; then continue tilt up "Kennedy rifle." Huge close-up of a hand holding an open jackknife. Montage of faces of Americans; they are anxious, perplexed, frightened.

AUDIO (Voice of Richard Nixon): "In recent years crime in this country has grown nine times as fast as the population. At the current rate, the crimes of violence in America will be double by 1972. We cannot accept that kind of future. We owe it to the decent and law-abiding citizens of America to take the offensive against the criminal forces that threaten their peace and security, and to rebuild respect for law across this country."

VIDEO: Line of hand-cuffed criminals standing by a brick wall, their faces concealed by their hands or coats.

AUDIO (Nixon): "I pledge to you that the wave of crime is not going to be the wave of the future in America."

VIDEO (Closing titles): THIS TIME VOTE LIKE YOUR WHOLE WORLD DEPENDED ON IT. NIXON.

One extremely effective spot, the "Woman" ad, presented a tension-building little melodrama that captured middle America's fear of crime:

WOMAN ad

VIDEO: Fade-up on a diagonal view down on a sidewalk. It is a wet night. Feet of a woman come into view.

AUDIO: Sound of the city. Sounds of clicking heels.

VIDEO: She is dressed in a cloth coat and looks to be about age 45. She is apparently coming home late from shopping or work. The camera begins to travel with her. Behind her a moving figure flows by the metal-gate covering of a locked storefront. It begins to get darker as the camera moves in for a medium close-up, and then a close-up as we continue to travel with her.

AUDIO (Announcer): "Crimes of violence in the United States have almost doubled in recent years. Today a violent crime is committed every sixty seconds. A robbery every two-and-a-half minutes. A mugging every six minutes. A murder every forty-three minutes. And it will get worse unless we take the offensive."

VIDEO: We are in close-up. The camera holds. The woman walks off down the sidewalk. Hold on this view as her figure grows smaller against the dark night.

AUDIO (Announcer): "Freedom from fear is a basic right of every American. We must restore it."

AUDIO: Distant heel clicks.

```
VIDEO (Closing titles): THIS TIME VOTE LIKE YOUR
                        WHOLE WORLD DEPENDED ON IT.
                        NIXON.
```

The "Woman" ad plays to film conventions that the viewing audience has learned from watching movies and television crime series. Viewers know that the woman will not make it home; they are expecting her to be mugged at any moment.

The Nixon ads similarly assigned retrospective blame and offered voters a choice of directions on the issue of welfarism. Nixon's antiwelfare stance is presented in juxtaposition to the activist government approach of Lyndon Johnson's Great Society and Hubert Humphrey's liberalism. The ads effectively tapped middle America's resentment of expanding, big-spending social programs. In one ad, Nixon narrates as voters are shown scenes of urban and rural decay and a sign on the street that reads "Government checks cashed here":

> For the past five years we've been deluged by programs for the unemployed, programs for the cities, programs for the poor. And we have reaped from these programs an ugly harvest of frustrations, violence, and failure across the land. Now our opponents will be offering more of the same. But I say we are on the wrong road. It is time to quit pouring billions of dollars into programs that have failed.

Issue-based images, not just personal-based images, were the hallmark of Nixon's advertising. To the extent that the Nixon media campaign worked, it did because it employed both issue-based and personal-based appeals. The campaign used different spots and different messages to reach different voters. Nixon offered voters a choice on the highly salient issues of the day.

The Vietnam issue, however, was not a strong influence on voting in the 1968 general election. The ability of voters to use issues to distinguish between the two major-party candidates in this area was diminished by the failure of both Nixon and Humphrey to identify a path of action one way or the other on Vietnam.[33] Citizens could not know for sure which candidate would continue, or which would draw down, the American military presence in Southeast Asia.

As we previously noted, the Survey Research Center found partisanship to be a much stronger influence than issues on voting in 1968. According to the Center, voter "evaluations of both

Humphrey and Nixon show a strong factor of traditional party allegiance suffocating most issue concerns into relative obscurity."[34] Yet, even given the strength of partisanship, the findings of the Center point out that issues were important in determining the outcome of an election as close as that of 1968. The Center found that issues were a prominent motivation for George Wallace's voters. More important yet was the Center's discovery that while most citizens voted their usual party allegiance in 1968, "switchers" nearly always moved in the correct direction according to the issue preferences.[35] These switchers provided the margin of victory in 1968.

1972: THE REJECTION OF MCGOVERN OR MCGOVERNISM?

In 1972, Richard Nixon won reelection by a landslide, beating George McGovern by 61 to 38 percent, virtually matching the scale of Lyndon Johnson's victory in 1964. McGovern even lost his home state, South Dakota, and carried only a single state, Massachusetts (leading Bay Staters to proudly sport bumper stickers after the election that read, "Don't Blame Me, I'm from Massachusetts!") and the District of Columbia.

The McGovern campaign was plagued by a series of candidate errors that undermined McGovern's image. Yet, postelection studies showed that it was not just personal image alone that hurt McGovern; issues were also an important influence on the outcome of the 1972 election. Mounting antiwar sentiment coupled with a reformed delegate selection process had led the Democrats to select an extreme liberal as their standard bearer—a candidate who was out-of-step with middle Americans on key issues.

The Democratic Race: Muskie Cries and the Politics of Momentum

At the beginning of 1972 it was not George McGovern but Maine Senator Edmund Muskie who appeared to have a virtual lock on the Democratic nomination. The story of Muskie's demise is an interesting tale that points to the power of the mass media to make and break a candidate's image.

Muskie's front-running position going into 1972 was the result of the favorable publicity he had received as Humphrey's running mate four years earlier. It was also the result of his performance in a single media event, a national broadcast he made on behalf of

Democratic candidates on the eve of the 1970 midterm elections. In this broadcast, Muskie appeared cool, relaxed, personable, and self-assured as he spoke to Americans from his Maine home. His image contrasted quite favorably with that of the more strident Richard Nixon that the Republicans had presented in a film clip in their broadcast that evening. Jeb Stuart Magruder, a member of Nixon's public relations team, would later remark, "It was like watching Grandma Moses debate the Boston strangler."[36]

But the front-runner's position actually worked to Muskie's disadvantage. When Muskie could not live up to the expectations that the media had set for him, press reports virtually destroyed his candidacy. Muskie's advisers had erred in contributing to the overexpectations of success by predicting outright victory; they had sought to create a bandwagon effect which would induce party leaders and followers to line up behind the Muskie effort. Muskie's own behavior also led reporters to question his presidential capabilities.

The key event in the demise of Edmund Muskie was the New Hampshire primary, a state where Muskie was expected to win big. *Washington Post* national politics reporter David Broder was not alone when he wrote in a January 9, 1972, story, "As the acknowledged front runner and a resident of the neighboring state, Muskie will have to win the support of at least half the New Hampshire Democrats in order to claim a victory."[37]

Muskie defeated George McGovern by a 46-to-37-percent margin in New Hampshire. But as Muskie had not met expectations, the media story that emerged was that of a Muskie "loss," not a victory. Because of this media-declared defeat, the Muskie campaign suffered reverse momentum and began its unstoppable slide.

Why did reporters go after Muskie in New Hampshire? In part, the demise of a front-runner provides a dramatic, big story that meets the requirements of horserace journalism. Also, as Timothy Crouse details, reporters covering Muskie had seen the candidate's fits of temper and were eager to expose his shortcoming.[38] Reporters seized on campaign incidents that allowed them to reveal their doubts of Muskie's personal abilities. As a result, the Muskie campaign in New Hampshire was dogged by a series of vicious rumors that found their way into print.

One rumor reported that Muskie had used the derogatory term "Canucks" in reference to the state's Canadian-American population. Another story portrayed Muskie's wife as a foul-mouthed woman with a fondness for drink. These and other such stories were gleefully repeated in the front-page, partisan-style reporting of William Loeb's *Manchester Union-Leader*, the most widely circulated newspaper in the state. After the election, the Watergate hearings would reveal that a number of these stories had their origins in the dirty-tricks unit of the Nixon campaign. Nixon's zealots sought to plant newspaper stories that would undermine the candidacy of the president's strongest potential November opponent.

Muskie personally resented these stories. He was especially taken aback by the slanderous attacks on his wife's character. In an emotional speech, he faced reporters in front of Loeb's offices to decry the smears. Tears filled his eyes as he hoarsely denounced the innuendo. Television cameras rolled as the tears flowed from Muskie's eyes and the snowflakes fell on his hair. This image was repeatedly shown on news broadcasts. For reporters, the outburst only confirmed that Muskie lacked the emotional stability to be president. The public, too, reacted to Muskie in highly personal terms. If he could not hold up under the pressure of the campaign in New Hampshire, how could he be expected to stand up to the Russians and the crushing burden of decision making in the White House?

In a tailspin from New Hampshire, Muskie finished fourth in the next primary, Florida, behind George Wallace, Hubert Humphrey, and Henry "Scoop" Jackson. The loss brought his candidacy to a virtual end. Interestingly, George McGovern finished even further down the line in sixth place, yet was not harmed by his poor finish. His managers had opined that as a dark horse McGovern lacked the time and money to campaign everywhere; he could only give one full day of campaigning to Florida. They downplayed McGovern's expectations in the state, and the press, to a great extent, bought the line.

When the initial nominating contests were over, Muskie had beaten McGovern four out of four times. He won the Iowa caucuses and the New Hampshire and Illinois primaries. Although he did poorly in Florida, he still outpolled McGovern in that state. Yet, because of press reports, Muskie was out of the race while McGovern remained not only a viable but an increasingly strong contender.

National opinion polls showed that until he sewed up the nomination, McGovern was not the first choice of Democratic voters. Yet, as a result of the intensity of conviction that motivated antiwar forces to turn out and dominate a fair number of delegate selection contests, McGovern was able to win the nomination.

McGovern's grassroots organization had helped to propel him to a strong 22 percent showing in the multicandidate field in Iowa, separating him from the rest of the crowded Democratic pack and providing the momentum that led to his dramatic showing in New Hampshire. He would then win Wisconsin. McGovern's organization also was very effective in packing caucuses and conventions. McGovern eventually gained delegates in such unlikely conservative states as Oklahoma and Virginia.

The McGovern insurgency produced a national party convention that was vastly more liberal than rank-and-file Democrats on such new cultural and social issues as welfare, busing, law and order, and the conduct of the war.[39] The party chose a presidential nominee who represented the views of the new issue activists but not those of the larger party-in-the-electorate.

McGovern sought to unify the party. He sought to have his delegates accept the seating of the challenged Illinois delegation, headed by Chicago Mayor Richard J. Daley. Daley could prove to be a valuable ally in November. The Illinois delegation had been selected according to state law but in clear violation of the party's new rules for openness. But McGovern could not control his supporters. It was their chance to take revenge against Daley for his taunts at the 1968 convention and his police department's brutal handling of demonstrators outside the convention hall. Viewers watching the 1972 convention on television saw delegates break out in spontaneous applause and cheers as the Daley delegation was unseated and was replaced by an alternative, unelected but demographically balanced delegation headed by Jesse Jackson and the then-liberal Alderman William Singer.[40] More centrist Democrats were left to wonder just whom this new Democratic party represented.

The Fall Campaign

McGovern faced a substantial problem in the general election: how to shift his appeal to a more centrist electorate than the one he mobilized during the nominating season. His handlers changed his campaign slogan from one that emphasized his issue purity—his primary season "McGovern, Right from the Start"—to the more general "McGovern, Democrat, for the People," which emphasized both party loyalty and broader populist appeal.

But McGovern could not pull off the transition. He could not shake the general public's perception of him as an extreme liberal, the candidate who stood for the three A's—acid, amnesty, and abortion. That perception had also been shaped by the controversial proposals that McGovern had staked out early in the primary campaign. In one controversial proposal, McGovern discussed the possibility of giving each American a welfare "demogrant" of $1,000.

Immediately after the convention, the Eagleton affair destroyed whatever presidential stature McGovern had remaining. McGovern had not looked very presidential at the convention in virtually begging Edward Kennedy and other prominent Democrats to join him on the Democratic ticket. McGovern finally settled on Missouri Senator Thomas Eagleton as his running mate. But the McGovern team did not adequately screen the senator's past. Press reports soon revealed that Eagleton had been under a psychiatrist's care and had undergone electroshock therapy to fight depression.

McGovern assured reporters that he had no intention of dropping the Missourian from the ticket. His staff then issued a notice stating that McGovern was "1,000 percent for Tom Eagleton." But only days later, in the face of the continued public clamour over his presence on the ticket, Eagleton—clearly with McGovern's assent—withdrew. He was replaced by Kennedy clan member Sargent Shriver.[41] In changing his mind after publicly declaring his support for Eagleton, McGovern once again looked wishy-washy. Already he had backed off his earlier $1,000 welfare demogrant and amnesty proposals. McGovern hardly looked presidential.

In an attempt to soften the public's view of McGovern as an extreme liberal, the McGovern commercials in the fall campaign were less specific than his spring ads in their discussion of issues.[42] In both spring and fall, the commercials used cinema verité footage to portray McGovern as a caring man of the people. These commercials typically pictured McGovern listening to groups of Americans—disabled Vietnam veterans, the elderly, blue-collar workers—and then responding to their concerns. McGovern expressed his own concern and his hopes to reestablish the kind of leadership that can help people. But he did not discuss program specifics, as the advocacy of new programs would have given the Republicans further ammunition in their charges against McGovern as a big-spending social liberal.

The ads failed because they did not adequately address voter concerns regarding race and welfare, issues that had led middle Americans and disaffected Democrats to view McGovern as too liberal. The ads further failed as they presented McGovern as a passive listener, not a dynamic leader.[43]

By the end of the campaign the cinema verité ads were withdrawn in favor of a new set of spots that utilized a somewhat unorthodox approach in an attempt to convey to voters the seriousness of the issues in the race. These ads presented no visuals other than the printed word on the television screen. An announcer read the words as they scrolled up from the bottom.

When it came to issues, though, it was the Republicans who enjoyed the clear advantage in the paid media campaign of 1972. The Nixon ads attacked McGovern's past campaign promises on welfare, defense spending, amnesty for draft evaders, and school busing. Probably the most effective ad of the entire campaign was a spot that visually dramatized the potential impact of McGovern's earlier defense proposal:

DEFENSE CUTS ad

VIDEO: A group of toy soldiers. A hand dramatically sweeps about a third of them off the table.

AUDIO (Announcer): "The McGovern defense plan. He would cut the marines by a third . . . "

VIDEO: Switch to another group of toy military figures. A hand sweeps a sizable number of them off the table.

AUDIO (Announcer): " . . . the Air Force by one-third."

VIDEO: Cut to other sets of toy soldiers, airplanes, ships, and carriers. In turn, a large portion of each group is similarly swept off the table. The camera than pans the destruction.

AUDIO (Announcer): "He would cut Navy personnel by one-fourth. He would cut interception planes by one-half, the Navy fleet by one-half, and carriers from sixteen to six. Senator Humphrey has this to say about the McGovern proposal: 'It isn't just cutting into the fat. It isn't just cutting into manpower. It is cutting into the very security of this country.'"

VIDEO: Picture of President Nixon standing with a naval officer aboard a ship.

AUDIO: Drum roll followed by the playing of "Hail to the Chief." (Announcer): "President Nixon doesn't believe we

should play games with our national security. He believes
in a strong America to negotiate for people from strength."

VIDEO (Closing sign): DEMOCRATS FOR NIXON

Another Republican ad charged McGovern with having submitted a welfare bill to Congress that "would make 47 percent of the people in the United States eligible for welfare," an "incredible proposal" that would cost 64 billion dollars in its the first years: "That's six times what we're spending now."

Critics charged that the Nixon ads presented such gross distortions of McGovern's proposals that they provided no basis for the serious discussion of public issues. The visual of toy ships being swept off the table, for instance, failed to address the question of what size American defense forces should be and how much fat could be cut from the military budget. The welfare ad attacks a proposal that McGovern claimed to have submitted to Congress only as a courtesy to the National Welfare Rights Organization.[44]

Still, whatever their distortions and incompletenesses, the ads quite clearly communicate the choice of policy directions offered by the candidates. McGovern was more disposed to welfare expansionism and was less tolerant of defense spending; Nixon took a tougher stance toward welfare and was more willing to spend on defense. The ads met the test of directional voting.

McGovern tried to make the break-in at the Democratic headquarters at the Watergate complex a campaign issue, but no one was listening. His charges were seen as little more than last-ditch desperation effort to turn around his much-troubled candidacy. It would not be until well after the election that voters would begin to see Watergate as anything more significant than a second-rate burglary.

Issue Voting in 1972

Postelection analyses point to the importance of issues in explaining the 1972 decision. The newer cultural issues represented in the McGovern insurgency destroyed the traditional class-based pattern of the vote; McGovern did no better among lower status voters than he did among higher status voters (see Table 7.1). The lowest status groups, those most in need of government social welfare programs, continued to support the

Table 7.1   Democratic Percentage of the Presidential Ballots, White Voters by Socioeconomic Position, 1948–1972

	1948	1960	1968	1972
All				
High SES	30	38	36	32
Middle SES	43	53	39	26
Low SES	57	61	38	32
Women				
High SES	29	35	42	34
Middle SES	42	52	40	25
Low SES	61	60	39	33
Under 30 years of age				
High SES	31	42	50	46
Middle SES	47	49	39	32
Low SES	64	52	32	36
College-educated	36	45	47	45
Noncollege	56	49	33	30

Source: Everett Carll Ladd, Jr., with Charles D. Hadley, *Transformations of the American Party System,* 2nd ed. (New York: W.W. Norton, 1978), p. 240

Democrats. But blue-collar and middle-class citizens voted less Democratic than normal as they were alienated by the welfarism, school busing, life-style liberalism, and the challenge to patriotism they perceived to be associated with McGovernism. On the other hand, better-educated, new elite voters—the intelligentsia—tended to be more sympathetic to the agenda of the McGovern movement. In 1972, there was no Republican upper-class versus Democratic lower-class pattern to the vote; instead, McGovern led a narrow "top-bottom coalition" against "the great middle."[45]

In contrast to 1968, the Vietnam War was a factor in the 1972 vote. Despite Nixon's ambiguous pledge of "peace with honor" and his administration's last-minute announcement that peace was at hand, voters were still able to see a distinct difference between the candidates on the war; McGovern was clearly the dove.[46]

But policy voting was not focused solely on the war. Racial integration was another area of policy voting in 1972. The candidates did not discuss race as much as they did Vietnam, but they did not have to. The different views of the candidates were easy to observe. McGovern professed a moral commitment to school integration, including the use of school busing. Nixon represented a more "go slow" approach to civil rights. In 1972, then, the "hard" issue of Vietnam—where voters could not easily identify a workable peace plan—and the "easy" issue of racial integration both yielded to policy voting.[47]

Policy voting was so apparent in 1972 that even the studies from the University of Michigan's Center for Political Studies (formerly the Survey Research Center) concluded that issues were an important influence on the outcome of the election. According to the Center, both personal images and issues were important determinants of the vote. One study observes that the 1972 election "was more heavily influenced by issue voting or voting on the basis of policy preferences than any election in the preceding two decades."[48] McGovern suffered his greatest loss of expected support among voters of the Center and the Silent Minority; he maintained the support of believers in the "New Politics."[49] Vietnam, economic, social, and cultural issues were all related to the vote independent of party identification.[50] Still another Center article concludes that voters met the requirements of issue voting; the preferred policy position of defecting Democrats was often to the right of Nixon.[51] The Center's article in the highly influential *American Political Science Review* argued that "a new issue politics" had emerged, as "policy disagreements strong enough to cause massive defections among rank and file Party supporters" became a new characteristic of American national politics.[52]

The evidence pointing to the importance of issues in the 1972 election seems overwhelming. Yet not all liberal activists and political scientists are willing to accept the conclusion that McGovern lost as a result of his extreme liberalism. Samuel Popkin and his colleagues argue that McGovern's policy positions, especially on economic policy and the war, were consistent with those of the majority of the public. Rather, according to Popkin, McGovern lost as a result of his perceived incompetence, not because of his stands on the issues. Even a large number of people who agreed with his policy positions did not vote for McGovern, for they doubted his capacity to deliver what he promised.[53] One of every ten voters mentioned the Eagleton fiasco in pointing to what they most disliked about McGovern. This ratio was higher than the ratio of those who disliked McGovern because of his positions on Vietnam and welfare.[54]

Popkin also suggests that McGovern "may have been hurt by voters' perceptions of the people standing by him: too many young people, too many blacks, too many welfare mothers."[55] But what Popkin fails to state is that citizens who cast their ballots in response to such perceptions are engaging in a form of issue voting. McGovern, not Nixon, is the candidate most likely to be influenced by these people and their causes. Voters who disliked these causes did well to reject McGovern; it was the rational choice before them.

SUMMARY: IMAGES AND ISSUES

Personal images were important factors in the presidential races of the 1964-1972 period. Goldwater and McGovern were rejected as extremists. McGovern further suffered from a perceived lack of presidential stature; he was viewed as indecisive and incompetent. In 1964, Nelson Rockefeller was hurt by the appearance of immorality; in 1968 he suffered from the image of vacillation. In 1968 George Romney's candidacy was destroyed by the "brainwashing" incident. In the Democratic nominating race, the followers of Eugene McCarthy and Robert Kennedy were divided more by concerns for candidate style and courage than by any great policy disagreements over the war in Vietnam. In 1972, Edmund Muskie learned that voters would not accept a presidential candidate who cries. Richard Nixon earned reelection as "the president."

Yet, purely personal images alone did not dictate the outcome of any of the elections of this period. As we have seen, partisanship continued to be a strong influence on voting in the elections of this period, particularly in 1968. The explanatory power of partisanship was on the wane, but it had not disappeared.

Issues, too, proved to be an important factor in the elections of this period. During the nominating race, the failure to establish and control a candidate's image could quickly lead to the death of a campaign. But issues also affected the nominating process. The conservative ideologues of 1964 and the antiwar activists of 1968 and 1972 were all motivated by issues.

In the general election, there is even less ambiguity. Issues, not just personal images and partisanship, were important in each of the elections of this period. While voters did not always have the specific knowledge necessary for prospective issue voting, they did possess sufficient information and capacity to engage in directional and retrospective voting. The electorate was unwilling to make the sharp changes of direction advocated by Goldwater and McGovern. In 1968, racial and social issues were also an important influence on the vote, just as the Vietnam War and school busing proved to be the most prominent of the issues that affected the vote in 1972.

The election year 1968 can also be interpreted as a retrospective rejection of Democratic liberalism, especially the Democratic administration's perceived excesses in the area of welfarism and its failure to quell riots and demonstrations. Similarly, 1972 can be seen as a retrospective endorsement for Nixon. Despite the continuing war in Vietnam, a relative quiet returned to the nation as the major inner-city and campus riots had for the most part faded into the past.

By 1972, political scientists had clearly come to recognize the role played by issues in presidential elections. Even the University of Michigan's Center for Political Studies, which had previously disparaged the level of issue voting in the United States, began to recognize its potential importance. The Center reported that issues were related to the George Wallace vote and party switching in 1968. Issues were even more clearly related to the vote in 1972.

THE POLITICS OF RETROSPECTIVE REJECTION: 1976-1980

8

By 1976, the great polarizations of the 1960s and early 1970s had receded into the past. The Vietnam War was over, and demonstrations on college campuses were relatively muted. Inner-city ghettos, too, were relatively quiescent. Richard Nixon had resigned in the midst of the Watergate scandal and was replaced by Gerald Ford, who characterized his term in office as "A Time to Heal."[1]

Issues had been important factors in presidential elections during the turbulent 1964–1972 period. Would they continue to be so as the United States entered a more calm political era?

Jimmy Carter's success in the 1976 Democratic primaries was the result of a campaign that emphasized personal imagery. Yet, as we shall see, candidate factors alone do not explain voting in the general election. In 1976, partisanship was once again an important influence on the presidential vote. Retrospective voting, too, was at work. The public ousted Gerald Ford because of his inability to handle the economy—one that was suffering from both high inflation and a prolonged recession. The public also held the Republicans accountable for Watergate. Four years later, retrospective evaluations would be even more closely related to the vote. Jimmy Carter was ousted from office because of his inability to handle both the economy and foreign policy.

1976: PERSONAL IMAGERY, PARTISANSHIP, AND RETROSPECTIVE VOTING

The Selling of Jimmy (not James Earl) Carter

Jimmy Carter and his campaign manager Hamilton Jordan were among the first to appreciate how greatly the reformed delegate selection rules and the proliferation of primaries had altered the nominating process. They adapted their campaign to the new delegate selection terrain. Carter, a party outsider, was marketed directly to caucus and primary voters without the benefit of working through party intermediaries.

Jordan's script for Carter was clear. As a dark horse, Carter had to enter and concentrate his limited resources on the early nominating contests. A win or even just a good showing in these early races was needed to establish Carter's viability, separate him from the rest of the Democratic pack, and attract media interest and new financial contributions.

Television was a key element in Carter's success. Carter won the first-in-the-nation Iowa caucuses by campaigning in the state as if it had a primary. His campaign did more than simply attempt to mobilize a small band of caucus participants, whom Carter met one-on-one in coffee-klatches and small group get-togethers. The Carter campaign also aired a relatively large volume of televised commercials that sought to sell the candidate to voters who had never before participated in the caucus process. No other candidate in 1976 made such extensive use of television in Iowa.

Jordan and other Carter advisers felt that the Watergate scandal had led to a renewed public focus on the personal qualities of a candidate. Carter sought to embody trustworthiness, competence, and integrity. He promised that he would never lie to the American people.

Carter, the relatively obscure former governor of Georgia, was not widely known. Gerald Rafshoon, the campaign's media specialist, saw his first task as establishing Carter's personal image.[2] In the campaign's early ads, Rafshoon presented Carter as a former naval commander, a nuclear engineer, a family man, a businessman, and a peanut farmer. The most famous of these early Carter ads showed the candidate clad in blue jeans and plaid shirt walking through his family's peanut fields in Plains, Georgia.

The Carter strategy worked even better than Jordan had dared hope. The surge of participation in the Iowa caucuses produced a Carter victory. Carter finished far ahead of any of the other candidates, although he still finished behind the number of delegates listed as "undecided." Carter had received very little national media attention while campaigning in Iowa. But his victory changed all that. The day after the Iowa victory, Carter was surrounded by news reporters as he continued his efforts in New Hampshire. The Iowa victory gave him the name recognition and momentum that led to a four-point victory in New Hampshire over the second-place finisher, self-styled progressive Arizona Congressman Morris Udall. The New Hampshire victory brought still greater sums of money and publicity to the campaign. Carter was now the front runner.

The primary season shifted to Florida. Carter's newfound national reputation allowed him to run as the more respectable voice of the South and thereby defeat George Wallace. It was a victory he could not have achieved without the momentum and stature provided by his earlier victories.[3] Wallace was further handicapped by doubts about his health. He had to campaign from a wheelchair, the legacy of a 1972 assassination attempt that left him partially paralyzed.

Carter enjoyed the great advantage of winning those initial contests when election story coverage was at its peak. Victories in later primaries and caucuses, even in larger states, did not always translate into equivalent coverage. Washington Senator Henry "Scoop" Jackson beat Carter in Massachusetts, just one week after New Hampshire, but Jackson did not receive the extensive publicity that Carter had received earlier. As Jackson adviser Ben Wattenberg complained:

> After the Massachusetts primary, Jackson, unlike Carter, was not on the cover of *Time*. He was not on the cover of *Newsweek*. We did not get articles about his cousin who has a worm farm. And that was the story of the Jackson campaign for the next six weeks, and that was what I think killed that campaign. Jackson had won a totally unanticipated victory, beyond what the press had expected, in a state with ten times as many delegates as New Hampshire, and the effect was barely visible. We were dismayed.[4]

Scoop Jackson was a centrist Democrat and a strong friend of both organized labor and Israel. He chose to bypass Iowa and New Hampshire, hoping to establish momentum by winning contests in the nation's larger and more industrial states. Jackson beat Carter in New York, a state where Jackson enjoyed great strength in the organized labor and Jewish communities. But he was never able to overcome Carter's early lead. A Carter victory over Jackson in Pennsylvania destroyed any notion of an unstoppable Jackson bandwagon and put the Washington senator out of the race.

Late entrants in the race—Idaho Senator Frank Church and the California Governor Edmund G. "Jerry" Brown—beat Carter in five of the last twelve nominating contests. But by then it was too late; the race for the nomination was effectively over. By running everywhere, Carter had continued to amass national convention delegates. Even in the states he lost, Carter won much-needed national convention votes as a result of the Democratic party's reformed rules requiring virtual proportional representation. By the end of the nominating season, Carter was far ahead of any other candidate in delegates won. Though he still lacked the majority needed at the convention to become the Democratic nominee, even old-line party leaders, such as Chicago Mayor Richard J. Daley, realized that they could do little but reaffirm the choice the voters had declared in the primaries.

The Republican Race: Ideological Challenge

On the Republican side, President Gerald Ford faced a stiff challenge from Ronald Reagan and the conservative wing of the GOP. President Nixon had named Ford as his vice president when Spiro Agnew resigned because of evidence that pointed to his involvement in scandals during his years as governor of Maryland. When Nixon, in turn, resigned in the wake of Watergate, Ford became president.

Ford enjoyed certain advantages of incumbency, but he was not in an especially strong political position. Having never run for national office, he lacked a national constituency. He also suffered from the image of being little more than an ordinary congressman who had risen above his abilities and who had done little as president. As he self-deprecatingly said in accepting the presidential office, "I'm a Ford, not a Lincoln."

Ford beat Reagan in New Hampshire by the narrowest of margins, one percentage point. New Hampshire would likely have been a media-declared victory for Reagan had it not been for the Reagan camp's strategic blunder of predicting outright victory. Reagan's advisers should have been hard at work in lowering the media's expectations of Reagan, pointing to the advantages that Ford possessed in being able to wrap himself up in the majesty of the presidential office and in being able to steer federal aid projects to key constituencies in New Hampshire. Instead, Reagan's camp had been carried away by favorable news coverage and poll ratings just prior to New Hampshire that pointed to Reagan's emerging strength. As a consequence, when the results of the New Hampshire contest came in, the front-page story nationwide was not that of Reagan's strength but of Ford's victory in fending off the Reagan challenge.

The momentum Ford gained from New Hampshire led to a string of early victories. Reagan lost the first four primaries to Ford. He also ceded virtually the entire Pennsylvania delegation to Ford without a challenge. A disastrous showing in Illinois all but eliminated Reagan from the race. But Reagan turned his campaign around with dramatic victories in North Carolina and Texas.

Numerous media critics have attributed Reagan's sudden re-birth to a switch in the campaign's advertising strategy beginning with North Carolina.[5] Until that primary, Reagan television ads featured short, man-in-the-arena film clips of Reagan speeches; the audience would applaud as Reagan confronted hostile questioners. The ads were created by Harry Treleavan and were reminiscent of the image-creation approach he took on Nixon's behalf in 1968. However, in 1976, the ads did not seem to be working. The campaign switched advertising formats.

In North Carolina, the Reagan campaign aired an edited version of an old Reagan speech. Reagan spoke simply and directly to viewers at home during a half-hour block of time purchased by the campaign. The speech contained the usual Reagan campaign lines; it would appeal to North Carolina's more conservative Republicans. Reagan won North Carolina with 52 percent of the vote.

The victory brought the campaign new money and momentum. A month later in Texas, Reagan soared to a dramatic two-to-one victory in winning the state's entire 100-person convention delegation. In the succeeding nominating contests he engaged Ford in a bitter battle for delegates. The fight for the nomination went down to the wire. The Republican convention was marked by enthusiastic floor demonstrations by the supporters of both candidates. Ford held on to win an extremely narrow 1187 to 1170 victory. The convention battle was so close that Reagan took the extraordinary step of attempting to win over marginal Ford delegates by announcing his vice-presidential choice in advance. If nominated, he would choose Pennsylvania Senator Richard Schweicker as his running mate.

But was it the new advertising approach that turned around the campaign for Reagan? The evidence points to an alternative explanation. In all likelihood, Reagan won North Carolina and Texas after losing the earlier rounds only because the Republican nominating contests had finally moved to the nation's more conservative states. Reagan's challenge to an incumbent president in his own party only drew sizable support in states with Republican constituencies responsive to his more ideological brand of conservatism. As political scientist Larry Bartels points out:

> Reagan's biggest primary victories came in Idaho, Nevada, Georgia, Texas, Alabama, and California—all strongly conservative Republican states in the West and South. By contrast, Ford's biggest victories came in New Jersey, Rhode Island, Michigan, and Massachusetts—all traditional strongholds of the moderate Republican establishment.[6]

It was ideology, not advertising, that dictated the state-by-state pattern of Reagan's successes and failures in 1976.

The General Election: "Are You Better Off . . .?"

Throughout the general election, Carter continued his personal image advertising. But his message was also one of retrospective rejection, urging voters to reject the mounting "stagflation" suffered under the Ford administration. The economic issue dominated the election. At the time of the first debate, unemployment was running at a national rate of 7.9 percent. Adding the unemployment and inflation rates together, according to Carter, amounted to a "misery index," which revealed the true extent of the nation's economic misfortunes under Ford. Democratic advertising attacked the nation's stagnating economic performance after eight years of Republican rule.

The Ford campaign was in fairly desperate trouble. Going into Labor Day, Ford trailed Carter by 18 points in the polls. The campaign had not even laid out an overall advertising strategy for the fall election; the president's political advisers had been too busy turning back the Reagan challenge and winning the nomination.

The initial Republican advertising approach was termed the "Rose Garden" strategy, as it attempted to wrap Ford in the symbols of the presidential office. These ads showed pictures of Ford hard at work in the Oval Office. Ford was the president; he was no mere candidate seeking to become president.

But as Carter's charges on the economic issue continued to hit home, the Ford campaign had to leave the Rose Garden strategy behind and rebut the Carter attacks. One Republican message was that Ford had brought down inflation. Eventually, the Republicans identified their theme—that people were feeling good about America and that Ford as President had restored respect and integrity to government. One campaign commercial featured a song written especially for the Ford effort. The visuals showed various images of proud and happy Americans at work and play while the voiceover sang out:

> *There's a change that's come over America*
> *A change that's great to see*
> *We're livin' here in peace again*
> *We're going back to work again*
> *It's better than it used to be.*
>
> *I'm feelin' good about America*
> *I feel it everywhere I go*
> *I'm feelin' good about America*
> *I thought you ought to know*
> *That I'm feelin' good about America*
> *It's something great to see*
> *I'm feelin' good about America*
> *I'm feelin' good about me!*[7]

The Republican ad campaign also sought to strengthen Ford's personal image, to offset the widespread impression that he was an unpresidential bumbler—a perception reinforced by Saturday Night Live comedian Chevy Chase, who repeatedly spoofed the president's clumsiness. The new Republican spots attempted to humanize Ford, even showing a picture of him in his football uniform at the University of Michigan. The new ads also sought to dispel any doubts about the president's intelligence: "He was graduated in the top third of Yale Law School, while holding a full-time job."

The Ford campaign rose from the depths. The final election was close; Carter won by only two points. To a great extent, Ford rebounded as the national economy began to recover. Ford's comeback was consistent with retrospective and "sociotropic" interpretations of voting: The public's support for the incumbent administration is greatly dependent on the broad perception of how well the economy is doing.[8] As political scientist Arthur Miller observes, the recovery in economic optimism in the few months prior to the election may have deflated the economic issue considerably.[9]

The story of Ford's comeback and its end is also the story of personal images built and lost in televised presidential debates. Postdebate polls showed that the public clearly saw Ford to be the winner of the first contest. Carter looked tentative and unsure of himself; he later admitted to having been somewhat intimidated in finding himself standing on the same platform confronting the president of the United States.

But Ford's momentum was brought to an abrupt halt by the second presidential debate. Press coverage of that debate, devoted to a discussion of foreign policy, was dominated by Ford's gaffe in responding to the question of whether or not the Soviets had gotten "the better of us" in certain signed agreements. As part of his question, *New York Times* associate editor Max Frankel asserted that "we've virtually signed in Helsinki an agreement that the Russians have dominance in Eastern Europe." Ford's response was to deny that there is Soviet domination of Eastern Europe and Poland. The reaction of the press was incredulous. In seeming not to be aware of the extent of Soviet domination of Poland and other Eastern European nations, Ford had again demonstrated his incapacities as president.

It is worth looking at Ford's comments in some detail to discover just what he said and how the press interpreted it. The most controversial of Ford's words are italicized:

> **Ford:** In the case of Helsinki, thirty-five nations signed an agreement, including the secretary of state for the Vatican. I can't under any circumstances believe that His Holiness the Pope would agree by signing that agreement that the thirty-five nations have turned over to the Warsaw Pact nations the domination of Eastern Europe. It just isn't true. And if Mr. Carter alleges that His Holiness by signing that has done it, he is totally inaccurate. Now, what has been accomplished by the Helsinki agreement? Number one, we have an agreement where they notify us and we notify them of any military maneuvers that are to be undertaken. They have done it in both cases where they've done so. *There is no Soviet domination of Eastern Europe* and there never will be under a Ford administration.

> **Frankel:** I'm sorry. Could I just follow? Did I understand you to say, sir, that the Russians are not using Eastern Europe as their own sphere of influence and occupying most of the countries there and making sure with their troops that it's a Communist zone, whereas on our side of the line, the Italians and the French are still flirting with the possibility of Communism?

> **Ford:** I don't believe, Mr. Frankel, that the Yugoslavians consider themselves dominated by the Soviet Union. I don't believe that the Romanians consider themselves dominated by the Soviet Union. *I don't believe that the Poles consider themselves dominated by the Soviet Union. Each of those countries is independent, autonomous.* It has its own territorial integrity. *And the United States does not concede that those countries are under the domination of the Soviet Union.* As a matter of fact, I visited Poland,

Yugoslavia, and Romania to make certain that the people of those countries understood that the president of the United States and the people of the United States are dedicated to their independence, the autonomy, and their freedom.

Moderator: Governor Carter, have you a response?

Carter: I would like to see Mr. Ford convince the Polish Americans and the Czech Americans and the Hungarian Americans in this country that those countries don't live under the domination and supervision of the Soviet Union behind the Iron Curtain.

Ford seemed unaware of the furor that his remarks would touch off. Frankel and Carter went in for the political kill.

What the postdebate commentary ignored was that Ford to a great extent was right! Ford had refrained from discussing the situation in Eastern Europe solely in terms of highly charged political stereotypes—stereotypes and emotions that Carter played to in his rebuttal to Ford. Ford was describing a pluralism in Eastern Europe that Americans as a whole, blinded by Cold War stereotypes, did not see. The Soviets did not control from the center all facets of life in Eastern European nations. Important variations and divisions continued to exist inside the Soviet bloc—as seen in the historic fissure between Yugoslavia and the Soviet Union, and in the continued strength of both the Solidarity movement and the Catholic church in Poland. The amazing events of 1989 and 1990—the success of the freedom movements in each of the East European nations, the reunification of Germany, and the elections of Vaclev Havel as president of Czechoslovakia and Solidarity leader Lech Walesa as president of Poland—would prove that Ford was right. The Soviets did not completely dominate Eastern Europe.

But the substantive accuracy of Ford's comments counted for little in the presidential politics of 1976. Carter had the politically astute sense to clearly identify himself with the cause of freedom-loving people in Eastern Europe. Yet, there was something absurd in seeing Carter attack Ford for failing to take a tougher stance on the Soviet presence in Eastern Europe "as if the conservative, hawkish President were soft on communism."[10] Throughout the campaign it was Ford, not Carter, who had insisted on a stronger commitment to defense spending. Carter's demagogic response to Ford's gaffe on Eastern Europe simply took advantage of "the bias of the news for the simple and symbolic."[11]

Voters saw Ford's remarks as significant only as the media told them they were. Viewers contacted within twelve hours of the second debate in fact saw Ford, not Carter, as the winner; 53 percent said Ford had won, and only 10 percent said the Poland remark was important. However, among voters contacted twelve to forty-eight hours after the debate, the results were much different. The percentage seeing Ford as the winner dropped to just 29 percent, and 60 percent saw the Poland remark as a major error.[12]

Studies show that the debates changed few voting decisions.[13] Still, in an election as close as 1976, Ford's stalled momentum in the wake of the second debate can be seen to have affected the final outcome.

A Partial Restoration of the New Deal Coalition

With the passing of the polarizations of the Vietnam era, the Democratic party enjoyed renewed unity. The Democratic New Deal coalition had been formed to a great extent in response to economic issues; and in 1976, economic issues once again dominated public concern.[14] As Warren E. Miller and Teresa E. Levitin observe in their summary of the polling data gathered by the Center for Political Studies, "[T]he 1976 election was as much a party election as those elections from the 1950s or early 1960s in which party was acknowledged to be a major determinant of voters' decisions."[15]

Social class had eroded as an influence on presidential voting behavior in 1968 and 1972. But in 1976, a class pattern to voting was once again apparent. Still, the class pattern observed in 1976 was less sharp than that observed during the New Deal, as typified by voting in the 1948 election (see Table 8.1). After the turmoil of the 1960s and early 1970s, the New Deal Democratic coalition could not be fully put back together again.[16]

Overall, in comparing the 1976 election with 1972, personal images were more important, ideology less important but still significant, and specific issues still less important than they had been four years previously.[17] In the wake of Watergate, both Ford and Carter attempted to persuade voters that they possessed the personal qualities of honesty, decency, integrity, and competence. Few prospective issue appeals were evident in 1976. One political scientist, J. David Gopoian, has observed the virtual absence of issue voting during the 1976 primaries.[18]

Yet, political observers who see the 1976 election as issueless do so only as they take a very strict and narrow definition of the issue voting.[19] Carter had asked voters if they were better off as a result of Republican rule. Few felt that they were. Ford's standing in the polls improved only when the economy showed signs of recovery. Voters divided along partisan lines in 1976, but this was

Table 8.1   Democratic Percentage of the Presidential Ballots, White Voters by Socioeconomic Position, Selected Years, 1948–1976

	1948	1960	1968	1972	1976
All					
High SES	30	38	36	32	41
Middle SES	43	53	39	26	49
Low SES	57	61	38	32	53
Women					
High SES	29	35	42	34	41
Middle SES	42	52	40	25	46
Low SES	61	60	39	33	53
Under 30 years of age					
High SES	31	42	50	46	46
Middle SES	47	49	39	32	48
Low SES	64	52	32	36	52
College-educated	36	45	47	45	44
Noncollege	56	49	33	30	51

Source: Everett Carll Ladd, Jr., with Charles D. Hadley, *Transformations of the American Party System*, 2nd ed. (New York: W.W. Norton, 1978), p. 289.

no mindless return to an earlier age of blind partisanship. Instead, economic issues were reflected in the partisan decision.[20]

The influence of both the economic issue and partisanship is evident if we take a look at Table 8.2. Economic performance evaluations are clearly related to the vote. Among self-identified Democrats, Republicans, and Independents alike, support for Carter was greatest among voters who gave the Ford government a poor rating on dealing with inflation. But partisanship, too,

Table 8.2   Vote by How Good a Job Government Was Doing Fighting Inflation, Controlling for Party Identification, 1976

	Democrats			Independents			Republicans		
	good job (6%)	fair (57%)	poor job (37%)	good job (16%)	fair (59%)	poor job (25%)	good job (22%)	fair (65%)	poor job (13%)
Vote									
Carter	62%	77%	93%	10%	41%	64%	7%	12%	31%
Ford	38	23	7	90	59	36	93	88	69
	100%	100%	100%	100%	100%	100%	100%	100%	100%

Source: Arthur H. Miller, "The Majority Party Reunited? A Comparison of the 1972 and 1976 Elections," in *Parties and Election in an Anti-Party Age*, ed. Jeff Fishel (Bloomington, IN: Indiana University Press, 1978), p. 129.

remained a strong influence on voting, so much so that Ford retained the loyalty of 69 percent of those Republicans who believed that the government did a bad job in handling inflation.[21]

Despite the candidates' purposeful attempts at ambiguity, surveys show that voters were able to distinguish between them in terms of their economic policies.[22] Voter concern over inflation and unemployment—especially unemployment—was the dominant issue in the 1972 election.[23] In the general election, Carter ran as a traditional Democrat. As the campaign progressed, voters increasingly associated Carter with the Democratic party's traditional positions on issues.[24] Voters saw Carter as liberal and Ford as conservative.[25]

Watergate was a second major issue in retrospective voting in 1976.[26] Voters blamed Ford for pardoning Nixon. Ford's approval rating as president dropped eighteen points, from 71 to 53 percent, in the first poll taken after the pardon.[27] Ford never recovered his popularity among key groups. Carter won an extremely narrow 270-to-240 electoral vote victory. Kristen Monroe concludes that "While it is impossible to say exactly how great an impact the pardon had on voter calculus in the 1976 election, the evidence here strongly suggests that the pardon of Richard Nixon cost Ford that margin of popular support he needed to win the election."[28]

Arthur Miller presents further evidence that opinion on the pardon was strongly related to the vote irrespective of partisanship (see Table 8.3).[29] Thirty percent of those Republicans who disapproved of the pardon defected to Carter!

Despite the personalization of campaigns after Watergate, 1976 was not an issueless battle of professionally mediated image campaigns. In the primaries, specific issues were important to pivotal electoral groups. In Iowa, Jimmy Carter won the votes of teachers and their families with his promise to create a cabinet-level Department of Education. Given the low level of participation in the caucuses, it can be argued that teachers and their families gave Carter his Iowa victory. Throughout the primaries Carter also won the votes of African-American citizens because of his record on civil rights. As governor of Georgia he had even placed a portrait of Martin Luther King on his wall, an extraordinary gesture for a white, Southern, elected official at that time. Union members and Jewish voters, however, supported not Carter but, instead, "Scoop" Jackson, a Senator whose voting record favored their causes.[30] Similarly, in the Republican primaries differences in ideology explained the state-by-state pattern of the Ford-Reagan vote.

Table 8.3   Vote by Attitude toward Ford's Pardon of Nixon

	Total		Democrats	
	approved (43%)	disapproved (57%)	approved (25%)	disapproved (75%)
Vote				
Carter	24%	75%	56%	88%
Ford	76	25	44	12
	100%	100%	100%	100%

	Independents		Republicans	
	approved (52%)	disapproved (48%)	approved (72%)	disapproved (28%)
Vote				
Carter	30%	61%	8%	30%
Ford	70	39	92	70
	100%	100%	100%	100%

Source: Arthur H. Miller, "The Majority Party Reunited? A Comparison of the 1972 and 1976 Elections," in *Parties and Elections in an Anti-Party Age,* ed. Jeff Fishel (Bloomington, IN: Indiana University Press, 1978), p. 132.

Even in the general election, issues proved important as personal image factors alone were not decisive in the final vote. After the Watergate scandal, voters sought a candidate that they could trust. But it was Ford, not Carter, who won this image battle in 1976; voters saw Ford as more trustworthy.[31] Carter won the election as a result of retrospective performance evaluations, not personal imagery. According to Morris Fiorina, a retrospective voting model can account for 85 to 90 percent of the vote in 1976.[32]

1980: ANYONE BUT CARTER

By 1980, Jimmy Carter was an unpopular president. Some of his aides blamed his unpopularity and reelection defeat on the Iranian hostage situation. In November 1979, more than fifty members of the American diplomatic mission were seized in Teheran, Iran. Television emphasized the gravity of the crisis. CBS News anchor Walter Cronkite ended each evening's broadcast by counting the number of days of captivity for Americans in Iran. ABC instituted a new late evening news broadcast it originally titled "America Held Hostage." After the hostage crisis, the broadcast continued as "ABC News Nightline."

Table 8.4   Carter Approval Ratings on Three Issues

	percentage approving						
	Nov. '79	Jan. '80	Feb. '80	Mar. '80	April '80	June '80	Aug. '80
Foreign Policy	28	45	48	34	31	20	18
Economy	21	27	26	23	21	18	19
Iran		55	63	49	30	29	31

Questions: (1) Do you approve or disapprove of the way Jimmy Carter is handling foreign policy? (2) Do you approve or disapprove of the way Jimmy Carter is handling the economy? (3) Do you approve or disapprove of the way Jimmy Carter is handling the crisis in Iran? Each percentage is the proportion approving Carter's actions on the stated issue.

Source: Kathleen A. Frankovic, "Public Opinion Trends," in *The Election of 1980*, ed. Gerald Pomper (Chatham, NJ: Chatham House, 1981), p. 100.

Had Carter been able to secure the release of the hostages before November, the outcome of the election might well have been different. In 1991, eleven years after the election and well after the revelations of the Iran-Contra affair, former Carter national security aide Gary Sick charged that the Reagan campaign secretly negotiated to give arms to Iran. In return, Iran agreed to delay until after the election the release of Americans held captive. In office, the Reagan administration did, in fact, help to arrange for the delivery of weapons to Iran. Yet, there was no firm evidence to support Sick's allegations of a preelection secret arrangement that included a delay in the release of the hostages.

Whether there existed a secret deal or not, Carter's defeat cannot be blamed solely or even primarily on the hostage situation. Polling data reveal that the president's approval ratings had plummeted due to the nation's mounting economic woes well before the Iranian crisis emerged.[33] During Carter's term in office, inflation hit 18 percent, the unemployment rate hovered around double-digit levels, and homebuyers faced the daunting prospect of having to pay 18 to 20 percent annual interest on loans. In the days immediately preceding the hostage-taking, only one in five Americans expressed their approval of the president's economic performance (see Table 8.4).

The Democratic Race: The Unmaking of "President" Kennedy and the Rediscovery of "President" Carter

Before the Iranian crisis altered the political landscape, Carter's unpopularity was so evident that the press, in a chorus of pack journalism, portrayed him as a one-term president.

According to many commentators, the Democratic nomination was Edward "Ted" Kennedy's for the taking.

But Carter fought off Kennedy in a divisive intraparty struggle. The press had understated the resources available to an incumbent president. Carter's appointees in the bureaucracy helped steer federal aid projects to key primary states, including New Hampshire. Kennedy's weaknesses as a candidate were also soon to become apparent.

As Kennedy moved closer to announcing, the press began to subject his candidacy to greater scrutiny. A special television program by CBS correspondent Roger Mudd was the key media event in Kennedy's undoing. Most damaging of all was the program's reenactment of the tragedy at Chappaquiddick, where Kennedy, a married man, on a summer evening in 1969, left a party on Martha's Vineyard in the company of a young political staffer, Mary Jo Kopechne. Kopechne drowned when the car driven by Kennedy plunged off a secondary bridge leading to the mainland. Kennedy did not immediately report the incident to authorities. Instead, in the hours immediately after the accident, he huddled with his close personal advisers. Kennedy claimed that his conduct was not improper, that in the dark he had inadvertently taken the wrong route to the main bridge. Kennedy also said that he did not immediately report the incident because he was suffering from a state of shock after having repeatedly plunged into the waters in an attempt to save Kopechne.

Mudd's television cameras seemingly contradicted Kennedy's account of the incident. Mudd showed that a definite turn had to be made for Kennedy's car to shift paths to the side road. As the car carrying CBS's camera left the main road, the television picture bounced up and down. No one could possibly have mistaken this secondary road for the main route to the bridge.

The Carter campaign exploited the opening offered by the morality issue. In one Carter man-in-the-street spot, both men and women voiced their doubts regarding Kennedy: "I don't think Kennedy's qualified to be president"; "I don't think he has any credibility"; "I don't trust him." Another Carter ad featured pictures of a happy and intact Carter family while an announcer informs viewers: "Husband, father, president. He's done these three jobs with distinction." Another ad was more biting still: "President Carter—He tells the truth."[34]

Put on the defensive, the Kennedy campaign attempted to reconstruct his personal image, as seen in the following excerpts from one biographical ad:

KENNEDY IMAGE ad (excerpt)

VIDEO: Shot of a family scene of Kennedy walking
   along the beach with his wife and children.

AUDIO (Kennedy): "I suppose that the greatest source of happiness
   in my life has been the relationships with my wife and my children, and my brothers, and my sisters, and my parents."

VIDEO: Switch to Kennedy sitting at home in a living room chair
   with a newspaper on his lap. He speaks to a teenage boy, who
   appears to be his son, carrying a lunch pail and a backpack.

AUDIO (Kennedy): "You're having a games day tomorrow?"

AUDIO (Boy): "Yeah. Yeah"

AUDIO (Kennedy): "Can I come, too?" (Laughter) "I want to
   play. Do they have the dads? Do they play, too?"

These Kennedy image ads, however, were generally ineffective. Voters had heard too much—about Chappaquiddick, allegations as to Kennedy's continued philanderings and marital
problems, and stories on his wife Joan's drinking problems—for
the new image-making to work.[35]
   But it was not simply the question of Kennedy's character that
turned around the Democratic race. The intrusion of both the
Iranian hostage situation and the Soviet invasion of Afghanistan
created a crisis situation that allowed Carter to act and look presidential, to regain his presidential stature. Americans tend to
unite behind the president in times of international crisis. This
rally-'round-the-flag pattern of public opinion was clearly apparent at the beginning of the hostage situation (see Table 8.4).
   Yet, as Table 8.4 shows, Carter's rebound in the polls was not
as high as might have been expected. Even the intrusion of a
foreign policy crisis could not totally resuscitate Carter's presidential image. Further, any rebound in the public's perceptions
of Carter resulting from the hostage crisis did not spill over into
the economic arena. In January and February, in the early
months of the crisis, still only one in four Americans approved
Carter's handling of the economy.

Carter responded to world events by adopting a "Rose Garden" strategy. In a time of crisis he would devote his full attention to the affairs of state. The news media covered his every pronouncement. In essence, he was campaigning by doing his job as president. His campaign ads only reinforced the image of a man hard at work handling the presidential job.

Carter's renewed presidential stature allowed him to easily beat Kennedy in the January Iowa caucuses and the February New Hampshire primary. Kennedy suffered a string of primary losses that virtually ensured Carter's renomination. Carter lost New York, in part due to the disaffection of Jewish voters outraged by the Carter administration's failure to veto a United Nations resolution condemning Israeli settlements on the West Bank.

As the hostage situation dragged on, the initial public rally behind the president began to fade (see Table 8.4). An ill-advised hostage rescue mission, aborted owing to the mechanical failure of three helicopters operating in desert conditions, only reinforced the public's perceptions of Carter's inabilities. Carter fared poorly in a number of the later primaries. But by then the race was already over; he had already amassed a large enough block of delegates to ensure his renomination.

The Republican Race: "I am paying for this microphone."

On the Republican side, Ronald Reagan, the front-runner, chose to bypass the Iowa caucuses where each of his lesser-known Republican rivals was attempting to gain the momentum of an early nominating season victory. It was a mistake. George Bush won Iowa and gained considerable publicity. In New Hampshire, Reagan would confront Bush directly.

Reagan effectively ambushed Bush in a pseudoevent that gained considerable media attention. After Iowa, Bush had sought to limit all Republican debates to the two top contenders, himself and Reagan. A local newspaper, the *Nashua Telegraph*, invited Bush and Reagan to participate in a two-person debate. But complications arose when the other Republican candidates complained and it was discovered that, under federal finance rules, the local television station's sponsorship of such a debate would amount to an illegal contribution to the Bush and Reagan campaigns. The Reagan campaign resolved the problem by paying for the air time for the debate.

While Bush and Reagan were seated ready to begin the debate, four other Republican candidates suddenly paraded out from behind the stage. When the debate moderator refused to change the format to allow their participation, Reagan spoke in their defense. The moderator ordered that Reagan's microphone be turned off; Reagan countered by sharply replying, "I am paying for this microphone." The crowd roared its approval; the four candidates standing behind Reagan and Bush literally applauded Reagan's words. Reagan came across as the champion of openness and fairness. He even shook the hand of one Republican rival, John Anderson, as he escorted the four uninvited guests off the stage. Compared to Reagan, Bush seemed petty, unfair, and afraid. Reagan beat Bush handily, 53 to 22 percent, in New Hampshire.

But it was not personal imagery alone that won New Hampshire. After Bush's victory in Iowa, the Reagan campaign switched to a more issue-oriented advertising approach that emphasized the conservative values popular in Republican party circles. In the new ads, for instance, Reagan stressed his doctrinaire opposition to communism—a sharp contrast to Bush's campaign ads that emphasized his resumé and showed the former Ambassador to China greeting Chairman Mao.[36]

The new ads also stressed Reagan's opposition to taxes. They also hit hard at the record of the Carter years:

JFK TAX CUT ad

VIDEO: Words scroll up from the bottom of the screen.

AUDIO (Announcer reads the words): "Ronald Reagan believes that when you tax something, you get less of it. We're taxing work, savings, and investment like never before. As a result we have less work, less savings, and less investment."

VIDEO: Reagan dressed in blue suit and red tie looks directly into the camera and speaks.

AUDIO (Reagan): "I didn't always agree with President Kennedy. But when his 30-percent federal tax cut became law, the economy did so well that every group in the country came out ahead. Even the government did so well that it gained $54 billion in unexpected revenues. If I become president, we're going to try that again."

News commentators criticized the distortions contained in the ad—whether the Kennedy tax cut was nearly as large as 30 percent and whether the government actually gained $54 billion in receipts because of the cut. Still, whatever its distortions, the ad proved effective in offering Americans a clear statement of policy direction; if elected, Ronald Reagan would cut taxes.

The General Election: Once Again, the Economy

Reagan's general election advertising contained a certain few specific policy promises intermixed with a clearly communicated sense of overall policy direction. In the October 17, 1980, "Reagan Speaks" commercial, Reagan sits on the edge of a desk in front of a twelfth-grade class at Luther High North in Chicago. He makes two specific prospective promises—to empower parents by enacting tuition tax credits and to replace the draft with a volunteer army:

> There is no reason for the nation to restore the draft at this time. And I am opposed to the advanced registration for the draft. I believe that we can make the volunteer military work if we adopt a pay scale commensurate with what we're asking the young men and women in uniform to do.

Reagan's ads promised a general conservative direction to government policy—to eliminate waste and inefficiency in government, to balance the budget, to look at the price tag before launching any federal programs, and to restore the nation's military defense capacity. Reagan also specifically promised to reduce taxes. Most importantly, though, the Reagan ads repeatedly hammered away at the Carter record, especially at the toll taken by the mounting rates of inflation during the Carter years.

REAGAN REPORTS FROM LIMA, OHIO ad (excerpts)

VIDEO: Reagan dressed in tie and white shirt stands in a supermarket and speaks directly into the camera.

AUDIO (Reagan): "Good evening. I've been campaigning today in western Ohio. And I'm speaking to you now from Lima, a community of about 60,000 persons. As I've traveled across the nation these past few months it's clear that there's one problem that cuts evenly across the board hurting everybody. And that's the common enemy of inflation. I'm here in a grocery store in Lima."

VIDEO: Camera pulls back to reveal a shopping cart full of groceries. Reagan pulls a package of hamburger from the cart and holds it up.

AUDIO (Reagan): "A mother, a father, four years ago, before Jimmy Carter was elected, could come in and buy a pound of hamburger for 89 cents. Today that same pound of hamburger costs $1.39. And if we continue the Carter economic policies for another four years, it will cost no less than $2.17 in 1984. The same thing is true for other staples."...

VIDEO: Reagan holds up a loaf of bread.

AUDIO: (Reagan): "A loaf of bread. Four years ago bread cost 39 cents a loaf. Today it's 85 cents. And with another four years of Carter inflation it will rise to $1.85. And so it goes. The inflation we've endured under Jimmy Carter, the worst inflation since the Second World War, is literally robbing millions of Americans of their chance to keep good food on the table."...

AUDIO (Reagan): "Yesterday, Jimmy Carter said that the reason for inflation was that revenues, tax revenues, had not kept pace with the increased amount of government, of public spending. In other words, his approach to solving inflation would be more taxes taken from you. There is another way—reduce the costs of government. And that can be done. And that's what I'd like to do. And at the same time I promise to begin reducing those taxes which are also so punitive. I know it can be done."...

BROKEN PROMISES ad

VIDEO: Still picture of a smiling face of Jimmy Carter.

AUDIO (Announcer): "Can we afford four more years of broken promises? In 1976 Jimmy Carter promised to hold inflation to 4 percent."

VIDEO: Picture rotates to reveal a still picture of a scowling Jimmy Carter.

AUDIO (Announcer): "Today it is 14 percent."

VIDEO: The picture continues to flip-flop back and forth as Carter's bright promises are contrasted with the present-day realities.

AUDIO (Announcer): "He promised to create more jobs. And now there are 8 million Americans out of work. He promised to balance the

budget. What he gave us was a $61 billion deficit. Can we afford
four more years?"

VIDEO (Closing pictures of Reagan and Bush with the words): REAGAN
& BUSH

AUDIO (Announcer): "The time is now for strong leadership. Reagan
for president."

The ads urge voters to retrospectively reject the Carter record.
Only in the area of budget deficits is the Reagan message troubling. As president, Reagan would incur budget deficits that
would dwarf those of the Carter administration.

The 1980 campaign was marked by the activity of many so-
called independent committees spurred on by the Supreme
Court's 1976 *Buckley v. Valeo* decision. Although spending data for
1980 is somewhat suspect, the Republican advantage resulting
from independent spending is considerable. In 1980, independent committees spent $13.3 million on behalf of Republican
candidates; in contrast only $171,000 was spent by independent
committees in ways that aided Democratic candidates.[37] Many
of the ads aired by independent political committees on behalf
of Reagan stressed retrospective evaluations of Carter's performance in office, especially in his handling of the economy:

 ARE YOU SATISFIED? ad

VIDEO: Still picture of the Capitol in Washington. Switch to a
still picture of a long unemployment line.

AUDIO (Announcer): "Jimmy Carter came to Washington promising to do
something about unemployment, to give people who were out of work
a chance to restore their hopes and dreams."

VIDEO: Film of Carter speaking directly into the camera. As he
speaks, a sign appears at the bottom of the screen: '76 Carter
Commercial.

AUDIO (Voice of Jimmy Carter): "7.8 percent unemployment is what
you arrive at when incompetent leaders follow outdated, insensitive, unjust, wasteful economic policies."

VIDEO: Camera scans down the list of candidates on a voting machine.

AUDIO (Announcer): "Jimmy Carter did do something about unemployment—2 million more people became unemployed this year alone."

VIDEO: Sign at the bottom of the screen reads: 2 Million More Unemployed.

AUDIO (Voice of Jimmy Carter): "Are we satisfied with what we have or are we ready to try to change it for the better?"

VIDEO (White words project out against a blue background): ARE YOU SATISFIED?

Carter's only hope of victory was for the public's focus to be shifted away from the record of the past four years to the dangers of electing Reagan as President. The Democratic strategy was to make the election a referendum on the personal qualities of the two men. Reagan's own exaggerations, verbal missteps, and memory lapses only fueled the public's doubts as to his presidential capacity.

In the only Reagan-Carter debate of the fall campaign, Carter steered discussion away from the economy. He attempted to focus the debate on foreign affairs, especially on the dangers of nuclear proliferation. According to Carter debate coach Samuel Popkin, Carter's strategy was to attack; he needed to goad Reagan into looking like "a man with dangerous tendencies, dubious judgment."[38] But Reagan deflected every Carter attack as a misrepresentation of his views. He began his response to one Carter attack with a simple and effective verbal parry, "There you go again." Reagan's steady performance reassured voters and put to rest the competency question.

Reagan concluded the debate with a virtual repeat of Carter's strong retrospective message of 1976. Reagan urged voters to ask themselves "Are you better off now than you were four years ago?"

A Third Candidate: "The Anderson Difference"

John Anderson, a moderate Republican leader, ran as an independent candidate for president in 1980 after first losing his attempt to gain the Republican nomination. His general election candidacy was novel. As a result, he provided the media with a good story and received news coverage disproportionate to the actual vote he finally received.[39]

He ran on the slogan of the "Anderson Difference," and appealed to "new collar" voters who identified with "new politics" issues. Anderson took strong stands on certain issues, which helped him to cultivate the image that he was different from most politicians—that he was an open, honest individual who was not afraid to take on special interests. Anderson publicly confronted the National Rifle Association on gun control. He also proposed a 50-cents-per-gallon tax on gasoline to promote energy conservation. His promise of a "bipartisan government of national unity," however, was vague, for he failed to delineate the principles on which a national consensus could be built or to detail just how he would be able to govern in the absence of party support in Congress.

Anderson faced monumental difficulties in gaining access to the ballot in the various states. Excessive signature requirements and early filing deadlines acted to preserve the two-party monopoly in most states. Anderson's success in forcing the revision of state electoral laws was notable, but the energy his campaign spent in petition campaigns and court fights diverted resources that could have been used to help build his general election appeal. Anderson also faced difficulty in borrowing money to run his campaign. It was not clear that he would win enough votes to receive public funding and thereby be able to pay back his creditors.

Polls showed that Anderson's support represented a greater threat to Carter than to Reagan. Despite his roots in the Republican party, Anderson's appeal was mostly to new liberals, voters who did not find Reagan at all acceptable. As a consequence, Carter sought to keep Anderson from being a factor in the fall election. Rulings by the administration made it more difficult for potential creditors to advance Anderson's strapped campaign badly needed funds. Carter also sought to deny Anderson parity. The president would not participate in any debates that included Anderson. The Carter campaign's message to voters was simple: as Anderson was a minor candidate, a vote for Anderson was a vote for Reagan.

Reagan, of course, found it to his advantage to keep Anderson's candidacy as viable as possible. Thus, Reagan insisted on Anderson's inclusion in the debates. Carter steadfastly refused. As a result, the first presidential debate, sponsored by the League of Women Voters, was a two-person affair between Reagan and Anderson.

Anderson suffered a serious blow when his standing in the polls fell below the 15 percent threshold arbitrarily set by the League of Women Voters for his inclusion in the debates. Consequently, the second debate, the one voters focused on, included only Reagan and Carter. Anderson was relegated to the heap of minor party candidates. He would finally finish with nearly 7 percent of the vote, enough to qualify for public funding.

A Retrospective Election, Not a Mandate: 1980

Studies show that there was no clear turn to the right by voters in 1980. Reagan beat Carter by 10 percentage points; yet the election was no prospective issue vote or ideological mandate for Reagan. According to polls, the public was more liberal than Reagan on a number of issues; on other issues the public had little idea where Reagan stood. As Kathleen Frankovic has shown, there was no strong shift to the right in public opinion from the time Jimmy Carter was elected in 1976 to Ronald Reagan's election in 1980 (see Table 8.5).[40]

Instead, the 1980 election was more simply a retrospective rejection of Carter's performance in office.[41] Poor economic conditions in particular helped to account for the voters' rejection of him.[42] Citizens were voting not so much for Reagan as they were against Carter. Issues were important only to the extent that they provided the reasons why voters rejected the president. Even during the primaries, retrospective evaluations of the president's handling of the economy proved to have a great influence in leading Democrats to vote for candidates other than Carter.[43]

Retrospective voting clearly dwarfed prospective issue voting in 1980. The work of Gregory Markus underscores the limited impact that prospective issues had on voter choice.[44] Markus reviews the surveys of the National Election Studies that polled voters throughout the course of the presidential campaign. As Table 8.6 shows, voters had no clear opinion whether the government should pursue inflation control even at the cost of increasing unemployment, or whether the government should reduce unemployment no matter what the effect on inflation. By October, 40 percent of the voters were unable to take any position on this issue, and an additional 22 percent located themselves at dead center. Voters were even less certain where Carter and Reagan stood on this issue. Apparently, the

Table 8.5   Ideological and Issue Preferences, 1976 to 1980*

ideology	November 1976	November 1980
Liberal	20%	18%
Moderate	48	51
Conservative	32	31

domestic spending	November 1976	November 1980
Increase	29%	12%
Decrease	45	49
Keep the same	26	33

welfare payments	July 1977	November 1980
Not needed	54%	51%
Necessary	31	39

payments for abortions	January 1978	November 1980
Favor	42%	38%
Oppose	50	55

business regulations	January 1978	November 1980
Too much regulation	58%	65%
Right amount	31	27

regulate pornography sales to adults	January 1978	November 1980
Yes	42%	32%
No	53	63

effect of '60s programs	January 1978	November 1980
Made things better	31%	30%
Made things worse	14	20
Had no effect	46	42

Questions: (1) Are you in favor of increasing government spending on domestic programs, reducing it, or keeping it about the same? (2) In your opinion, do you think that most people who receive money from welfare could get along without it if they tried, or do you think they really need this help? (3) The government should help a poor woman with her medical bills if she wants an abortion. Do you agree or disagree? (4) The government has gone too far in regulating business and interfering with the free enterprise system. Do you agree or disagree? (5) Should government, at some level, restrict the sale of pornography to adults, or should adults be permitted to buy and read whatever they wish? (6) There were many government programs created in the 1960s to try and improve the condition of poor people in this country. Do you think these programs generally made things better, or made things worse, or do you think they didn't have much impact one way or the other?

Source: Kathleen A. Frankovic, "Public Opinion Trends," in *The Election of 1980*, ed. Gerald Pomper (Chatham, NJ: Chatham House, 1981), p. 114.

Table 8.6   Respondent and Perceived Candidate Positions on the
Inflation-Unemployment Trade-off (percent)

	reduce inflation (1-2)	3	4	5	reduce unemployment (6-7)	DK
Respondent						
February	15	10	24	10	11	31
April	17	12	23	8	11	30
June	16	11	22	9	12	29
September	9	10	22	11	10	38
October	8	9	22	11	9	40
Carter						
February	4	7	18	16	17	38
April	11	11	18	13	11	36
June	13	12	17	12	11	35
September	6	9	17	12	10	45
October	6	7	14	14	12	47
Reagan						
February	10	11	10	8	5	56
April	14	11	13	10	5	47
June	11	13	16	9	4	47
September	11	12	12	10	5	51
October	11	11	12	9	5	52

Source: Gregory B. Markus, "Political Attitudes During an Election Year: A Report on the 1980 NES Panel Study," *American Political Science Review* 76 (September 1982): p. 543.

unemployment-inflation trade-off issue was too "hard" to guide most voters in 1976.

Voters showed less but still substantial confusion on the questions of whether federal expenditures for health, education, and related services should be cut (see Table 8.7). There is no consensus among voters for a sharp reduction in these services. In October, more than a third of the voters could not even identify Reagan's position on this important domestic issue. On the whole, voters were able to see some difference between the candidates, with Carter being in support of maintaining services and Reagan being in favor of cuts. It was Carter, not Reagan, who was somewhat closer to the average voter on this issue! Voters in 1980 do not appear to have used their ballots to provide government with a clear sense of policy direction on the issue of domestic spending. Of course, voter opinion would have been quite different had the question asked solely about cuts in welfare.

In the area of defense spending the results are a bit different (see Table 8.8). Again, many voters had a difficult time placing where the candidates stood on the issue. But overall the voters

Table 8.7   Respondent and Perceived Candidate Positions on Domestic Services Expenditures (percent)

	cut in services (1-2)	3	4	5	no cut in services (6-7)	DK
Respondent						
February	13	11	15	16	29	17
April	15	12	15	12	28	18
June	14	12	15	12	27	20
September	16	13	15	13	26	17
October	16	11	17	11	26	18
Carter						
February	4	6	18	20	26	26
April	6	11	19	19	20	26
June	5	7	18	22	21	27
September	3	7	16	23	24	27
October	3	5	12	22	28	28
Reagan						
February	13	11	14	8	7	46
April	17	14	14	10	5	40
June	16	13	15	10	6	39
September	19	16	15	9	6	34
October	19	15	15	8	8	35

Source: Gregory B. Markus, "Political Attitudes During an Election Year: A Report on the 1980 NES Panel Study," *American Political Science Review* 76 (September 1982): p. 544.

favored increased spending for defense, an opinion that accurately reflected Reagan's position on the issue. As Markus notes, Reagan's stance on this issue may have contributed to his advantage over Carter.

That issues can dominate over personal imagery in a presidential election is easily demonstrated by the results of the 1980 campaign in the South. Democratic ads aired in that region attempted to exploit the fact that President Carter was a native southerner. Carter kicked off his fall campaign with a Labor Day speech at Tuscumbia, Alabama. Clips from this event were used to create commercials that emphasized Carter's solidarity with the region and the sense of pride that southerners felt in seeing one of their own in the White House. These ads showed pictures of a large, enthusiastic crowd lining the parade route as Carter arrived at the airport. Parade viewers commented: "He picked the best place—that's the South"; "I'm proud that he's a southerner"; and "He's coming back home." The announcer intones: "The arrival of the president is always a special event. But never more so than when he comes home to the South." Carter speaks

Table 8.8   Respondent and Perceived Candidate Positions on Defense
Spending (percent)

	reduce spending (1-2)	3	4	5	increase spending (6-7)	DK
Respondent						
February	4	4	13	23	41	15
April	5	5	15	22	37	17
June	5	6	15	24	36	15
September	3	4	15	21	41	14
October	6	4	16	21	39	15
Carter						
February	5	10	18	22	22	22
April	10	13	23	20	12	23
June	11	13	23	20	11	21
September	12	16	23	18	9	22
October	16	19	18	12	10	25
Reagan						
February	4	4	9	13	23	47
April	3	7	11	17	25	37
June	3	4	11	19	27	36
September	3	3	7	18	41	29
October	2	4	6	15	43	30

Source: Gregory B. Markus, "Political Attitudes During an Election Year: A Report on the 1980 NES Panel Study," *American Political Science Review* 76 (September 1982): p. 544.

from behind a podium with the presidential seal: "In the last few years, I've been to a lot of places, and I've seen a lot of people. But I just want to say how great it is to be with folks who don't talk with an accent." The crowd laughs and cheers.

Yet, despite this personal-image merchandising, Carter lost the South to an outsider. Carter won the votes of southern blacks. But white southerners knew too much about Carter's liberalism for his "good ole boy" and southern-roots imagery to work. It was Reagan's conservative ideology that had a stronger appeal in this traditionalist region. As Kathleen Hall Jamieson observes, personal imagery cannot overcome deeply held beliefs and information:

> If, as [Carter media adviser Gerald] Rafshoon believes, Carter lost his southern base in 1980 because he had proven more liberal than white southerners had expected him to be, then no appeals to southern values could have saved him. Advertising, whether brilliant or banal, is powerless to dislodge deeply held convictions anchored in an ample amount of credible information.[45]

The Republican nominating contest in 1980 further demonstrates that good advertising by itself cannot win a presidential election. Senate Majority Leader Howard Baker was a fresh candidate whose campaign for the Republican nomination was noted for its advertising excellence. Carefully chosen camera angles and skillful editing made the diminutive Baker appear to be a towering, powerful, dramatic leader. In one quite famous commercial, Baker is shown verbally putting down an Iranian student protester, much to the delight and amplified cheers and applause of his audience. Yet, Baker lost in Iowa and his campaign quickly dissolved. Good media was not enough.[46]

THE POLITICS OF RETROSPECTIVE APPROVAL: 1984

9

I n 1984, Ronald Reagan won reelection by a landslide. He won 59 percent of the popular vote and forty-nine states. Democrat Walter Mondale carried only his home state of Minnesota and the District of Columbia.

The 1984 election was an overwhelming retrospective vote of endorsement for the Reagan administration. The country was at peace, inflation had eased, and a sense of growth and prosperity had returned. As the Reagan ads proclaimed, "It's morning again in America." There was little reason for Americans to vote for a change.

Retrospective performance evaluations dominated the fall election. Image politics, particularly the vaguely defined sense of candidate "momentum," had dominated the Democratic primaries. Yet, as we shall see, broad issue choices were at stake in both the spring and fall. Walter Mondale and Gary Hart drew support from quite different constituencies in the Democratic party. In the general election, Reagan and Mondale offered voters a clear choice of governmental directions. The electorate gave its endorsement to the changes Reagan had initiated during his first term in office. They voted to continue—not to reverse and not to expand—the general course of action as set by

Reagan. The issue of taxes also proved to be an important factor in the fall election.

The 1980 and 1984 elections were no mandates for extreme conservatism. In 1980, Americans voted to oust a President, Jimmy Carter, who could not handle the nation's mounting economic crisis. In 1984, Americans voted to return a president, Ronald Reagan, whose performance showed that he could do so.

THE 1982 MIDTERM ELECTIONS: REAGAN'S NADIR

The retrospective basis of voting in the 1980s becomes all the more apparent if we look at an election, the 1982 midterm congressional elections, at a time when Reagan and the Republicans were not so popular. In 1982, unemployment rates were at their highest since the Great Depression. The Republicans controlled both the presidency and the Senate. In 1982, unlike the presidential election two years previous, voters would blame the Republicans, the party of government, for the nation's poor economic performance.

In 1982, the Republicans lost twenty-six House seats—a major loss for the party of an incumbent president in a midterm congressional election. In a way, the Republicans were fortunate; they barely held on to a number of sharply contested Senate seats. There had been no mandate for Republicanism or conservatism in 1980. The public had simply rejected Carter's and the Democrats' performance in office. Now, in 1982, they were rejecting the Republican performance as well.

Democratic ads seized on the poor state of the economy under the Republicans:

STATE UNEMPLOYMENT ad

VIDEO: Scenes, shot in color, of people standing in what is
    meant to be a present-day unemployment line.

AUDIO (Announcer): "The Republicans in this state say that the
    record unemployment is only temporary. High taxes, only
    temporary. 'High unemployment is topping out,' the Republi-
    cans say. 'Why, prosperity is just around the corner.'"

VIDEO: The picture suddenly turns to black-and-white, as the
    contemporary unemployment line blends into one of Depression-
    era clad people—a line of unemployed people during the
    Great Depression. Finish with a close-up of the face of one
    of the persons standing in line, that of a stereotypical,
    Depression-era elderly gentleman.

AUDIO (Announcer): "Of course, the Republicans have said that
    before. The President was Hoover. The year was 1929."

VIDEO: White letters against a black background read:
    LET'S GET OUR STATE WORKING AGAIN

AUDIO (Announcer): "Let's get our state working again."

AUDIO AND VIDEO: Closing message to vote for the
    local Democratic candidate by name.

One particularly effective 1982 Democratic spot was a play off a Republican commercial that had aired two years previous. In their 1980 ad, the Republicans hired James "Buzz" Willders, a stereotypical blue-collar worker, to stand inside a closed factory and argue that if the Democrats are so good for working people, then why are so many people not working? The spot had two objectives. It hit at the poor state of the economy under Carter. It targeted blue-collar voters who, dissatisfied with Democratic welfarism and social liberalism, were no longer firmly anchored in the New Deal Democratic coalition and might be persuaded to cross party lines. Reagan won a majority of white working-class voters in 1980.

But by 1982, it was a Republican administration that presided over a deepening recession. Democratic National Committee advertising specialist Robert Hirschfeld heard rumors that Willders was dissatisfied with the treatment and favors he had received from the Republicans. Hirschfeld traveled to Baltimore to ask Willders to do a new ad for the Democrats. But Hirschfeld added that he was interested in producing the new spot only if Willders would agree to appear in it without pay. The result was a classic retrospective appeal that urged a targeted group of voters to reject the poor economic performance of the incumbent administration:

BALTIMORE WORKER ad

VIDEO: A worker clad in T-shirt and blue jeans walks through an idle factory.

AUDIO (Worker addresses viewers): "Remember me? In 1980 the Republicans paid me to go on television because they promised us they would make things better. And I believed them."

VIDEO: The worker's name appears at the bottom of the screen: James A. Willders, Baltimore, MD.

AUDIO (Willders continues): "Well, since they've been in control, unemployment is the highest since the Great Depression. And businesses are closing down every day. Millions are without jobs, and we've got to do something."

VIDEO: Willders turns and looks directly into the camera. For emphasis, he first points to himself, and then to the audience.

AUDIO (Willders): "I'm a Democrat, but I voted Republican once. It's a mistake I'll never make again. And I didn't get paid to say that!"

VIDEO: The words "Democrats will get this country working!" are overlaid across Willders' picture on the screen.

AUDIO (Announcer): "Democrats will get this country working!"

The Democrats also attacked the lack of fairness in the tax and spending cuts initiated by the Republicans. The fairness issue was an important factor in 1982:

SOCIAL SECURITY ad

VIDEO: Super close-up of a Social Security card.

AUDIO (Announcer): "The Republicans all say they believe in Social Security, a sacred contract with the American people. That's what they say. Look what they do."

VIDEO: Pull back to show a pair of scissors repeatedly clipping off portions of the Social Security card until there's almost nothing left.

AUDIO (Announcer): "In 1981 they tried to cut Social Security by $60 billion. In 1982 they said either increase Social Security taxes or cut $40 billion just to balance the budget. When are they going to stop? Not until it hurts."

VIDEO: Still frame of scissors cutting the small portion of the Social Security card that still remains. Across the picture appear the words: "It isn't fair. It's Republican."

AUDIO (Announcer): "It isn't fair. It's Republican."

TRICKLE DOWN ad

AUDIO: Sounds of water dripping into a tin cup.

VIDEO: Water drips into a tin cup held by an arm clad in a plaid shirt, apparently that of a working man.

AUDIO (Announcer): "The big Republican tax cut. What does it mean to the average working person? About four bucks a pay check. Not much! But it means a lot to the wealthy!"

VIDEO: Suddenly a champagne glass, held by a hand clad in what appears to be a tuxedo, intercepts the trickle of water. The trickle suddenly turns into a gushing flow of champagne. The champagne overflows into the champagne glasses held apparently by other well-dressed party-goers.

AUDIO: Sounds of laughter at a high-class party.

AUDIO (Announcer): "It's the Republican theory called Trickle Down. Give to the rich, and it will eventually trickle down to every body else."

VIDEO: From the last champagne glass a few drops of water finally trickle down all the way to the bottom—into the tin cup.

AUDIO (Announcer): "But you have to ask yourself: just how much is trickling down to you lately?"

> VIDEO: The tin cup is turned over to reveal that it is
>   virtually empty. Freeze frame of the empty tin cup next
>   to the words: "It isn't fair. It's Republican."
>
> AUDIO (Announcer): "That's what we thought. It isn't
>   fair. It's Republican."

The Republicans countered with ads of their own urging voters to "Stay the Course!" and complete the difficult job of cutting government spending and turning the economy around. The Republican ads also pointed out that Reagan had brought down inflation and interest rates from their exorbitant highs of the Carter years. The ads also pointed out that the Republicans had given the nation the greatest tax cut in its history.

The ads on both sides were incomplete and contained numerous distortions. For instance, the Democratic ad on Social Security did not mention that reforms were urgently needed to put the program on more solid fiscal footing. The ad also misled voters by seeming to imply that cuts had been made in the benefits provided the elderly. In fact, the initial cuts had been predominantly in the more peripheral Social Security programs. Likewise Republican ads on the Reagan tax cut did not address the question of who was receiving the lion's share of new tax reductions.

Still, despite distortions and incompleteness, the ads offered voters a choice of policy directions. A viewer who saw both parties' ads and heard the competing claims and arguments could choose accordingly. A citizen who wanted tax cuts and believed that bitter medicine was needed to control inflation and turn the economy around could vote Republican to stay the course. A citizen more concerned with fairness, protecting Social Security benefits, and the urgency of dealing with the recession could vote Democratic.

Given the poor state of the economy in 1982, it was the Democratic message that resonated with the public. Retrospective voting on the economy and the fairness issue both contributed to the Democratic victory. "Stay the course!" was the best argument that a Republican administration could muster in the midst of such difficult economic times; but it was not one that had great appeal to citizens suffering the hardships of the recession.

Only the lack of finances and the resulting inability of the Democrats to widely broadcast their message kept the Democrats from picking up even more extensive congressional gains in 1982. The Democratic National Committee prepared the spots but lacked the money to air them nationwide. It was left up to each local Democratic campaign to decide whether to use the spots and to find the money to pay for air time. As a result, the Democratic generic spots were not seen in many congressional districts.

Tactical decisions by national Republican party officials further helped to mute the impact of the advantages enjoyed by the Democrats. The Republican party worked hard to recruit and train a good class of congressional candidates. National party officials also made sure that funds, computer services, and other forms of party campaign technical assistance were targeted to Republican candidates in competitive races. In contrast, much of the Democratic funds were spent and effectively wasted by incumbents in relatively safe districts.[1]

Overall, the 1982 House elections were a referendum on President Reagan.[2] They were a retrospective vote against the Republican record.

1984: THE ECONOMY AND REAGAN CAME BACK

In February 1983, in the depths of the recession, Reagan's approval rating fell, in at least one national poll, to a low point of 35 percent.[3] But the president's ratings would soon rise with the improvement in national economic conditions. As Scott Keeter has shown, Reagan's popularity virtually tracks the gains made in employment (see Figure 9.1).[4]

By 1984, unemployment was no longer the dominant issue that it had been in 1982. The economy had rebounded. The 1984 election would be a referendum on peace and prosperity.

IMAGES AND ISSUES IN THE DEMOCRATIC PRIMARIES

The race for the Democratic nomination in 1984 turned on images and the influence of momentum. Yet, as we shall see, issues—the broad choice of policy direction—were not absent from the Democratic contest. Different constituencies in the Democratic party voted for different candidates.

Walter Mondale, the front-runner, ran as an establishment liberal committed to the party's New Deal and civil rights traditions. However, Mondale suffered serious image problems. His opponents charged that he represented a tired, outdated political philosophy that was incapable of meeting the challenges of the 1980s. Mondale also gained endorsements from numerous

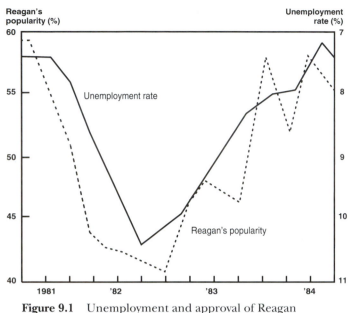

Figure 9.1   Unemployment and approval of Reagan

Source: Scott Keeter, "Public Opinion in 1984, " in *The Election of 1984: Reports and Interpretations,* ed. Gerald Pomper (Chatham, NJ: Chatham House Publishers, 1985), p. 94.

organizations, including the National Organization of Women, the National Education Association, and the first-ever presidential endorsement of the AFL-CIO. These endorsements seemed to provide further evidence of Mondale's ties to the old political order. His opponents charged that he was the captive of special interests. As the former vice president, Mondale also bore the albatross of the failed policies of the Carter administration—an image problem that would hurt him in the general election more than in the Democratic primaries.

Ohio Senator John Glenn and Colorado Senator Gary Hart both offered themselves as candidates who represented the nation's future. Glenn's handlers hoped that their campaign would benefit from the Hollywood release of *The Right Stuff,* a film that glorified the early years of, and Glenn's role as an astronaut in, America's man-in-space program. Glenn's commercials were generally recognized to be of high quality. They projected his heroism, patriotism, and sensible centrism. But they could not overcome the handicaps stemming from the senator's dull public-speaking style (he did not do well in candidate debates) and his campaign's general lack of organization.[5]

The Meteoric Rise. . .

Hart ran on a new generation image but sought to avoid Glenn's more conservative tag. Hart was deliberately ambiguous in the ideological image he projected. He sought to attract votes from all factions of the party dissatisfied with Mondale, from both conservatives and "new collar" antiestablishment liberals alike.[6]

Hart entered the first-in-the-nation Iowa caucuses as a relative unknown. He hoped that a good showing in Iowa would establish him as a major candidate and boost his chances for success the next week in New Hampshire. As Hart explained: "You can get awful famous in this country in seven days."

Mondale won the Iowa caucuses with 45 to 49 percent of the vote. (The exact percentage of vote that Mondale received is unclear as complex caucus voting procedures at times allow the supporters of a losing candidate to reallocate their votes to another candidate.) Yet it was Hart who emerged from Iowa as the big winner. Hart gained considerable momentum with 15 to 16 percent of the vote and a second-place finish that effectively separated him from the rest of the Democratic field. News coverage of the Hart campaign grew tenfold during the week following the Iowa caucuses, and equaled that given Mondale. Equally important, the new media coverage given Hart was virtually all upbeat.[7]

Hart's 37-to-32-percent upset win in the first-in-the-nation New Hampshire primary was a stunning surprise. One week later, Hart did even better, winning an amazing 70 percent of the vote in Vermont's nonbinding primary. Momentum was clearly with Hart. According to CBS/*New York Times* polls, Hart had been the choice of only 1 percent of Democrats before Iowa. One week after New Hampshire, Democrats said that they preferred Hart to Mondale by a 38-to-31-percent margin.[8]

. . . and Fall of Gary Hart

But as Hart moved clearly to the front, the press began to subject his candidacy to greater scrutiny. The press got tough on Hart; "compensatory journalism" began to slow his momentum.[9] News stories criticized Hart for aping John Kennedy's mannerisms, for allegedly lying about his age, and for having changed his name from Hartpence.

Hart had run on a program of "new ideas." He called for a streamlined national defense that relied on smaller, more flexible, and cost-effective weapons systems. He proposed a national industrial policy geared to increased productivity and the development of high-technology industries. He rejected trade protectionism for insulating American industry from the demands of competition and adaptation. As a senator he had angered organized labor by being one of the few Democrats to vote against the Chrysler bailout.

Since the beginning of the campaign, when Hart was still "Gary Who?" his organization had dutifully fed the press reams of position papers. The press, with few exceptions, ignored them. Issues were boring. A detailed examination of policy proposals did not make for interesting stories. Some members of the press derisively dismissed Hart as the thinking-man's candidate. But all this changed when Hart emerged as the new front-runner. The media now began to question whether there was any substance to Hart's new ideas.

In a March debate, Mondale borrowed a line from the Wendy's hamburger ads that had become part of the popular culture. Mondale said that when thinking about Hart's new ideas he was tempted to ask: "Where's the beef?" The sound bite was picked up and repeated nationwide. At various campaign rallies thereafter, Mondale would hold up an empty hamburger bun much to the delight of his supporters.

Mondale's "Where's the beef?" charge hit home, as Hart had not been clear in identifying himself as either a liberal or conservative. According to political scientist Larry Bartels, ambiguity can be an effective strategy for a candidate early in the primary season, for voters can project their own preferred policy views onto a candidate who fails to take clear stands on issues. But later in the campaign, a candidate like Hart pays a price for this strategy as the press subjects his issue positions to more critical scrutiny.[10] Hart had tried to gain votes both from conservatives who saw Mondale as too liberal and from new liberals who saw Mondale as too conservative. But now many Americans began to wonder if Hart had any substance at all.

In addition, new rules changes in the Democratic party worked to Mondale's advantage, but to Gary Hart's and Jesse Jackson's disadvantage. As one of the changes, the Hunt Commission increased to 568 the number of seats awarded automatically to senators, congressional representatives, key state and local elected officials, and party officeholders. Few of these superdelegates could be expected to support a political loner such as Hart or an outsider such as Jackson. Mondale, in contrast, had long-established contacts with many of these superdelegates. He had even campaigned and raised money for a number of them. As a result, Mondale had the support of an estimated 450 to 500 of the 568 superdelegates.

Mondale and Hart had finished the primary season virtually even in terms of the number of delegates actually won in the primaries and caucuses. As the primary trail progressed, however, it was Mondale's edge in superdelegates that helped influence public perception as to his lead.[11] Mondale's support among superdelegates also gave him effective control of the national convention.

A second change in the nominating rules shortened the primary season to make it more difficult for a dark horse candidate to use an early primary or caucus victory to build the resources necessary to win later races. However, compression of the primary schedule actually worked to Hart's advantage at first. The momentum from his Iowa showing carried him to victory the next week in New Hampshire. There was insufficient time for a new critical attitude in the press to emerge and burst the Hart bubble.

Soon thereafter, the compressed and frontloaded primary calendar worked as predicted. Hart was forced to take on Mondale in five states on a single day, Super Tuesday, only two weeks after New Hampshire. The Hart campaign by necessity had focused virtually every resource it had in Iowa and New Hampshire. As a result, the campaign had made almost no advance effort in the three southern Super Tuesday states. His organization lacked time to redeploy staff and take full advantage of the surge of financial contributions that flowed into the campaign following its success in New Hampshire.

When Super Tuesday came, Hart could not deliver the knockout blow the press expected. Hart won the Massachusetts, Rhode Island, and Florida primaries. But the big story of the day was Mondale's survival, as the former vice president won Alabama and Georgia.

Momentum was no longer with Hart. Mondale regained the lead as the primary trail shifted north to Illinois and other major industrial states.

Momentum and Ideology in 1984

Momentum was a key factor in the rise and fall of Gary Hart. Yet, ideology was also related to the vote in the Democratic primaries. Hart's greatest appeal was to the young, to yuppies, and to new collar voters. He made no special promises to blacks or labor and, therefore, found little support among those groups.[12] Hart did well in the early contests in more rural and ideologically moderate states and thereby established his momentum. But when the primaries moved to the more urban and industrial states, Hart found that he was campaigning among more traditional Democratic constituencies. His new ideas message was not well received by constituencies that preferred the civil rights and job protectionism promises of Mondale.[13]

Jesse Jackson had attempted to build a "rainbow coalition" of forgotten Americans of all colors. But this broad range of support for Jackson did not materialize in 1984. Jackson's support was centered in the nation's black communities. His best showings came in those southern and northern industrial states with large African-American populations.

As Hart had virtually no support among African-Americans, Jackson's showing came essentially at Mondale's expense. Had Jackson not been in the race, Mondale would have had an easier time putting down Hart's challenge. Jackson's candidacy probably cost Mondale victories in Wisconsin, Louisiana, Indiana, Ohio, and California.[14]

The media, as previously observed, generally did a poor job in covering the policy views of the candidates. Hart ran as the candidate of new ideas; but according to a CBS poll, only 9 percent of voters could identify any specific Hart new idea.[15]

Still, as Larry Bartels shows, despite the glaring inadequacies of news coverage, as the 1984 primary season progressed, voters learned much about the candidates and their ideologies, not only about their personal traits. General issue orientations did matter in 1984, even if voters did not clearly see the differences between Mondale and Hart on specific issues. New Deal adherents preferred Mondale to Hart, and social traditionalists viewed Mondale more favorably than they did the new-style liberal Hart. In contrast, younger, more upscale voters preferred Hart. Hart and Mondale were viewed by their respective constituencies as they should have been. If voters did not quite learn about candidates' stances on specific issues, they did as least learn about candidates' general styles and issue dispositions.[16]

Mondale won the nomination, but he did not win the loyalty of those more independent Democrats who supported Hart. According to a CBS/*New York Times* poll, one-third of those Democrats who supported Hart in the primaries defected to Reagan in the general election. Two-thirds of the self-described independents who supported Hart also voted for Reagan in November.[17]

THE GENERAL ELECTION

The Reagan campaign ads sought to make the 1984 election a referendum on the incumbent, on the president's handling of the economy and foreign policy. Reagan had brought inflation to heel. The nation was feeling a new sense of vibrancy. It was a nation at peace and a nation with renewed respect abroad.

During the spring, the Tuesday Team, as Reagan's advertising professionals were called, aired upbeat, warm-feeling ads that dwelled on the nation's improved economy and sought to associate the president with the images of a content and well-off America at work and on the move:

PROUDER, STRONGER, BETTER ad

VIDEO: Picture of a city harbor at daybreak. A fishing boat goes to work.

AUDIO (Narrator): "It's morning again in America."

VIDEO: Various shots of people at work—a businessman getting out of a taxi, a farmer on a tractor, a boy on his bicycle delivering newspapers, and a suburbanite on his way to work. Switch to a scene of a man and young boy carrying a new carpet into a home.

AUDIO: "Today more men and women will go to work than ever before in our country's history. With interest rates at about half the record highs of 1980, nearly 2,000 families today will buy new homes, more than at any time in the past four years."

VIDEO: Stereotypical scenes of a small-town wedding. An elderly lady dressed in white virtually explodes with happiness. A couple exchanges marital vows. The bride smiles. The happy couple kisses.

AUDIO: "This afternoon 6,500 young men and women will be married. And with inflation at less than half of what it was just four years ago, they can look forward with confidence to the future."

VIDEO: Picture of the U.S. Capitol at night. Switch to a picture of a young boy looking up as the American flag is raised. Various scenes of a small-town flag-raising. Close-up on Old Glory as it waves in the breeze.

AUDIO: "It's morning again in America. And under the leadership of President Reagan, our country is prouder, and

stronger, and better. Why would we ever want to return
to where we were less than four short years ago?"

VIDEO (Closing picture of Reagan next to the American
flag, accompanied by the words): President Reagan:
Leadership That's Working.

It was almost as if Reagan personally deserved credit for every
young couple that married or every family that moved into a
new home. The early Reagan ads emphasized imagery, but it
was imagery based not on a candidate's personal attributes but
on retrospective performance:

STATUE OF LIBERTY ad

VIDEO: Shots of people at work on a heavy industrial job.
Male and female workers welding, hoisting, and so on.

AUDIO (Narrator): "It was a dream that built a nation. The
freedom to work at the job of your choice, to reap the rewards of your labor, to leave a richer life for your children and their children beyond."

VIDEO: Camera pulls back to reveal that the workers have been
on the scaffolding of the Statue of Liberty, working on the
much-celebrated restoration of that national monument.
Close with a shot of the Statue of Liberty, enveloped in
its scaffolding, standing majestically in New York Harbor.

AUDIO: "Today the dream lives again. Today jobs are coming
back. The economy is coming back. And America is coming
back, standing tall in the world once again."

VISUAL (Closing picture of Reagan next to the American flag, accompanied by the words): President Reagan: Leadership That's Working.

AUDIO: "President Reagan. Rebuilding the American Dream."

A number of the themes of the Reagan campaign were en-
capsulated in a seventeen-minute biographic retrospective of the
Reagan presidency, aired at the Republican convention and later

televised as a paid broadcast. The program, as did all Reagan ads, mixed images and issues. The program detailed both Reagan's personal qualities for leadership and his achievements in office. The film even included pictures of a physically vigorous president riding horseback and chopping wood at his ranch outside Santa Barbara, California. These pictures were meant to dispel any qualms that the public may have had about Reagan's advanced age, that he was too old to serve another full term in office.

In the program, a cross-section of Americans talk about their new-felt sense of pride in America and how America is once again on the move owing to Reagan's presidency. Reagan himself recalls for viewers the vast gains in the economy made during his four years in office. The film associates Reagan with this renewed sense of patriotism and well-being. Numerous shots of a flag-waving and a strong America at work are shown while the words "I'm Proud to Be an American…God Bless the U.S.A." (from Lee Greenwood's song "God Bless the U.S.A.") are sung in the background. The song became the reelection campaign's unofficial anthem.

The film's image-building sought to underscore the faith that Americans can have in Reagan as a take-charge and effective world leader. The president, dressed in a military jacket, prays and dines with American troops stationed in Korea. He walks the Great Wall of China and shakes hands with Chinese officials at a banquet.

Yet, the most moving part of the film is not a simple personal-image appeal; rather, it mixes images with a message. Most poignant of all is the program's extended treatment of Reagan's emotional speech on the beaches of Normandy in commemoration of the fortieth anniversary of the D-Day invasion. Speaking on a windswept beach, the president tells the story of the heroism of the sixty-two rangers who, in the first wave of the assault, scaled the cliffs: "These are the boys of Pointe du Hoc. These are the men who took the cliffs." The camera pans the now aging veterans and their families in the audience, who later stand and applaud the President's remarks. Reagan continues:

> They were what General Marshall called our secret weapon, the best damn kids in the world. Where do we find them? Where do we find such men? And the answer came almost as quickly as I'd asked the question. Where we've always found them in this country. On the farms. In the shops, and the stores, and the offices. They just are the product of the freest society the world has ever known.

The D-Day memorial sequence concludes with Reagan reading the words of the daughter of one of the veterans, a man who died of cancer eight years previous to the memorial. Her father had "promised that he would return to Normandy," and she, in turn, promised her father:

> I'm going there, Dad. And I'll see the beaches and the barricades and the monuments. I'll see the graves, and I'll put flowers there just like you wanted to do. I'll feel all the things you made me feel through your stories and your eyes. I'll never forget what you went through, Dad. Nor will I let anyone else forget. And Dad (Reagan's voice breaks as he continues to read), I'll always be proud.

The camera switches to the audience where the woman in question, the daughter of the deceased veteran, is crying. Reagan concludes: "We will always remember. We will also be prepared so we may be always free."

The D-Day speech is not just a simple appeal to emotional imagery and patriotism. It is also meant to underscore Reagan's message of peace through strength, the need to be vigilantly armed in a dangerous world. Reagan's approach to national defense entailed military spending at levels far above those advocated by the Democrats.

Throughout the campaign, the Tuesday Team felt that the theme of leadership and America's regained international respect had great appeal to younger voters. Economics was a second area that the campaign saw as a key to getting the votes of young people. The Republican ads portrayed Reagan's policies of economic growth as providing today's younger citizens with continued opportunity. Throughout the fall campaign, the Tuesday Team contrasted Reagan's strength and the alleged indecisiveness of the Carter-Mondale White House. On election day, the oldest presidential nominee in the history of the nation would carry a majority of the nation's youngest voters.[18]

The only ray of hope for Mondale came as a result of the first presidential debate. Reagan's unfocused and rambling answers, especially toward the end of the ninety-minute encounter, once again raised the age issue. Was the seventy-three-year-old President too old to serve another term in office? Reagan's poor debate performance only reinforced doubts raised by rumors of his daily afternoon naps. Reagan did not seem to be fully in control of the White House.

Media reports and commentary on the debate served to magnify the political significance of Reagan's showing. Immediately after the debate, 43 percent of the public saw Mondale and 34 percent saw Reagan to be the winner. But two days after the debate, after press discussions of Reagan's performance had time to sink in, public opinion polls showed Mondale's victory margin to be much greater—66 to 17 percent.[19]

In the wake of the president's faltering debate performance, his campaign handlers decided on two strategy changes. First, the Tuesday Team would reassure voters by airing commercials that featured visuals of an effective, take-charge president in the Oval Office. In a five-minute ad and in two thirty-second spots, Reagan spoke directly to television viewers. Second, the campaign went on the offensive by airing stronger anti-Mondale ads. These ads would make Mondale's promise to raise taxes the key prospective issue in the campaign.

Mondale had made his extraordinary tax promise in a desperate gamble to revive his flagging campaign. He had little hope of victory unless he could focus the public's attention on the more unsatisfactory aspects of Reagan's governance, particularly the mounting budget deficits of the Reagan years. In his televised acceptance speech at the Democratic national convention, Mondale argued that a tax increase would be necessary to ease the deficit, no matter who was elected president in November: "Mr. Reagan will raise taxes, and so will I. He won't tell you. I just did."

Mondale's tax vow was not popular with voters, and the Republicans took advantage of it. A generic ad run on behalf of Republican congressional candidates showed a Democratic congressman stuck in an elevator frantically pressing buttons in an effort to escape as voters asked him whether or not he supported Mondale's proposed tax increase. A second Republican ad compared Reaganomics and Mondalenomics, listing "Raise Taxes" again and again on the Mondale side of the screen. The Tuesday Team also hit home on the tax issue in what was arguably the most effective single spot of the 1984 race:

TAX VIGNETTES ad

VIDEO: A grimy, sweaty construction worker is hard at work breaking a street with a pickaxe. A truck unloads gravel in the background.

AUDIO: Sounds of city traffic.

AUDIO (Announcer): "Walter Mondale thinks that if you put in more overtime, you could pay for his promises with your taxes. What do you think?"

AUDIO AND VIDEO: Construction worker with the pickaxe looks up in frustration and says with great sarcasm: "Right!"

VIDEO: Scene of a housewife in a busy kitchen. In the background, her children fight, and the family dog barks. The housewife scrapes peanut butter from a jar and tries to spread it thinly among a number of sandwiches.

AUDIO: Sounds of kids playing and fighting and the dog barking.

AUDIO (Announcer): "Walter Mondale thinks you can squeeze more tax money out of your budget. What do you think?"

VIDEO: Housewife gives a look that could kill.

VIDEO: A farmer is busy lifting bales of hay.

AUDIO: Sounds of farm machinery.

AUDIO (Announcer): "Walter Mondale thinks that if you stay out in the field longer you could pay more taxes. What do you think?"

VIDEO: The farmer looks up in obvious disgust.

VIDEO (Closing picture of Reagan next to the American flag, accompanied by the words): "President Reagan: Leadership That's Working."

AUDIO (Announcer): "Vote for President Reagan. You have better things to do with your money than to pay for Walter Mondale's promises."

The second debate, which was to focus on foreign policy, would allow Reagan the opportunity to undo any of the damage done in the first debate. Alternatively, a second bad performance could compound his troubles and accelerate a voter move toward Mondale.

During the days preceding the debate, the Tuesday Team sought to run ads that would make the public more receptive to Reagan's foreign policy message. The ads generally underscored the peace that the United States enjoyed during the Reagan years. The most well-known political spot of the 1984 campaign, "The Bear," was run for six consecutive days.

THE BEAR ad

AUDIO: Eerie music and sounds of heartbeat-like drum-beats.

VIDEO: Various scenes of a grizzly bear lumbering through the woods.

AUDIO (Announcer): "There's a bear in the woods. For some people, the bear is easy to see. Others don't see it at all. Some people say the bear is tame. Others say it is vi-cious and dangerous. Since no one can be sure who is right, isn't it smart to be as strong as the bear?"

VIDEO: The bear looks up and sees a man with what appears to be a rifle slung across his shoulder. The bear sud-denly stops and appears to take a step backward.

AUDIO (Announcer): "If there is a bear." (Ominous background music trails off.)

AUDIO: Drumbeat continues. Then only the eerie music.

VIDEO (Closing picture of President Reagan accompanied by the words): PRESIDENT REAGAN. PREPARED FOR PEACE.

The bear in the ad, of course, was meant to symbolize the Soviet Union. The ad was designed to provoke public discussion of the United States' need to continue to deal with the Soviets from a position of strength.

The Bear ad was probably the most heavily tested political spot in history. It was shown to no fewer than 100 focus groups and got an amazingly high 75-percent recall among viewers.[20] The ad succeeded in provoking commentary. Yet, the spot was probably too obscure and abstruse to be truly effective. Many viewers did not know what the bear represented; many did not even recognize that it was a political ad. A number of television viewers even thought that the ad was a commercial for "The Life and Times of Grizzly Adams," a once-popular television show.

A Reagan quip in the early moments of the second debate quickly dashed any hopes that Mondale may have had for a comeback victory in November. Panelist Henry Trewitt of the Baltimore *Sun* asked Reagan about his continued ability to perform in office despite being "the oldest president in history." Reagan responded: "I want you to know also that I will not make age an issue in this campaign. I am not going to exploit for political purposes my opponent's youth and inexperience." The audience roared its laughter and approval. Reagan looked sharp and reassuring. As the debate continued, he effectively parried Mondale's thrusts on the dangers of an accelerated arms race and continued nuclear proliferation. But the substance of the debate and the candidates' stands on policy matters counted for little. Reagan's performance had laid the age issue to rest.

Reagan's lead over Mondale had fallen to 12 percent in the wake of the first-debate disaster. His performance in the second debate, however, helped to restore a more comfortable ballot edge of 20 to 22 points.[21] Reagan's reelection was well in hand, enough that the president's advertising team chose not to use the tougher negative ads it had created attacking Mondale's two-faced voting record and his indecision on Grenada.

Instead, the campaign returned to its retrospective themes. In the campaign's final ads, Reagan once again spoke of the nation's economic accomplishments, his record of peace, and the hopes for a better future that his policies offered young people. One ad featured pictures of a parade and flag-waving celebration as the people turn out to greet the president's train, according to the announcer, as if to tell the president thank you for all that he has done.

Mondale, in contrast, was unable to find a message that hit home. As a result, he switched from issue to issue in an effort to find one that would reach voters. A number of his ads attacked Reagan's deficits for the "mortgaging" of America that would be a burden on future generations. Another ad used the visuals of a roller coaster to challenge the up-and-down performance of the Reagan economic record. Perhaps the most effective Mondale ads were those that tapped the public's fear of nuclear catastrophe by pointing to the policy area that polls showed to be the one glaring weakness in Reagan's record—his failure to negotiate an arms control treaty.

THE GENDER GAP AND THE FERRARO FACTOR?

Walter Mondale picked New York Congresswoman Geraldine Ferraro as his vice-presidential running mate. It was a landmark choice. Ferraro was the first female major party nominee for the vice-presidency.

Mondale's choice of Ferraro was designed to exploit the **gender gap**. Women in the United States differ from men somewhat in their policy attitudes and candidate preferences. In the 1980 presidential and 1982 midterm congressional elections, women voted less Republican than did men. Women as a whole are less supportive of militarism than are men. Women are also more prone to support caring social service programs. Reagan's advocacy of escalated military budgets and reduced social spending only served to raise the salience of those issues at the root of the gender gap. But any advantage that Mondale hoped to gain from this choice quickly dissipated as the press grilled Ferraro on the question of her tax returns and those of her businessman-developer husband.

In the November 1984 presidential vote, the gender gap was once again observed.[22] The exact size of the gender gap remained unclear, as it varied from poll to poll. Depending on the poll, women voted 4 to 9 points less Republican for president than did men. Still, Reagan's popularity was so great that he carried the majority of female and male voters alike.

Overall, the nomination of Ferraro for vice president had little impact on the final vote. Perhaps the choice of Ferraro appealed to those more feminist voters who, for the most part, were already disposed to vote Democratic. The first-ever major-party nomination of a woman neither greatly helped nor greatly hurt the Democratic ticket.

RETROSPECTIVE VOTING AND CANDIDATE IDEOLOGY IN 1984

The 1984 election can most simply be understood as a retrospective endorsement of the Reagan administration's performance in office. The Tuesday Team had presented the public attractive images based more on performance than on personality. The public's favorable evaluations of Reagan were colored by positive evaluations of his performance in office.[23] The public's assessments of Reagan's effectiveness as President overshadowed the more personal evaluations of Reagan.[24] His record in office, not his acting skills or Teflon coating, determined his reelection.

The 1984 election was essentially a referendum on the state of the economy.[25] Annual inflation was down from 12 percent to 4 percent. Interest rates similarly were down sharply, from 21.5 percent to 12 percent. Even unemployment, while still somewhat troublesome, stood at 7 percent, below the 10 percent level of 1982.[26] As the economy improved, Americans were answering that all-important economic question positively: Yes! They were better off now than they were four years ago.[27]

Mondale could not hope to win an election focused on retrospective performance evaluations. The Democrats had to shift voter concerns to other matters, more specifically to the impact of rising budgetary deficits on future generations and the dangers that could result from Reagan's reluctance to negotiate new controls on the nuclear arms race. Mondale was asking voters to look not simply at the past but also to the future.

But Mondale was not successful in these efforts. For most voters, present-day pocketbook concerns outweighed questions about possible future policy consequences. On one prospective issue the voters did have a clear opinion; they did not want Mondale's new taxes.

Mondale also faced the difficult task of getting a broad spectrum of Americans to address such hard issues as the arms race and the budget. Most of the public had little understanding of Strategic Defense Initiative technology—its capabilities, its costs, and its relative merits compared to alternative weapons systems. Similarly, few Americans could appreciate the exact size of the nation's annual budget deficits or the possible long-term economic harm posed by the accumulated national debt. Reagan's budget-cutting rhetoric and the traditional image of the Republicans as the party of fiscal conservatism only further confused the public about how bad the budget situation was and who was to blame.[28] The return of peace and prosperity, in contrast, was much easier for voters to feel and comprehend.

Whereas retrospective economic evaluations were paramount in 1984, the electorate's behavior in 1984 cannot fully be understood solely by retrospective voting. Mondale and Reagan also offered Americans fundamentally different visions.[29] As was the case in 1972 the presidential candidates in 1984 tended to take distinct stands on the policy issues. The public responded accordingly. The electorate clearly saw Mondale as the more liberal of the two major-party candidates. The voters were also able to see differences between the candidates when it came to specific issues. Paul Abramson and his colleagues studied public opinion in seven different issues areas in the 1984 election. They found that voters' issues positions were strongly related to candidate choice.[30]

Still, we should be cautious not to overstate the impact of specific issues, other than taxes, on the 1984 election. According to the work of Martin Wattenberg, the public saw itself as closer to Mondale than to Reagan on the issues. Wattenberg sees the 1984 election as a vote of endorsement for Reagan's performance in office, not for his specific policy positions.[31]

The 1984 election was a mandate for neither conservatism nor Republicanism. In their separate studies of national polling data gathered by the Center for Political Studies, both Paul Abramson and Warren Miller have concluded that the public in 1984 had a preference for moderate policies. They further report that in a number of policy areas the public preferred more liberal policy alternatives than those advocated with Reagan.[32] While the public approved of the general conservative direction of Reagan's first four years in office, they were skeptical of initiatives that would move the country in a still more conservative direction:

> The Reagan administration had achieved many of its domestic program cuts and had increased spending for defense. In both cases, the average respondent was saying that the shift in policy was just about right. There was no longer any overall sentiment for further domestic program reductions nor for increased spending for defense.[33]

As Miller concludes: "Ronald Reagan may have been reelected in part because he had moved the government to the ideological right; he was *not* reelected with a mandate to move further toward the goals of his conservative supporters.[34]

Overall, retrospective voting was the key to Reagan's reelection. But economic performance alone does not explain Reagan's success. Foreign policy performance constitutes a second important element in voter positive evaluations of the Reagan years. Theodore Lowi has traced public opinion trends and observed that Reagan's upswing in popularity starting in his third year in office is associated with key international events with which the president shrewdly associated himself.[35] One big jump in the president's approval rating came after his strong rhetorical denunciation of the Soviets for shooting down a Korean Air Lines passenger plane. Another sharp upswing in his approval

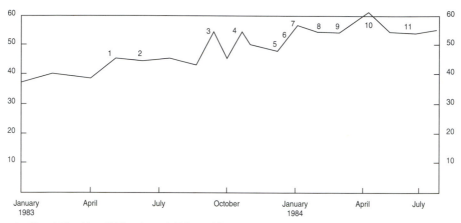

1. Terrorist bombing of U.S. embassy in Beirut and Reagan denunciation thereof; Secretary Shultz dispatched to Beirut.
2. Economic summit, Williamsburg, Va.
3. South Korean airliner downed; 2,000 more Marines to Lebanon.
4. Terrorist attack, killing 241 Marines in Beirut; Grenada invaded.
5. U.S. air attacks on Syrian positions near Beirut; 2 U.S. jets downed; Lt. Robert Goodman captured by Syria.
6. U.S. ships attack Syrian aircraft near Beirut.
7. Lt. Goodman released by Syria.
8. Redeployment of U.S. Marines, Beirut; Andropov dies.
9. Chernenko new Russian leader.
10. President's trip to China.
11. Presdent's trip to Ireland and Normandy.

Figure 9.2   A profile of Ronald Reagan's popularity, 1983–1984

Source: Theordore J. Lowi, *The Personal President: Power Invested, Promise Unfulfilled* (Ithaca, NY: Cornell University Press, 1985), p. 18. Reprinted in *The Elections of 1984*, ed. Michael Nelson (Washington, DC: CQ Press, 1985), p. 283.

rating came after the Grenada invasion, a swift and successful action that proved immensely popular with Americans (see Figure 9.2). John Aldrich and his colleagues, too, have concluded that foreign policy was an important influence on the vote in both the 1980 and 1984 presidential elections.[36]

SUMMARY

Performance-based, not personal-based, images dominated the 1984 election. The year was an integral part of a retrospective voting era in American presidential elections:

> In sum, it would seem reasonable to conclude that the 1976 election, with its razor-thin edge going to Carter, was a very narrow rejection of Ford's incumbency, and 1980 was a clear and strong rejection of

Carter's. In 1984, Reagan won in large part because he was seen as having performed well and because Mondale was unable to convince the public that he would do better.[37]

But it would be a mistake to view voting in 1984 purely in retrospective terms. Policy choices were at stake in 1972, when Richard Nixon and George McGovern offered Americans a clear-cut choice of policy directions. In 1984, Mondale and Reagan offered voters a similarly clear choice. Once again, voters were able to see distinct and important differences between the candidates.[38] The choice was pristinely clear on one particular issue. The voters knew what they did not want; they did not want Walter Mondale's proposed tax increase.

Both retrospective and prospective issue voting were at work in 1984. As Paul Abramson and his colleagues conclude: "[T]he 1984 election appears to be more like that of 1972, in that the retrospective evaluations were more important than the issue preferences, but the latter remained an important factor in the vote."[39] Substance—issues and performance evaluations, not simply personal-based imagery—determined the results.

THE TRIUMPH OF ISSUE-BASED IMAGES: 1988

Popular accounts that were circulated about the "flag and furlough campaign of 1988"[1] see the election to have turned on the creation of powerful televised images. Peter Goldman and Tom Mathews made these observations:

> What was disturbing about the 1988 election, both for itself and as a harbinger of our future, was that ideals were never really in play. It was instead a contest between two men who could not say with any precision why they wanted to be president, or why they ought to be. In the circumstances, there was no agenda to fight for, only victory for its own sake. The result was a contest at manipulation, a war between high-tech button-pushers unburdened by contending vision or issues, and, whatever else one made of the outcome, the better button men surely won.[2]

Political scientist Marjorie Randon Hershey observes that media coverage of the three televised debates centered not on the substance of the candidates' issue positions but "on which candidate seemed the most relaxed, the most likable, with the

best one-liners, as though the election were to result in the selection of a dinner guest, not a president."[3] It was "politics as
spectator sport" where "[m]edia values had almost completely
supplanted the values of governing."[4] Hershey's overall assessment is pejorative: "For when the 1988 presidential campaign
came down to a choice between Willie Horton and the Pledge
of Allegiance, the only people enriched were the campaign
consultants."[5]

But was the 1988 campaign nothing more than a battle of
personal images? As we shall see, the critics are in part right. In
1988, personal-based candidate images or, more accurately, the
destruction of carefully cultivated candidate images, dominated the primary season. But the general election offered voters
more—a fundamental choice between competing visions. Voting studies point to the importance of issues in the 1988 election.[6] Personal imagery alone did not win the day; instead, the
fusion of issues and images—the promulgation of issue-based
images—turned the tide for George Bush. In both the paid and
the free media, Bush evoked powerful symbols that underscored
the fundamental alternative that he offered to the more liberal
policy directions of Michael Dukakis.

Retrospective evaluations were also important in 1988.
Bush's victory could not have been gained in the absence of the
Reagan economic prosperity. Nineteen eighty-eight was essentially the second presidential election that turned on voter evaluations of the performance of the Reagan administration.[7]

CANDIDATE IMAGERY IN THE DEMOCRATIC RACE

The 1988 race for the Democratic nomination underscores the
extent to which the presidential race is not in the total control of
professional image-makers. Campaign managers and consultants
cannot control the actions of the candidate. Nor can they dictate
the course of events and the reactions of the news media. As a result, 1988 saw the rapid deterioration of the presidential image
of a number of Democratic contenders, who were rapidly eliminated from the primary field.

Certain candidacies just never got off the ground despite
the efforts of campaign handlers. Arizona Governor Bruce Babbitt and Illinois Senator Paul Simon both lacked the flair to come
across well on television. Babbitt courageously called for raising
taxes to reduce the national deficit. Well behind in the polls, he

had little to lose by doing so. Simon, sporting an old-fashioned bow tie, sought to represent a return to the Democratic party's ideals of the New Deal era. Simon finished a somewhat distant second in Iowa caucuses and lost momentum. He needed a better showing in a state neighboring his native Illinois.

Gary Hart and Joe Biden: Monkey Business and Plagiarism

The campaigns of two of the Democratic contenders, Gary Hart and Joe Biden, virtually self-destructed as the media focused on questions of personal character. Hart, the former Colorado Senator, was the clear early leader in the race owing to his nearly successful challenge for the Democratic nomination four years earlier. But he could not survive the scrutiny that the press gives a front-runner. Hart, dogged by repeated rumors as to his extramarital philanderings, sought to lay the suspicions to rest by challenging anyone interested in his sex life to "put a tail" on him. According to Hart, "They'd be very bored."

The Miami Herald responded to Hart's challenge. Following up a telephone tip, *Herald* reporters staked out and kept watch on the ex-Senator's Washington townhouse on a night when Hart's wife was out of town. The resulting exposé was anything but boring. Hart spent the night with a buxom model, Donna Rice. Rice, herself, later revealed under questioning that she and Hart had previously spent a night on a yacht off Bimini. The yacht, quite appropriately, was named *Monkey Business. Washington Post* reporter Paul Taylor asked Hart the unprecedented question of whether he had ever committed adultery. Commentators in the press continued to speculate about the psychological and compulsive roots of Hart's behavior. Hart soon dropped from the race.

Delaware Senator Joe Biden was similarly forced to withdraw when media stories effectively demolished public perceptions of his presidential stature. Not counting Jesse Jackson, Biden was perhaps the most effective orator in the Democratic field, copying, it was said, John F. Kennedy's mannerisms. Unfortunately, that was not all that Biden copied. In an Iowa speech, he virtually repeated word-for-word, without attribution, a long section from a speech by British Labour Party Leader Neil Kinnock. With the media's attention now focused on Biden, it was soon uncovered that he had also lifted phrases from speeches by Robert Kennedy, that he inflated his college and law school grades, and that he had received an F in law school for plagiarizing a law review article.

The quick drop of public support for these two contenders illustrates how voters learn from political campaigns. According to Samuel Popkin, voters often extrapolate a candidate's future performance as president from what they know about the candidate's past private behavior. People find it easier to project from personal data than from political data. The result is a "Gresham's law of information" where "small amounts of new information can dominate large amounts of impersonal information."[8] Popkin uses the phrase **low-information rationality** to describe the process of voter learning that relies on extrapolations and informational shortcuts.[9]

Yet, do voters always draw valid inferences from such fragments of information? Larry Sabato questions the assumption that private action always yields valid insight as to a candidate's future public action. As Gary Hart argued, whatever his personal past, he would never lie to Congress or shred government documents. Sabato further doubts that the press provides sufficient or balanced evidence for the public to make accurate judgments as to a candidate's character. The news media in its **feeding frenzies** tends to dwell on the most sensational and negative episodes of candidate behavior.[10]

Richard Gephardt: Self-Styled Populist

Missouri Congressman Richard Gephardt hoped to repeat Jimmy Carter's 1976 strategy of using an early win in Iowa to establish the momentum that would carry him to the nomination. Gephardt was, in fact, a Washington insider on the fast-track to a leadership position in Congress.[11] But as such a reputation would not sell in Iowa, Gephardt was recast for the campaign as a populist outsider running on behalf of the people against powerful established interests. He campaigned in Iowa as the champion of the family farm against corporate agriculture. By the end of the Iowa campaign, Gephardt's handlers even had him "shucking off his navy-blue business suits in favor of bright red parkas and farmer's caps."[12]

Gephardt also sought the votes of blue-collar workers by stressing the issue of trade protectionism and his record on tax reform. Gephardt hit hard against the allegedly unfair trade practices of Japan and South Korea. One powerful Gephardt ad claimed that Americans would have to pay $48,000 for a Korean-made Hyundai if the United States were to place the same taxes and tariffs on imported cars that Korea had placed on American-made cars. His "people's"-oriented message was encapsulated in the campaign slogan created by media adviser David Doak: "It's your fight, too."[13]

Gephardt won Iowa, but his focus on that state left him little time and money to adequately campaign in the New Hampshire primary, only one week away. Defeated by Michael Dukakis in New Hampshire, Gephardt was in a poor financial and organizational position to battle on Super Tuesday, when twenty-one states chose nearly one-third of the nominating convention delegates in a single day. Dukakis's ads effectively demolished Gephardt's populist image. These ads questioned how Gephardt could be fighting for the people when he had accepted large campaign contributions from corporate political action committees. On Super Tuesday, Gephardt won only one contest, his home state of Missouri.

Albert Gore: An Alternative Candidate

Conservative elements in the Democratic party had crafted Super Tuesday with the hope that the early prominence of southern primaries would weed out liberal candidates and propel a southerner or conservative to the front of the pack. Senator Albert Gore of Tennessee hoped to vault into the race with a strong showing on Super Tuesday. Gore sought to portray himself as the only centrist or conservative candidate in a field of liberal contenders. Some commentators pointed to the liberal aspects of the senator's voting record, which belied the candidate's campaign image.

Gore won six states on Super Tuesday but still found himself hopelessly behind Dukakis, who had the better-financed and more extensive national campaign organization. Still, Gore's victories in the South confirm that money and media advertising do not by themselves win presidential primary elections. Dukakis's campaign was well-financed, and the Massachusetts governor was rated positively by most voters on Super Tuesday. Yet, despite Dukakis's positive personal image, native southerners still preferred Gore, the "favorite son of the South" who had the message better tailored to voters in the region.[14]

Gore's lack of a national base, however, quickly became evident. He made virtually no showing in the Illinois primary only a week after Super Tuesday. His candidacy came to an end in New York, where he gained only 10 percent of the vote, finishing far behind both Dukakis and Jackson.

Jesse Jackson: Learning from the Mistakes of 1984

Jesse Jackson learned from the mistakes of his 1984 campaign and sought to broaden his base of support. In 1988 Jackson ran as a populist and did surprisingly well among white voters in economically depressed rural areas in Iowa, Minnesota, Maine, Vermont (where he received 25 percent of the vote among a virtually all-white electorate), Michigan, and Wisconsin.

Still, Jackson's best showings came in contests where black voters composed a large percentage of the turnout. His campaign took on the appearance of a crusade among African-Americans. Black churches provided much of the strategic resources for the campaign, especially during its early stages. In the South, networks provided by black churches were particularly helpful to Jackson.[15] On Super Tuesday, he mobilized his base of black supporters in the region to win contests in Alabama, Georgia, Louisiana, Mississippi, and Virginia. Two weeks later, Jackson scored a stunning upset in the Michigan caucuses where, because of a low turnout statewide, the outpouring of the vote in black communities constituted a large percentage of the total vote. Black churches in Michigan had acted as the de facto precinct organization of the Jackson campaign.[16] Jackson also gained votes from the Detroit area's sizable Arab-American population as a result of his embracing the Palestinian cause. In uniting black and Arab-American voters in the Michigan primary, Jackson had forged "an alliance of church and mosque."[17]

Despite these precedent-shattering victories, Jackson had no real chance at the nomination. He was still perceived by many whites as too extreme, inexperienced, and untrustworthy—especially in the critical area of foreign policy—to get their votes.

"Mike the Greek" Dukakis: Managerial Competence

The Dukakis campaign sought to win support from the diverse working-class and middle-class constituencies of the Democratic party by emphasizing the Governor's hard-working and ethnic roots. John Sasso, chief strategist for the Dukakis campaign, had transformed a technocratic governor, the son of a suburban doctor, into "Mike the Greek, a tough little ethnic scrapper fighting for the American Dream because his family had been blessed by it."[18] At the Democratic National Convention, Dukakis told how his parents, like millions of others, came to this country as immigrants and got ahead through hard work:

"I believe in the American dream." The halls rang out with the strains of Neil Diamond's song, "Coming to America."

To a great extent, Dukakis won the nomination on the basis of an image campaign that stressed his managerial record and presidential abilities. After eight years of the Reagan administration, Dukakis, Sasso, and other members of the campaign staff figured that voters had had enough of divisive ideology. Instead of ideology, Dukakis would offer technocratic competence. His candidacy sought to offer the economic revival known as the "Massachusetts miracle" to the entire nation. In his acceptance speech, Dukakis proclaimed: "This election is not about ideology, it's about competence."

The Dukakis campaign suffered a damaging blow when John Sasso, implicated in leaking proof of Biden's plagiarism to the press, was forced to resign. In the absence of Sasso, the campaign lacked a capable, guiding strategist. Sasso would be brought back on board with just two months remaining before election day, way too late, when it was clear that the Dukakis campaign was in great trouble.

ISSUES IN THE DEMOCRATIC PRIMARIES

It would be a mistake to conclude that voters in the 1988 primaries were manipulated by manufactured candidate images. Ideology and policy priorities were related to the Dukakis vote—and to the vote for the other Democratic candidates as well.

Dukakis was able to withstand the prospect of numerous losses on Super Tuesday only as a result of his appeal to more liberal areas of the country. Ideology coupled with the superior financial position of the Dukakis effort allowed the Massachusetts governor to offset his strategic weakness in the South, especially the Deep South, with victories elsewhere. Dukakis's "four corners" offense on Super Tuesday focused on winning more liberal states outside or on the rim of the South—including Massachusetts, Rhode Island, and Maryland in the Northeast and East, and the Washington caucuses in the Northwest. In the Southwest corner, his ability to speak Spanish coupled with his economic liberalism allowed Dukakis to reach the large Latino community in Texas and win that state's important primary. In the Southeast corner, Dukakis won the Florida primary by appealing to the large number of retirees and Jewish voters who had migrated to the state from other parts of the country.[19]

In 1988, Super Tuesday did not have the effect, as its creators had intended, of tilting the nomination toward a more conservative or moderate candidate favored by the southern wing of the Democratic party. While Tennessean Al Gore's candidacy was momentarily energized by Super Tuesday, Dukakis was able to secure a sufficient number of victories to continue his progress toward the nomination. The most liberal candidate in the Democratic field, Jesse Jackson, also did quite well, winning five Super Tuesday contests and nearly winning Texas and Virginia. Dukakis and Jackson showed that, in a crowded field, liberals could do well on Super Tuesday. Not only could liberals do well in contests outside the region, the South is more varied than the organizers of Super Tuesday had recognized. Dukakis and Jackson were able to appeal to specialized constituencies instead of the southern issues as a whole.[20] It would not be until 1992 that Super Tuesday would at long last work as its creators had envisioned, helping to propel native son southerner Bill Clinton toward the White House.

Exit polls and other voting studies show that the policy priorities of the candidates were of exceptional importance in the Super Tuesday primaries. Voters learned about and responded to those issues that the candidates chose to emphasize. Voters concerned with unemployment and poverty voted for Jackson; those more concerned with foreign trade voted for Gephardt. Candidates's campaign themes were, indeed, related to the vote.[21]

But voters learned not just about candidates' policy priorities but also about their chances of winning. On Super Tuesday, many voters engaged in **sophisticated voting** or **strategic voting,** incorporating both substantive policy concerns and assessments as to candidate viability into their voting decision. Voters who preferred not to waste their votes on likely losers cast their ballots for their second- and third-choice candidates. However, supporters of Jesse Jackson and, in the Republican party, supporters of the Reverend Pat Robertson remained intensely loyal to their preferred candidate despite the low chances that he would win the nomination.[22]

THE DE-WIMPING OF GEORGE BUSH

The Republican candidacies of Delaware Governor Pierre DuPont, Congressman Jack Kemp, and former Secretary of State Al Haig never caught on in 1988. These candidates tried, but failed, to grab the mantle of Reagan conservatism. They tried other ploys as well. DuPont, a member of the wealthy Delaware family, dropped the aristocratic-sounding monicker of Pierre and campaigned simply as the more everyday "Pete" DuPont. It did not work.

Pat Robertson, host of "The 700 Club," a religion-oriented television talk show, was able to mobilize his fundamentalist Christian following to good showings in the preliminary rounds of such low-turnout affairs as the Republican caucuses in Michigan and an advisory straw poll in Iowa. Robertson charged briefly into the national spotlight when he took nearly 25 percent of the vote in a second-place finish in the Iowa caucuses. But many Americans still distrusted Robertson; they were suspicious of a man they saw as a television preacher. It was an image that Robertson would unsuccessfully try to shake during the campaign. The press, not knowing how to treat a candidate whose religious claims were considered fantastic by many Americans, had been reluctant to criticize Robertson. But the press gained its opportunity to question Robertson's credibility when he alleged without evidence that Soviet missiles were based in Cuba—an allegation that was quickly denied by the Reagan administration.

Robertson's grassroots Christian following did not fit the stereotype of "elite" Republicans. Some of his supporters even wore blue jeans to Republican conventions. Deeply concerned about religious, family, and moral issues, they were to a great extent newcomers to Republican party affairs.[23] Intensely motivated, they could pack party caucuses and exert great influence in small-turnout caucus affairs. But when the race turned to states with primaries that required a more broad base of popular support, Robertson faded.[24]

The Republican race was essentially a two-man contest between Senate Minority Leader Robert Dole and Vice-President George Bush. Dole campaigned in Iowa as the champion of farmers. He tried to build on the record he had established in representing farmers in his home state of Kansas. Dole talked about his life growing up in a Kansas farm town during the Great Depression. Dole's handlers also convinced the senator, who walked with a noticeable limp, to talk about the injuries he had sustained in the service during World War II, a matter that he had previously been reticent to discuss throughout his public life. Dole would be sold to the voters as a courageous, tough, and patriotic, yet caring, leader. His handlers portrayed Dole as a man of the people. In turn, they sought to paint Bush as the candidate of wealth and privilege.

Bush finished an embarrassing third place in Iowa, In part, the vice president had been victimized by the wrath of Iowa voters who blamed him and the Reagan administration's farm policy for the state's depressed farm economy.

Bush was also fighting what *Newsweek* magazine in a cover story labeled "The Wimp Factor," the public perception that he was a kind, decent, yet somewhat ineffective, man.[25] Bush was seen as Reagan's perpetual second-banana, the ever-loyal vice president who lacked the capacity to be president. Bush was also seen as a preppie. As the son of a United States senator from Connecticut, he had attended elite schools Andover and Yale.

Bush's image-makers would dispel the wimp notion. They recast Bush as a Texan, a man of the people who knew both bravery and the rigors of hard work. His campaign commercials showed vintage footage of Bush, then a young World War II aviator, stepping onto a naval ship after his plane had been shot down on a mission. Bush was shown to have spurned privilege, setting out on his own after the war to make his fortune in the rough and tumble days of the oil business in Texas. In interviews, Bush professed a love for fried pork rinds and country music. He also declared his voting residence to be in Texas, despite the time he spent at the Bush family compound in Kennebunkport, Maine. Actually, the vice president's Texas residence amounted only to a hotel suite in Houston.

Roger Ailes worked with the vice president to make him a more effective public speaker. Bush was coached to be more assertive with his hand gestures and to avoid his penchant for using such unbecoming phrases as "deep doo-doo."

A "defining moment" for the Bush campaign, to use the lexicon of Ailes and campaign manager Lee Atwater, came in a January 25, 1988, live television interview with "CBS Evening News" anchor Dan Rather. Atwater feared that Rather would attempt to use the opportunity to undo Bush's candidacy, just the way that CBS reporter Roger Mudd had critically injured Ted Kennedy's 1980 presidential campaign with a disastrous taped program and interview. Ailes insisted that Rather conduct the interview live in order not to allow CBS an opportunity to edit Bush's responses to the vice president's disadvantage.

As Atwater feared, Rather did intend to focus the interview almost exclusively on the vice president's role in the Iran-Contra affair. American arms had been sold to Iran to raise funds for the Nicaraguan Contras, apparently in violation of federal law at the time. CBS planned to lead into the interview with a five-minute film that reviewed the Iran-Contra affair, pinpointing questions as to the vice president's involvement. Some staffers at CBS were bragging that the broadcast would be the end of the Bush campaign. However, Bush's handlers got wind of CBS's plans and alerted the vice president as to how he should respond to the trap.

Bush came out swinging. Instead of directly responding to Rather's first question following the film, Bush went on the offensive: "I find this to be a rehash and a little bit, if you'll excuse me, of a misrepresentation on the part of CBS, who said you're doing political profiles of all the candidates." Bush was challenging Rather, who, despite his own Texas roots, was now perceived by the public as a million-dollar, pampered, elite, New York network anchor. If Bush could do it right, it would be Rather, not Bush, who was put on public trial. When Rather declared that he did not mean to be argumentative, Bush's response was sharp and personal: "You do, Dan."

The strategy underlying Bush's response was similar to that of the man-in-the-arena format that Ailes had used in creating ads for the 1968 Nixon and 1976 Reagan campaigns. The sympathies of viewers back home rush to a besieged candidate who responds to an attack with self-assurance and courage. In his exchange with Rather, Bush came across as a fighter, a street brawler, anything but a wimp. Atwater was enthusiastic: "I think it was the most important event of the entire primary campaign."[26]

In New Hampshire, Bush stepped up his increasingly aggressive style of campaigning. During the weekend before the primary, the Bush campaign flooded the state with a negative ad portraying Robert Dole as a two-faced senator who straddled votes on taxes and other key issues.[27] Badly organized, the Dole campaign was unable to muster new television ads to respond to this late broadside. Bush won the primary by nine points. The race had turned.

Dole was despondent over the turn of events. His televised comments after the returns came in only served to make matters worse. He sourly asked Bush to "stop lying" about his record. Dole looked unpresidential, very much like an embittered loser. If he could not stand up to Bush's attack in New Hampshire, how well could he stand up to the Soviets and all the other pressures of the presidential office?

THE MEDIA CAMPAIGN: PERSONAL AND ISSUE-BASED IMAGERY

At the time the Republican convention was to convene in New Orleans, the Bush campaign was in serious trouble. The size of Dukakis's lead had diminished a bit as the afterglow of the

Democratic convention wore off. It was expected to diminish further, still, as the Republicans dominated the nation's airwaves with their week of speeches and festivities. Still, Dukakis's lead appeared strong. Furthermore, the Iran-Contra affair and revelations of the United States's dealings with the Panamanian dictator and drug trafficker Manuel Noriega had taken some of the gloss off the Reagan record. Unless something was done, the momentum seemed to be with Dukakis.

Bush campaign pollster Robert Teeter pointed to data that underscored a possible Republican opportunity. Voters had no strong impressions of Dukakis. For the most part, the governor of Massachusetts remained an undefined quantity in the eyes of the public. The Bush media campaign would seize the opportunity and define Dukakis for the public. The liberal elements in Dukakis's record would provide the Bush team with all the ammunition required. Dukakis's liberalism would become the dirty L-word of the 1988 campaign. Even Dukakis's past membership in the American Civil Liberties Union—an organization that opposed organized prayer in public schools—would be used to portray the Democrat as a left-winger out of step with the American public.

The pictures that had emanated over the airwaves from the Democratic convention in Atlanta made the Republican task easier. Jesse Jackson's supporters were bitterly disappointed when Dukakis asked Texas Senator Lloyd Bentsen, and not Jackson, to be his running mate. After all, their candidate was the second largest vote-getter in the Democratic primaries. They were outraged by what appeared to be a gratuitous snub when Dukakis did not even inform Jackson of his choice. Jackson learned of the decision from reporters at the airport; he was visibly stunned. The Dukakis team was confronted by the prospects of an embarrassing fight and large-scale revolt at the convention. This was not the image of managerial competence they had hoped to portray.

Dukakis's handlers quickly moved to patch up the spat. But it was not easy. The dispute, an interesting story in an otherwise storyless convention, dominated media coverage. Jackson was interviewed on one network after another. Some of his demands regarding reforms in the conduct of intraparty affairs were met. He was also given a prominent position on the convention schedule to address the concerns of the constituencies for which he spoke. While Jackson dominated the airwaves, Dukakis did not—at least until his acceptance speech at the convention's close. To the viewer at home it sometimes seemed that Jackson, not Dukakis, was the party's flag bearer. Furthermore, was Dukakis really presidential if he could be so easily forced to yield dominance to Jackson? The Democrats on television appeared to be the party of Dukakis *and* Jackson, an image that the Republicans would exploit in certain states, especially in the South, in the fall campaign.

Though the 1988 campaign is known for its negative ads, there were plenty of positive appeals as well. Dukakis stressed the upbeat message that "The best America is yet to come." Bush's handlers followed the maxim that a successful campaign could not simply go negative. You had to first establish positive images of your candidate to offer voters a credible alternative. Also, in the weeks before the November election, the Bush campaign closed with upbeat advertising, recounting the vice president's personal qualities and broad leadership experience. Such positive image creation was necessary for Bush to escape some of the stigma associated with negative campaigning.

Even at the Republican convention, the twenty-minute film used to introduce Bush reviewed his career experience and achievements and presented him as a warm and caring family man. The film contained images that would be used again and again in the various positive commercials run throughout the Fall campaign:

FAMILY/CHILDREN ad

VIDEO: Young child running, probably one of Bush's grandchildren. Bush walks with his wife Barbara and the grandchildren. Child runs into Bush's arms. Scenes of Bush at a family picnic. Bush plays with the grandchildren; he makes a playful face at one. Switch to films of Bush's past, among them: Bush as a young World War II pilot boarding a submarine after his plane was downed; Bush as the U.S. Ambassador to the United Nations; Bush being sworn in as vice president; Bush with British Prime Minister Margaret Thatcher. Close with Bush lifting and kissing his grandchild.

AUDIO AND VIDEO (Barbara Bush on camera): "I wish people could see him as I see him, thousands of people see him. You know, I always loved the time someone said to George, 'How can you run for President? You don't have any constituency.' And George

```
said, 'Well, you know, I got a great big family and
thousands of friends.' And that's what he has."
```

```
AUDIO (Announcer): "For more than forty years George
    Bush has met every challenge the country and the
    world has offered up to him. The truth is, the more
    you learn about George Bush, the more you realize
    that perhaps no one in this century is better pre-
    pared to be President of the United States."
```

```
CLOSING VIDEO: GEORGE BUSH
               EXPERIENCED LEADERSHIP
               FOR AMERICA'S FUTURE.
```

Bush's performance in delivering his acceptance speech was masterful. He appeared calm and in control. He paced his delivery well, pausing strategically, and using hand gestures where appropriate for emphasis. He spoke of the remarkable achievements of the Reagan legacy and portrayed himself as Reagan's loyal vice president. He then spent the rest of the speech setting himself out as his own man, attacking Dukakis, and establishing himself as presidential timber. He attacked the Massachusetts governor for opposing the death penalty and for failing to support the mandatory recitation of the Pledge of Allegiance in schools. He repeated his prior assault on Dukakis's record on prison furloughs and taxes. His own opposition to taxes was clear: "Read my lips. No new taxes!" He closed by leading the convention in reciting the Pledge of Allegiance.

The well-crafted speech was initially penned by Peggy Noonan, the noted Reagan speechwriter whom the campaign had recruited to help in what had been a previously troubled area.[28] The speech was far from negative in its tone. Bush reminded America of its strength and diversity, of the thousands of ethnic associations and voluntary and community organizations that were like the stars twinkling in the heavens, "a thousand points of light." Bush called for a "kinder, gentler nation." In a bit of personal imagery, he recounted how he had "learned a few things about life in a place called Texas," setting out after the war to run a business, living in a house with just one room for the three of them. It was a life of "high school football on Friday nights" and neighborhood barbecues. George Bush was one of us.

The convention conveyed the desired message to the public. By the time it was over, Bush was again leading in the polls, despite the flap that arose over the selection of Dan Quayle as the Republican vice-presidential nominee.

Still, it was the negativism of the attack ads that dominated the fall campaign and gave the 1988 general election its special flavor. At the end of May, when Bush was still trailing Dukakis by nearly 20 points, most of the Republican campaign braintrust— Robert Teeter, Lee Atwater, Roger Ailes, Nicholas Brady, and the vice president's chief of staff Craig Fuller—had assembled in Paramus, New Jersey, to help identify the themes they could use to turn around the election. From behind a one-way mirror, they viewed a focus group in which a Republican spokesperson informed thirty or so Democrats who had voted for Reagan in 1984 about numerous aspects of the Dukakis record. The Reagan Democrats were seen by the Republican campaign staff as the key to Bush's election chances. The Republicans were still narrowly the nation's minority party. A Republican candidate for the presidency needed the crossover vote of independents and disaffected Democrats. Reagan won this key constituency twice, but, as Teeter's polls showed, these voters were not yet there for Bush.

The focus group moderator informed the group that Dukakis had once vetoed a bill requiring teachers to lead the recitation of the Pledge of Allegiance in class. He also informed the group that Dukakis, a member of the ACLU, supported the nuclear freeze and gun control, but opposed the death penalty and prayer in schools. The Massachusetts governor also allowed Boston Harbor to become one of the filthiest city harbors in the nation. The spokesperson told the group the story about Willie Horton, a black man and a convicted murderer who was ineligible for parole but had been let out of Massachusetts prisons ten times on furlough. During his tenth furlough, Horton escaped to Maryland where he kidnapped a white couple, stabbing the man and raping the woman.

The results were dramatic. Prior to the session, the members of the focus group had been leaning toward Dukakis. After learning of the new information, half of the group said that they were switching to Bush. Lee Atwater assessed the situation: "I realized right there that we had the wherewithal to win."[29] Atwater told a Republican forum, "If I can make Willie Horton a household name, we'll win this election."[30] Ailes was reported as saying, with a touch of sarcasm, that the only question left in the campaign was in which of Horton's hands should they portray him holding the knife.[31]

The single most dominant ad in the campaign was the thirty-second Bush spot that used good visuals to portray Dukakis's furlough program as a revolving door.

REVOLVING DOOR ad

AUDIO: Opening "clang," a prison sound, followed by sounds of a guard's footsteps on metal prison steps.

VIDEO: Armed prison guard climbs a guard tower. Another guard patrols with a rifle. A long line of prisoners go in and then immediately back out of a revolving-door entrance to the prison.

AUDIO (Announcer): "As governor, Michael Dukakis vetoed mandatory sentences for drug dealers. He vetoed the death penalty. His revolving-door prison policy gave weekend furloughs to first-degree murderers not eligible for parole."

VIDEO: Sign across the bottom of the screen reads: 268 ESCAPED. It is followed by another sign that reads: MANY ARE STILL AT LARGE.

AUDIO (Announcer): "While out, many committed other crimes like kidnapping and rape. And many are still at large. Now Michael Dukakis says he wants to do for America what he's done for Massachusetts. America can't afford that risk."

CLOSING VIDEO: An armed guard on a prison wall.

Ailes had been careful to try to insulate the campaign against charges of racism stemming from the ad; few black faces appeared in the endless line of prisoners that filed through the turnstyle. Horton was not mentioned by name, nor was his picture shown. Ailes asserted that the Republicans would have used the furlough issue even if Horton had been white.

Still, critics charged that the ad played on white stereotypes of blacks as criminals. At the time the ad was shown, the Horton story was already well known. The vice president had mentioned it in his speeches, and the media had discussed the Republican charges at length. The commercial could evoke these preconceptions and fears without having to directly mention Horton or show his face.

Horton's face did appear in a televised ad, although not in one produced by the official Bush campaign. In California, an independent group showed an ad that lingered on a picture of Horton. The Bush campaign disavowed the spot, pointing out that independent committees do not clear their actions with the official campaign.[32] But critics questioned just how independent such groups really are. They charged that the Bush campaign effectively had its cake and ate it too. The Republicans could deny direct involvement; yet the fact that Horton was black was raised and extensively repeated by the media. Most viewers saw the ad and Willie Horton's face only through its exposure on the free media of television news.

An amateurish attempt at image-building by the Dukakis camp provided Bush's advertising consultants with the opportunity to create another effective thirty-second spot. The Dukakis campaign had staged a pseudoevent to counter perceptions that the Massachusetts Democrat was soft on defense. Wearing a tank driver's helmet and headset, Dukakis rode a new tank that had just come off the assembly line. He looked out of place and ridiculous, and media commentators had a field day deriding the event. Footage of the ride provided the grist for a Republican ad that quite effectively exploited perceptions of Dukakis's weakness on defense:

TANK RIDE ad

VIDEO: Filmed footage of Dukakis, with helmet, riding
in the gun turret of a tank. Words scroll up from
the bottom of the screen. The announcer reads them
to underscore their seriousness.

AUDIO (Announcer): "Michael Dukakis has opposed virtually every new defense system we developed. He
opposed new aircraft carriers. He opposed anti-
satellite weapons. He opposed four missile systems,
including Pershing II missile deployment. Dukakis
opposed the Stealth bomber and a ground emergency
warning system against nuclear attack. He even

criticized our rescue mission to Grenada and our
strike on Libya."

VIDEO: "Words no longer appear on the screen. Camera
moves in for a close-up on Dukakis, who appears to
be smirking.

AUDIO (Announcer): "And now he wants to be our commander-in-chief. America can't afford that risk."

CLOSING VIDEO: AMERICA CAN'T AFFORD THAT RISK

The prison turnstyle and Dukakis-tank-ride spots were
among the most famous of the campaign ads produced in 1988.
Other ads produced by Ailes hit hard at Dukakis's claims to competence. They sought to debunk any notion that the governor
had an economic miracle in Massachusetts. The ads portrayed
Massachusetts as suffering from continued economic woes due
to a series of Dukakis tax hikes. A controversial ad sought both to
destroy Dukakis's image of managerial competence and seize
the advantage on the environmental issue:

 BOSTON HARBOR ad

VIDEO: Opening sign reads: THE HARBOR. Switch to
shots of floating garbage, oil slicks, and other
disgusting pictures of pollution of the harbor.
Close-up of a sign on the edge of the water that
reads: DANGER. RADIATION. NO SWIMMING.

AUDIO (Announcer): "As a candidate, Michael Dukakis
called Boston Harbor an 'open sewer.' As governor
he had the opportunity to do something about it but
chose not to. The Environmental Protection Agency
called his lack of action the most expensive public
policy mistake in the history of New England. Now,
Boston Harbor, the dirtiest harbor in America, will
cost residents $6 million to clean. And Michael
Dukakis promises to do for America what he's done
for Massachusetts."

Critics of the Republican campaign charge that the focus-group method allowed the Bush team to identify "phony" issues that were not really important to the governance of the country. The Bush campaign shifted public discussion to Willie Horton and away from such vital matters as developing plans to address the savings and loan bailout and deficit reduction.

Yet the focus-group methodology can be defended. In probing the attitudes of a small number of people in depth, the focus-group technique may prove superior to public opinion polling in revealing issues of concern to the people. Focus groups "can reveal inchoate attitudes that people are usually reluctant to express unless they are validated or reinforced by others."[33]

The adeptness of the Republican campaign was not confined only to the paid media. Skillful orchestration even allowed the Republican campaign to escape what could have been its single great political disaster, the selection of Dan Quayle as the vice-presidential nominee. After Quayle's selection, it was revealed that he had gotten into an Indiana National Guard unit during the height of the Vietnam War, apparently with the help of his family's political connections. In the midst of an otherwise quiet convention and with little to do, reporters focused on the Quayle story. Reporters soon discovered that, in college, Quayle had been a better golfer and socializer than a student. Overall, Quayle looked to be a lightweight, a man incapable of handling the responsibilities of the Oval Office if called on to do so.

The top Republican campaign echelon met to discuss a damage limitation strategy. Bush had to maintain his image of looking strong and presidential; Quayle would not be dumped from the ticket. The Republicans would not repeat the mistake made by Democrat George McGovern who looked weak in giving in to the pressure to remove Thomas Eagleton from the ticket in 1972 after the press revealed that Eagleton had undergone electroshock therapy to treat depression.

The campaign group made the decision to play to the press's norm of neutrality to get the press to back off the Quayle story. Republican spokespersons again and again publicly accused the press of engaging in a "feeding frenzy" in covering the story out of proportion to its merits. Immediately after the Republican convention, Quayle was flown to his hometown, Huntington, Indiana, to meet the press before a public forum. In a variant of the man-in-the-arena format, a partisan hometown crowd booed reporters as they pressed their questions. The cheers and jeers from the audience cued television viewers at home.

The sympathies of television viewers rushed to Quayle as he fended off the attack by the press.

The charges of a feeding frenzy rang true with the public, as there were excuses in the media's focus on the Quayle affair. The press's coverage of Quayle's problems suffered from exaggeration and a lack of balance. The press went beyond an investigation of Quayle's National Guard service and raised a flurry of other allegation, including unsubstantiated charges that Quayle had smoked marijuana and engaged in academic cheating while a student at DePauw. The press even resurrected "a counterfeit, dead-and-buried episode" hinting that the youthful senator had cheated on his wife and been involved with "party girl/lobbyist" Parla Parkinson."[34]

The press had inadvertently become part of the story. With its own objectivity now under attack, the press gave less emphasis to the Quayle affair. For the rest of the campaign, the Republican handlers did their best to hide Quayle, having him speak only in safe states and in secondary media markets where he would not draw a large press following.

Dukakis did not quickly respond to Bush's negative campaigning. He did not believe that the voters would be greatly influenced by charges he saw as so tangential to the presidency. However, by the time Dukakis finally responded, the Bush ads and themes had already defined the playing field for the campaign.

In an act of desperation, a series of Dukakis ads attempted to warn voters against being manipulated by the Bush ad team. These spots portrayed a group of well-dressed, professional Republican campaign consultants discussing how they purposely twisted and distorted Dukakis's record. In one of the ads a younger consultant asks, "How long do you expect to get away with this?" The obviously senior consultant replies by calling out, "How long to the election, Bernie?" They cynically laugh. While the ads were good theater, they were too complex and confusing to have any real impact on voters. Viewers only casually glancing at their television sets would not even know if they were watching a Bush or a Dukakis campaign ad.[35] Furthermore, the ads offered no convincing reasons for people to vote for Dukakis.

Dukakis finally appeared in other ads saying "I'm sick of it"—regarding distortions contained in the Republican spots. Bush ads retorted that it was Dukakis who was distorting the truth.

THE DEBATES: ONE LAST CHANCE

The spirits of the Dukakis campaign were briefly revived during the vice-presidential debate in which Democrat Lloyd Bentsen appeared eminently more distinguished and presidential than Quayle. When, in responding to a question, Quayle observed that he had as much experience as John Kennedy when Kennedy was elected president, Bentsen went for the jugular with a sound bite that was picked up by virtually every news program across the nation: "Senator, I served with Jack Kennedy. Jack Kennedy was a friend of mine. Senator, you're no Jack Kennedy." Democratic ads played on the public's fears of having Quayle only a heartbeat away from the presidency.

For all intents and purposes, the last chance for Dukakis came down to the final televised debate. He had to carry the attack to Bush. He would have to give Americans a clear reason to vote for him. And he would have to dispel voter perceptions of him as overly dispassionate and distant; a cool and detached robot.

Unfortunately for Dukakis, his chance came to an end in his answer to the first question, put to him by CNN reporter Bernard Shaw: "If Kitty Dukakis were raped and murdered, would you favor an irrevocable death penalty for the killer?" Dukakis answered the question in legalistic fashion by repeating his opposition to capital punishment and pointing to alternative crime control measures. He did not mention his wife, Kitty, in his answer. Nor did he respond with any visible emotion to the hypothetical situation of seeing his wife raped and murdered. Many voters need to see their president as a warm and caring human being. Dukakis's answer came across as cold, almost inhuman. He had compounded his image problem. Nor did he appear "tough" on crime.

On election day, Bush won handily, carrying forty states to a 426 to 112 electoral-vote victory. The only rays of hope for presidential Democrats were that, despite having run an inept campaign, their candidate did better than expected in holding Bush to 54 percent of the popular vote. The Democrats also did fairly well in the upper Midwest and the West, regions that had not been very kind to the Democrats in recent presidential elections. In these regions Dukakis won Iowa, Wisconsin, Minnesota, Washington, and Oregon; he also made good showings in Michigan, Ohio, Illinois, Missouri, and California.

In Congress, the Democrats did even better. The strength of incumbency and the rise of split-ticket voting acted to insulate incumbents against any presidential trend. Bush had virtually no coattails. He not only failed to bring new Republican legislators into office with him; Republicans actually lost one Senate and three House seats.[36]

THE ISSUES IN 1988: WHAT VOTING STUDIES SHOW

Dramatic televised images dominated the fall election. Yet, the choice presented voters was not simply one of competing personal images. Americans were able to distinguish meaningful differences between the candidates in 1988. As Paul Abramson, John Aldrich, and David Rohde note in introducing their extensive data analysis of the 1988 campaign:

> Clearly, the election offered policy alternatives, and as we shall see, voters saw clear policy differences between Bush and Dukakis. Although voters could not reelect Reagan, they could vote to continue his policies. Electing Dukakis would not overturn Reagan's reforms, but it would clearly lead to major revisions. Americans could also vote to support the traditional values espoused by Bush or the more liberal views advanced by Dukakis.[37]

Abramson and his colleagues report that voters were able to distinguish differences between the candidates on issues in 1988, more so than in several other contemporary presidential elections. Voters could even see differences when it came to prospective issues, what the candidates promised to do in the future. And 62 percent voted for the candidate they saw to be closer to them on the issues,[38] leading to the conclusion "that prospective issues were quite important in the 1988 election, but they cannot account for Bush's victory."[39] Citizens also cast ballots retrospectively to continue the general policy directions of the Reagan administration.

Issues were important in 1988. Martin Wattenberg has shown performance evaluations to be more important than policy issues in determining the 1988 vote. Yet, in examining voter responses to the open-ended questions of the National Election Study, Wattenberg also found that voters gave five issues prominent mention—crime, abortion, taxes, a weak military position, and liberal ideology—in explaining why they voted against Dukakis.[40]

Perhaps of most importance are the works of J. David Gopoian, J. Merrill Shanks, and Warren Miller analyzing the extensive survey data yielded by the 1988 National Election Study. Gopoian found that issue voters outnumbered image voters in 1992, that image and personal quality assessments were not as crucial to the election's outcome as the conventional wisdom would have us believe. Despite the negative Republican campaign and contrary to the conventional wisdom, Dukakis even enjoyed a slight edge among image voters. Had the election been decided on the basis of voter assessment of candidate's leadership traits, Bush would have lost.[41] Issue voters, especially voters who objected to Democratic welfarism and redistributional spending, provided Bush with his decisive edge. Bush's attack on Democratic liberalism, the "L-word," succeeded in defining the issue arena for the 1988 election.

Shanks and Miller confirm that the 1988 election was decided by policy considerations, not personal images. Bush's election was the product of the voters' choice of policy directions coupled with a retrospective endorsement of the performance of the Reagan administration. Voters expressed a high level of agreement with the policy of the previous eight years. However, some new sense of economic insecurity cut the Republican margin of victory in 1988 as compared to 1984.[42]

Bush was given a substantial edge by voters in terms of his ability to handle crime. But Dukakis enjoyed a favorable edge when it came to management of the environment.[43] Apparently the Willie Horton and the revolving door ad worked, yet the Boston Harbor proved far less persuasive. The message of the Boston Harbor ad was muted by alternative sources of information that voters had regarding the Republican administration's environmental record.

Contrary to the popular commentary at the time of the election, it was not personal image evaluations that lost the race for Dukakis. Despite the comments of political pundits, Dukakis did not come across as a "cold fish." Instead, survey evidence shows that he was well received in personal terms and was rated just about the same as Bush when it came to personal characteristics and leadership traits.[44] Directional and retrospective voting, not personal imagery, determined the outcome in 1988.

THE ISSUES WERE IN THE ADS

The importance of issues can be denied only by critics who consider crime, the Pledge of Allegiance, and welfarism to be only matters of secondary importance that diverted voter attention away from the more pressing concerns of the day. These critics charge that the voters ignored the real issues—important issues like the deficit and the savings and loan bailout—while focusing on phony issues concocted by campaign strategists.

Yet, it is elitist for self-proclaimed experts to assume that they know just what issues voters should have focused on in an election. For many voters, crime and redistribution issues were more pressing matters than was the subject of the mounting budget deficit. Other Americans were concerned with maintaining a strong and vigilant position of national defense. Other voters, still, were concerned with the patriotism inherent in the Pledge debate. Candidates can only successfully push those concerns that citizens are willing to see as issues. It is worth repeating Jean Bethke Elshtain's observation that "[v]oters and candidates are co-constructors of issues." As Elshtain goes on to explain: "To claim, then, that candidates are trafficking in nonissues because they immerse themselves in weighty symbolism is to presume that which does not exist—a clear-cut division between the symbolic and the real, between issues and emotional appeals."[45]

The policy area of criminal justice cannot be dismissed as irrelevant or of only secondary importance when choosing a president. The president appoints an attorney general and sets the nation's law enforcement posture. He helps to determine the priorities and budgets of law enforcement agencies. He also nominates Supreme Court justices. Over time, the president thereby indirectly helps to determine the permissibility of certain law enforcement procedures and even the constitutionality of the death penalty.

Of course, the candidates did not offer the voters clear policy choices in all areas. Bush's promise to be the environmental president and the education president blurred any voter perceptions of stark policy differences in these areas. When it came to child care, Dukakis promised expanded grants-in-aid for child care while Bush offered a program of tax credits. The difference was lost on most voters. Both candidates also failed to detail plans for reducing the budget deficit. Bush's call for a "flexible freeze" on federal spending was especially vague. Still, there was one policy area in which there was a basic difference. Bush was adamant in opposing new taxes; Dukakis was more equivocal.

The candidates were clearly distinguishable in other areas besides taxes. Dukakis was pro-abortion; Bush was pro-life. Voters could also discern a choice on national defense, as Barbara

Farah and Ethel Klein underscore in reviewing public opinion trends:

> Bush's lead was based on values implicit in keeping America strong, rather than on a policy of increased militarism . . . . Voters withdrew their support from Dukakis because they feared he would weaken the nation's defenses. Nothing in the Dukakis campaign made voters think that he would keep America strong. Instead, what voters heard about were all the weapon systems that the Democrat would get rid of and the inexperience of Dukakis in dealing with other nations . . . . Two weeks before the general election, 41 percent agreed that Dukakis would weaken national security.[46]

Bush had used his Republican convention speech to clarify the choice offered voters when it came to international action in world affairs: "He [Dukakis] sees America as another pleasant country in the U.N. roll call, somewhere between Albania and Zimbabwe. And I see America as leader, the unique nation with a special role in the world." Bush continued, "Strength and clarity lead to peace; weakness and ambivalence lead to war." Bush was describing a clarity of vision that would lead him as president to use force in Panama and the Persian Gulf. When it came to international affairs, Bush and Dukakis had offered Americans an extremely important choice of action orientations.

The Tank Ride ad further served to distinguish Bush from Dukakis on the issue of national defense. The ad cited the governor's opposition to numerous weapons systems. Dukakis's camp cried that the ad was deceptive in that the Democratic candidate did indeed support a number of weapons systems.

Kathleen Hall Jamieson argues that the Tank Ride ad not only distorted facts but actually impeded rational discussion of the issues at hand. The ad only tells voters what weapons systems Dukakis is against, not what weapons systems Bush supports. Nor does the ad identify just which of the weapons systems it lists are necessary and worth the cost. After the election, Bush abolished two of the weapons systems that the ad attacked Dukakis for opposing! Further, the ad does not allow the public to evaluate the relative merits of Dukakis's proposal to strengthen America's reliance on conventional weaponry, including tanks, as an alternative to the Republican administration's build-up of nuclear weapons. Instead of fairly discussing the competing Republican and Democratic positions, the spot reduces Dukakis's military proposals to a simplistic "weak on defense." Reporting of the controversy followed the reductionist shorthand of the ad.

Political pundits interpreted the Dukakis tank ride as a tactical gimmick used by the Democrats in an attempt to compensate for their candidate's weakness on defense. The overgeneralizations and reductionism inspired by the Tank Ride ad crowded out any meaningful discussion of the United States's changing defense needs.[47]

Yet, despite the factual and rhetorical shortcomings of the ad, the Tank Ride spot does succeed in communicating a basic difference between the candidates on an issue of importance to voters. As the ad reveals, Dukakis was less disposed than Bush to continue high levels of defense spending. This in and of itself is an important difference. Voters are not Pentagon analysts who are equipped to evaluate the relative merits and costs of individual weapons systems. Yet these voters wanted to be assured that the United States would continue to maintain its military preparedness and command respect abroad. Despite the relative merits and demerits of any specific weapons system, Dukakis's lesser inclination than Bush to spend on military weaponry rendered him suspect in this critical area of voter concern.

Crime was another area where differences between the candidates were easily perceived. Bush supported the death penalty; Dukakis did not. Marjorie Randon Hershey, who as we earlier observed is underwhelmed by the level of issue discussion in 1988, has admitted that broad, general differences in orientations could be observed in the field of crime: "Ads featuring Willie Horton and the ACLU did suggest that George Bush associated himself with a different vision of crime and punishment than did Michael Dukakis."[48]

Overall, important differences between the candidates did emerge in 1988. Even *Washington Post* journalist Paul Taylor, who is otherwise so critical of the "mediaocracy" evident in the 1988 election, concludes that voter preferences had a lot to do with the election's outcome: "[T]he voters in fact wanted a great many contradictory things (more services *and* lower taxes, for example) and by the time they weighed them all, the rational choice was George Bush."[49]

Taylor continues, "in a video-literate society" citizens "know how to cut through what Key called the 'buncombe' of campaigns."[50] In 1988, the media campaign gave voters reasons why they should vote for or reject a candidate. Even in the 1988 primaries, George Bush's comeback in New Hampshire was due to his clear stance on the tax issue: His stern opposition to new taxes contrasted with Robert Dole's more vacillating position on the matter.

In the fall election, the candidates continued to offer the voters a choice of direction in several policy areas. Bush, for instance, staked out his opposition to the ill effects of government over-regulation of business. Dukakis, in contrast, pointed to the necessity of workplace regulation. Dukakis specifically contrasted his support of legislation requiring a business to give workers a sixty-day notice in case of a plant closing with Bush's vote against such a measure. One Dukakis ad showed pictures of Bush and Quayle with the word "NO" stamped across the words "60 Days' Notice of Plant Closings?" The spot ended with the narrator declaring that, "The choice is clear." The ad underscored the clear and contrasting specific stands that the candidates had taken on the issue.

Another Dukakis spot used the visual of a young man of college age tossing dough in a pizza parlor. This young man could have attended college, but, as the narrator in the ad informs viewers, the Republican administration had cut student loans for working-class families. Dukakis, on the other hand, promised a new college loan program to ensure that any student could afford to go to college. Even without spelling out the specifics of the proposed loan program, this ad was an issue ad. It informed voters of the contrasting policy directions offered by the candidates.

In the closing days of the campaign, Dukakis clearly and unabashedly laid out the choice before voters. In the "On Your Side" ads, Dukakis spoke directly into the camera and asked:

> On the things that matter most to you, who do you trust to be on your side? We know where Mr. Bush stands. He wants to cut taxes by $30,000 a year for the wealthiest one percent of this nation. He's on their side. I want to see us teach our children, and house our homeless, and care for our elderly, and ask once again what we can do for our country and not just ourselves.

A clear choice of policy orientations was at stake in 1988 but was missed by critics who expected more: that election campaigns would present voters with a dialogue on the relative merits of detailed policy proposals. No contemporary major national American campaign can meet such a rigid test. Only broader choices are at stake in an election. If voters in 1988 were not quite offered specific formulations on each issue, they were presented with a basic choice of policy directions or values.[51]

RETROSPECTIVE VOTING IN 1988

Even where prospective issues were avoided, the Republicans raised questions of retrospective judgment and evaluation. In ad after ad they asked voters if they wanted to continue the policies of the past administration that had brought peace and prosperity, the nation's longest period of economic expansion. Apparently the voters did.

Democratic claims that the Republicans had purchased this prosperity only at the cost of an outrageous national debt that had mortgaged the future of America's children fell on deaf ears. Martin Wattenberg's study of presidential approval ratings in 1988 found that the public's performance assessment of the economy and national security were the most important factors in explaining Reagan's popularity. Attitudes toward the national debt did not seem to greatly affect the public's attitude toward Reagan: "People apparently cared little about a balanced budget as long as the state of the nation remained healthy."[52] Even though many voters saw the deficit as an important problem, they continued to feel that the Republican Party, not the Democrats, would do a better job in handling this issue in the future.[53]

Bush won not just because he had the better advertising team but also because he had the better message; he had the broad issue themes that best fit the times. Had the nature of the times been different, a quite different set of issues and images would likely have dominated the election. Four years later, a prolonged recession would raise a quite different set of issues and images, and the themes that Bush used so capably in 1988 would not work to gain him reelection.

Performance evaluations were key to explaining Bush's success in 1988 and his subsequent defeat in 1992. Voters in the candidate-centered age have an increased tendency to base their evaluations on short-term results, especially on results that are economic in nature. Bush won in 1988 despite voter disagreement with him in a number of policy areas. As Wattenberg writes, in the 1980s "many voters were torn between the candidate they thought would adopt the best policies and the candidate they thought would perform better."[54] In 1988 the public's attitudes toward Bush were determined more by performance evaluations than by policy concerns.[55]

ASSESSING NEGATIVE ADVERTISING IN 1988

There is a disturbing note in the 1988 campaign. It goes beyond charges of racism implicit in the Willie Horton issue. It even goes beyond the alienation of citizens from the electoral process that has been exacerbated by the seemingly endless exchange of unsubstantiated allegations and personal attacks. The most troubling note of the 1988 campaign stems not from the negative nature of much of the campaigning but from the distortions in the ads that undermined the ability of citizens to use elections as instruments of policy control and government accountability.

Communications expert Kathleen Hall Jamieson and other critics have scored the serious deceptions inherent in political advertising. Jamieson is particularly scornful of the erroneous impressions purposely left by such ads as the Revolving Door spot. The Revolving Door spot gives viewers the impression that, during Dukakis's term in office, many murderers and dangerous prisoners escaped and that many are still at large. In fact, only four of the 268 escapees were first-degree murderers; and fewer than one percent of the convicts on furlough escaped. She further observes that the audience at home views such ads from the conventions of entertainment television, with the tendency to "suspend disbelief and all critical acuity."[56] Viewers tend to uncritically accept staged showings as representations of reality.

The Revolving Door ad clearly contains intentionally misleading inferences. The setting is also unreal. Paid actors go in and out of a door in a prison that, as Jamieson notes, is actually in Utah, not Massachusetts. The revolving door itself is a stage prop. But all this really is of little import. The ad effectively portrays candidate differences in policy orientations in an area that many Americans deemed to be of great importance.

Nor could Dukakis's supporters successfully decry that the ad was misleading in that it blamed Dukakis for a furlough program that had in fact been enacted by his Republican predecessor. The furlough program, they point out, was also later repealed. They also charge that a large number of convicts on furlough had escaped from federal prisons during the Reagan-Bush administration. The Dukakis campaign made these arguments, belatedly, in ads of its own. The voters simply were not convinced. Dukakis was a progressive on penal matters, and the voters did not want a progressive in this issue area.

As governor, Dukakis had commuted the life sentences of twenty-eight murderers.[57] He had shown little inclination to curtail

Massachusetts' furlough program, even in the immediate wake of the Willie Horton episode. The furlough program was repealed not as a result of the governor's actions but by the state legislature in response to a public referendum. There was a basic difference between Bush's and Dukakis's orientations toward criminal justice. The Revolving Door ad underscored this difference. So did Dukakis's intellectual but weak response in refusing to endorse the death penalty even when asked what he would do if his wife had been raped and murdered.

Negative ads can provide information that helps citizens to distinguish candidates' issue positions and dispositions. Attack campaigning is not intrinsically bad. Of course, like positive ads, negative ads tell only part of the story, the part that the candidate wants voters to know. An opponent in turn has the opportunity to present ads that offer competing facts and interpretations and tell the other side of the story. The voters can then choose.

Electioneering by its nature entails the partial or one-sided representation of arguable claims. Virtually all political advertising—pamphlets, broadsides, partisan speeches, public addresses, print ads, radio ads, and television spots—contain distortions. No candidate admits weaknesses or discloses countervailing facts that can be used against his arguments or policy positions.

But positive ads can deceive just as well as negative ads. For instance, in 1988 one Republican ad clearly overclaimed the vice president's role in arms control. The narrator informs television viewers that "It was George Bush who led the way" in signing the 1988 arms reduction treaty. An informed follower of public affairs would have to wonder at this rewriting of history. Just what role did President Reagan play in opposing arms reductions agreements for so long before finally, later during his term in office, negotiating this treaty? It was President Reagan, not Vice-President Bush, whose actions determined the nation's policy in this critical area.

More serious distortions occur when a candidate or his or her handlers misrepresent events to mislead voters in attempting to escape the political consequences of unpopular actions. The most blatant distortion in the 1988 campaign involved not the Willie Horton and Revolving Door ads but Bush's Boston Harbor ad. The Boston Harbor spot implied that Dukakis bore responsibility for the toxicity of the city's filthy harbor. Dukakis's administrative incapacities in failing to clean up the harbor were certainly fair target for a Republican attack. But it was the Reagan administration, not the Dukakis administration, that had the poorer environmental record, especially in the area of pollution control. It was the Republican administration in Washington that had sought to relax the enforcement of environmental protection statutes and free business from some of the harmful effects of regulation.[58]

The power of the Boston Harbor ad results from its deceptive use of visuals. The ad was shot on a drizzly, dreary day that made the water in the harbor look worse. An open pipe that dribbled waste into the harbor looked more offensive in sloweddown, stop-frame treatment. The sign that read "Danger/Radiation Hazard/No Swimming" had been left over from a long-closed submarine base.[59]

The ad succeeded on two levels. It inoculated Bush in an issue area that, because of the Reagan administration's record, had been a political soft spot for Republicans. By pinning the blame for the lack of pollution enforcement on Dukakis, the ad also questioned Dukakis's record on the environment and his managerial capacities as governor.

Later in the campaign, Dukakis would counter that it was the Republican administration that had undercut effective pollution control. But his response was too little, too late. By then, the image of a sickly Boston Harbor had been fixed in the public's mind.

Taxation is another issue area where it can be argued that deceptive rhetoric undercut the ability of voters to use elections as instruments of policy control. In 1990, only two years into his presidency, Bush retreated from his vow against new taxes. He had opposed new taxes throughout his first year in office, but now he approved an agreement negotiated with congressional leaders that called for tax increases to help balance the budget.

If Bush knew during his 1988 campaign that the mounting national debt would eventually force a tax increase, then his nonew-tax vow was deceptive. On the other hand, Bush as president had opposed a number of proposals for new taxation. His midterm change on the issue can be seen as a necessary adjustment to the demands of governance in the face of changing fiscal and political realities. Presidents need to be flexible; to be able to learn in office.

In the New Hampshire primary, Bush had used the Straddle ad to skewer Bob Dole on the tax issue. Dole was fresh from his victory in Iowa. Bush's victory in New Hampshire ended the momentum of the Dole campaign and changed the contours of the 1988 Republican nominating race. In 1990, just two years after the New Hampshire contest, Dole as Senate Minority Leader was asked by President Bush to help round up votes for a budget package that contained tax increases. One can only wonder what Dole felt.

SUMMARY

The 1988 election shows the ability of modern political handlers to manufacture carefully constructed and powerful symbolic images. The ability of the Bush paid-media effort to define the campaign dialogue was especially effective because the Dukakis campaign did not initially choose to challenge the claims advanced by the Bush campaign.

Yet, it is too easy to see the 1988 election solely as a battle of professional image merchants. Retrospective performance evaluations were prominently related to the vote in 1988. Voters could also discern important policy differences between the candidates. Indeed, the paid media effort, including the negative ads, helped voters to discern the competing action orientations of Bush and Dukakis in such issue areas as crime and defense spending. Negative ads provided the voters with information. The informational value of certain negative ads, however, was diminished by the distortions contained in those ads.

1992: "IT'S THE ECONOMY, STUPID."

In 1992, the presidential candidates appealed to voters through various entertainment programs and other non-traditional media forums. Larry King Live, Arsenio Hall, Oprah, Donahue, and MTV were only the most notable of the many entertainment shows that hosted the candidates. In his appearance on Arsenio Hall, Clinton donned sunglasses and played the saxophone. His appearance was a triumph, despite pundits at the time who cried, quite incorrectly, that Clinton would never again be taken seriously as a potential president. Eventually, even President Bush, who had earlier spurned such appearances as demeaning to his presidential stature, accepted invitations to appear on Larry King Live and other talk shows.

The nation's prolonged economic slump was the dominant issue in 1992. The public was concerned with the health of the economy, not Clinton's personal history or George Bush's foreign policy experience and successes. Some observers argue that, objectively, the condition of the national economy was not all that bleak; while growth had stagnated, unemployment rates were not that severe, and certain indicators pointed to the beginning of a recovery. Still, if the recession was not deep, it was deep enough for most voters; and it seemed to go on forever. The media focused on the nation's slow economic growth, not the more complex story inherent in the mix of economic indicators. By his own actions and statements, Bush only contributed to the public perception that he was not taking the economy seriously.[1]

Bill Clinton won despite personal allegations and image problems that would have sunk most presidential campaigns. Had voters been concerned only with personal character, Clinton in all likelihood would have lost. But the nation's focus was on issues—the economy and domestic policy—not on the personal. Performance evaluations and issue concerns determined the outcome of the 1992 election. The sign above master strategist James Carville's desk at Clinton's Little Rock campaign headquarters pointed to the number one issue and the focus of Clinton's strategy in 1992: "It's the economy, stupid."

THE NEW-STYLE MEDIA CAMPAIGN OF 1992

The new-style television campaigning of 1992 has received much criticism. In both talk shows and citizen town meetings broadcast during air time purchased by a campaign, candidates respond directly to voters' and interviewers' questions with stock, rehearsed answers. In such forums, candidates appear responsive. Yet, candidates risk very little inasmuch as they are able to circumvent more established news shows where professional news reporters, armed with background research, can ask tougher questions. Talk show host Larry King admits to being not a political expert but an interviewer-entertainer whose job it is to hold the interest of his audience. Call-in shows and televised town meetings (initially popularized by Ross Perot) fail to provide adequate opportunity for follow-up questions or a sustained probe of a candidate's views in any one area; the subject quickly shifts from one topic to whatever else is raised by the next caller.

But the fears of "mediaocracy" are largely misplaced. The new-style campaigning of 1992 offered voters substance as well as images. Candidate debates, televised town meetings, and the call-in interview shows all offered voters new opportunities to view the candidates. The campaign was brought to the people. During the seemingly endless series of debates and candidate forums during the Democratic primaries and the fall election, citizens as well as reporters had the opportunity to bring their concerns directly into the election process.

Rather than detracting from the political debate, the call-in talk shows and televised town meetings actually contributed to the public dialogue in 1992. These new formats allowed citizens to raise their concern over crime and other issues that were to a great extent overlooked by professional news reporters and commentators. The call-in talk shows also gave the candidates an extended opportunity to present their domestic programs to the public. Talk show hosts like Phil Donahue could also ask tough and embarrassing questions—although at times their questions were highly personal, not policy oriented. Candidate forums and call-in talk shows constituted "user-friendly news formats" that allowed voters to frame the questions, thereby adding to voter understanding of the general policy orientations of the candidates. While the more conventional news media continued to focus more on the horse race and strategic aspects of the presidential contest, the nontraditional media forums allowed candidates to elaborate their substantive positions.[2]

A study of Bill Clinton's talk show appearances from June 2 to July 22 reveals that viewer questions focused not on the personal but on issues, particularly domestic policy issues. In his answers, Clinton offered fairly detailed policy information. The talk shows allowed Clinton to convey his substantive message to voters at a time when his campaign themes were largely ignored by a press focused on the strategic aspects of the presidential race during the postconvention period.[3]

Earlier in the election year, the press had reported Bill Clinton's alleged extramarital involvements, pursuing an unsubstantiated story that first appeared in a supermarket tabloid. They also focused on how Clinton as a student avoided the military draft—a story that would return during the closing stages of the fall election. The call-in shows allowed voters to steer the public dialogue away from the personal charges and back toward domestic policy concerns.

Another innovation in the 1992 race was the use of television commercials to direct viewers to more detailed statements of a candidate's issue positions. Beginning in New Hampshire, Bill Clinton and Paul Tsongas used television commercials to direct voters to read booklets that elaborated their plans for America in unprecedented detail. Clinton's "A Plan for America's Future" and Tsongas's 86-page "A Call to Economic Arms" were widely distributed to voters. Copies were also placed in local libraries. In the general election, even the incumbent president of the United States, George Bush, had to issue a booklet of his own in an effort to convince voters that he had a concrete plan for America's economic recovery. But the Bush plan was quite sketchy and vague as contrasted to the more specific proposals spelled out in the Clinton and especially in the Tsongas booklets.

THE DEMOCRATIC RACE

The Emergence of a "New Democrat"

In the wake of the February 1991 Gulf War, George Bush's job rating soared to a stratospheric 90 percent public approval. With the president's reelection seemingly preordained, none of the often-mentioned Democratic "heavyweights"—Lloyd Bensten, Richard Gephardt, Bill Bradley, Al Gore, Sam Nunn—were willing to take the necessary steps toward candidacy. New York Governor Mario Cuomo, too, was hesitant to enter the race. He had criticized the war. He also did not know if he had the "fire in the belly" to make the arduous national campaign. Suddenly, the presidential field was open to lesser-known Democrats who in other years would have had little chance at the nomination.

Paul Tsongas, the former senator from Massachusetts, was the first to enter the race. He foresaw an economic downturn and reasoned that Bush's popularity would quickly tumble. Tsongas ran on a program that emphasized the urgency of economic restructuring. As president, he would declare an "economic emergency" and implement far-sweeping changes. Tsongas's budget-cutting and economic revitalization plans included such controversial measures as greater reliance on nuclear energy, an increase of up to 50 cents in the tax on gasoline, and reduced Social Security benefits for better-off recipients. Tsongas also attempted to make a virtue out of his lack of media charisma; his somber tone seemingly underscored the seriousness of his message.

Iowa Senator Tom Harkin emphasized a return to old-fashioned liberalism to correct growing inequalities of the Reagan-Bush era. But the voters were not receptive to Harkin's seeming embrace of big government. Another candidate, fiscally conservative Virginia Governor Douglas Wilder, failed to articulate a clear message or organize a serious national campaign effort and withdrew before the first primary.

Nebraska Senator Bob Kerrey attempted a new generational appeal similar to that of Gary Hart in 1984. Kerrey announced his candidacy to the music of Bruce Springsteen's "Born in the U.S.A.," but his early campaign lacked focus. Showing no movement in the polls, Kerrey changed his media consultants. His new television commercials in New Hampshire centered on the promise of national health care. But Kerrey's promise failed to distinguish him from the other Democrats, all of whom were promising a national health plan.

The media firm of Doak, Schrum, Harris, Sherman, and Donlon briefly revived Kerrey's flagging campaign in New Hampshire with a 30-second spot that showed Kerrey talking tough on trade while standing before a net on an indoor hockey rink: "Other nations guard their goal to keep products out while we leave our net wide open." But Tsongas effectively countered Kerrey's message by charging the Nebraskan with simplistic Japan-bashing. One Tsongas ad charged that "others just blame the Japanese" while Tsongas seeks to enact the tough measures necessary to restore the United States's international competitiveness. Only late in the campaign did Kerrey's ads finally emphasize his attractive biography: as a Navy Seal in Vietnam, Kerrey had lost a leg and won the Congressional Medal of Honor. But by that time, momentum had already bypassed Kerrey.

The absence of the Democratic heavyweights offered Bill Clinton a unique chance in 1992. Without Bradley and Gore in the race, Clinton would not have to share the votes of moderates with other more centrist candidates. Especially in the races on Super Tuesday in the South, Clinton would not have to divide the region's more moderate vote with Gore. With Jesse Jackson choosing to sit out the race, Clinton was also able to pick up the votes of African-Americans, especially in his native South. Further, Clinton's national connections meant that he was the only Democrat in the reduced field who had a substantial campaign war chest and national organizational base.

Clinton ran as a "new Democrat" committed to a program of middle-class populism. Like Tom Harkin and former California Governor Jerry Brown, still another of the Democratic presidential hopefuls, Clinton appealed to the public's resentment of the growing inequalities of the Reagan-Bush era.[4] But unlike his two more liberal rivals, Clinton stressed policy provisions and programs that appealed to a middle-class constituency, not just to party liberals, the poor, and racial minorities. Clinton promised a middle-class tax cut, a two-year limit on welfare, and a program of national health protection for those who faced rising premiums and those who risked the loss of health coverage when they switched jobs. Clinton affirmed his support of the death penalty; as governor of Arkansas, he refused to intervene and stop the execution of a prisoner. At a progressive conference dominated by labor unions, he was booed by the audience when he refused to promise that as president he would lead the fight to repeal the right-to-work provisions of the Taft-Hartley law. At a conference sponsored by Jesse Jackson, Clinton publicly criticized rap singer Sister Souljah for her remarks that blacks should take a week off from killing each other and kill whites instead. Throughout the campaign, he kept his distance from Jackson. But in many other ways, Clinton was a new southerner who appeared natural and genuine in his visits to black churches and the African-American community.

Clinton's "new Democrat" approach was more than just a facile manipulation of campaign imagery. It represented his philosophy of government, a philosophy that was rooted in the predominantly southern Democratic Leadership Council (DLC), which Clinton chaired. The DLC was an organization dedicated to steering the Democratic party back to a more moderate, less ideologically liberal, political philosophy. The DLC sought to redefine the policy goals, ideology, and "identity" of the Democratic party.[5] The DLC provided the Clinton campaign with its philosophical impetus as well as its early organizational muscle. Contrary to Paul Tsongas's charges that Clinton was a "pander bear" who constantly shifted his views to accommodate public opinion, Clinton throughout the campaign reiterated the middle-class oriented policy positions that he had been taking for a number of years.[6]

As the Democratic field conceded the Iowa caucuses to home state Senator Tom Harkin, the New Hampshire primary was the first important contest in 1992. Clinton campaign strategists sought to deliver a programmatic message in New Hampshire. They believed that voters were becoming increasingly resistant to political campaigns based on 30-second promises and sound bites. Their first commercial in New Hampshire was designed to do something different from the usual political spot; in it, Clinton offered voters a "plan" to turn the economy around.[7] As if to underscore the appearance of substance, the ad was 60-seconds in length, twice as long as the usual political spot. Clinton spoke directly to voters without the assistance of sophisticated visuals:

CLINTON PLAN ad:

VIDEO: Clinton, wearing a dark jacket and red tie, is perched atop an office desk in front of an American flag. As he speaks directly into the camera, the identification line "Gov. Bill Clinton" appears on the bottom of the screen.

AUDIO (Clinton): "The people of New Hampshire know better than anyone America's in trouble, our people are really hurting. In the eighties, the rich got richer, the middle class declined, poverty exploded, politicians in Washington raised their pay and pointed their finger, but no one took responsibility. It's time we had a president who cares, who takes responsibility, who has a plan for change."

VIDEO: As the camera moves in for a close-up, writing on the bottom of the screen reads: "For a copy of the plan, call (603) 668-1992 or visit your local library."

AUDIO (Clinton): "I'm Bill Clinton. And I believe that you deserve more than 30-second ads and vague promises. That's why I've offered a comprehensive plan to get our economy moving again, to take care of our own people and regain our economic leadership. It starts with a tax cut for the middle class and asks the rich to pay their fair share again. It includes national health insurance, a major investment in education, training for our workers, tough trade laws, and no more tax breaks for corporations to move our jobs overseas. Take a look at our plan and let me know what you think."

VIDEO: At the bottom of the screen: "Join Us. (603) 668-1992."

AUDIO (Clinton): "I hope you'll join us in this crusade for change. Together we can put government back on the side of the forgotten middle class and restore the American dream."

AUDIO (Announcer): "Paid for by Clinton for President."

The Clinton Plan ad is neither a pure image ad nor a pure issue ad. Instead, it mixes both image and substance. On the one hand, the plan ad seemingly provides only the appearance of moving beyond glib, image advertising. The ad gives viewers no detail as to how Clinton proposes to reach and pay for his broad policy goals. Yet, such criticism understates the thematic content that is in the ad. The ad provides a clear indication of Clinton's middle-class populism, an approach that offers a competing direction to the liberalism of Harkin and Cuomo and the harsher economic prescriptions of Tsongas. The Plan ad and similar Clinton ads also tie in to more specific issue appeals; they offer voters the opportunity to find out the details of Clinton's proposals. Clinton media adviser Frank Greer claims that by the end of the campaign in New Hampshire, the campaign had received over 15,000 phone calls and requests for copies of the plan. An abbreviated copy of the plan was also sent to virtually every registered Democrat in the state and, as has already been noted, was placed in local libraries.

But as the New Hampshire primary date neared, the Clinton campaign was pummelled by the extensive media coverage given to allegations that Clinton, during his tenure as governor, had committed adultery by sleeping with former local news reporter and cabaret performer Gennifer Flowers. The allegations first appeared in *The Star,* a supermarket tabloid that paid Flowers for her story. More responsible media at first attempted to downplay the unverified allegations. *The New York Times* initially reported the story on the bottom of one of its inside pages. But the media could not resist the story for long.

Suffering politically, the Clinton campaign team decided to confront the charges head on. To maximize coverage given to their defense, Bill and Hillary Clinton chose to go on the popular CBS news magazine program "Sixty Minutes." Their "Sixty Minutes" appearance was in many ways a master stroke of image building. Throughout the interview, Bill and Hillary Clinton sat extremely close to each other, side by side. Hillary looked into Bill's face as he spoke. Their arms comfortably rested on each other's. Clinton denied allegations that he had a 12-year affair with Gennifer Flowers, but he refused to answer the question as to whether or not he has ever had an extramarital affair. Instead, the Clintons portrayed themselves as average Americans. They explained that they, like a great many Americans, have had troubled moments in their marriage, and that they have worked over the years to build their marriage. If a divorced person can become president, surely, Bill asserted, so can an individual who has overcome personal problems and kept a marriage together.

The Clintons further argued that no American should be put in the uncomfortable period of having to answer, in public, questions concerning the most private, aspects of his or her life:

"SIXTY MINUTES" interview (excerpt):

VIDEO: Bill and Hillary Clinton sit close together on a love seat by the fire in a hotel room. CBS reporter Steve Kroft sits directly across and asks questions.

AUDIO (Kroft): "I think that most Americans would agree that it's very admirable that you've stayed together, that you've worked your problems out, that you've seemed to reach some sort of understanding and an arrangement..."

VIDEO: Switch to a close-up of Bill Clinton as he interrupts.

AUDIO (Bill Clinton): "Wait a minute, wait a minute. You're looking at two people who love each other. This is not an arrangement or an understanding. This is a marriage. That's a very different thing."

VIDEO: Switch to close-up of Hillary Clinton. Pull the camera back to show Bill taking her hand and looking into her face as she speaks.

AUDIO (Hillary Clinton): "You know, I'm not sitting here as some little woman standing by my man like Tammy Wynette. I'm sitting here because I love him, and I honor what he's been through and what we've been through together. And, you know, if that's not good enough for people, then, heck, don't vote for him."

The loving-couple appearance of the Clintons stood in marked contrast to the obviously strained performance given four years earlier by Lee Hart when she was flown in to defend her husband Gary against charges of adultery.

The exaggerated coverage given the Gennifer Flowers allegation was a classic case of pack journalism. But as intense as the media coverage was, reporters soon retreated and renewed their focus on other aspects of the race. The norms governing media coverage of politics were in the process of changing in 1992. Reporters felt that emphasis should be placed on the political, not the personal. Reporters could not see the relevance of a story which, even if true, was part of the past. Reporters saw a Clinton affair as something quite different from the Gary Hart episode, where a presidential candidate almost seemed to court disaster by continuing an adulterous affair in the midst of the intensive media scrutiny of a presidential campaign. Reporters also felt guilty for having given such great play to a story run by a supermarket tabloid that did not abide by professional norms of objective reporting. To many of the reporters, Flowers's story had a false ring to it; Flowers had responded to a tabloid that had repeatedly offered money in an effort to find a woman who would admit to a past sexual liaison with Clinton.

Tsongas's early start and concentration of resources in New Hampshire helped produce his surprise victory. Still, Clinton's 25-percentage point, second-place finish was good enough to place him in serious contention. As the results were coming in, Clinton adeptly seized the media forum in an early evening speech to his supporters, providing the sound bite that helped shape the next day's news coverage. Having survived all his misfortunes, Clinton declared himself the "comeback kid."

The Democrats Get Nasty: A Battle of Issues

The New Hampshire results to a very great extent made the Democratic race a two-candidate affair. But Tsongas was short on resources as he sought to quickly mount a campaign in the state primaries that followed New Hampshire.

Tsongas's troubles, though, were substantive as well as financial. The Clinton campaign used focus groups to identify issues that they could profitably use against Tsongas. Their strategy in the races that followed New Hampshire was to contrast Clinton's "people first" message with the harshness of Tsongas's pro-business plan.[8] With Cuomo's refusal to enter the race, Clinton could emphasize how his plan, not Tsongas's, was more compatible with traditional Democratic party values: "I believe that you can have growth and fairness in this country."

As the race turned to Georgia and Maryland on Junior Tuesday, and then to Super Tuesday, both the free media and the paid media campaigns underscored the competing policy directions offered by the two leading Democrats. Clinton ads contrasted his middle-class prescriptions with the Republican-style "trickle-down economics" of Tsongas's "A Call to Economic Arms." Clinton ads castigated Tsongas's promise to be "the best friend Wall Street ever had." Clinton also attacked Tsongas for endorsing nuclear power, a 50-cent a gallon hike in the gas tax, and a reduction in the "capital gains tax for the rich" while opposing a tax cut for the middle class. Tsongas, in return, continued his assault on Clinton's "gimmick" and demagoguery of promising a middle-class tax cut at a time of high budget deficits.

In Florida, Clinton targeted issue appeals to that states' large number of retirees. Clinton ads attacked the "Tsongas Plan" for proposing a "Cut in cost of living adjustments for older Americans." The charge was technically true but invited misinterpretation. The ad seemingly implied that Tsongas threatened to cut Social Security benefits for a vast number of older Americans. Tsongas's proposal was, in fact, much narrower. Tsongas had said that he was "looking at" reducing benefits for retirees with incomes over $125,000. Left unsaid in the Clinton ads was the fact that Clinton, too, had proposed a similar alteration in entitlement benefits for the elderly; Clinton had said that he was considering having the well-to-do elderly pay a portion of their Medicare premium.

Clinton's issue-based attacks wounded Tsongas, who responded by stepping up his attacks against Clinton. The narrator of one 30-second political spot contrasts Tsongas's character to Clinton's: "He's no Bill Clinton, that's for sure. He's the exact opposite. Paul Tsongas, he's not afraid of the truth." By joining in the political fray, however, Tsongas sacrificed the moral high ground that he had occupied earlier in the campaign.

In primary after primary, a breakdown of Tsongas's supporters showed the limited nature of the senator's programmatic appeal. Tsongas drew his greatest support from upper-income and highly educated white-collar voters. Clinton, in contrast, received his strongest support from lesser-educated, blue-collar voters and African-Americans, voters who were less financially able to bear the sacrifice demanded by the Tsongas plan.[9] After his poor showing on Super Tuesday and in the Midwest, Tsongas effectively terminated his active candidacy.

Clinton's opposition for the rest of the primary season was provided by former California Governor Jerry Brown. After New Hampshire, Brown climbed back into the race with a victory in the Maine caucuses—a race that the other candidates for the most part chose to bypass—and Colorado. Days after Tsongas's virtual withdrawal, Brown won a dramatic victory in Connecticut. Brown was the only alternative available for Democrats hoping to stop a Clinton nomination.

In Michigan, Brown donned a union jacket to symbolize his solidarity with automobile workers dissatisfied with Clinton's failure to adhere to strict trade protectionism and pro-union orthodoxy. In other states, however, Brown's appeal was primarily to younger, college-educated constituencies attracted to his environmentalism and his campaign against America's elites. Brown's "take back America" campaign was directed against the entire political system corrupted by the influence accorded money and privileged interests. Brown refused big donations and initially announced that he would accept no more than $100 from any individual. He appealed for small-money contributions and announced his campaign's toll-free 800 number at every conceivable media opportunity.

Overall, however, Brown's message was not mainstream enough to draw wide support. As it had with Tsongas, the Clinton campaign again emphasized the policy differences between Clinton and his chief opponent. Clinton ads attacked the unfairness and regressivity of Brown's proposed 13-percent flat tax. In New York, Clinton commercials pointed to the havoc that Brown's flat tax proposal might wreak on the financing of Social Security.[10] Clinton sewed up the nomination well in advance of the party's national convention.

RE-TOOLING FOR THE GENERAL ELECTION

The 1992 presidential campaign was "the most aggressively 'focus grouped' ever."[11] The various candidates' efforts used focus groups as well as opinion polls to refine candidate images and hone substantive messages.

As the primary season came to an end, attitudinal research conducted by Mandy Grunwald and Stan Greenberg in the Clinton campaign showed that Clinton suffered a serious image problem. The public deduced from the schools Clinton attended—Georgetown, Oxford, and Yale—that he had lived a privileged life. The Clinton campaign needed to correct this misperception; otherwise he would be less successful in casting himself as the "people's" candidate against an uncaring, aristocratic George Bush. Further, in the fall, the Republicans would capitalize on any public's resentment against the perception of Clinton as a spoiled, elite liberal. Earlier biographic ads, which had informed viewers that Clinton had worked his way through college, obviously had been insufficient to counter the candidate's image problem. The Clinton media campaign would have to communicate the candidate's personal story more visually and dramatically.

Clinton strategists used the national convention as the focal point of their effort to paint Clinton as a common man who had worked hard to overcome adversity.[12] The humanizing of Bill Clinton was accomplished in a biographic film which was aired both at the convention and later in the fall as an election eve broadcast. Parts of the program were also excerpted in biographic spot ads. In the film, some of the most private parts of Bill Clinton's life as a youth were paraded before the public. At a very early age, Bill Clinton is left at home in Hope, Arkansas, while his mother seeks a way to support her family. The young Bill Clinton protects his mother by standing up to his alcoholic stepfather. Just in case anyone misses the point, Hillary Clinton states the morale of the story—Bill Clinton was no rich kid:

Clinton's THE MAN FROM HOPE national convention film and election eve broadcast (excerpts):

Bill Clinton: "She (my mother) went back to New Orleans to finish her nursing education. She became a nurse anesthetist. And it was, you know, tough for her to leave me. And during this time she was away, one time, my grandmother and I went down on a train to visit her. And I remember one time we pulled out of the station, and my mother kneeled at the side of the track and cried because she felt so bad that I was leaving. It's one of my most vivid memories of childhood."

Hillary Clinton (interviewed on an outdoor patio): "Some people think that Bill must have been born wealthy, and raised wealthy, you know, and he had all of the privileges that you could ever imagine. But instead of being born with a silver spoon in his mouth, he was really born into a house that had an outhouse in the back yard."

Bill Clinton: "My stepfather, as you know, we had some problems growing up. But he was very good to me."

Virginia Kelley (Bill Clinton's mother): "Roger Clinton was an alcoholic. A good man. And if he ever loved anything in this world, it was Bill."

Bill Clinton: "When I was in the ninth grade, I think, he kind of got violent with my mother one night. And I bulled through the door and told him he wasn't going to do that any more. And I said..."

Virginia Kelley (recalling the words of her son): "'...Stand up! I have something to say to you.' And obviously he couldn't stand up. So he got in his face and said, 'Daddy, if you're not able to stand up, I'll help you. You must stand to hear what I have to say.' And some way or another he stood. And Bill told him then, 'Don't you ever, ever lay your hand on my mother again.'"

Clinton's choice of a vice-presidential running-mate was used to reinforce his "new Democratic" message and to underscore the break that 1992 Democratic ticket had made with the big-government liberalism of the party's past. Al Gore possessed solid environmental credentials and could help Clinton reach out to the environmentalist wing of the Democratic party. But other than that, the selection of Gore defied the usual concern for ticket balancing. Gore was not a liberal whose selection could appeal to the party's more ideological factions disaffected by Clinton's centrism. A Clinton-Gore ticket also spurned regional balance. Instead, a presidential ticket of two southerners promised to carry the Democratic campaign into the Republican presidential heartland in Dixie. The ticket would force the Republicans to expend valuable resources to protect their base in the South.

The Clinton-Gore ticket bespoke of a new generational politics. The Democratic convention itself was run in an effort to appeal to voters accustomed to the visuals, music, and pacing of MTV and VH1. The pacing of the convention was sped up. The new Democratic ticket celebrated to Fleetwood Mac's "Don't Stop Thinking About Tomorrow." While not the most current rock music, the song still marked a generational appeal quite different from a replay of Franklin Roosevelt's "Happy Days Are Here Again." Gore's environmentalism, too, was an asset among younger voters.

THE REPUBLICAN BATTLE: KING GEORGE?

Confident of reelection after the wake of the Gulf War, George Bush felt comfortable in delaying any real foray into campaign activity. Even when his poll ratings began to drop, Bush spurned the advice of his political handlers to begin campaigning; he would not switch from his "governing mode" to his "campaign mode." But Bush did not foresee the parallel between his postwar electoral fortunes and those of Great Britain's Winston Churchill. Churchill, too, was ousted by an electorate focused on domestic policy concerns only months after he had led his nation to military victory.

By the 1992 elections, the Gulf War was already a distant memory for most voters. The Republicans gained little political credit for both America's victory in the Gulf and the 1989 collapse of communism ending the Cold War. Foreign policy concerns were swamped by the swelling public discontent with the economy.

The fall 1991 defeat of former Bush Attorney General Richard Thornburgh in the Pennsylvania senate race was a crude wake-up call for the White House. Democrat Harris Wofford not only stressed his promise of national health insurance, he made the election a virtual referendum on the performance of the Bush administration. In an election that helped signal the extent of voter disaffection with Washington, Wofford overcame a 44-percentage point deficit in early polls.[13]

The Bush administration responded to Thornburgh's defeat in a reactive, almost panicked manner. The White House postponed a presidential visit to Japan as they feared the trip would reinforce the public's perception of Bush as a foreign policy president unconcerned with domestic affairs. The trip was later undertaken only when White House spin doctors redefined the mission to give it a new economic policy focus: The president was flying to Japan to reduce trade barriers and thereby create new jobs for Americans. But the president looked weak in appearing to beg the Japanese to change their protectionist policies. The news media had no major trade gains to report. Instead, televised news stories repeatedly showed clips of an ill President Bush vomiting on the laps of his hosts at a state dinner.

The growing strength of Patrick Buchanan's support in New Hampshire polls also pointed to the president's vulnerability. Buchanan, a conservative columnist and co-host of CNN's "Crossfire," believed that Bush lacked a clear philosophical core and had sold out the Reagan revolution. Buchanan sought to reenergize conservative Republican forces, move the party back toward the Right, and influence the future direction of Republican presidential politics.

Buchanan's campaign was highly issued-focused. He offered Republicans specific reasons to reject George Bush. In particular, Buchanan honed in on the President's broken tax vow. One ad provides a clip of George Bush making his famous 1988 "Read my lips. No new taxes!" pledge. The series of messages displayed on the screen underscored the narrator's words: "In 1988 we *Believed* George Bush when he took the tax pledge." "LARGEST TAX INCREASE." "Bush Betrayed our Trust. He Raised Our Taxes." "Can we afford four more years of Broken Promises?"

Buchanan's 37 percent of the Republican vote in the New Hampshire primary was seen as a rebuke to Bush. The president won New Hampshire by 16 percentage points, but Buchanan won the media victory. Still, despite the issue-orientedness of Buchanan's appeals, the Buchanan vote was not in its entirety a call for conservatism. While many New Hampshire Republicans voted for a return to Reagan-style purism, others used Buchanan only to register their dissatisfaction with George Bush's handling of the economy. Like the vote for Democrat Eugene McCarthy in New Hampshire in 1968, the Buchanan vote was a vehicle of protest, not simply a vote for a specific political philosophy

The Bush campaign had committed a serious strategic error in New Hampshire by failing to respond to the Buchanan insurgency. Buchanan, not Bush, had largely defined the issues that dominated the New Hampshire primary. The president's campaign would not repeat that mistake after New Hampshire. Instead, they sought to drive up Buchanan's "negatives" by pointing to his more unpopular policy positions. In the South, especially in Georgia, the president's ads pointed to a difference that might be important to the large military population of the region:

Bush campaign's P.X. KELLEY ad:

VIDEO: A gentleman wearing a tie and jacket talks directly into the camera.

AUDIO (P. X. Kelley): "When Pat Buchanan opposed Desert Storm, it was a disappointment to all military people and a disappointment to all Americans who supported the Gulf War. And I took it personally."

VIDEO: The identification line "Gen. P.X. Kelley, Commandant, US Marine Corps, ret." appears on the bottom of the screen.

AUDIO (Kelley): "I served with many of the marines who fought in Desert Storm. The last thing we need in the White House is an isolationist like Pat Buchanan. If he doesn't think America should lead the world, how can we trust him to lead America?"

VIDEO: White letter against black background read: "Pat Buchanan...Wrong on Desert Storm. Wrong for America."

The ad offered voters a clear choice, capably distinguishing Bush's action orientation in foreign policy from Buchanan's more isolationist posture. Still, the ad was deceptive. As CNN's Brooks Jackson pointed out in one of his many "Special Assignment" reports on political advertising in 1992, the ad led viewers to believe that Kelley actually served with the troops in the Gulf when, in fact, he had retired over three years before Desert Storm.

Other Bush ads continued to distinguish him from the more extreme Buchanan. One ad repeated a Buchanan quotation that women are "less psychologically equipped" to succeed in the workplace. In Michigan, a Bush ad virtually accused Buchanan of hypocrisy in his "America First" campaign for trade protectionism. As the ad shows still photographs of a closed automobile factory, a scowling Buchanan, and a Mercedes Benz, a

narrator observes: "While our auto industry suffers, Pat
Buchanan chose to buy a foreign car, a Mercedes Benz. Pat
Buchanan called his American cars, quote, Lemons. Pat
Buchanan. It's 'America First' in his speeches, but a foreign-
made car in his driveway."

Buchanan, too, stepped up his attacks on "King George"
who was out of touch with the concerns of the American people.
The Buchanan assault went beyond the president's reversal of his
tax vow. Buchanan ads attacked Bush for caving in to pressures
and signing into law a civil rights statute that the president had
previously opposed as authorizing racial quotas: "Fall 1991.
BUSH BROKE His PROMISE and signed a QUOTA Bill."

In the most extreme attack of the campaign, first aired in
Georgia, Buchanan even accused Bush of "investing tax dollars
in pornographic and blasphemous art:"

 Buchanan's TONGUES UNTIED ad:

VIDEO: Half-naked and leather-clad men dance in the
    street in what appears to be a gay rights celebra-
    tion or demonstration. Throughout most of the ad
    the message "Bush Used Your Tax $$$ For This" ac-
    companies Bush's picture on the bottom of the
    screen. The announcer reads the words that scroll
    up from the bottom:

VIDEO and AUDIO (Narrator): "In the last three years,
    the Bush Administration has invested our tax dol-
    lars in pornographic and blasphemous art, too
    shocking to show. This so called art has glorified
    homosexuality, exploited children, and perverted
    the image of Jesus Christ. Even after good people
    protested, Bush continued to fund this kind of art.
    Send Bush a Message!"

AUDIO (Narrator): "We need a leader who will fight
    for what we believe in. Vote Pat Buchanan for Pres-
    ident."

VIDEO: Picture of Buchanan before an American flag,
    next to the words: "We Need a Real Leader. Vote
    Buchanan for President."

The ad was deceptive as well as homophobic. National Endowment for the Arts funding for the film "Tongues Untied," with its gay rights celebration scenes, was granted during Reagan's, not Bush's, tenure as president. The filmmaker did not receive a grant directly from the NEA, but instead obtained partial funding for the film, only $5,000, from another organization that had received NEA funds.

The Tongues Untied ad was so outrageous that it not only proved ineffective but it may have even produced a small backlash against Buchanan. CNN's Brooks Jackson reported that polling in Georgia showed that 63 percent of Republican voters who viewed the ad called it unfair. More respondents said that the ad helped to increase their support for Bush than for Buchanan![14] The focus group work of Kathleen Hall Jamieson, too, revealed that voters viewed the ad negatively.[15] Political advertising is not all-powerful but most work within the confines of what voters already know. Americans knew too much about George Bush to believe the exaggerated claims contained in the ad.

After his successes in the early spring races, Buchanan's percentage share of the primary vote fell to the twenties. He failed to win a single state. Bush's renomination was assured. Buchanan suspended his active candidacy but did not withdraw from the race.

The Bush-Quayle strategists believed that, for the president to win the election, he had to first solidify his support among the party's conservatives. In an attempt to appease the Right, the Bush forces turned the writing of the party platform over to conservatives.[16] The platform endorsed a U.S. Constitutional amendment to ban abortions in all instances, with no exceptions for rape or incest. Further, in an effort to bring Buchanan into the fold, Bush-Quayle officials struck a deal that gave him a virtual keynote speech slot at the Republican national convention. In fact, the opening day of the convention was given over to the party's conservatives. Buchanan's speech and fervency of belief stood in marked contrast with Bush's more pragmatic governing approach. Buchanan's religiosity and warning of a "cultural war" was echoed by the Reverend Pat Robertson. Throughout the convention, Republican speakers, especially Dan and Marilyn Quayle, repeated the party's devotion to traditional, conservative, family values. Where the Democrats used their national convention to broaden the appeal of their ticket to younger and more centrist voters, the Republican convention alienated younger and more moderate voters, especially the growing number of Americans who did not fit the Republican convention's ideal of the two-parent family.

THE IN-AND-OUT PEROT CANDIDACY

The candidacy of Ross Perot fascinated reporters and voters alike. Ross Perot's campaign was initially fueled by a genuine grassroots organization of clubs and headquarters that popped up across the country. The sudden appearance of this extensive grassroots effort was perhaps the most notable phenomenon of the spring primary season.

For most of the winter and spring, Perot enjoyed good media. Early news stories focused on the curiosities of the citizens' movement and Perot as the self-made multi-billionaire and the rogue corporate venturer who financed a rescue mission into Iran to free two of his employees. Only when Perot's political standing continued to remain high in the polls did media coverage become more critical, focusing on some of the more troubling, authoritarian aspects in Perot's background and personality.[17] In May and June, before he suddenly withdrew from the race, public opinion polls actually showed Perot to be leading the three-candidate presidential field. He reentered the race with a little more than a month to go before the fall election.

Perot defied conventional politics. He made his personal appearances on Larry King the base of his campaign. He announced an 800 number that citizens could call and join the "United We Stand" effort. The United We Stand organization gave citizens a new opportunity for grassroots involvement in politics, although, as the campaign progressed, the indigenous organizers of many of the local United We Stand headquarters found themselves ousted by operatives paid by Perot. Perot spoke eloquently on the need to take strong measures to cut the budget deficit and reform government in order to give it back to the people. But other than his call for continued town meetings and term limitations, his promises lacked specificity. In his spring campaign, Perot did not back up his budget-cutting claims with figures; he did not show how he could cut the budget, obtain the huge savings that he projected, and still preserve the entitlement programs that people valued. When he returned in the fall, Perot did mention some specific program cuts and did provide budgetary figures. But the figures were not realistic; instead,

Perot relied on unspecified and fantastic gains to be made in efficiency to bring the budget in balance.

An unorthodox politician, Perot refused to be marketed or handled by campaign professionals. Two well-known political consultants, former Reagan political operative Ed Rollins and Jimmy Carter's campaign manager Hamilton Jordan, joined the Perot campaign, and reportedly received lucrative salaries. Rollins tapped the talents of Hal Riney, the creator of Reagan's "Morning in America" ads. But Perot, the business executive used to holding power in his hands, refused Rollins's advice on how to structure an effective national campaign. Perot was not impressed with the political professionals. He rejected the draft ads and Rollins's nationwide advertising strategy that sought to define Perot by emphasizing his personal qualities. Why, Perot reasoned, should he spend so much money on paid media when he was reaching the public via the talk shows for free? Also, Perot felt that his own business people could produce ads that were equally effective for much less cost. Riney was dismissed.

Perot was also angered when Rollins removed him from the safety of the television studio in an effort to broaden his supportive constituency. Previously, Perot's few live appearances were before enthusiastic groups of people who had already given him their support. Perot was not used to being vigorously questioned by persons who did not share his antigovernment orientation. Consequently, he was surprised and angered by the vigorous criticism he received as a result of his appearance before the National Association for the Advancement of Colored People, an event where Perot referred to blacks as "you people." After that blow-up, Perot refused future public appearances, as campaigning for the White House was no longer "fun." Rollins, frustrated by Perot's unwillingness to heed political advice, quit the campaign, publicly complaining about Perot's instability and egotism.

In a stunning move coincident with the Democratic National Convention, Perot announced that he would not run for president. According to Perot, a reinvigorated Democratic party had incorporated much of his message. But, Perot left himself an entry back into the race: He remained on the ballot in all 50 states. He also left the core of his organization in place in each state, often under the direction of a paid "volunteer" or two.[18] In October, he announced his reentry into that race by saying that he was responding to the wishes of his supporters (wishes that were registered, in part, by a rigged phone-in poll where all calls were automatically counted as a "yes"!).

Appearing on "Sixty Minutes" a little more than a week before the election, Perot provided a much different account of his July withdrawal. Perot sounded almost paranoid, declaring that he had withdrawn from the race because he did not want to see his daughter's wedding disrupted by a GOP plot that entailed the distribution of phony, scandalous pictures. The "Sixty Minutes" interview showed Perot to be a man concerned with rumors, internecine plots, and espionage.

Perot's fall campaign never recaptured the magic of the late spring and early summer. Fall polls showed that he was destined to finish no better than third. Perot's talk-show interviews and paid advertisements were supplemented by only a handful of personal appearances before friendly audiences. According to one estimate, in just his first two weeks back, Perot spent $24 million on paid television, more than the Bush and Clinton campaigns combined.[19] Perot's half-hour "infomercials," in which the candidate held up and explained amateurish charts, proved exceeding popular; they appealed to voters upset with the continued budget deficits and the performance of Washington. The ads also gave Perot the appearance of being issue-oriented, even if he actually proposed little of substance in each half hour. Perot's shorter ads featured no fancy visuals but relied on words that scrolled up or down the screen, again conveying the image that the campaign was devoted to substance—an image that was not merited by the virtual contentless nature of Perot's broad attacks.

THE FALL ELECTION

Immediately after the Democratic convention, the Clinton/Gore ticket took a triumphant bus ride through the upper Midwest and the Ohio Valley. Enthusiastic crowds greeted the Democratic motorcade. Traveling by bus seemingly provided symbolic confirmation that Clinton and Gore were candidates in touch with the people. The bus tour also helped to cement the ticket's support in states that were critical for a Democratic victory.

In an effort to institutionalize presidential debates and take them out of the hands of the individual campaign organizations, the League of Women Voters had arranged a series of presidential encounters for 1992. After some question, the League invited Perot to participate, as they said he met the organization's test of viability.

The candidates' representatives argued over debate formats. The Bush campaign wanted a series of forums mediated by reporters who would likely bring up questions concerning Clinton's alleged marital infidelity, draft problems, and truthfulness. As the exchanges continued, the scheduled time for the first League debate came and went without Bush's assent to participate. Democrats had persons dressed in chicken suits shadow "Chicken George" at Bush campaign rallies.

Behind in the polls, Bush needed the debates to focus new attention on Clinton. A major gaffe by Clinton could also change the contours of a race that polls showed the president was losing. The Bush campaign finally accepted a combination of formats for three presidential debates and a vice-presidential debate that included more informal encounters that were suited to Clinton's, not Bush's, personal style.

In the first meeting, Bush attacked Clinton's lack of patriotism. Bush contrasted his record of having flown missions off an aircraft carrier during World War II with Clinton's opposition to the Vietnam War while a student at Oxford. Bush declared that he found it impossible to understand how a person in a foreign land could demonstrate against his own country at a time when Americans were held prisoner. Clinton, however, was prepared for the attack and had an effective retort that referred to the president's father, the former Senator Prescott Bush: "Your father was right to stand up to Joe McCarthy. You were wrong to attack my patriotism." Clinton's assertion that there had been "enough division" was greeted with audience applause.

Bush was obviously uncomfortable with the format of the second debate in which the candidates faced questions from a live audience. Bush appeared formal and stiff, Clinton, in contrast, was used to the format, as he had engaged in a series of similar debates in the primaries. Clinton rose from his stool and approached members of the audience in Phil Donahue–like fashion. ABC's Carole Simpson, the debate moderator, effectively neutralized a number of possible Bush attacks when, at the beginning, she declared that the voters were sick of hearing the candidates talk about dirt, not issues. The president was hurt, further still, when he appeared to be unable to answer a young woman's question about how he personally had been affected by the recession. Bush may not have understood the question, which was poorly phrased. Nonetheless, his reply, which contained the unfortunate phrase "I am not sure I get it," was weak and only re-inforced appearances that the president was out of touch with the daily lives and economic anxieties of average Americans. By the end of the debate, Bush even appeared to be glancing down at his watch.

In the third debate, Bush was much more assured, com-posed, and presidential. Overall, the debates did little to change the parameters of the race. No serious sound bites or mortal blows were landed. Clinton made no major gaffe.

Near its end, the Bush campaign was reduced essentially to a series of aggressive, negative attacks on Clinton's character and record. In one series of ads, nothing was conveyed to viewers other than the words of various men and women in the street (or, more commonly, sitting at a diner) who repeatedly attacked Clinton's lack of trustworthiness and integrity:

Bush INTEGRITY ad:

VIDEO: White letters against a black background read "On Integrity. October 1992." Close-ups of various men and women, at a diner and outdoors. Unsteady, hand-held camera shots add to cinema verité, the appearance of authenticity.

AUDIO: Sounds of dishes and people talking in a diner. Some of the words that follow are not easy to understand, as if these are tapes of real, un-staged interviews:

VIDEO AND AUDIO:

(Man in diner booth): "If you're going to be presi-dent, you have to be honest."

(Diner #2): Bill Clinton's not telling anything hon-estly to the American people."

(Woman in park): "The man just tells people what they want to hear."

(Back to diner #2): "...by dodging the draft."

(Elderly woman in park): "I just think he's full of hot air."

(Man in park): "I wouldn't trust him at all to be commander-in-chief."

(Woman in diner): "I think that there's a pattern. I just, just don't trust Bill Clinton."

(Woman #2 in diner): "I don't think he's honorable. And I don't think he's trustworthy."

(Man holding a child): "You can't have a president who says one thing and does another."

(Woman standing before flag bunting): "It scares me. He worries me. And he'll just go one way or another..."

VIDEO (Closing sign): "To be continued tomorrow..."

The personal vilification of Bill Clinton was even carried out on the floor of the U.S. House of Representatives, where conservative Republican Bob Dornan used C-SPAN's television coverage to promote the story that Clinton, during his student days at Oxford, had demonstrated against his country and even visited the Soviet Union to provide aid to the Communists. President Bush repeated the charges in an interview with Larry King.

Other Bush ads provided at least the appearance of a more substantive basis for their anti-Clinton charges. But the claims, facts, and figures presented in the ads were quite arguable. In one Republican ad, Clinton's Arkansas was presented as a devastated, almost surreal landscape:

Bush ARKANSAS RECORD ad:

AUDIO: Sound of wind blowing as in a storm.

VIDEO: Black-and-white scenes of an approaching storm. All scenes are shown in slow motion with a tint to the pictures to make the scenes appear especially ominous. Leaves fall from a tree. Storm clouds roll in. Trees bend in the wind. More storm clouds roll in accompanied by a bolt of lightning. Shots of an isolated landscape, of an isolated farm windmill in the storm.

AUDIO (Female announcer): "In his 12 years as governor, Bill Clinton has doubled his state's debt, doubled government spending, and signed the largest tax increase in his state's history. Yet his state remains the 45th worst in which to work, the 45th worst for children. It has the worst environmental policy. And the FBI says Arkansas has America's biggest increase in the rate of serious crime."

VIDEO: The following signs accompany the narrator's words and are overlaid on the storm scenes. Sources, where given, are printed in smaller letters across the bottom of the screen:

"Doubled State's Debt."

"Doubled Government Spending."

"45th Worst in Which to Work*

    *Source: The Corporation for Enterprise Development."

"45th Worst for Children*

    *Source: The Center for the Study of Social Policy."

"Worst Environmental Policy*

    *Source: The Institute for Southern Studies."

"Biggest Increase in Serious Crime Rate*

    *Source: The FBI."

AUDIO (Announcer): "And now Bill Clinton says he wants to do for America what he's done for Arkansas. America can't take that risk."

VIDEO: Shadowy shot of a large bird, maybe a vulture, sitting atop a leafless tree against the stormy sky. Fade. Replace with closing sign: "America Can't Take That Risk."

The Clinton campaign had learned lessons from Dukakis's failure in 1988. Clinton's ad people quickly responded to virtually every Republican allegation. Grunwald and Greenberg had even used focus groups to test possible response lines to expected

Republican attacks.[20] Clinton ads responded to Republican charges in the Arkansas *Record* ad and similar spots by providing alternative facts that highlighted Clinton's record of managerial success: that Arkansas had the second lowest tax burden in the country, and that Arkansas was first in the nation in job growth.

Perhaps the most effective Republican spot was an ad that charged that Clinton's plans would raise taxes:

Bush CLINTON ECONOMICS/FEDERAL TAXES ad:

AUDIO: Somber, almost moody music. (Female announcer in a hushed, serious tone): "Bill Clinton says he'll only raise the taxes of the rich to pay for his campaign promises. But here's what Clinton economics could mean for you. $1,088 more in taxes. $2,072 more in taxes."

VIDEO: In white lettering on black background:

"To Pay for His Campaign Promises."

"Here's What Clinton Economics Could Mean To You."

Cut to shots of typical Americans, their names in small print in the upper left of the screen, and the indicated amount that they would pay in increased taxes in larger print across the bottom of the screen:

(Man, dressed in blue work clothes, carrying a large pipe wrench): "John Cannes, Steamfitter: $1,088 More In Taxes."

(Woman dressed in a black top and jeans, carrying a hard hat): "Lori Huntoon, Scientist: $2,072 More in Taxes."

AUDIO (Announcer): "One hundred leading economists say his plan means higher taxes and larger deficits."

VIDEO: Switch to new screens of white letters against black background:

"100 Economists Say."

"Higher Taxes…Bigger Deficits."

Cut to more typical Americans:

(Business couple with briefcases): "Julie and Larry Schwartz, Sales Reps: $1,191 More In Taxes."

(Black man in a business suit): "Wyman Winston, Housing Lender: $2,072 More In Taxes."

AUDIO (Announcer): "$1,191 more in taxes. $2,072 more in taxes. You can't trust Clinton economics. It's wrong for you. It's wrong for America."

VIDEO (Closing signs): "Clinton Economics, Wrong For You. Wrong for America"

The tax issue was potentially damaging to Clinton. But "ad watch" stories in newspapers and on television pointed out that Republican analyses may have overestimated the cost of the Clinton programs as well as underpredicted the revenues that would be generated by an economic rebound. More importantly, the ad just did not appear convincing. Voters had come to understand that the apparently factual claims in the ad were the exaggerations of political rhetoric. Viewers had some awareness that the tax figures presented were, at least in part, phony, as no one could accurately cost out programs that were yet to be enacted.

The Clinton campaign also responded with ads of its own to limit the damage. One Clinton ad pointed out that the Bush tax charges were labelled "Misleading" by the *Washington Post*. The same ad also quoted the *Wall Street Journal* to the effect that "Clinton has proposed to <u>cut taxes</u> for the sort of people featured in [Bush's] ad." Another Democratic ad observed that the Clinton plan has been endorsed by over 600 economists and ten Nobel Prize winners. The Clinton forces also sought to reassure voters, as they had earlier in the campaign, by returning to more positive themes and offering copies of the Clinton plan that voters could obtain by calling a toll-free 800 number. Clinton also reemphasized his middle-class, new Democrat image. One ad explicitly stated that Clinton and Gore were "a new generation of Democrats" who "don't think the way the old Democratic party did."

The sustained Republican attacks did succeed in driving up the "negatives" in the public's ratings of Bill Clinton. Perhaps the ads were a factor if the daily tracking polls at the time, notorious for their imprecision, were correct in reporting that Clinton's lead had narrowed. But the ads hurt Bush as well as Clinton! Voters viewed Bush more negatively as a result of the unrelenting negativism of the final days of the campaign, especially as many of the claims in the ads were not seen as credible.

Viewers were not reliant on the information contained in the Republican ads. They had other information that they used to assess the credibility of the Republican charges. After its experience in the 1988 campaign, the press was more vigilant in policing the ads, examining and contradicting a number of the charges made. Democratic advertising also provided competing information. Clinton's "new Democrat" image and promise to end "welfare as we know it" had effectively inoculated him against attacks that he was another big-spending, liberal Democrat.[21] Most importantly, the Republican ads did little to counter what voters had already learned about the state of the economy and George Bush's economic performance.

The limited impact of the Republican ads is evident in voter responses to open-ended survey questions. Voters evaluated Clinton positively on a number of factors despite the Republican assault. They saw Clinton as empathetic and caring; they also rated him highly on leadership and competence, more than counterbalancing their ambivalence when it came to questions as to his "integrity." It was Bush, not Clinton, who received negative evaluations from voters, reflecting of the president's failed economic stewardship and his reversal of his tax pledge.[22] While voters saw Bush's reversal of his tax vow as significant, they for the most part spurned the charges against Clinton's character as irrelevant. As Kathleen Frankovic has observed in her review of polling data from 1992, voters decided what matters were relevant; they looked at "character" with "a political, not a personal, meaning."[23] Retrospective assessments, not personal politics, decided the election in 1992.

A RETROSPECTIVE VOTE

The popular vote was no runaway: Clinton received 43 percent to Bush 38's percent. Clinton's clear-cut 370-to-168 vote victory in the Electoral College, however, helped to legitimize his presidency.

Perot's 19 percent of the vote was the largest received by a third-party presidential candidate since Theodore Roosevelt's Bull Moose revolt in 1912. In Maine and Utah, Perot finished in second, not third, place.

The economic issue was clearly the most dominant factor in explaining the Democratic rebound from 1988. According to Democratic pollster Peter Hart, 60 percent of the voters cited the economy and the need for change as the most important factor in their vote. Only one-third cited trust, foreign policy, or any of the competing campaign themes pushed by Bush.[24] By the beginning of the Republican National Convention, the public's rating of George Bush's management of the economy had fallen below even Jimmy Carter's previous all-time low.[25] Changes in the economy also produced changes in partisanship. Throughout the campaign, Democratic gains in partisanship paralleled changes in the unemployment figures; as the recession grew, so did the number of Democratic supporters.[26] Economically hard-hit California went Democratic for the first time in seven presidential elections. The economy had so foreordained the results in California that, late in the campaign, the Bush organization virtually ceded the state's 54 electoral votes to the Democrats in order to concentrate its efforts on less troubled and more winnable states.

Clinton's appeal to the middle class allowed Democrats disaffected with the liberalism of the party's previous presidential candidates to come home. Clinton's vote largely resembled the Democratic New Deal coalition. He fared better among lower-income than among higher-income voters. He picked up 83 percent of the votes of black voters and 80 percent of the votes of Jews. He did well among Catholics, Latinos, and union voters—although he failed to win a majority of union voters, as some union families, disaffected with Clinton's weak stand on trade protectionism and NAFTA, voted for Perot.[27] He also did better in the white South than did the Democratic candidates who preceded him.

Yet, the white South was the one element of the New Deal coalition that was clearly no longer allegiant to the Democratic banner. In 1992, Bush gained his strongest support in the South despite the fact that two southerners headed the Democratic ticket. Carll Everett Ladd argues that the 1992 election in effect marked the completion of the pro-Republican realignment of the South. Whites in the region not only voted Republican for president but also voted Republican in races for the House of Representatives by a margin of roughly 3 to 2.[28]

The moderation of Democratic presidential ideology does not by itself explain Clinton's success. While he fared better than any Democrat in the last twenty years among moderate voters, paradoxically, voters overall still perceived Clinton's ideological position as liberal, not centrist.[29] Retrospective assessments of the economy, not ideology, provided the impetus for voters to return to the Democratic party.

Clinton/Gore did very well among younger voters, getting about a 60–40 break among the 18–29 age group. In the 1980s, Reagan and Bush had secured sizable majorities among younger voters. But in 1992, younger voters were the strongest age cohort for Clinton. The turnout of younger voters was also significantly higher in 1992 than in the previous two elections.[30] It is, however, too early to tell if younger voters will stay with the Democratic party. Much depends on Clinton's performance in office and the performance of the economy. Some observers argue that the influx of younger voters into the Democratic column may mean that the political balance of the electorate is in the process of changing, ending the Republican dominance that has characterized presidential elections since the late 1960s. Just as Ronald Reagan's presidential campaigns brought new adherents to the Republican party, the Clinton/Gore campaign themes brought new activists to the Democratic party, leading one political scientist to conclude: "Whatever the impact of Clinton's presidency, the generational and ideological shifts embodied in his 1992 campaign will structure partisan conflict into the next century."[31] However, the major gains made by the Republicans in the 1994 mid-year elections suggest that we skeptically view any thesis pointing to a changed electorate more disposed to the Democrats.

The economy was not the only issue concern that affected the vote 1992. Bush's reversal of his no-new-tax vow also lost him votes. On the other hand, the Republican ticket attracted voters with strong concerns for "family values."[32] The Bush campaign may have even gained votes as a result of its stance on abortion; the right-to-life minority was more likely to cast its vote in response to a candidate's stand on this issue than were pro-choice supporters.[33] But, overall, the liberalization of public attitudes on abortion and other issues since 1988 aided the Democrats. By 1992, the electorate had become less conservative, and had moved closer to the Democrats on such issues as defense spending, health insurance, and roles for women.[34]

The rhetoric and advertising of the media campaign helped voters to understand the basic directional choice offered by the two major candidates. The issue of health care provides a case in point. One Bush ad aired at the end of the campaign showed a businessman sitting uncomfortably and impatiently in a hectic, overcrowded waiting room. The narrator in the ad attacks the Clinton health care plan for "putting the government in control" of a program that will "ration health care," a program known as "socialized medicine." Few voters were familiar with the details of the Clinton and Bush health approaches. Yet, political advertising in 1992 did help voters to understand the broad difference in approaches offered by Bush and Clinton: Clinton offered the more comprehensive vision of health care; Bush was resistant to the intrusions of more extensive government health care. Unfortunately for the Republicans, the polls show that Clinton's position was, at the time, the one more in tune with the prevailing voter demands for more extensive health protection. Only after Clinton, in office, proposed a specific health plan did a sustained barrage of criticism and attack ads convince Americans of the ills of this particular big-government health effort.

THE PEROT VOTE

Perot voters were a diverse constituency joined only by their rejection of the existing political system. In Silicon Valley, highly educated, upper-income voters were attracted to Perot's technocratic virtues and his promise to run government more like a corporation. But in Texas, Perot's vote was much less upscale; Texas voters for Perot were not political information-seekers or activists, but "semi-participants," many of whom were unlikely to vote in future elections.[35] Indeed, Perot drew support across the income spectrum; his vote from the highest income bracket was nearly equal to that which he received from the lowest.[36]

Perot's vote lacked a clear social group or ideological base of support. Perot voters tended to be independents who exhibited extreme levels of alienation and discontent. One study of a representative sample of voters who called Perot's 800 number found near unanimity (96.9 percent) in the opinion that government was run by a few big interests instead of for all the people.[37] Perot activists were angered by the size of budget deficits, by the loss of American jobs overseas, and by politics as usual; they sought to restrict sharply government's role.[38] But other than that, Perot activists were a diverse group who had little ideological clarity or consensus on issues.

Survey results underscore the lack of a clear issue basis to the Perot vote. Unlike the supporters of third-party presidential candidate George Wallace in 1968, Perot's followers were not united in their stances on specific issues.[39] They were united only in their rejection of the existing system and the major two parties. Their attachment was more to Perot and to his style of politics than to any clear-cut philosophy or set of issue positions—other than the urgency of deficit reduction.[40] Indeed, the personal rather than substantive basis of Perot's appeal was most clearly revealed during the spring campaign, when his support in the polls grew despite his refusal to spell out his position on the issues or to provide the details of his budget-cutting plans.[41] Given their diversity, it is unlikely that Perot voters will provide the basis for a strong, ongoing, third-party movement in the absence of the charismatic influence of Ross Perot.

THE YEAR OF THE WOMAN?

The year 1992 was allegedly the political year of the woman. Many women were outraged by what they saw to be the mistreatment of Anita Hill at the hands of an all-male Senate Judiciary Committee during its October 1991 hearings on the nomination of Clarence Thomas to the Supreme Court. Motivated by a new sense of the unfairness of gender-based power inequities, 11 women ran for the Senate in 1992; another 106 received nominations to the U.S. House of Representatives. The Democrats made women's political gains the theme of the party's national convention.

In 1992, four women—Carol Mosely-Braun of Illinois, Barbara Boxer and Dianne Feinstein of California, and the self-styled "mom in tennis shoes" Patty Murray of Washington—were elected to the U.S. Senate, increasing the number of women in the institution to a grand total of six. In Pennsylvania, Lynn Yaekel lost to Arlen Specter, the senator who had aggressively grilled Anita Hill in the live televised hearings. Twenty-eight women were newly elected to the House of Representatives. Women made good use of their gender as a mark of their "outsiderism" in a year when voters highly valued it.[42]

The Anita Hill hearings, however, were not the only force that motivated the political mobilization of women. Another important factor was the Supreme Court's 1989 *Webster* decision that seemingly put abortion rights in danger, which had the effect of raising the salience of the abortion issue as well as decreasing public support for abortion regulations and George Bush's pro-life position.[43]

Hillary Clinton broke gender barriers in the presidential race, in a number of ways defying the passive and supportive role traditionally expected of potential "first ladies." The future president's wife had built an impressive career of her own in legal work, advocacy, and public service. During the primaries, Bill Clinton observed that he and Hillary represented a new generation with a revised definition of gender roles. He promised a modern partnership; you vote for one and you get two.

But the "liberation" represented by Hillary Clinton was less than total. She drew extensive criticism for defying traditional role expectations. Early in the campaign she had earned the ire of some portions of the public when, in response to criticism of her feminism, she said tartly that she could have stayed home and baked cookies. Her "Sixty Minutes" interview comment that she was "not some little woman standing by my man" also drew criticism. Right-wing commentators ridiculed her policy strengths, derisively observing that a Democratic administration would be run by "Hillary." Conservatives misrepresented her writings outlining the legal rights of children as "antifamily." At the Republican National Convention, Patrick Buchanan attacked radical feminism and the agenda of "Clinton and Clinton." Marilyn Quayle, the vice president's wife, offered herself as an alternative embodiment of the feminist ideal, a woman who sacrificed her own professional ambitions for the good of her husband's career and family.

As the campaign progressed, the Clinton campaign lowered Hillary's profile in an attempt to mute the "Hillary factor." She also engaged in actions clearly meant to portray her in the more traditional roles of supportive wife and mother. She even offered her Democratic chocolate chip cookie recipe in a bake-off against Barbara Bush's recipe. Focus group results had revealed that a large portion of the public believed that the Clintons were childless. In response, the Democratic campaign featured Hillary and 12-year old daughter Chelsea more prominently in photo opportunities, portraying the Clintons as the wholesome, typical American family. Only after the campaign was over and the election won did Hillary finally feel it was safe to let reporters know that she preferred to be referred to as Hillary Rodham Clinton, not simply Hillary Clinton.

The 1992 national conventions proved that the Democratic and Republican parties were polarized around the issue of feminism. The parties did not seek to moderate their views by going to the center of public opinion. Instead, they offered clearly competing views as to the role that women should play in society.[44] The differences went beyond abortion. Bill Clinton promised more extensive day care as well as a program of family and medical leave. In contrast, Vice President Dan Quayle attacked TV sitcom character Murphy Brown for having a child out of wedlock. Evangelicals pushed the Republican platform to the right not just on abortion but also on such issues as gay rights and "family values." The party's convention denounced efforts to "redefine the traditional American family." Contrary to journalistic accounts at the time, there was no coup by the Republican party's right that seized control of the platform process. Rather, Bush-Quayle campaign operatives appointed conservatives to chair the writing of the platform in an effort to mollify Buchanan supporters and convince the party faithful that Bush, indeed, was a genuine conservative.[45] The National Organization of Women (NOW) and the National Abortion Rights Action League (NARAL) demonstrated outside the convention hall in an effort to gain media attention and educate the public on women's issues.[46]

At the 1992 Democratic convention, women's issues were incorporated into the party's platform. Abortion was no longer seen as a debatable issue in the Democratic party.[47] Convention chair and Texas Governor Ann Richards denied Pennsylvania Governor Robert Casey's request to speak against a platform that he considered to be supportive of "abortion on demand." A Women's Caucus, open to outsiders as well as to convention delegates, held daily meetings, and Bill Clinton appeared before it.

A number of feminists saw the Democratic party as the vehicle to future progress. Others, however, felt that substantial gains could not be made within the umbrella of the two-party structure and the compromises forced by conventional politics. NOW announced the formation of a new Twenty-first Century Party. The choice facing NOW and other feminists in the future is to decide whether their agenda can most profitably be furthered by pursuing the third-party route or by joining the Democratic party and pushing it to the left.[48]

As has been the case in presidential elections since 1980, there was a **gender gap** in 1992 as women continued to vote somewhat differently from men. Women voted Democratic for president at a 5 to 6 percentage point greater rate than did men.[49] Among women, Clinton beat Bush by a 9 percentage point margin; among men, his advantage was only 3 points. Perhaps the gender gap would have been greater still had perceived economic conditions not led men, as well as women, to reject the incumbent Republican administration.

The gender gap was greatest among highly educated voters. Among those with graduate training, the gender gap was 18 percent, with Clinton beating Bush by a whopping 55 to 30 margin among women, as compared to his narrower 7-point margin among men (see Table 11.1). Highly educated, professional women were the group most alienated by the Republican emphasis on family values, which seemingly attempted to restrict women to more conventional roles. In what can be termed a **marital gap,** Clinton also enjoyed substantial margins of support among voters who were single, divorced, separated, or widowed; Bush, in contrast, won a slight edge among married couples.[50] While the GOP convention may have helped consolidate Bush's strength among conservatives, the strategy was "disastrous" in helping to turn away college-educated, suburban, and middle-income voters.[51]

The gender gap was larger at the subpresidential level than in the presidential race.[52] The difference between male and female voting patterns ranged from a low of 3 points in the Arizona senate race to highs of 27 and 28 points in the two California senate races.[53] In every senate race where a woman ran against a man, female voters gave a larger share of their vote to the woman than did male voters. In 1994, the gender gap reemerged in strengthened form in House and Senate races. While Democrats did well among women, Republicans gained control of Congress as a result of their support from men.

The voting patterns outlined above suggest that a woman running for the presidency might be the political beneficiary of a "gender gapped" vote. Yet, other aspects of the race may offset any advantage that a female presidential candidate may enjoy. Stereotypes persist; a woman still faces the presumption by many voters that she does not have the personal characteristics and strength demanded of a president. In 1988, the press focused on Colorado Representative Patricia Schroeder's tears when she announced her withdrawal from the presidential field, as if her

Table 11.1 Big Gender Differences in the 1992 Voting Between Highly Educated Women and Men

Vote for President	% for Clinton	% for Bush	% for Perot	Dems. Margin	Gender Gap
High School Graduate					
Women	43	38	18	5	
Men	43	33	24	10	–5
College Graduate					
Women	44	40	16	4	
Men	34	43	23	–9	13
Graduate Training					
Women	55	30	15	25	
Men	47	40	13	7	18

Source: Everett Carll Ladd, "The 1992 Vote for President Clinton: Another Brittle Mandate?" *Political Science Quarterly* 108, 1 (1993), p. 3.

crying were any indicator of her lack of suitability for the presidency. In 1992, no women actively sought the Democratic and Republican nominations, and none were considered seriously for vice president.

In 1992, the two major parties offered distinctly different views as to the role women should play in American society. If the parties continue to diverge on the issue of feminism, culture—not class—may prove to be a new defining line in future presidential elections.[54]

SUMMARY

The 1992 election showed the power of the economic issue and retrospective voting. Had the economy been better, the outcome might have been different. Clinton backed many progressive Democratic policies, but his was a populism with a twist, a populism targeted to the middle class, not solely to the poor and the disadvantaged. During the primaries, Clinton's middle-class orientation helped him build a biracial coalition. As University of Chicago sociologist William Julius Wilson observed, Clinton's promise of middle-class tax relief and programs intended for all low- to moderate-income groups, not just minorities, acted to "unite, not divide, racial minorities and whites."[55] In the fall election, the Republican effort to portray Clinton as an extreme liberal was unpersuasive given what voters had already learned about him throughout the campaign. Clinton's candidacy reenergized the Democratic party, recasting it as standing for something other than big-government liberalism, as well as attracting new voters and the young to the party. However, just two years later, the Clinton record gave the Republicans yet another opportunity to portray the Democrats as the party of big-government liberalism.

Bush attempted to make the 1992 election a referendum on Bill Clinton's personal character, but he failed. Instead, the 1992 election revolved around issues. As Martin Wattenberg concludes from his study of National Election Survey data, the issues that the candidates chose to stress are the dynamic factor that explains the change in election outcomes from 1988 to 1992: "Contrary to the fears of many, candidate-centered politics has not led to presidential election being determined by the personalities of the nominees."[56] In 1992, the public focused not so much on individual pocketbook concerns but on the nation's economic well-being, including looming economic problems and health care concerns.[57] Prospective and retrospective issue voting both contributed to Clinton's victory.[58] In 1992, issues made the difference!

THE FUTURE OF AMERICAN POLITICS

12

As we have seen in this book, issues exert a much greater influence on presidential elections than many commentators admit. Whereas Americans seldom meet the standards for prospective issue voting, presidential voting has, nonetheless, a substantive basis. Voters are capable of retrospectively evaluating a candidate's past performance. Economic evaluations have become a dominant factor in national elections. Voters are also able to distinguish the basic choices of direction offered by the two major-party candidates. They are capable of responding to the most salient issues of the day—especially "easy" issues.

Partisanship exerts a declining, but still significant, pull on voting behavior. Personal imagery continues to be part of the presidential race. The electorate will not vote for a candidate who appears unpresidential. But partisanship and personal imagery do not alone determine the outcome of presidential elections. Substantive evaluations of the candidates are important, too.

THE DIALOGUE OF TELEVISED DEMOCRACY:
THE ISSUES ARE IN THE ADS

Many commentators continue to bemoan the lack of issue voting and the poor quality of public debate in presidential campaigns. These commentators portray presidential elections as little more than the product of the behind-the-scenes manipulation of advertising consultants and other media strategists. According to this critique, the campaign dialogue is geared to sound bites and puffery. Candidates seldom present voters with a reasoned, coherent argument and a meaningful discussion of policy alternatives.[1] The voter is thereby deprived of a significant choice at the ballot box.

Yet, despite the much-alleged poor quality of issue discussion in presidential elections, the public has, in fact, been able to differentiate between presidential candidates. In certain elections—1964 (Johnson-Goldwater), 1972 (Nixon-McGovern), and 1984 (Reagan-Mondale)—the differences between the candidates were sharply drawn by the elite dialogue; the public could easily discern competing issue dispositions. But even in an election such as in 1988, where one candidate failed to effectively participate in the campaign debate and where (as critics charge) phony issues dominated the campaign dialogue, the public was still able to see important differences between the candidates. Dukakis was perceived as the more liberal candidate. Bush was seen as the candidate more clearly opposed to new taxes, but more willing to spend on national defense.

Why is it that the pejorative view of presidential campaigns has missed the role played by issues? With its focus on the rise of the professionally mediated televised campaign, the critics of the American presidential election process have failed to recognize one important point: The issues are often in the advertisements! Of course, campaign strategists and advertising consultants continue to portray presidential candidates as embodying desirable personal leadership attributes. Presidential campaigns utilize *both* personal image ads and more substantively based ads. Different appeals are used to reach different markets of voters.

One notable study has pointed to the issue-based nature of contemporary presidential advertising. Thomas E. Patterson and Robert D. McClure found that 42 percent of the televised ads in the 1972 race were "primarily issue communications" while another 28 percent "contained substantial issue material."[2]

According to Patterson and McClure, the ads presented voters with "solid reasons" based on "issue appeals."[3] Although the information provided in the ads was far from complete and lacking in richness and nuance, the information was no more one-sided or incomplete than that contained in candidate speeches, party campaign pamphlets, and other more traditional campaign media. Patterson and McClure find that their evidence leads them to dismiss the pejorative view of contemporary presidential campaigns:

> Political spots, then, are not entirely the mindless creatures developed in advertising darkrooms that some observers have claimed them to be. Presidential advertising is instead a blend of soft imagery and hard issue material. The image content is intended to draw an emotional reaction. The issue content is intended to make voters think. In the past, commentary about televised political advertising has fixed on the image content, condemned it, and ignored the issue content.[4]

Critics charge that the degree of issue-orientation of the 1972 ads may be a bit atypical. The issue-based character of the 1972 ads may be simply a result of the McGovern insurgency or the extraordinary politicization of the late–Vietnam War era. The issue-based dialogue of the paid media in 1972 may also reflect the relatively long length of the ads featured in the campaign. Only two percent of the ads shown in 1972 were thirty-second spots—the vehicle that has proved so popular in more recent presidential campaigns.

But a study of the paid advertising twenty years later, in 1992, shows that 1972 was not an aberration. A content analysis of the paid ads used in the 1992 general election shows that a majority were issue-based. Image ads, though, were more dominant in the primaries.[5] Contrary to the pejorative view, presidential advertising, at least in the general election, contains messages of substance.

Yet, Richard Joslyn rejects the proposition that presidential advertising communicates substantive issue material. Joslyn observes that the learning from the 1972 ads was quite limited and was greatest among low-interest voters. More concerned citizens learned little from paid television. The information presented in the ads was likely to be redundant.[6]

Joslyn's point of view is fortified by his review of an admittedly unscientific sample of 506 televised political commercials used in presidential and nonpresidential races. He finds that political ads tend to market candidates on the basis of their personal attributes, often doing little more than attempting to portray a candidate as a benevolent leader. Whereas political ads may emphasize retrospective satisfaction or dissatisfaction with performance, future actions or policy intentions are seldom revealed. According to Joslyn, only 15 percent of the ads contain appeals based on prospective policy choices. He concludes that televised spot ads do little to enable effective citizen participation or to educate the public regarding the policy alternatives represented by the candidates.[7]

Joslyn's assessment, however, can be challenged on several grounds. First of all, retrospective voting is based on relevant, not inconsequential, substantive evaluations. Retrospective performance may even provide a more dependable basis than prospective promises for assessing the action orientations of presidential candidates. Second, even when voters do cast their ballots on a candidate's personal qualities, those personal qualities are often relevant to the demands of the presidential job.

Third, Joslyn's findings are influenced by the inclusion of nonpresidential ads in his sample. In relatively invisible elections for lesser offices where voters know little about the candidates, personal-image appeals may well prove to be the core of a winning advertising strategy. However, in a presidential race where virtually all voters are likely to know *something* about the candidates or have opinions on salient issues, personal-image appeals by themselves do not suffice.

Most importantly, Joslyn understates the issue content of the ads he analyzes. This understatement is readily apparent if we review his treatment of the televised advertising of the 1964 election—especially two ads that we reviewed in Chapter 7. Joslyn classifies the Daisy Girl and Khrushchev (Pledge of Allegiance) spots not as issue ads but only as "elections-as-ritual appeals" that evoke symbolic appeals to prevailing norms of cultural values. Joslyn considers Daisy Girl merely a "minimelodrama," a "truncated and simplistic" commercial that uses the "elements of intensified peril, conflict, suspense, and villainy to communicate a message."[8] He likewise excoriates Barry Goldwater's Khrushchev ad for appealing to prevailing cultural stereotypes and for its simplistic message "that if one is opposed to communism then one should vote a particular way."[9]

What Joslyn fails to see, however, is that the two ads in question did, in fact, succeed in informing viewers of clear differences between the candidates on matters of national significance. Daisy Girl and similar ads aired on behalf of Lyndon Johnson reminded voters of Goldwater's less-than-prudent statements on the use of nuclear weapons—an issue certainly of great importance to the future of both the nation and the world. As we already discussed in Chapter 7, this difference in action orientations may well have been of monumental importance in the post-1964 period. Faced with a failing war effort in Vietnam and his loosening hold on the presidency, Johnson did not resort to the use of nuclear weapons in Southeast Asia. It is uncertain whether Goldwater, given his statements on the nuclear weapons issue, would have shown equal restraint as president.

Goldwater's Khrushchev (Pledge of Allegiance) ad likewise presented voters with a choice on another issue of importance. The ad showed Goldwater to be the more intent of the two candidates on stopping the spread of communism. Critics of the campaign dialogue in 1964 point out that Johnson was no dove. As president, he acted to greatly escalate the United States's involvement in the war in Vietnam. But Johnson also called periodic bombing halts and placed numerous restrictions on American military action in an effort to pursue a negotiated peace. Goldwater sharply criticized each of these restrictions and the pauses in the bombing. Goldwater was, as his ads had shown, the more strident in his opposition to communism. He would not fight a limited war; nor would he likely risk bombing halts in the pursuit of peace.

Both the Khrushchev and Daisy Girl ads contained substantive messages that went beyond mere melodrama or ritual. Both used symbolism—but it was symbolism that effectively communicated the competing action dispositions of the two presidential candidates. As Samuel Popkin observes, we cannot easily divide between "fluff and substance" in a political campaign.[10] Symbolic appeals can reveal more about the issue dispositions of a candidate than do the self-serving homilies that candidates often spout when talking about issues:

> When a George Wallace crowns a beauty queen who is black, or a Rockefeller eats a knish, each man is communicating important changes in his relations with and attitudes about ethnic and religious minorities. When the southern governor who promised "segregation forever" congratulates the homecoming queen who is black, does this have less significant implications for policy than posturing about gun control or drug control?[11]

For "issue voting" to occur, voters need only a general awareness of the positions of the candidates and parties; voters do not need to know about specific pieces of legislation or the details of alternative policy proposals. Voters do not need a public policy expert's understanding of program details. They generally care about ends, not the means or the methods by which results are achieved.[12] Critics of presidential campaigns set unnecessarily high standards for public discourse. Joslyn's idealized standards of issue voting ignore the way many citizens incorporate issues into their voting decisions. Voters need only to discern and understand the basic choice of policy directions offered to them by the two major-party candidates. Do they want more of what the Democratic or the Republican candidate has to offer? Do they want to continue the present course of policy or do they want a change?

Evidence from 1988 would seem to show that presidential ads increase citizen learning. In answering open-ended questions about reasons for voting against Dukakis, respondents identified Dukakis's lenient attitude toward crime, his weakness on military and defense issues, and his support of taxes—themes that dominated the Republican media effort.[13]

Voters learn from television—from paid advertising. Televised political dialogue is in many ways shallow and far from perfect—just as its critics have charged. Yet, the televised debate is far from issueless. In the race for the presidency, the issues are in the ads. We only have to be willing to look to see them.

COPING WITH NEGATIVE ADVERTISING

Contemporary accounts of presidential elections have focused on the supposed ills of negative or attack campaigning. Yet, any serious discussion of this phenomenon must come to grips with the different forms of attack advertising. Some negative ads focus on legitimate questions of policy and performance. This form of advertising actually adds to voter knowledge of the records and positions of the candidates. These ads provide a more issue-oriented basis for the voting decision than do vacuous positive ads that do little more than celebrate a candidate's leadership traits or present him as being a family man in tune with everything that is good about America.

Negative ads are one-sided. They never do full justice to the discussion of an issue. But positive ads are equally blameworthy in this regard. They, too, exaggerate claims, resort to the manipulation of symbols, and present equally shallow and distorted discussions of complex issues. No political ad—positive or negative—readily admits what is suspect in a campaign's position or what is defensible in an opponent's position. Yet democracy does not require that each candidate make an opponent's arguments. Instead, it is up to the voters to choose among the competing claims and arguments of the candidates.

Yet, not all forms of negative advertising are as salutary as the more issue-oriented negative ads discussed above. Spot ads that circulate unsubstantiated allegations, launch personal attacks irrelevant to job performance, or purposely distort a candidate's policy positions and past records provide no useful information in a democracy. They only increase the public's cynicism regarding politics.

Within elections is a safeguard against the excesses of negative advertising. Each candidate has the ability to respond with news conferences and ads of his or her own that point to the unfairnesses, distortions, and exaggerations in the opponent's attack. Perhaps negative campaigning was so influential in 1988 because Michael Dukakis failed to respond quickly and effectively to the initial Republican attacks.

Dukakis's failure, though, will help ensure against a repeat situation in the future. Bill Clinton and other presidential candidates have learned the lesson of 1988; they must respond immediately and effectively to each attack ad. The technology of the modern electoral politics has evolved to the point that a well-organized campaign can even put together and air a response to an attack levied during the weekend before election day. The quick-response style of the 1992 Clinton campaign, not the lethargy of the Dukakis effort, is the likely model for future presidential efforts.

During the primaries, however, accessibility of the airwaves is very much dependent on a candidate's finances. A candidate strapped for funds has only a limited ability to respond to an opponent's attack. In the general election, in contrast, public funding has helped to ensure that the two major party candidates have relatively equal media access. Each has the ability to answer the other's charges. However, independent spending by political action committees (PACs) has helped to undo some the equality of media access.

PAC sponsorship of negative ads raises additional problems by undoing some of the natural policing built into American campaigns. No presidential candidate can afford to push an attack that is seen to be too personal or too unfair. Such an attack risks a backlash against the candidate who launched or sponsored the attack. But hard-hitting, even scurrilous, attacks can be launched with impunity by independent organizations. The candidate who benefits from the attack can deny responsibility for the ad in question. He may even point to the law that prohibits coordination between the independent committee and his official campaign organization. This was the strategy George Bush adopted when questioned about the more controversial Willie Horton attack ad.

One piece of proposed legislation has sought to deal with the problem of attacks from independent committees by requiring that broadcast stations give candidates free air time to respond to certain ads sponsored by independent committees. But the merits of this legislative proposal are open to debate. Legislation that limits what can be said in a political ad may violate First Amendment free speech rights and may not survive court challenge. Also, as few organizations will pay for an ad giving an opponent free response time, the proposed piece of legislation in question, if enacted, may lead to the virtual elimination of such ads. This would have the detrimental effect of diminishing the volume of information available to the voting public.[14] Citizens need to hear competing claims and charges. They need to hear free debate regarding possible deficiencies in a candidate's past record or proposed program.

Another proposed measure for dealing with the problem of negative advertising seeks to bar ads that refer to an opponent unless a candidate appears personally in the ad to make the charge. Here again, the proposed measure might be a violation of free speech protections. But even if constitutional, such a measure would make for boring, ineffective ads with messages that are not likely to be remembered. Any reform measure must come to terms with the fact that different citizens have different learning processes. Lower-status voters tend to get their information from spot ads. As Alexander Heard reminds us: "Advertising is a way of retailing information that narrows the 'information gap' between better-informed citizens and those traditionally less knowledgeable about public affairs—the young and the old, the poor, the less educated, women."[15] Any proposed reform measure to restrict political advertising must be cautious not to limit the volume of information provided the general public.

An alternative route for dealing with the problem posed by negative advertising calls for greater press responsibility and vigilance. Radio and television stations, for instance, can be urged to place independent ads under greater scrutiny than they do at the present. Broadcast stations are not obligated by law to air the ads of independent committees, and, in fact, may be held liable for any defamatory material contained within the ads. As a result, station managers have at times refused to run ads that contain defamatory, false, or misleading accusations.[16] Yet, there is a peril for free speech if we set up station managers as the guardians of truth. Do we really want station managers to have the power to decide just which of the conflicting claims in a political campaign are meritorious enough to deserve broadcast?

More aggressive reporting by the media can also help to mitigate some of the problems posed by negative advertising. Indeed, after the advertising excesses of 1988, television and print journalists in 1992 increasingly monitored the claims presented in political ads. CNN labeled suspect advertising claims as "False" or "Misleading." CBS subjected political claims to a "Reality Check." ABC reported on "The Facts," placing a universal "No" sign (a circle with a diagonal line drawn through it) when an ad's claims did not quite fit the facts. The new, more aggressive journalistic approach was typified by the press's treatment of Patrick Buchanan's Tongues Untied ad that used film clips of militant gays to accuse Bush of supporting pornographic and blasphemous art. Critical reporting diminished the power of the ad and helped to create a small backlash against Buchanan.[17]

Yet, there is a limit to what such vigilant reporting can hope to achieve. Throughout the course of a campaign, viewers are likely to see the exaggerated and distorted claims of an ad many times. They may see the news media's critical analysis of that ad once, if at all.[18] News coverage of and commentary on a controversial ad may even inadvertently give wider circulation to the claims contained in the spot—as was the case when the free media in 1988 repeatedly broadcast the message of the Willie Horton and the Revolving Door ads.

In 1992, television journalists tried to avoid inadvertently spreading an attack ad's factual inaccuracies in their reports. News commentators demonstrated considerable restraint wherever possible in showing only portions of a controversial ad, not the entire ad in question. Television stations also placed clips of the ads inside a cartoon-like television box in order to diminish their effect on the viewing audience. Recognizing that television is primarily a visual medium, news commentators also used visuals to clearly stamp an ad as false or misleading.

But journalists are ill-equipped to deal with the more subtle distortions contained in political spots. Reporters will point out claims that are fabricated. But they are less likely to question ads that are truthful in their statement of facts but unfair in the unspoken inferences that readers draw. For example, reporters are not likely to point to the subtle deceptions that occur when the video or soundtrack in an ad is creatively altered, or when a negative ad juxtaposes audio and video so as to exaggerate the sense of foreboding or the seeming ill that has been alleged.[19]

Some political observers have called for the resurrection of the Fair Campaign Practices Committee (FCPC) from the 1950s.[20] The FCPC was a blue-ribbon, nonprofit citizens' organization that tried to instill a sense of morality into the conduct of political campaigns. The Committee possessed no statutory or coercive power. It could only investigate and publicize violations of a code of fair campaign practices.

The findings of such a committee today could provide the basis for news stories pointing to the excesses of a political campaign.[21] But, as we pointed out above, such news stories devoted to negative campaigning are unlikely to have nearly as much impact as the ads in question. Furthermore, as the decisions of the FCPC do not make for a good news story, they are unlikely to receive extensive media coverage.

More creative measures for offsetting the role of negative advertising have been proposed. Journalist Paul Taylor has advanced one such proposal.[22] Instead of attempting to eliminate or restrict attack ads, which might be contrary to democracy in action, Taylor has proposed that a new forum of communications be created to compete with the political spot. During the last five weeks of the campaign, each major candidate for president would be given five minutes of free air time a night—on alternating nights—to appear personally on every television and radio station in the country. Continuous appearances before a national forum would virtually force candidates to enunciate substantive policy positions. Candidates would also have a forum to respond almost immediately to attacks made by an opponent or independent committee.

The feasibility of Taylor's proposal remains to be seen. As Taylor admits, there is no constituency for the free-time proposal. Broadcasters can be expected to strongly line up against the proposal unless they are reimbursed for lost air time. Also, just what constitutes fair access accorded to third-party candidates is still the subject of much debate.

An alternative reform proposal entails the setting aside of nine Sunday evenings between Labor Day and election day for debates and candidate telecasts. The underlying principle of the proposal is to allow candidates substantial periods of time to speak directly to the people. In many way, the 1992 election realized the goals of the "Nine Sundays" proposal as the candidates engaged in four debates and took advantage of call-in shows and other "new media" formats.[23] Yet, despite the contribution of these forums to the campaign dialogue, they did little to temper the negative tone of the paid media campaigns.

Kathleen Hall Jamieson similarly seeks to diminish the influence of negative campaigning by structuring alternative campaign forums likely to yield more fruitful discussion of issues. Jamieson proposes grouping together the primaries of states with similar problems and challenges. If such a reform were enacted, sustained attention could be given to a particular set of issues. One week would find candidates focused on the problems of farm states. Another week would see candidates paying attention to the issues of declining work opportunities in industrial states such as Pennsylvania and Michigan. While oppositional or negative campaigning would continue, the grouping of primaries would place candidates before similar audiences and will likely result in an extended discussion of a set of related policy concerns. Coordinated primaries would also allow the press to focus more on issues and solutions as opposed to campaign strategy.[24]

Jamieson similarly proposes that debate formats be altered "to eliminate the debate-ads that now masquerade as debates."[25] Candidate acceptance of public funds can be conditioned upon participation in presidential debates. Debate formats should be altered to allow candidates sufficient time for thought-worthy responses. Reporters should be allowed follow-up questions. The studio audience should be banned in order to diminish the applause that cues viewers at home and rewards candidates for responding with sound bites.

Alternative debate formats might be tried. Some of the more reasoned discussion of the 1992 primary season was seen in a Bill Clinton–Jerry Brown debate that had no panel of reporters asking questions of the candidates. Going head-to-head, with the occasional intervention of a moderator, the candidates talked substance. Each was reluctant to bear the risk of adverse public reaction by launching a direct, personal attack against the other. There was no reporter to do the "dirty work" for a candidate by bringing up personal charges. The sober tone of the

Clinton-Brown encounter stood in marked contrast to the rhetorical flashes and exaggerated attacks of the Clinton-Brown exchanges that directly preceded it.

Negative advertising is here to stay. Candidates will resort to negative attacks as long as voters respond to them. The good news is that negative campaigning no longer has the legendary reputation it enjoyed as a result of the 1988 Bush-Dukakis race. The 1992 anti-Clinton ads simply did not work all that well. Voters had information other than that presented in the Republican ads which they could use to evaluate Clinton and his record. The Republican ads also failed to convince voters on the issue that mattered most—the state of the economy. Negative ads are most influential when they present credible evidence on issues of salience to the American voter. Both the press and voters alike have become a bit more sophisticated in their response to the claims presented in negative ads.

Still, successful candidates will find it necessary to rebut attacks. Sophisticated candidates will attempt to inoculate themselves against expected negative attacks. John Kennedy's handling of the religious issue in 1960 provides a classic example as to how a candidate can anticipate an attack in an identified area of weakness. Kennedy did not wait for the question of his religion to hurt his campaign effort. Instead, he sought to preempt the issue in both his campaign advertising and his appearances before conventions of ministers and other audiences by appealing to the best of America's values: "Now you cannot tell me the day I was born it was said I could never run for president because I wouldn't meet my oath of office."[26]

In 1992, Bill Clinton similarly inoculated himself against expected Republican charges that he was just another big-government, liberal Democrat. By supporting middle-class programs, by declaring his support for the death penalty and a two-year limitation on welfare, by keeping his distance from Jesse Jackson, and even by attacking the rap music of Sister Souljah, Clinton established himself as a "new Democrat," not a "liberal." Clinton campaign operatives also directly rebutted Republican attacks with response ads that featured facts buttressed by quotes from newspapers and other authoritative sources. There would be no repeat of 1988, where Republican strategists were able to turn the election on the question of Dukakis's liberalism.

Not all negative attacks distort voter understanding of the issues. On the contrary, substantively accurate negative ads are needed to contribute to the accuracy of voter issue perceptions.

Voters often falsely project their issue preferences onto their preferred candidate; they have a psychological tendency to believe that their favorite candidate shares their views on issues, even when that is not the case. Negative advertising provides "information to the contrary" that helps break down these false voter projections.[27]

Whatever its shortcomings, negative advertising raises issues and adds information to a campaign. As Samuel Popkin notes, campaigns cannot deal with anything substantive if they cannot "make noise."[28] Attack campaigning or "dirty politics" raises issues in a way that gets the public's attention: "The tradition of genteel populism in America, and the predictable use of sanitary metaphors to condemn politicians and their modes of communication, says more about the distaste of the people who use the sanitary metaphors for American society than it does about the failings of the politicians."[29] If the nastiness of the 1994 midterm elections is any indicator, negative advertising will continue to be a prominent part of national campaigns.

DEALIGNMENT AND REALIGNMENT: A NEW ELECTORAL ERA?

Does Bill Clinton's election mark the beginning of a new electoral decade? If so, we would say that the 1992 election was a "realigning" election. Or did voting behavior in the 1992 election for the most part represent a continuity with past patterns? If so, the 1992 election would only be considered a "maintaining" or "deviating" election.

Political scientists classify elections according to their long-term significance.[30] An election that produces nothing other than a continuation of prevailing voter patterns is called a **maintaining election**—the expected party wins and there are no fundamentally long-term alterations in voting allegiances. A **deviating election** occurs when the "wrong" party wins the election due to short-term forces but no permanent changes in voter behavior or loyalty take place. Once the short-term disruptive forces disappear, normal voting patterns reemerge. As we saw in Chapter 6, Dwight Eisenhower's victories in 1952 and 1956 are commonly classified as deviating elections as they did not usher in a new era of Republicanism but marked only a temporary interruption of Democratic party dominance during the New Deal era. The term **realignment** is reserved for those periods when a fundamental alteration in the electoral balance of power occurs as a result of a shift in partisan allegiances and voting behavior of large groups of voters. In a **realigning election** the new policy and partisan preference of a significant group of voters not only send a new party to the White House but alter the balance of power in elections for the next two decades or so.

In looking back over elections of the past two and a half decades, one conclusion is undeniable: Some fundamental reorientation or realignment of voter preferences has taken place. The Democratic New Deal majority no longer dominates presidential elections. In fact, as Republicans won five of the six elections for the White House from 1968 to 1988, it might even be more accurate to talk about a Republican as opposed to Democratic presidential majority. The 1994 mid-term election results, with Republicans winning control of Congress, only underscore the conservative, if not always Republican, sympathies of the national electorate.

Yet, whatever realignment took place in the period from the mid-1960s through the 1980s was incomplete. No clear-cut majority of Republican identifiers-in-the-electorate emerged to replace the Democratic majority of the New Deal era. Also, despite their disastrous record in presidential elections during the late 1960s, 1970s, and 1980s, the Democrats continued to win the majority of congressional and statehouse races, a result that was sharply reversed in the Republican victories of 1994.

Instead of ushering in a new Republican majority at all levels, the realignment of this period resulted only in a new era of voter independence and volatility—a period of **rootless politics** characterized by high levels of party switching between elections, split tickets, split results, and divided government. Many voters no longer saw the sense of establishing new partisan affiliations. These voters were alienated from both major parties. Voter dealignment undermined the extent of partisan realignment that could occur.

The **post–New Deal system**[31] that emerged during this period was characterized by an inversion of the New Deal class order, where high-status whites proved more supportive than low-status whites of liberal or equalizing change. Also notable was the emergence of a two-tier party system where the dynamics of candidate selection and voting at the presidential level are quite different from the dynamics of congressional elections.[32] The Republicans successfully emphasized broad ideological themes to capture the presidency. The Democrats, for a long time, parlayed their edge in partisanship and the advantages of incumbency and redistricting to retain control of congressional, especially House, elections. More recent polling data, however, show that the Democratic edge in partisanship has slipped substantially over time. The 1994 congressional elections may mark, at long last, the emergence of a Republican era.

The change in voter alignments has come gradually. Its roots can be found in 1948, when the white South, in reaction to the civil rights planks of the Democratic platform, began to split off from the national Democratic party. The changes continued over three decades. Ladd notes that the group alignments evident by 1984 were vastly different from those of the New Deal era. In 1936, 85 percent of white southerners voted for Roosevelt; twenty-eight years later, just over a quarter voted for Mondale. The 1994 election confirmed the emergence of a new Republican South, where the GOP controlled a majority of the Senate seats, House seats, and governorships in the 11 states of the old Confederacy.

White southerners were not the only group to alter their voting allegiances. During the New Deal alignment, blue-collar voters and Catholics were mainstays of the Democratic coalition. In 1984, in sharp contrast to the New Deal patterns, the majority of voters in each of these groups cast their ballots for Reagan, not Mondale. African-Americans today are more solidly aligned with the Democratic party than they were during the New Deal era.[33]

The issue of race alone does not fully explain the change in voting alignments. Economics, too, played a large role. Changing times redefined the economic issue. While economic hard times, especially during a Republican administration, will work to the political advantage of the Democrats, it was the Republicans during this period—not the Democrats—who enjoyed the advantage on such economic issues as inflation, taxes, and management of the economy. The Democrats could no longer rely on economic issues to rally a presidential majority as they did during the New Deal era. There was no longer a Depression-era, submerged middle class in need of the economic and social assistance programs promised by the Democrats. Voters took for granted major Democratic legislative victories, including the enactment of Social Security, Medicare, and other basic social welfare protections. At the same time, many of these voters resented rising taxes, inflation and the extension of programs to provide benefits to the undeserving poor.

During the New Deal era, the Democrats were seen as the

party of recovery and prosperity; the Republicans, in contrast, were the party of Depression and Hoovervilles. But memories of Hoover, Roosevelt, the Depression, and the New Deal, all faded deep into the past. They were supplanted by general partisan images of a more recent vintage—of Jimmy Carter's and the Democrats' inability to handle the economy compared to the general economic prosperity brought by the Reagan years. Younger voters, in particular, were influenced by perceptions based on more recent political events. The Democrats could no longer win by running on what was essentially a New Deal, or even a Great Society, platform.

Did the 1992 election mark the beginning of a new electoral era? Or was it merely the continuation of the post–New Deal system? The long-term significance of 1992 cannot be fully gauged until we see the result of future presidential contests and find out whether Clinton's election is followed by a series of Democratic or Republican victories. Still, a number of preliminary observations can be ventured.

The 1992 election was obviously not a maintaining election, as the "wrong" party won. Clinton's election marked a departure in the apparent Republican "lock" on the White House during the post–New Deal era. It also appears that 1992 was not likely a realigning election, as there was little happening in the mix of party identification and policy preferences of various social groups.[34] Further, there was no "critical event" along the order of magnitude of a Great Depression to crystallize a change in voter loyalties. The extensive Democratic losses in 1994 would also appear to indicate that no pro-Democratic realignment took place in 1992. Instead of having clear, long-term significance, 1992 looks more like a deviating election in which the out-of-power party won the White House for the first time in sixteen years, primarily as a result of short-term forces.

Retrospective voter rejection of Bush's handling of the economy gave the Democrats the White House in 1992, but there is no guarantee that retrospective economic evaluations will work to the Democrats' advantage in future elections. Nor does the 1992 election represent a mandate for an age of Democratic activism. The amazing Republican victories in the 1994 mid-term elections represent a clear rejection of such activism. Clinton electoral strategist James Carville best described the nature of the Democratic presidential victory in 1992: "We didn't break the GOP electoral lock on the White House—we just picked it."[35]

The end of the Cold War, too, may turn out to be only a short-term electoral factor that abetted Democratic victory in 1992. The break-up of the Soviet empire removed an issue that had worked to the Republican's advantage. In the 1970s and 1980s, voters judged the Republicans as the party better capable of handling national defense. However, there is no guarantee that the low priority given national defense concerns in 1992 will characterize future presidential elections.[36]

The fundamental structure of elections over the past two decades—a dealigned electorate and a split-level system under which Republicans do better in the presidential contest as compared to congressional races—remained intact in 1992. Despite the deviating result of a Democratic presidential win, 1992 saw essentially a continuation of electoral patterns set in the mid-1960s through the 1980s.[37]

The white South continued its move away from its strong Democratic loyalties of the New Deal alignment. In fact, the South should now be considered as presidentially Republican. It was the only region of the country where George Bush won a plurality of the votes in 1992. Clinton's success in the region was due primarily to his strength among black voters.[38]

Catholics, too, continued their drift away from their strong Democratic affinities of the New Deal alignment. In 1992, the Democratic voting edge among white Catholics was a mere 5 percent[39]—far below the margins the Democratic party enjoyed during the New Deal era.

The gender gap, another feature of voting patterns in the post-New Deal era, was also evident in 1992. Various polls show that Clinton did 5 to 6 points better among women than among men.[40] The gender gap was most evident among voters with college and graduate training. Among women with graduate school training, Clinton led Bush by a whopping 25 points.[41] College- and graduate-school-educated women can be viewed as part of an "intelligentsia"[42] more comfortable with Democratic as opposed to Republican views on social change. The "cultural war" speeches of Patrick Buchanan and Pat Robertson at the 1992 GOP convention contributed to the fears of these women.

The relationship of age to the vote in 1992 continued for the most part as it had during the 1980s. Republicans were strongest among younger voters and weakest among voters whose political experiences were formed during the New Deal era. Still, the Democrats were able to improve substantially their performance among younger voters. In terms of party identification, the parties were virtually even among persons 18 to 29 years of age.[43] The economic recession of the later Bush years had taken the bloom off the Republican rose. Where younger voters were once attracted to Reagan and the Republicans as the means of a promising economic future, in 1992 these voters were willing once again to look toward the Democrats.

In sum, while Clinton attracted new voters to the Democratic banner, his election does not appear to mark a realignment where the Democratic party uncovered new and permanent sources of voter support. Instead, the 1992 election appears to be a continuation of contemporary voting patterns. Clinton won by piecing together traditional elements in the Democratic voting base, elements that had rejected the "liberalism" of Democratic presidential aspirants in preceding elections. The Clinton campaign especially focused on winning the traditional Democratic base in "northern tier" industrial states.[44] The Clinton-Gore post-convention bus trip of 1992 was targeted at Democrats in these states.

Clinton found the key to Democratic success in 1992. But there was no guarantee that Democrats will be able to repeat that success in the future. The republican capture of Congress in 1994 underscores the tenuous nature of the Democratic victory two years previous.

THE PEROT FACTOR

The long-term significance of H. Ross Perot's unexpectedly large share of the 1992 vote, 19 percent, cannot yet be fully seen. On the one hand, such a surprising third-party vote underscores the deviating nature of the 1992 election. Alternatively, strong third-party showings often act as the precursor of voter realignment. The appearance of a third party indicates new fault lines in American politics—new social tensions and the dissatisfaction of large numbers of voters with the way existing political parties are handling newly emerging issues.

An upswing in voter intensity is another feature associated with the realignment process.[45] In 1992, voter turnout increased to 55 percent, a notable reversal of the decline in participation in the immediately preceding presidential elections. Part of this increased turnout is currently attributable to Perot's candidacy. Perot attracted numerous voters, angry at the system, who were voting for the first time or had not voted in recent years.[46]

The large vote for Perot in 1992 may indicate that voter anger with politics-as-usual may have reached the point at which normal voting patterns are disrupted. The Perot movement points to the possible emergence of a new defining issue in American politics—the politics of deficit reduction. While the Democratic and Republican parties can be expected to take steps to coopt the Perotist movement, neither party may be capable of absorbing what may prove to be a new force in American politics—large numbers of voters seriously intent on deficit reduction. The Democratic party will not be able to effect the major cuts in social spending required for elimination of the deficit. A proposed Clinton health and welfare policy that adds billions in new spending only further enraged voters demanding a downsizing of government. The Republican party, too, is unlikely to support deficit reduction strategies that entail either increased taxes or major cuts in defense spending.

Will Perotism be a factor that influences elections beginning in 1996? Much depends on the salience not just of the budget deficit but also of the economic conditions that fueled populist resentment in 1992. Perot's supporters in 1992 were angered not just by George Bush's reversal of his no-new-taxes vow but also by his inability to handle the economy. Will that motivating sense of outrage at an incumbent administration and the political system in general be there if the economy improves? If the answer is "No," then the Perotist movement will likely prove to be a one-time expression of anger that quickly burns itself out. Perot's ability to run as a "dissident hero" may not provide the basis for long-term support.[47] While Perot endorsed a number of candidates who lost in 1994 (as well as some who won), overall the 1994 results point o a reservoir of anti-washington resentment that Perot may tap.

The future impact of the Perot factor also depends on H. Ross Perot himself. Realignments are not just mass-based but are also elite-led. The Perotist movement may prove capable of evolving into a genuine third party only if Ross Perot himself chooses to take it in that direction. But in 1992 and the period immediately after the election, Perot showed no indications of any such interest. Instead, he preferred to run United We Stand as his personal electoral vehicle. As the 1992 campaign progressed, local United We Stand chapters were partially financed by Perot and run top-down by the candidate and his designated appointees. At times the grassroots actors who initially organized the local Perot office chafed at the new constraints placed on them from above. Quite often, United We Stand chapters were prevented by fiat from recruiting candidates for other offices.

Should Perot decide not to run for president, the electoral cloud of United We Stand will likely quickly fade. But even if Perot decides to continue his pursuit of the presidency, much depends on whether he chooses to run as a third-party/independent or as a Republican. Ross Perot spent billions on his 1992 campaign. He must decide whether it makes sense to continue to spend such vast sums of money on an independent or third-party route that offers little chance of electoral success.

Perot's remarkable vote in 1992 shows that the structural and behavior roots of the American two-party system may not be as deeply rooted as political scientists have often assumed. Still, significant institutional and behavioral barriers remain and are likely to be sufficient to bar a third-party or independent candidate from winning the White House. A reading of the strategic environment can lead to the following conclusion: An attempt at the Republican nomination offers Perot his best chance of winning the presidency.

Perot's natural base of support lies in the Republican, as opposed to the Democratic, party. Perot's vote in 1992 came disproportionately, in terms of social status and political outlook, from groups that vote Republican in presidential elections. Perot's supporters tended to be white, western, and male, and favored cutting taxes even at the cost of reducing government services.[48] National surveys since the election also point to the fact the Perot voters, while highly independent, lean decidedly to the Republican party. This trend among Perotist voters in the Southwest was especially evident in the 1993 special election for senate in Texas. Immediately after the primaries, one survey showed that Perot voters supported Republican Kay Bailey Hutchison over interim Democratic Senator Bob Krueger by an overwhelming 69 percent to 7 percent margin.[49] Three weeks later, Texas United We Stand, America—the local Perotist organization—endorsed Hutchison. Exit polls in 1994 showed Perot supporters voting about 2 to1 for the Republicans.

Perot could prove to be a formidable candidate in the Republican nominating races.[50] United We Stand offers him the virtue of a strong, grassroots organization. The intense motivation of his followers would prove to be an important electoral asset in the Iowa caucuses and other early or low-turnout contests. His ability to spend billions of his own money means that

Perot will not confront the same financial constraints faced by other candidates. Subject only to his willingness to spend his own fortune, Perot has the money to campaign widely. Should the spending rules for 1996 remain as they were in 1992, Perot can spurn public funding and wind up possibly as the only candidate not subject to the Federal spending limits that accompany public funds. Unlike other candidates, Perot can spend lavishly on the initial contests, and still have sufficient money for the Super Tuesday and big-state races that immediately follow in an increasingly frontloaded primary system.

The move of the California primary from early June to late April also offers Perot a considerable opportunity should he choose to make a run for the Republican nomination. California has proven to be a hotbed of Perotist support. Perot's personal wealth and exemption from spending ceilings mean that he could be one of the few candidates, if not the only candidate, with the financial ability to campaign effectively in this expensive, media-intensive state. If the Republicans keep their virtual winner-take-all rules for California, Perot could conceivably find himself in a multicandidate field with an excellent chance of winning the convention delegates of the entire California delegation.

The renewed prominence of the California primary also helps Perot's prospects in other states. Competing candidates, facing limited budgets and Federal spending regulations, will likely find it necessary to divert limited funds from other primaries to the critical California primary. Perot will be under less pressure to make such a diversion. Only changes in the public financing laws can diminish the considerable financial advantages that Perot would enjoy in a 1996 bid for the Republican presidential nomination.

DEMOCRATIC STRATEGY

Bill Clinton's 1992 election strategy seemingly provides Democrats with a road map to the White House. Clinton studiously sought to avoid the "liberal" tag that had so hurt the presidential efforts of Walter Mondale and Michael Dukakis. Clinton's candidacy was based on the recognition that the 1970s had changed the political terrain. As *Washington Post* columnist and political observer E.J. Dionne described, "The 1970s did to liberals and the Democrats what the 1920s did to businessmen and the Republicans."[51] The public had come to reject what liberals and liberalism—at least in its extremes—stood for: "Liberals, the folks who gave us the New Deal and our victory in World War II, came to be seen as impractical souls who picked the pockets of the middle class."[52]

Clinton ran as a centrist—a middle-class-oriented, moderate-liberal Democrat. If Clinton was a populist, his was a populism of the middle class not of the poor. Clinton sought to win back many of the blue-collar "Reagan Democrats" who had deserted the Democratic Party in previous elections. At campaign stops he surrounded himself with flags to express his acceptance of American patriotism. He sought to express the work-oriented values of middle-class Americans. By avoiding the posture of an extreme liberal, Clinton was able to keep the public's attention on the record of the Bush administration, not on the ideological disposition of the Democratic nominee.

But once in office, Clinton strayed from his promise of middle-class populism. He abandoned the idea of a middle-class tax cut in order to fund deficit reduction. His proposal for national health care seemed unwieldy and complex. By 1994, many voters saw clinton not as a centrist but as part of the Washington establishment; they voted Republican. Yet not all Democrats are satisfied with a centrist route to the White House. Writing before the 1992 election, William Crotty, for instance, criticized what he saw as efforts to move the Democratic party to the right. Crotty was particularly critical of the actions of the Democratic Leadership Council (DLC), an organization dominated by southern and border-state moderates, which attempted to redirect the party's agenda back toward the "political mainstream." As Crotty asked in the title of his article: "Who Needs Two Republican Parties?"[53]

The Democratic party's more liberal factions argue that the electorate has not fundamentally changed its policy orientations over time, that Democrats can still win by appealing to the best of their party's principles and traditions. They argue that Democratic presidential campaigns prior to Clinton's lost for reasons other than ideology. And they argue that Humphrey lost in 1968 because the Democratic party was divided by the Vietnam war. In 1968, Nixon also had the advantage of a superior advertising team. In 1972, McGovern's presidential image was destroyed by the Eagleton fiasco. In 1980, Reagan was elected as a repudiation of Jimmy Carter's inadequacies as president. In 1988, the Democrats lost an election they could have won because Republican strategists rescued a failing Bush presidential effort and Dukakis failed to inoculate himself against the attacks.[54] In the wake of the 1994 electoral disaster, Demoocratic liberals urged that the party offer a clear progressive message to mobilize its base of support.

For the more liberal wing of the Democratic party, there are only limited lessons to be learned from the long drought that characterized Democratic presidential efforts during the 1968–1988 period. Instead of refashioning the basis of the party's appeal to a post–New Deal-era electorate, liberals advise Democratic nominees to learn the art of "candidate self-presentation" and campaign communication.[55] Democratic nominees are counseled not to moderate their liberal message but only to learn how to say it better. According to this perspective, Dukakis's defeat stemmed from his self-presentation as a technocratic manager, his failure to give a positive meaning to liberalism, his inability to come across as a caring and passionate individual, and his loss of control over the media agenda.[56] The only compromise that is required is that a Democrat use the word "moderate" in place of "liberal."[57] The liberal wing of the party argues that Democrats need to offer a message of hope and justice that mobilizes the Democratic vote among key constituencies—nonvoters, African-Americans, Latinos, and women.[58] This is the "rainbow coalition" strategy advocated by Jesse Jackson.

The liberal approach to the White House is taken to task by William Galston and Elaine Ciulla Kamarck, two activists in more moderate Democratic organizations, who expose the flaws in the liberal/progressive strategy. Contrary to the assertions of the liberal activists, the mobilization of nonvoters will not guarantee Democrats electoral success. Why? Democrats no longer enjoy the large edge in voter registration that characterized the earlier New Deal era. Further, class lines no longer predict voting patterns to the same extent that they did during the New Deal. Peripheral voters are not necessarily that much more Democratic than is the active electorate. These peripheral voters are also quite difficult to mobilize. Any hoped-for Democratic gains from the activation of marginal voters into the active electorate will be insufficient to compensate for the decline in support among middle-class voters that the Democratic party has suffered since the end of the New Deal era.[59]

Selective mobilization will not produce victory. Black and Hispanic turnout would have to be increased far above white levels in order to compensate for the disappearing Democratic middle.[60] The Hispanic community is also so heterogeneous that it cannot be relied upon to provide solid margins of support for Democratic presidential candidates. Programmatic appeals that increase minority turnout will also act to certify the "liberal" nature of the Democratic party, thereby causing further defections among white middle-class voters.

Similarly, efforts to mobilize a "women's vote" will likely fail to produce a Democratic victory. The women's vote is more heterogenous than gender gap enthusiasts assume. The Democrats may already enjoy whatever edge they hope to gain as a result of gender gap issues. There may be little room for extensive Democratic party gains in this area. Further, the gender gap may be more indicative of the problems associated with, not the electoral potential of, Democratic liberalism. As Galston and Kamarck note, the gender gap may be more the result of a decline in Democratic support among men than a surge in Democratic support among women. In 1994, the Republicans rode the solid support of white male voters to sweeping congressional and statehouse victories.[61]

The Democratic party's presidential weakness cannot be cured by a strategy based on increased turnouts and selective mobilization. Nor is it rooted in a simple failure of image merchandising. Instead the party's presidential problem stems from a "liberal fundamentalism" where the party's presidential coalition has been "increasingly dominated by minority groups and white elites—a coalition viewed by the middle class as unsympathetic to its interests and its values."[62] As a result of liberal programmatic rigidity, the public has begun to associate the Democrats with taxing and spending, welfarism, indifference to crime, and indifference to American interests abroad.

The risks inherent in pursuing the liberal mobilization strategy are clear. The liberal/progressive strategy acts to cement in place the image of a too-liberal Democratic party, an image that will lead the public to reject the Democratic party not only in the election immediately at hand but in future presidential elections as well.

In the **cementing elections** immediately following the critical elections of 1896 and 1932, the losing party refused to shift away from what had proven to be a disastrous course of action four years earlier.[63] Similarly in the 1970s and 1980s, the Democrats resisted change and nominated liberal candidates with diminishing voter appeal—candidates who cemented in place partisan images that worked to the Democrats' disadvantage. Clinton's nomination and election offered the Democratic party a chance to reexamine its principles and redefine its public image.

More liberal Democrats object that a centrist strategy represents a sell-out of the party's traditions and principles. Yet, a Democratic presidential nominee can be politically viable and still offer voters a program substantially to the left of that offered by the Republicans.

Clinton showed that even an allegedly centrist Democrat can offer progressive policies. Clinton promised to extend unemployment insurance and to take a more proactive government role in job creation. He promised to expand the Earned Income Tax Credit—an important subsidy program for the working poor. He promised to repeal executive orders that limited abortion counseling and fetal-tissue research. He promised more extensive reductions in America's defense spending than those proffered by President Bush. Clinton also promised universal health care—a monumental program clearly consistent with Democratic party traditions. Liberals might object that Clinton did not seize the chance to establish a single-payer, Canadian-style system. But voters were not willing to accept the taxes and bureaucratization associated with a single-payer system.

A Democratic presidential nominee does not need to be a conservative in order to be politically viable. Studies have shown that presidential elections in the 1980s did not constitute a mandate for specific conservative or Republican programs. In many policy areas, the Republicans were perceived to be more conservative than the public at large. To win, the Democrats do not need to mimic the Republican platform. But they do need to offer candidates and a general policy orientation that voters are willing to accept.

Concern for winning does not denote a sacrifice of the party's principles. Winning is important. Only by winning can the Democratic party advance its programs in the areas of anti-poverty policy, civil rights, women's rights, workplace regulation, environmental protection, nuclear nonproliferation, and foreign affairs. Only by winning the presidency can the Democrats gain control of nominations to the Supreme Court and redirect the Court away from its Reagan-era conservative drift on civil rights, civil liberties, and abortion rights.

To win, Democrats must learn which issues they should emphasize and which they should not in presidential elections. First of all, Democrats must recognize the **ideological/operational split** in American public opinion.[64] More Americans identify themselves as conservative than as liberal. When asked about government in a broad ideological sense, Americans tend to give conservative answers. They oppose activist big government, taxation, regulation, welfarism, and redistribution. They prefer state and local power to national power. Yet, when asked about specific programs—that is, when broad principles are given operational definition—the public proves much more supportive of government action. The public supports continued expenditures for Social Security, Medicare, unemployment assistance, antipoverty programs (as long as they are not labeled "welfare"), the relief of homelessness, the rebuilding of cities, job training, improving the economic conditions of minorities, student aid, and the provision of assistance to needy children. Voters claim to be against government regulation, but they support strengthened measures to ensure airline and workplace safety, environmental protection, and the regulation of day-care centers.

The lesson for Democrats is clear. They should avoid broad, philosophical statements regarding the role of the government in the social and political economies. Instead, they need to argue for the virtues of specific programs where the public can clearly see the benefits of government action.

As Kevin Phillips has pointed out, the Democrats can also remain true to their party's populist heritage by attacking the intensifying inequalities of the Reagan and Bush years. Especially if the post-1994 Republican Congress reduces the taxes on investors, the Democrats can once again paint the Republicans as the party of the rich: the party of billionaires and yacht owners insensitive to the needs of everyday working people. The rich prosper. Yet, the homeless populate America's streets, newlyweds face the lost dream of owning a home of their own, and even two-income families find it difficult to pay for their children's education at the college of their choice.[65]

Democrats can carry the populist attack to the Republicans on the issue of taxes. Democrats must repeatedly point out that Republicans during the Reagan-Bush era cut the top income tax bracket from 70 percent to 28 percent, created the "bubble" under which many middle-class Americans pay a higher tax rate than do millionaires, and reduced taxes on corporations and unearned income.[66]

Democrats must be careful to avoid Walter Mondale's grave political mistake of advocating new taxes as the path to deficit reduction. The advocacy of new taxes is an abandonment of populism. Middle-class voters are suspicious that they will be the ones to bear the brunt of any new levy, even when they are promised that the burden of a new tax will fall on the rich. Even if new taxes are needed to cope with the deficit, the Democrats must ensure that Republicans in Congress initiate such taxes. Given the public's demand for deficit reduction, Clinton's 1993 increase in the gas tax by 4.2 cents per gallon was probably small enough to be politically acceptable. It still, though, risked giving the Republicans an issue with which they can continue to cast the Democrats as the party of taxation.

The new inequalities of the Reagan era also afford the Democrats new political opportunities in the nation's heartland. Traditional Democratic job-based appeals and promises to save the family farm should win votes in much-troubled farm states and economically depressed rustbelt cities in the Midwest.[67] Clinton clearly took advantage of this opportunity in 1992.

Democrats can also argue for equalizing programs that provide benefits across class lines. By pursuing the passage of programs that provide benefits to the middle class and the poor, the Democrats can remain true to their party's progressive traditions and still avoid the electorally damaging stigma of welfaristic liberalism. The Democrats can count on continued public support (especially among the elderly) for Social Security and Medicare. They can also count on middle-class support for public education and new programs in the areas of college tuition assistance, day-care provision, and health-care financing. The provision of assistance to first-time homebuyers represents still another program area where positive government action can attract middle-class votes.

Democrats can even target assistance to the poor as long as they are careful to emphasize benefit programs tied to education and the workplace. Democrats can propose expanded funding for schools, job training, day care, and even cash relief tied to a recipient's work effort. The benefits provided by these job training and social assistance programs can be generous, but they must be conditioned on a recipient's efforts at self-improvement. Democratic proposals for welfare reform do not need to mimic the harsh prescriptions offered by Republicans. Still, any Democratic policy of conditioned assistance must also recognize the value that the American public places on work.

The environment represents a potentially potent issue for Democrats. Americans overwhelmingly support more aggressive governmental action in the area of environmental protection.[68] Democratic presidential candidates can push for an activist program of environmental protection, including measures for recycling, pollution reduction, toxic waste clean-up, and energy conservation.

Yet, Democrats must still be cautious in approaching this issue. Public opinion behind environmental protection certainly seems strong. Seventy percent of the public views environmental regulations as "not strong enough," and 78 percent agree that environmental standards cannot be too high and that environmental improvements must be continued regardless of the cost. Yet, when an October 1989 Gallup poll asked "Would you be willing to pay $200 more taxes each year to increase federal spending for...reducing air pollution?" 71 percent said no. More than half the public also expressed their opposition to a 25-cent-per-gallon gasoline tax increase that would be used to control pollution.[69] Democrats must be careful not to advance proposals that lead the public (and the Republicans!) to focus on the costs rather than the benefits of environmental clean-up.

The Democrats can also take advantage of the public's support for women's rights. Younger and more professional women may be attracted to the Republican party's conservative economic philosophy, but they are less comfortable with the Republicans' record on women's and lifestyle issues. The Republicans have been too tied to the profamily orientations of New Right traditionalists to respond to the more liberal lifestyle concerns of younger, career-oriented women. The image of the New Right and the "two Pats"—Patrick Buchanan and Pat Robertson—at the 1992 Republican Convention can be used to instill fear in the hearts of younger voters.

Social and lifestyle issues alone, however, will not win back younger voters for the Democrats. Reagan and Bush won the votes of younger Americans who saw the Republicans as the party of a better economic future. To win the votes of younger Americans, Democrats, too, must be seen as the party of economic opportunity. Democrats must favor partnerships with business to promote economic adaptation and a growing economic pie. While Democrats can propose more equitable measures than those of the rapacious profiteering of the Reagan boom period, they must seek to become known as the party that promotes growth and prepares America for a high-tech economic future.

In foreign and defense policy, the Democrats can take advantage of the public's fears of nuclear war. Democrats can campaign for arms reduction and nuclear nonproliferation. But Democrats must also recognize that a policy of nuclear arms reduction will not be enough to win voter confidence in the foreign policy area. Assessments of a candidate's ability to handle foreign policy are crucial when Americans go to the polls to elect a president. Americans want a president who can lead, one who is supportive of necessary military spending and capable of taking decisive action especially in times of crisis. In the area of national defense, voters have not seen Democratic candidates as potential world leaders. Instead, many view the Democrats as though they are still the party of George McGovern, a party so plagued by the post-Vietnam War syndrome that it is incapable of using force when needed in foreign policy.

Democrats must also learn the importance of political symbols. Patriotism, the Pledge of Allegiance, and respect for the flag are not minor or inconsequential issues in a presidential race. Nor are they simply the specious creations of advertising specialists. Instead, they are important issues to the millions of Americans who express outrage when they see these cherished symbols violated.

Democrats can win presidential elections, but only if their program and candidates escape the taint of big-government, welfaristic, dovish-on-defense liberalism. The L-word hurt Dukakis in 1988. Clinton showed that the label can be avoided. To win, the Democrats need to find a candidate who can escape the liberal tag, yet remain true to the party's progressive traditions. The candidate must be capable of unifying the diverse constituencies that make up the party but still be able to reach out to more independent voters. When in the year 2000 Clinton cannot be renominated, it will be no easy task for the Democrats to find such a candidate. Even if they do, there is no guarantee that he or she will survive the primary and caucus selection system.

Geography provides one additional clue to the path of a possible Democratic presidential victory. The 1990 census recorded the further shift of population and electoral votes to the Sunbelt. National Democrats have not done well in the South in recent years, and there is little guarantee that the Democrats will be able to repeat the 1992 success of Clinton-Gore in Dixie.

However, the Pacific states—California, Oregon, and Washington—each contain strong pockets of social and political liberalism. These states may well provide the pivotal battleground for future presidential races. If so, the Democrats may do well to recruit candidates who can appeal to voters in these Pacific states and not just to traditional Democratic constituencies in the Northeast and the Midwest. In choosing a presidential candidate, Democrats can profitably heed the advice: "Go West, Young Democrat!"[70]

Too often, advocates of political realism have suggested that Democrats structure their appeal to win back white moderates in the South. This is the exact strategy suggested by Earl and Merle Black who, in their book *The Vital South,* argue that the Democrats must break the commanding Electoral College advantage that Republicans enjoy as a result of the Republican presidentialism of the white South.[71]

Still, the "southernness" of the 1992 Democratic strategy should not be overstated. As Jerome Mileur explains, Clinton won not simply by targeting the South but by building on Dukakis's strength in the Pacific Northwest and by winning back traditional Democratic constituencies in the central East and Midwest, particularly in states along the Ohio River. The Bill and Hillary Clinton and Al and Tipper Gore bus tour the week after the Democratic convention points to what the Clinton campaign saw to be the crucial battleground. The bus did not go South. Instead, the Democratic team visited enthusiastic old Democratic bastions in New Jersey, Pennsylvania, West Virginia, Ohio, Illinois, and Missouri. Except for Dan Quayle's home state of Indiana, which the bus passed through, the Democratic ticket swept these states in the fall.[72] The 1994 congressional election results further confirm the picture of Democratic weakness in the South.

Mileur is correct. Democrats need not "go South" or nominate a conservative to win. Still, they need to moderate extreme positions in order to be acceptable to pivotal middle voters no matter in which region of the country these voters reside. Clinton's moderation allowed him to reclaim key constituencies in both the North and the South.

REPUBLICAN STRATEGY

Like the Democrats, the Republican party is similarly divided when it comes to the question of future presidential strategy. Once again, the division is essentially between party members who prefer a more ideological course of action and those who prefer a more pragmatic or centrist strategy.[73]

The more ideological faction of the GOP argues that the party can win by nominating a true, principled conservative who offers the public a clear set of easily definable policy positions that embody American values. Ronald Reagan was just such a communicator and leader; George Bush was not.

George Bush lost the White House because he stood for no clear policy principles or direction. The Bush White House was rudderless. Rather than stake out clear policy positions and take on the Democratic Congress on key questions of programmatic direction, Bush sought a middle ground and cooperated with the Congress in order to achieve workable governance. As a result, voters did not know whom to blame for new taxes, increases in social spending, a failure to control the deficit, and the passage of a civil rights act that appeared to allow affirmative action and racial preferences. Bush appeared to lack any purpose other than maintaining power. Voters in 1992 were forced to look elsewhere for leadership.

The conservative wing of the Republican party is certainly correct in pointing to Bush's leadership failures. Voting alignments and realignments are to a great extent elite-led. Political leaders, including presidents, give definition to a political party and articulate the issues to which the public responds.[74] George Bush failed to define a clear political philosophy that would have attracted voters to the Republican banner. Ronald Reagan's initial election in 1980 may have been not a clear public endorsement of conservatism but only a retrospective rejection of the failures of the Carter administration. Yet, once in office, Reagan used the presidency as a pulpit to persuade people of the virtues of low taxation, limited government at home, and a strong national defense. As a result, by 1984 the Republican party succeeded in attracting new adherents whose loyalty it had not yet commanded in the previous election.[75]

Yet the more moderate faction of the Republican party counters that there is great risk in pursuing an ideologically conservative road to the White House. While the party's centrist leaders agree that issues are the key to the party's future success, they argue that conservative advocates too often emphasize the wrong issues—issues that lose the Republicans votes and risk losing the presidency. Pragmatic Republicans argue that American presidential elections are normally won or lost in the political center. They argue that George Bush lost in 1992 not because he was insufficiently conservative but because he was seen as too distant from the average American voter. Bush did not respond quickly or thoroughly to the economic anxieties of middle Americans in a troubled economy. As a consequence of his inaction, Bush also ceded the emerging health care issue to the Democrats. To win the White House, the Republican party must respond to the concerns of voters in such areas as health care, the economy, the

environment, and access to education. The party must especially seek to respond to the concerns held by highly independent
younger voters; to run only as the party of limited government
and limited taxation is not enough.

More centrist Republican leaders emphasize the harm in-
flicted on the 1992 GOP ticket by a national party convention
dominated by the highly charged speeches of Pat Robertson and
Patrick Buchanan. The GOP is unlikely to win the presidency if it
is perceived by voters to be extreme, judgmental, and intolerant
on such cultural and lifestyle issues as women's rights, abortions,
alternatives to the nuclear family, and personal relationships and
sexuality. Younger voters finding the party's economic conservatism attractive will be turned off by a party that has seemingly
rejected their social and lifestyle choices. Strident Republican
opposition to abortion—especially to *all* abortions, including
abortions in cases of rape and incest—will lose the party some
support among younger and more moderate voters.

What constitutes the most feasible Republican path to the
White House? Put most simply, Republicans should follow the
same broad strategy that gave the party its dominance of presidential elections from 1968 to 1988, as well as its congressional
victory in 1994, but update that strategy to the changed political
contours of the 1990s. Minimal government at home and American strength abroad are no longer enough to win elections. Republicans must continue their antitax, antigovernment agenda
but recognize the dangers inherent in carrying positions to an
extreme. The public's demands for change—including economic fairness and the effective provision of health care and education—pose limitations as to the extent of budget reductions
that Republicans can safely enact. Republican support for militarism also needs to be tempered in the wake of the end of the
Cold War.

As much as possible, Republicans should keep the campaign
dialogue at the ideological level where the public is attuned to the
party's more conservative appeal. Republicans should seize upon
symbols—patriotic symbols included—in tune with America's ideological conservatism. They should continue to portray themselves
as the party of the sensible middle as contrasted with a Democratic party captured by an effete, trendy, liberal intellectual elite that
is out of touch with the values of a majority of Americans.

Republican candidates need to underscore their staunch
opposition to big government, taxes, bureaucracy, and regulation. They need to portray the Clinton administration and

Democrats as big spenders. They need to produce persuasive evidence that the Clinton budgets provide little real deficit reduction but lots of new governmental spending and tax increases. Republicans can take particular advantage of the tactical openings offered by Clinton's increase in the gasoline tax and by those features of the Clinton health care plan that threatened to raise health care premiums or taxes for millions of Americans.

Of course, given the retrospective basis of the public's economic evaluations, much depends on the health of the economy at the time of an election. Still, the area of economic policy offers Republicans a critical issue that they can exploit. The Republicans can continue to present themselves as the party of a prosperous economic future. Republican economic policies are designed to preserve jobs at home by making American industry more competitive globally. When Democrats charge that Republican tax and economic policies are inequitable, the Republican response is simple: The Republicans give tax cuts and a brighter economic future to all Americans! Democrats, in contrast, offer only the antiquated prescriptions of another era. The GOP needs to portray the Democrats as a party too constrained by its obligations to big labor and other special interests to undertake those actions that will make the American economy more competitive and bring benefits to everyone.

In the domestic arena, five other specific issues afford the Republicans great electoral advantage. First is the issue of crime. As the 1988 election showed, many Americans continue to see the Democrats as soft on crime. The crime issue remains ripe for Republican exploitation.

The second area is affirmative action. A majority of Americans do not accept the arguments made on behalf of affirmative action. Instead they see it simply as reverse discrimination, a policy that violates merit principles by awarding unfair advantages to certain individuals on the basis of skin color, gender, or ethnicity. Given the constituent make-up of the Democratic party, Democratic presidential candidates in all likelihood will continue to support affirmative action programs, if not quite numerical quotas. The Republicans should argue aggressively that there is no real difference between affirmative action programs and quotas. By pressing their attack on affirmative action and quotas, the Republicans also increase their chances of gaining new support among Asians, Jews, and other racial and ethnic groups who see their opportunities limited by the hiring and promotional preferences given to others.

Third, the 1994 elections and the overwhelming passage of Proposition 187 in California show the power of the illegal immigration issue. Voters in California, burdened by high taxes and the state's economic downturn, voted to deny most social and educational services to persons who enter the country illegally. The Republicans can exploit this issue, arguing that Americans who work hard and play by the book should not be taxed to support services for those who break the rules.

The fourth issue, school prayer, has not been a salient factor in recent presidential elections. Yet, it has indirectly affected presidential elections by helping to shape the general public's perceptions of the two parties. Public opinion surveys reveal overwhelming support for prayer in public schools. While civil libertarians and Democrats may object that organized school prayer violates the separation of church and state, such arguments carry little weight with voters. Republicans can use the school prayer issue to paint the Democrats as a party more in touch with the ACLU than with the values of everyday Americans. In dealing with school prayer and other religion-related issues, though, Republicans must be cautious not to be seen as the agents of New Right, Christian fundamentalist groups— groups that do not enjoy great public confidence.

The final issue, public choice, crosses several substantive policy areas. Republicans have made increased public choice part of their governing philosophy. Americans are dissatisfied with the state of public services and with their dependence on public bureaucracies. Americans are particularly dissatisfied with the state of public schooling. Republicans can offer the public tax credits, vouchers, and other public choice programs that will give parents the ability to reclaim control over their children's education. These programs will allow parents to withdraw their children from schools that perform poorly and send them to schools that perform better. Republicans can offer competition, restructuring, and reform as the answers in education. They can attack Democratic solutions as rewarding unionized teacher bureaucracies and doing little more than throwing good money after bad to schools that do not teach.

Of course, choice programs need not be restricted to the area of education. A program of tax credits can expand the public's choice of day-care and adult-care arrangements. Tax incentives can also increase the variety of health insurance plans offered by employers to workers.

But Republicans must be cautious in proposing choice plans. The 1993 defeat of a school voucher initiative in California shows that the public is not willing to accept choice plans that are so extreme that they appear to be a raid on the public treasury or a ruse for aiding elite private academies to the detriment of public education.

Republicans must be aware of the electoral pitfalls that face national candidates who run afoul of America's operational liberalism. Republican policy proposals must not be so antigovernment that the GOP loses the votes of middle-class Americans. A conservative revolution that leads to major service cuts in programs favored by the middle class can only endanger Republican political standing. Republicans can effect cuts in Social Security, health care, tuition assistance, and other big-spending, middle-class programs only at great political risk.

The Republicans run a similar risk of alienating voter affections if they pursue deregulation and economic growth policies that are harmful to the environment. The environment has become a new and important political symbol. Republicans recognized this in 1988 in using the Boston Harbor ad to turn the environmental issue on Dukakis. George Bush further recognized the electoral significance of this issue in his promise to become the nation's environmental president. Future Republican presidential candidates will find themselves on safer political ground if they follow the more balanced environmentalist stance of George Bush as opposed to the more ideological, antienvironment policies of Ronald Reagan.

The area of foreign and defense policy has proven to be an electoral asset for Republicans. The Republicans can continue to run as the party of proven strength and leadership in foreign policy. Yet, with the end of the Cold War, Republicans must be aware of voters' ambivalence in the areas of foreign and defense policy. Americans want the nation to be adequately prepared in the area of defense, and they want a president who is capable of exerting effective foreign policy leadership. Yet Americans do not support a buccaneering foreign policy that will drain the country's economy and jeopardize the lives of American soldiers. The constraints that limited American intervention in Somalia, Haiti, and Bosnia during the early Clinton administration all point to the public's limited tolerance for protracted American engagement in trouble spots overseas. Republicans can seek to contrast their perceived strength and competence in the foreign policy arena with the inconsistencies that characterized the handling of American foreign policy abroad in the early Clinton administration as it approached regional conflicts.

Overall, Republicans should present themselves as the party of the sensible middle as opposed to Democratic elite liberalism. To do so they must avoid being captured by the party's more ideological and evangelical wing. The Republicans will be popular only so long as they continue to run the sort of candidates and advocate those policies that Americans approve. An extreme Republican party that ignores the policy concerns of more moderate voters faces the risk of political rejection.

CONCLUSION

This book is written in the tradition of V. O. Key, Jr. The voters are not fools. Image manipulation and television alone do not win presidential elections. Today's more independent electorate responds to broad-based issue concerns as well as to images. The most effective political campaigns are those that mix personal-based images with issue-based themes.

The lesson of this book is simple. When Americans go to the polls to choose a president, they know why they vote as they do. The political party that ignores their values and issue preferences will, in all likelihood, lose.

NOTES

Chapter 1. Campaigning in the Television Age

1. One notable dissenting voice argues that estimates of the growing number of independent voters are frequently overstated. According to this critique, the growth of true voter independence peaked in the 1970s and has been slowly ebbing since then. Many self-professed independents today are, in fact, closet Democrats and Republicans who do not admit their partisan tendencies. See Bruce E. Keith, David B. Magleby, Candice J. Nelson, Elizabeth Orr, Mark C. Westlye, and Raymond E. Wolfinger, *The Myth of the Independent Voter* (Berkeley, CA: U. of California Press, 1992).
2. Samuel L. Popkin, *The Reasoning Voter* (Chicago: U. of Chicago Press, 1991).
3. Ibid.

Chapter 2. The Stages of the Presidential Selection Process

1. Larry M. Bartels, *Presidential Primaries and the Dynamics of Public Choice* (Princeton, NJ: Princeton U. Press, 1988), pp. 105–107.
2. Anthony Corrado, "Presidential Candidate PACs and the Future of Campaign Finance Reform," in *The Quest for National Office: Readings on Elections,* eds. Stephen J. Wayne and Clyde Wilcox (New York: St. Martin's, 1992), p. 318.

323

3. Richard L. Berke, "Dole Takes First Real Steps Toward '96 Presidential Race," *The New York Times,* June 15, 1994.

4. E.J. Dionne, Jr., "The Illusion of Technique: The Impact of Polls on Reporters and Democracy," in *Media Polls in American Politics,* eds. Thomas E. Mann and Gary R. Orren (Washington, DC: Brookings Institution Press, 1992), p. 155.

5. Charles D. Hadley and Harold W. Stanley, "Surviving the 1992 Presidential Nomination Contest," in *America's Choice: The Election of 1992,* ed. William Crotty (Guilford, CT: Dushkin Publishing Group, 1993), p. 34.

6. Alan I. Abramowitz, Ronald B. Rapoport, and Walter J. Stone, "Up Close and Personal: The 1988 Iowa Caucuses and Presidential Politics," in *Nominating the President,* eds. Emmett H. Buell, Jr., and Lee Sigelman (Knoxville, TN: U. of Tennessee Press, 1991), pp. 65–67.

7. Robert T. Nakamura, "Yes—Convention Delegates Should Be Formally Pledged," in *Controversial Issues in Presidential Selection,* ed. Gary L. Rose (Albany, NY: State University of New York Press, 1991), pp. 59–66.

8. Howard l. Reiter, *Selecting the President: The Nominating Process in Transition* (Philadelphia: U. of Pennsylvania Press, 1985).

9. L. Sandy Maisel, "The Platform-Writing Process: Candidate-Centered Platforms in 1992," *Political Science Quarterly* 108, 4 (1993–94): 671–98.

10. Larry David Smith and Dan Nimmo, *Cordial Concurrence: Orchestrating National Party Conventions in the Telepolitical Age* (New York: Praeger, 1991); Byron E. Shafer, *Bifurcated Politics: Evolution and Reform in the National Party Convention* (Cambridge, MA: Harvard U. Press, 1988); and, Donald M. Timmerman and Larry David Smith, "The 1992 Presidential Nominating Conventions: Cordial Concurrence Revisited," in *The 1992 Presidential Campaign: A Communication Perspective,* ed. Robert B. Denton, Jr. (Westport, CN: Praeger Publishers, 1994), pp. 65–87.

11. Lynda Lee Kaid, "Paid Advertising in the 1992 Campaign," in *The 1992 Presidential Campaign: A Communication Perspective,* ed. Robert E. Denton, Jr. (Westport, CN: Praeger Publishers, 1994), pp. 116–17; and L. Patrick Devlin, "Contrasts in Presidential Campaign Commercials of 1992," *American Behavioral Scientist* 37 (November 1993): 287–88.

12. For a review of workings of the Electoral College and competing evaluations of various plans for its reform, see: David W. Abbott and James P. Levine, *Wrong Winner: The Coming Debacle in the Electoral College* (New York: Praeger, 1991); Judith Best, *The Case Against Direct Election of the President: A Defense of the Electoral College* (Ithaca, NY: Cornell U. Press, 1975); Michael J. Glennon, *When No Majority Rules: The Electoral College and Presidential Selection* (Washington, DC: CQ Press, 1992); Lawrence D. Longley and James D. Dana, Jr., "The Biases of the Electoral College in the 1990s," *Polity* 25 (Fall 1992): 123–45; Neal R. Peirce and Lawrence D. Longley, *The People's President: The Electoral College in American History and the Direct-Vote Alternative,* rev. ed. (New Haven, CT: Yale U. Press, 1981); Nelson W. Polsby and Aaron Wildavsky, *Presidential Elections,* 8th ed. (New York: Free Press, 1991), pp. 307–17; Wallace S. Sayre and Judith H. Parris, *Voting for the President: The Electoral College and the American Political System* (Washington, DC: Brookings Institution, 1970); and Allen P. Sindler, "Basic Change Aborted: The Failure to Secure Direct Popular Election of the President," in *Policy and Politics in America: Six Case Studies,* ed. Sindler (Boston: Little Brown, 1973), pp. 31–80.

13. For an example of this argument, see Denny Pilant, "No—The Electoral College Should Not Be Abolished," in *Controversial Issues in Presidential Selection,* ed. Gary L. Rose (Albany, NY: State University of New York Press, 1991), pp. 216–26.

Chapter 3. The Changed Setting of Presidential Elections: Media Wizardry and Partisan Dealignment

1. Joe McGinniss, *The Selling of the President 1968* (New York: Trident Press, 1969).

2. Theodore White, *The Making of the President 1960* (New York: Atheneum, 1961).

3. Paul Taylor, *See How They Run: Electing the President in the Age of Mediaocracy* (New York: Alfred A. Knopf, 1990), pp. 207–8.

4. See Chapter 5 for a review of the literature pointing to the increased influence of issues in contemporary presidential elections.

5. John Kenneth White, *The New Politics of Old Values,* 2nd ed. (Hanover, NH: University Press of New England, 1988), pp. 145–84.

6. Jean Bethke Elshtain, "Issues and Themes in the 1988 Campaign," in *The Election of 1988,* ed. Michael Nelson (Washington, DC: CQ Press, 1989), p. 117.

7. Bruce E. Keith, David B. Magleby, Candice J. Nelson, Elizabeth Orr, Mark C. Westlye, and Raymond E. Wolfinger, *The Myth of the Independent Voter* (Berkeley, CA: U. of California Press, 1992).

8. Walter DeVries and V. Lance Tarrance, *The Ticket-Splitter: A New Force in American Politics* (Grand Rapids, MI: Eerdmans, 1972), pp. 48–55.

9. Ibid., pp. 57–90; Walter Dean Burnham, *Critical Elections and the Mainsprings of American Politics* (New York: W.W. Norton, 1970), pp. 127–30, observes similar characteristics in the "new breed" of American independent.

10. Angus Campbell, Philip E. Converse, Warren E. Miller, and Donald E. Stokes, *The American Voter,* abridged ed. (New York: John Wiley & Sons, 1964), pp. 83–85.

11. Keith et al., *The Myth of the Independent Voter,* chapters 3 and 7.

12. Martin P. Wattenberg, *The Decline of American Political Parties, 1952–1992* (Cambridge, MA: Harvard U. Press, 1994), chap. 10.

13. Herbert F. Weisberg, with David C. Kimball, "The 1992 Presidential Election: Party Identification and Beyond," paper presented at the annual meeting of the American Political Science Association, Washington, DC, September 1993.

14. Michael B. MacKuen, Robert Erikson, and James A. Stimson, "Macropartisanship," *American Political Science Review* 83 (December 1989): 1125–42; Herbert F. Weisberg and Charles E. Smith, Jr., "The Influence of the Economy on Party Identification in the Reagan Years," *Journal of Politics* 53 (November 1991): 1077–92.

15. Raymond E. Wolfinger and Steven J. Rosenstone, *Who Votes?* (New Haven, CT: Yale U. Press, 1982), pp. 13–36, 89–93.

16. Martin P. Wattenberg, *The Decline of American Political Parties, 1952–1988* (Cambridge, MA: Harvard U. Press, 1990), p. 139.

17. Weisberg, "The 1992 Presidential Election: Party Identification and Beyond"; Paul R. Abramson, John H. Aldrich, and David W. Rohde, *Change*

and Continuity in the 1992 Elections (Washington, DC: CQ Press, 1994), pp. 221–49, too, conclude that that as a result of Bush's weak performance in office, the Republicans in 1992 lost the slight edge in partisanship that they had built up during the Reagan years.

18. Ruy A. Teixeira, *The Disappearing American Voter* (Washington, DC: Brookings Institution, 1992), presents an overview of the various reasons for low voter turnout in American elections.

19. Abramson, Aldrich and Rohde, *Change and Continuity in the 1992 Elections*, pp. 120–23; Frank B. Feigert, "The Ross Perot Candidacy and Its Significance," in *America's Choice: The Election of 1992*, ed. William Crotty (Guilford, CT.: Dushkin Publishing Group, 1993), p. 85; Steve Knack, "Perot, Recession, MTV, and Motor Voter: Explaining the '92 Turnout Rise," paper presented to the annual meeting of The American Political Science Association, Washington, DC, September 2–5, 1993.

20. Steven J. Rosenstone, John Mark Hansen, Paul Freedman, and Marguerite Grabarek, "Voter Turnout: Myth and Reality in the 1992 Election," paper presented to the annual meeting of The American Political Science Association, Washington, DC, September 2–5, 1993.

21. Teixeira, *The Disappearing American Voter*, pp. 154–85.

22. Ibid., pp. 92–94.

23. Ibid., pp. 95–96.

24. Abramson, Aldrich, and Rohde, *Change and Continuity in the 1992 Elections*, pp. 123–28.

25. Burnham, *Critical Elections and the Mainsprings of American Politics*, pp. 90–134.

26. Wattenberg, *The Decline of American Political Parties, 1952–1988*, pp. 92–98.

27. Keith et al., *The Myth of the Independent Voter*, pp. 131–32.

28. L. Sandy Maisel, "The Platform-Writing Process: Candidate-Centered Platforms in 1992," *Political Science Quarterly* 108, 4 (1993–94): 671–98.

29. Wattenberg, *The Decline of American Political Parties, 1952–1989*, pp. 92–98.

30. Everett Carll Ladd, Jr., with Charles D. Hadley, *Transformations of the American Party System* (New York: W.W. Norton, 1978), pp. 19–27 and 275–76; James L. Sundquist, *Dynamics of the Party System: Alignment and Realignment of Political Parties in the United States* (Washington, DC: Brookings Institution, 1973), pp. 376–411.

31. Thomas Byrne Edsall and Mary D. Edsall, *Chain Reaction: The Impact of Race, Rights, and Taxes on American Politics* (New York: W.W. Norton, 1991).

32. Paul Allen Beck, "A Socialization Theory of Partisan Realignment," in *Controversies in American Voting Behavior*, eds. Richard G. Niemi and Herbert F. Weisberg (San Francisco: W.H. Freeman, 1973), pp. 396–411.

33. Wattenberg, *The Decline of American Political Parties, 1952–1988*, pp. 120–24.

34. Keith et al., *The Myth of the Independent Voter*, pp. 125–26.

35. Ibid., pp. 125 and 199.

36. Ladd and Hadley, *Transformations of the American Party System*, pp. 162–69.

37. See, for example, Donald Kinder and D. Roderick Kiewiet, "Sociotropic Politics: The American Case," *British Journal of Political Science* 11 (1981): 129–61.

38. Gary C. Jacobson, "The Misallocation of Resources in Congressional Elections," in *Congress Reconsidered*, 5th ed., eds. Lawrence C. Dodd and Bruce I. Oppenheimer (Washington, DC: CQ Press, 1993), pp. 115–40. Also see Jacobson, *The Electoral Origins of Divided Government* (Boulder, CO: Westview Press, 1990).

39. Walter Dean Burnham, "Insulation and Responsiveness in Congressional Elections," *Political Science Quarterly* 90 (1975): 411–35.

40. A quite different view of divided government is presented by David Mayhew, *Divided We Govern* (New Haven: Yale U. Press, 1991). Mayhew argues that the policy results of divided government are not that different from that of unified government, where one party controls both the Congress and the executive. The passage of innovative legislation is affected more by the "public mood" and other factors that by whether there is unified or divided control of government.

41. For examples of this argument, see Burnham, *Critical Elections and the Mainsprings of American Politics;* and Ladd and Hadley, *Transformations of the American Party System.*

42. Keith et al., *The Myth of the Independent Voter,* pp. 198–200.

43. Ibid., p. 167.

Chapter 4. The Nominating System and Campaign Finance Reform: The Rules of the Game

1. Byron E. Shafer, *Bifurcated Politics: Evolution and Reform in the National Party Convention* (Cambridge, MA: Harvard U. Press, 1988), pp. 32–39.

2. William Crotty and John S. Jackson III, *Presidential Primaries and Nominations* (Washington, DC: CQ Press, 1985), p. 28. Crotty and Jacobson provide a good overview of the reforms of the nominating process and their effects.

3. Martin Plissner and Warren J. Mitofsky, "The Making of the Delegates, 1968–1988," *Public Opinion* (September/October 1988): 47; John S. Jackson III, "Yes—The Nominating System Is Representative," in *Controversial Issues in Presidential Selection,* ed. Gary L. Rose (Albany, NY: State University of New York Press, 1991), pp. 27–30.

4. Shafer, *Bifurcated Politics,* pp. 97–103.

5. Crotty and Jackson, *Presidential Primaries and Nominations,* pp. 34–35.

6. Crotty and Jackson, *Presidential Primaries and Nominations,* pp. 44–49, detail the more limited delegate selection reforms instituted by the Republicans.

7. Plissner and Mitofsky, "The Making of the Delegates, 1968–1988," p. 47.

8. The Democratic rules allow two exceptions or modifications to strict proportional representation—the "bonus" system where extra delegates are awarded to the winner of a congressional district, and the "loophole primary," a complex system where voters both register a presidential preference and vote directly for delegates. For a description of which states use which of the variety of delegate selection systems allowed by party rules in both the Democratic and Republican parties, see Emmett H. Buell, Jr., and James W. Davis, "Win Early and Often: Candidates and the Strategic Environment of 1988," in *Nominating the President,* eds. Emmett H. Buell, Jr. and Lee Sigelman (Knoxville, TN: U. of Tennessee Press, 1991), pp. 8–12.

9. Denis G. Sullivan, Jeffrey L. Pressman, Benjamin I. Page, and John J. Lyons, *The Politics of Representation: The Democratic Convention, 1972* (New York: St. Martin's Press, 1974), pp. 17–40.

10. Jeane Kirkpatrick, *The New Presidential Elite: Men and Women in National Politics* (New York: Russell Sage Foundation, Twentieth Century Fund, 1976), pp. 299–308.

11. Ibid., pp. 3–34, 281–331. Also see Austin Ranney, *Curing the Mischiefs of Faction: Party Reform in America* (Berkeley, CA: U. of California Press, 1975), pp. 150–54; and Sullivan et al., *The Politics of Representation*, pp. 17–40.

12. Kirkpatrick, *The New Presidential Elite*, pp. 53–54.

13. Thomas R. Marshall, "Turnout and Representation: Caucuses versus Primaries," *American Journal of Political Science* 22 (February 1978): 169–82.

14. Alan I. Abramowitz, Ronald B. Rapoport, and Walter J. Stone, "Up Close and Personal: The 1988 Iowa Caucuses and Presidential Politics," in *Nominating the President*, eds. Emmett H. Buell, Jr. and Lee Sigelman (Knoxville, TN: U. of Tennessee Press, 1991), pp. 44–57, 68–69.

15. Herbert Kritzer, "Representativeness of the 1972 Presidential Primaries," in *The Party Symbol*, ed. William Crotty (San Francisco: W. H. Freeman, 1980), pp. 148–54.

16. Crotty and Jackson, *Presidential Primaries and Nominations*, pp. 89–95.

17. Herbert McClosky, Paul J. Hoffman, and Rosemary O'Hara, "Issue Conflict and Consensus Among Party Leaders and Followers," *American Political Science Review* 56 (June 1960): 406–29.

18. Warren E. Miller and M. Kent Jennings, with Barbara G. Farah, *Parties in Transition: A Longitudinal Study of Party Leaders and Party Supporters* (New York: Russell Sage Foundation, 1986). Also see Nelson W. Polsby and Aaron Wildavsky, *Presidential Elections*, 7th ed. (New York: Free Press, 1988), pp. 127–30.

19. Walter J. Stone, "Asymmetries in the Electoral Bases of Representation, Nomination Politics, and Partisan Change," in *New Perspectives on American Politics*, eds. Lawrence C. Dodd and Calvin Jillson (Washington, DC: CQ Press, 1994), p. 109.

20. Plissner and Mitofsky, "The Making of the Delegates, 1968–1988," p. 47; Polsby and Wildavsky, *Presidential Elections*, p. 135.

21. Shafer, *Bifurcated Politics*, pp. 100–07.

22. Crotty and Jackson, *Presidential Primaries and Nominations*, p. 137.

23. Polsby and Wildavsky, *Presidential Elections*, pp. 127–43.

24. Shafer, *Bifurcated Politics*, pp. 223–25.

25. Ibid., pp. 121–29.

26. Ibid., pp. 118–21.

27. Candice J. Nelson, "Money and Its Role in the Election," in *America's Choice: The Election of 1992*, ed. William Crotty (Guilford, CT: Dushkin Publishing Group, 1993), p. 106.

28. Richard L. Berke, "U.S. Eases Spending Rules in Presidential Primaries," *The New York Times*, December 18, 1991.

29. Anthony Corrado, *Creative Spending: PACs and the Presidential Selection Process* (Boulder, CO: Westview Press, 1992), pp. 216–18.

30. Herbert E. Alexander and Monica Bauer, *Financing the 1988 Election* (Boulder, CO: Westview Press, 1991), p. 83.

31. Nelson, "Money and Its Role in the Election," p. 106.

32. Herbert E. Alexander, *Financing Politics: Money, Elections, and Political Reform*, 4th ed. (Washington, DC: CQ Press, 1992), pp. 56–58.

33. *Buckley v. Valeo*, 424 U.S. 1 (1976). In *FEC v. NCPAC*, 105 S.Ct. 1459 (1985), the Supreme Court essentially reaffirmed its view as to the constitutional protection afforded independent expenditures, even in campaigns that otherwise are publicly funded.

34. Alexander, *Financing Politics*, 4th ed., p. 104.

35. Corrado, *Creative Campaigning*, pp. 1–3.

36. Ibid., p. 122.
37. Herbert E. Alexander and Brian A. Haggerty, *Financing the 1984 Election* (Lexington, MA: Lexington Books, 1987), p. 403. Also see Corrado, *Creative Campaigning.*
38. Alexander, *Financing Politics,* 4th ed., p. 115.
39. Chuck Alston, "Big Money Slips Back Into Government," *Congressional Quarterly Weekly Reports* (March 7, 1992): 590.
40. Alexander, *Financing Politics,* p. 105.
41. Beth Donovan, "Parties Turned Soft Money Law Into Hard and Fast Spending," *Congressional Quarterly Weekly Reports* (May 15, 1993): 1197.
42. Nelson, "Money and Its Role in the Election," p. 104.
43. Alexander, *Financing Politics,* 4th ed., p. 69.
44. Alexander and Bauer, *Financing the 1988 Election,* p. 80.
45. Frank J. Sorauf, *Inside Campaign Finance: Myths and Realities* (New Haven, CT: Yale U. Press, 1992), pp. 137–40. The quotation is from p. 140.
46. Ibid., p. 137.
47. Ibid., pp. 147–51 and 218–19.
48. Herbert E. Alexander, "Making Sense about Dollars in the 1980 Presidential Campaigns," in *Money and Politics in the United States,* ed. Michael J. Malbin (Chatham, NJ: Chatham House, 1984), pp. 19–24; Alexander and Haggerty, *Financing the 1984 Election,* pp. 329–31; Alexander and Bauer, *Financing the 1988 Election,* pp. 40–43.
49. In 1992, Bush and Clinton each received $55.24 million in federal grants to run their general election limited campaigns. The two major parties also received a little over $11 million each for their national conventions. These figures do not include $12.1 million in federal matching funds that Clinton received and the $10.1 million that Bush received during the primary season. See Nelson, "Money and Its Role in the Election," pp. 102–04.
50. Alexander and Bauer, *Financing the 1988 Election,* p. 42.
51. Nelson, "Money and Its Role in the Election," p. 102.

Chapter 5. The Debate over Issue Voting

1. Richard G. Niemi and Herbert E. Weisberg, eds., *Controversies in Voting Behavior* (Washington, DC: CQ Press, 1984), p. 102.
2. Angus Campbell, Philip E. Converse, Warren E. Miller, and Donald E. Stokes, *The American Voter* (New York: John Wiley & Sons, 1960). Page references to *The American Voter* cited in this chapter will be to the abridged edition published in 1964.
3. Paul F. Lazarsfeld, Bernard Berelson, and Hazel Gaudet, *The People's Choice* (New York: Columbia U. of Chicago Press, 1954).
4. Bernard R. Berelson, Paul F. Lazarsfeld, and William N. McPhee, *Voting* (Chicago: U. of Chicago Press, 1954).
5. Ibid., pp. 19–21.
6. Ibid., p. 27.
7. Ibid., p. 322.
8. Angus Campbell, Philip E. Converse, Warren E. Miller, and Donald E. Stokes, *Elections and the Political Order* (New York: John Wiley & Sons, 1966).
9. Campbell et al., *The American Voter,* p. 33.
10. Ibid., p. 72.

11. Ibid., p. 76.
12. Ibid., p. 29.
13. Ibid., p. 44. Also see Herbert McClosky, Paul J. Hoffman, and Rosemary O'Hara, "Issue Conflict and Consensus Among Party Leaders and Followers," *American Political Science Review* 54 (June 1960): 406–27.
14. Campbell et al., *The American Voter,* p. 98.
15. Ibid., p. 105
16. Philip E. Converse, "the Nature of Belief Systems in Mass Publics," in *Ideology and Discontent,* ed. David E. Apter (New York: Free Press, 1964), Chap. 6. Christopher A. Achen, "Mass Political Attitudes and Survey Response," *American Political Science Review* 69 (December 1975): 1218–31, criticizes that some of the low correlations over time reported by Converse are the artifact of inadequate survey methods, more precisely the low reliability of survey questions. As the choices in questions do not closely match voter beliefs, respondents' answers vary a bit over time, even when their opinions do not change. When Achen corrects for the lack of reliability of the survey instrument, he finds that voters have more stable opinions. Other political scientists, however, charge that Achen has inadvertently inflated the apparent level of ideological thinking by overcompensating for the lack of reliability of survey questions.
17. Campbell et al., *The American Voter,* pp. 116–17, 135.
18. Ibid., p. 142.
19. V.O. Key, Jr., *The Responsible Electorate* (New York: Vintage Books, 1966), pp. 7–8.
20. Ibid., p. 37.
21. Ibid., p. 55
22. Ibid., p. 92
23. Ibid., p. 56.
24. Also see Everett Carll Ladd, Jr., with Charles D. Hadley, *Transformations of the American Party System,* 2d ed. (New York: W. W. Norton, 1978), pp. 129–30.
25. Key, *The Responsible Electorate,* p. 57. Also see Arthur H. Miller and Martin P. Wattenberg, "Throwing the Rascals Out: Policy Evaluations of Presidential Candidates, 1952–1980," *American Political Science Review* 79 (1985): 359–72.
26. Also see Miller and Wattenberg, "Throwing the Rascals Out," p. 365.
27. Richard G. Niemi and Herbert F. Weisberg, eds., *Controversies in American Voting Behavior* (San Francisco: W. H. Freeman, 1973), pp. 165–66.
28. Michael Margolis, "From Confusion to Confusion: Issues and Voters, 1952–1972," in *Parties and Elections in an Anti-Party Age,* ed. Jeff Fishel (Bloomington, IN: U. of Indiana Press, 1978), pp. 116–17.
29. David E. RePass, "Issue Salience and Party Choice," *American Political Science Review* 65 (June 1971): 389–400. The quotation appears on p. 390.
30. Margolis, "From Confusion to Confusion," pp. 120–21.
31. Ibid., p. 119.
32. Gerald Pomper, "The Impact of *The American Voter* on Political Science," *Political Science Quarterly* 93 (Winter 1978): 625.
33. Norman H. Nie, Sidney Verba, John R. Petrocik, *The Changing American Voter* (Cambridge, MA: Harvard U. Press, 1976), pp. 70–73.
34. Ladd and Hadley, *Transformations of the American Party System,* p. 320.
35. Gerald Pomper, *Voters' Choice* (New York: Dodd, Mead, 1975), p. xiii. Also see Pomper, "From Confusion to Clarity: Issues and American Voters, 1952–1968," *American Political Science Review* 66 (June 1972): 415–28.
36. Ibid., pp. 11–12.

37. Ibid., p. 180.
38. Ibid., p. 114.
39. Ibid., pp. 170–73.
40. Ibid., p. 178.
41. Margolis, "From Confusion to Confusion," p. 117.
42. Ibid., pp. 117–19
43. Nie et al., *The Changing American Voter,* especially Chapter 8. Also see Norman H. Nie and Kristi Anderson, "Mass Belief Systems Revisited: Political Change and Attitude Structure," *Journal of Politics* 36 (August 1974): 540–90.
44. Converse, "The Nature of Belief Systems in Mass Publics."
45. George F. Bishop, Alfred J. Tuchfarber, and Robert W. Oldendick, "Change in the Structure of American Political Attitudes: The Nagging Question of Question Wording," *American Journal of Political Science* 22 (May 1978): 250–69; and Eric R. A. N. Smith, *The Unchanging American Voter* (Berkeley : U. of California Press, 1989), pp. 117–35.
46. John L. Sullivan, James E. Piereson, and George E. Marcus, "Ideological Constraint in the Mass Public: A Methodological Critique and Some New Findings," *American Journal of Political Science* 22 (May 1978): 233–49.
47. Norman H. Nie and James N. Rabjohn, "Revisiting Mass Belief Systems Revisited: Or, Doing Research Is Like Watching a Tennis Match," *American Journal of Political Science* 23 (February 1979): 139–75.
48. John L. Sullivan, James E. Piereson, George E. Marcus, and Stanley Feldman, "The More Things Change, the More They Stay the Same: The Stability of Mass Belief Systems," *American Journal of Political Science* 23 (February 1979): 176–86; and George F. Bishop, Alfred J. Tuchfarber, Robert W. Oldendick, and Stephen E. Bennett, "Questions About Question Wording: A Rejoinder to Revisiting Mass Belief Systems Revisited," *American Journal of Political Science* 23 (February 1979): 187–92.
49. Philip E. Converse and Gregory B. Markus, "Plus ça change...: The New CPS Election Study Panel," *American Political Science Review* 73 (March 1979): 32–49.
50. Philip E. Converse, Warren E. Miller, Jerrold G. Rusk, and Arthur G. Wolfe, "Continuity and Change in American Politics: Parties and Issues in the 1968 Election," *American Political Science Review* 63 (December 1969): 1083–1105.
51. Arthur H. Miller, Warren E. Miller, Alden S. Raine, and Thad A. Brown, "A Majority Party in Disarray: Policy Polarization in the 1972 Election," *American Political Science Review* 30 (September 1976): 753–78; Warren E. Miller and Teresa E. Levitin, *Leadership and Change: The New Politics of the American Electorate* (Cambridge, MA: Winthrop, 1976), pp. 45–62, 119–66.
52. Edward G. Carmines and James A. Stimson, "The Two Faces of Issue Voting," *American Political Science Review* 74 (March 1980): 78–91.
53. Morris P. Fiorina, *Retrospective Voting in American National Elections* (New Haven, CT: Yale U. Press, 1981), p. 83 and chap. 6; John E. Jackson, "Issues, Party Choices, and Presidential Votes," *American Journal of Political Science* 19 (May 1975): 161–85; and Charles H. Franklin, "Issue Preferences, Socialization, and the Evolution of Party Identification," *American Journal of Political Science* 28 (August 1984): 459–78. For a brief review of the revisionist literature that sees party identification as a response to adult political experiences and policy attitudes, see Michael M. Gant and Norman R. Luttbeg, *American Electoral Behavior* (Itasca, IL: F. E. Peacock, 1991), pp. 30–33.
54. Michael B. MacKuen, Robert S. Erikson, and James A. Stimson, "Macropartisanship," *American Political Science Review* 83 (1989): 1125–42.

55. Not all political scientists agree that partisanship is a response to issue and performance assessments. Some charge that the fluctuations in partisanship are not the result of voter assessments of current affairs but simply the result of methodological failings and the inability of lesser involved voters to give consistent answers to polling questions over time. See: Donald Philip Green and Bradley Palmquist, "Of Artifacts and Partisan Instability," *American Journal of Political Science* 34 (August 1990): 872–902; and, Bruce E. Keith, David B. Magleby, Candice J. Nelson, Elizabeth Orr, Mark C. Westlye, and Raymond E. Wolfinger, *The Myth of the Independent Voter* (Berkeley: U. of California Press, 1992), pp. 85–87.

56. Fiorina, *Retrospective Voting in American National Elections*, p. 200. Emphasis in the original.

57. Carmines and Stimson, "The Two Faces of Issue Voting," p. 79.

58. Fiorina, *Retrospective Voting in American National Elections*, pp. 10–11.

59. Ibid., p. 10.

60. Ibid., p. 5.

61. This point is also made by Anthony Downs, *An Economic Theory of Democracy* (New York: Harper and Row, 1957), pp. 38–40.

62. See, for instance, D. Roderick Kiewiet, "Policy-Oriented Voting in Response to Economic Issues," *American Political Science Review* 75 (1981): 448–59; Donald R. Kinder and D. Roderick Kiewiet, "Sociotropic Politics: The American Case," *British Journal of Political Science* 11 (1981): 129–61; Donald R. Kinder, Gordon S. Adams, and Paul W. Gronke, "Economics and Politics in the 1984 Presidential Election," *American Journal of Political Science* 33 (May 1989): 491–515; and Robert S. Erikson, "Economic Conditions and the Presidential Vote," *American Political Science Review* 83 (June 1989): 567–73.

63. Fiorina, *Retrospective Voting in American National Elections*, pp. 100, 127–28; and Arthur H. Miller, "Partisanship Reinstated? A Comparison of the 1972 and 1976 United States Presidential Elections," *British Journal of Political Science* 8 (1978): 129–52.

64. Kathleen A. Frankovic, "Public Opinion Trends," in *The Election of 1980*, ed. Gerald M. Pomper (Chatham, NJ: Chatham House, 1981), pp. 97–118; Gregory B. Markus, "Political Attitudes During a Presidential Year: A Report on the 1980 NES Panel Study," *American Political Science Review* 76 (1982): 538–60.

65. George Rabinowitz and Stuart Elaine Macdonald, "A Directional Theory of Issue Voting," *American Political Science Review* 83 (1989): 93–121.

66. Irwin L. Morris, "Issue Voting and the Coexistence of Directional and Proximity Voters," paper presented at the annual meeting of the American Political Science Association, Washington, DC, September 2–5, 1993; George Rabinowitz, Stuart Elaine Macdonald, and Ola Listhaug, "Competing Theories of Issue Voting: Is Discounting the Explanation?," paper presented at the annual meeting of the American Political Science Association, Washington, DC. September 2–5, 1993.

67. Rabinowitz and Macdonald, "A Directional Theory of Issue Voting," p. 94.

68. Ibid., p. 115.

69. Rabinowitz, Macdonald, and Listhaug, "Competing Theories of Issue Voting."

70. Morris, "Issue Voting and the Coexistence of Directional and Proximity Voters."

71. Carmines and Stimson, "The Two Faces of Issue Voting," pp. 78–91.

72. It should be noted that the Carmines and Stimson article analyzes the impact of the Vietnam War and race on voting in the 1972 presidential election. It is likely that their conclusions also apply to the 1968 election. In their book *Issue Evolution: Race and the Transformation of American Politics* (Princeton, NJ: Princeton U. Press, 1989), pp. 123, 137, Carmines and Stimson state that race was at the center of voters' ideology or "issue bundles" in 1968.

73. See Carmines and Stimson, *Issue Evolution: Race and the Transformation of American Politics,* pp. 11–12.

74. Samuel L. Popkin, *The Reasoning Voter* (Chicago: U. of Chicago Press, 1991).

75. Downs, *An Economic Theory of Democracy,* too, argues that it is irrational (speaking in the strictest economic sense of the word) for voters to pursue new information when they derive so little direct benefit from becoming a more informed voter.

76. Popkin, *The Reasoning Voter,* pp. 15–16.

77. Ibid., p. 78; On the interconnectedness of issues and images, see Lawrence R. Jacobs and Robert Y. Shapiro, "Issues, Candidate Image, and Running: The Use of Private Polls in Kennedy's 1960 Presidential Campaign," *American Political Science Review* 88 (September 1994): 527–540.

78. Popkin, *The Reasoning Voter,* pp. 78–79.

79. Ibid., p. 7.

80. Ibid., pp. 1–4.

81. Ibid., p. 3.

82. Edwin Diamond, Martha McKay, and Robert Silverman, "Pop Goes Politics: New Media, Interactive Formats, and the 1992 Presidential Campaign," *American Behavioral Scientist* 37 (November 1993): 258.

83. Richard G. Niemi and Herbert F. Weisberg, *Classics in Voting Behavior* (Washington, DC: CQ Press, 1993), p. 99.

Chapter 6. The New Deal Era

1. Gerald Pomper, "The Impact of *The American Voter* on Political Science," *Political Science Quarterly* 93 (Winter 1978): 625.

2. V. O. Key, Jr., *The Responsible Electorate* (New York: Vintage Books, 1966).

3. V. O. Key, Jr., "A Theory of Critical Elections," *Journal of Politics* 17 (February 1955): 3–18; Walter Dean Burnham, *Critical Elections and the Mainsprings of American Politics* (New York: W. W. Norton, 1970), pp. 1–10.

4. Walter Dean Burnham, "The Changing Shape of the Political Universe," *American Political Science Review* 59 (March 1965): 7–28, reprinted in Walter Dean Burnham, *The Current Crisis in American Politics* (New York: Oxford U. Press, 1982), p. 49.

5. Samuel Lubell, *The Future of American Politics,* 2d ed. (Garden City, NY: Doubleday, 1951, 1956), p. 40.

6. Ibid. The nature of Bryan's appeal is also discussed by Everett Carll Ladd, Jr., *American Political Parties: Social Change and Political Response* (New York: W. W. Norton, 1970), pp. 120–24.

7. E. E. Schattschneider, *The Semi-Sovereign People* (New York: Holt, Rinehart & Winston, 1960), p. 79. The phrase "the system of 1896" is also from Schattschneider.

8. Burnham, "The Changing Shape of the Political Universe," p. 50.

9. Lubell, *The Future of American Politics,* pp. 35–43. Also see Key, "A Theory of Critical Elections," pp. 4–11.

10. Gerald H. Gamm, *The Making of New Deal Democrats* (Chicago: U. of Chicago Press, 1989), pp. 188–90; Duncan MacRae, Jr., and James A. Meldrum, "Critical Elections in Illinois: 1888–1958," *American Political Science Review* 54 (1960): 669–83; and Jerome M. Clubb and Howard W. Allen, "The Cities and the Election of 1928: Partisan Realignment?" *American Historical Review* 74 (April 1969): 1205–20.

11. Kristi Anderson, "Generation, Partisan Shift, and Realignment: A Glance Back to the New Deal," in Norman H. Nie, Sidney Verba, and John R. Petrocik, *The Changing American Voter* (Cambridge, MA.: Harvard U. Press, 1976), pp. 74–95. Everett Carll Ladd, Jr., with Charles D. Hadley, *Transformations of the American Party System,* 2d ed. (New York: W. W. Norton, 1978), pp. 31–87, presents the opposite point of view, that the "conversion" of former Republicans, not "generational replacement," accounts for realignment. The argument that both conversion and generational replacement occurred during a continuing process of realignment is made by Robert S. Erikson and Kent L. Tedin, "The 1928–1936 Partisan Realignment: The Case for the Conversion Hypothesis," *American Political Science Review* 75 (December 1981): 951–62; and Courtney Brown, "Mass Dynamics of U.S. Presidential Competitions, 1928–1936," *American Political Science Review* 82 (December 1988): 1153–81.

12. Gamm, *The Making of New Deal Democrats,* pp. 3–104, 183–202.

13. Paul Allen Beck, "A Socialization Theory of Partisan Realignment," in *Controversies in American Voting Behavior,* eds. Richard G. Niemi and Herbert F. Weisberg (San Francisco: W. H. Freeman, 1973), pp. 396–411.

14. Edwin Diamond and Stephen Bates, *The Spot: The Rise of Political Advertising on Television* (Cambridge, MA: MIT Press, 1984), p. 41.

15. Ibid., pp. 46–47.

16. J. Leonard Reinsch, *Getting Elected: From Radio and Roosevelt to Television and Reagan* (New York: Hippocrene Books, 1988), pp. 79–80.

17. Ibid., p. 82.

18. Diamond and Bates, *The Spot,* p. 52.

19. Ibid., p. 54; and Stanley Kelley, Jr., *Professional Public Relations and Political Power* (Baltimore: Johns Hopkins Press, 1956), p. 188.

20. Kelley, *Professional Public Relations and Political Power,* pp. 193–95.

21. Nixon's strategy in preparing for the Checkers speech is discussed by Diamond and Bates, *The Spot,* pp. 66–75; Kelley, *Professional Public Relations and Political Power,* pp. 177–84; and Kurt Lang and Gladys Engel Lang, *Politics and Television* (Chicago: Quadrangle Books, 1968), pp. 24–29.

22. Angus Campbell, "A Classification of the Presidential Elections," in *Elections and the Political Order,* eds. Angus Campbell, Philip E. Converse, Warren E. Miller, and Donald E. Stokes (New York: John Wiley & Sons, 1966), pp. 69–79.

23. Richard W. Boyd and Maura Solomon, "The Influence of Foreign Policy Issues in the 1952 Election," paper presented at the annual meeting of the Midwest Political Science Association, Chicago, April 13–17, 1993.

24. Samuel L. Popkin, *The Reasoning Voter* (Chicago: U. of Chicago Press, 1991), p. 62.

25. Ibid., p. 110.

26. Diamond and Bates, *The Spot,* pp. 95–96.
27. Philip Converse, "Religion and Politics: The 1960 Election," in *Elections and the Political Order,* eds. Campbell et al., p. 124.
28. Ithiel de Sola Pool, Robert P. Abelson, and Samuel L. Popkin, *Candidates, Issues, and Strategies: A Computer Simulation of the 1960 Presidential Election* (Cambridge, MA: MIT Press, 1964), p. 117. See their more extensive discussion, pp. 115–18.
29. According to Kathleen Hall Jamieson, *Packaging the Presidency: A History and Criticism of Presidential Campaign Advertising* (New York: Oxford U. Press, 1984), pp. 136–39, the Kennedy campaign also used the saga of the PT-109 rescue mission to portray a physically vigorous and quite capable Kennedy, thereby keeping under wraps Kennedy's affliction with Addison's disease.
30. Marshall McLuhan, *Understanding Media* (New York: McGraw-Hill, 1964), pp. 287–88. Reinsch, *Getting Elected,* pp. 133–53, provides a good account of the strategy involved in the debates from the perspective of the Kennedy camp.
31. Evron M. Kirkpatrick, "Presidential Candidate `Debates': What Can We Learn From 1960?" in *The Past and Future of Presidential Debates,* ed. Austin Ranney (Washington, DC: American Enterprise Institute, 1979), pp. 29–32.
32. Lang and Lang, *Politics and Television,* pp. 212–49, and Sidney Kraus, ed., *The Great Debates* (Bloomington, IN: U. of Indiana Press, 1962), analyze the impact of the 1960 debates.
33. Key *The Responsible Electorate,* p. 56.
34. Ibid., p. 57. Also see Arthur H. Miller and Martin P. Wattenberg, "Throwing the Rascals Out: Policy Evaluations of Presidential Candidates, 1952–1980," *American Political Science Review* 79 (1985): 359–72.
35. Arthur H. Miller, Martin P. Wattenberg, and Oksana Malanchuk, "Schematic Assessments of Presidential Candidates," *American Political Science Review* 80 (1986): 521–40.
36. Miller and Wattenberg, "Throwing the Rascals Out," p. 365.

Chapter 7. The Rise of Issues in Presidential Elections: 1964–1972

1. Edwin Diamond and Stephen Bates, *The Spot: The Rise of Political Advertising on Television* (Cambridge, MA.: MIT Press, 1984), pp. 122–24.
2. Ibid., pp. 124–26.
3. Aaron Wildavsky, ``The Goldwater Phenomenon: Purists, Politicians, and the Two-Party System," *Review of Politics* 27 (1965): 386–413.
4. For details about the Johnson campaign's continued use of the nuclear weapons issue even after the withdrawal of the Daisy Girl ad, see Diamond and Bates, *The Spot,* pp. 129–36.
5. Kathleen Hall Jamieson, *Packaging the Presidency: A History and Criticism of Presidential Campaign Advertising* (New York: Oxford U. Press, 1964), pp. 177–78.
6. Ibid., p. 176.
7. David E. RePass, "Issue Salience and Party Choice," *American Political Science Review* 65 (June 1971): 389–400.
8. Norman H. Nie, Sidney Verba, John R. Petrocik, *The Changing American Voter* (Cambridge, MA: Harvard U. Press, 1976), pp. 123–30. Also see Norman

H. Nie and Kristi Anderson, "Mass Belief Systems Revisited: Political Change and Attitudinal Structure," *Journal of Politics* 36 (August 1974): 540–87.

9. Nie, Verba, and Petrocik, *The Changing American Voter,* p. 336.

10. Gerald Pomper, *Voters' Choice: Varieties of American Electoral Behavior* (New York: Dodd, Mead, 1975), p. 178.

11. Donald E. Stokes, ``Some Dynamic Elements of Contests for the Presidency," *American Political Science Review* 60 (March 1966): 19–28.

12. Aage R. Clausen, Philip E. Converse, and Warren E. Miller, "Electoral Myth and Reality: The 1964 Election," *American Political Science Review* 59 (June 1965): 321–32.

13. Ibid., p. 331.

14. Ibid.

15. Arthur H. Miller, Martin P. Wattenberg, and Oksana Malanchuk, "Schematic Assessments of Presidential Candidates," *American Political Science Review* 80 (1986): 528–29.

16. R. Kenneth Godwin, *One Billion Dollars of Influence* (Chatham, NJ: Chatham House, 1988), pp. 101–2; Herbert E. Alexander, *Financing the 1964 Election* (Princeton, NJ: Citizens' Research Foundation, 1966); and Frank J. Sorauf, *Money in American Elections* (Glenview, IL: Scott, Foresman; Boston: Little, Brown, 1988), p. 26.

17. Theodore H. White, *The Making of the President 1968* (New York: Atheneum, 1969), p. 61.

18. Ibid., pp. 3–5.

19. Ibid., pp. 71–72.

20. Ibid., p. 70.

21. Timothy Crouse, *The Boys on the Bus* (New York: Ballantine, 1972), p. 196.

22. Richard M. Scammon and Ben J. Wattenberg, *The Real Majority* (New York: Coward-McCann, 1970), pp. 85–87.

23. Philip E. Converse, Warren E. Miller, Jerrold G. Rusk, and Arthur G. Wolfe, "Continuity and Change in American Politics: Parties and Issues in the 1968 Election," *American Political Science Review* 63 (December 1969): 1095. Also see Scammon and Wattenberg, *The Real Majority,* p. 91.

24. Nelson W. Polsby, *Consequences of Party Reform* (New York: Oxford U. Press, 1983), pp. 24–26; White, *The Making of the President 1968,* p. 218.

25. Scammon and Wattenberg, *The Real Majority,* p. 142.

26. Joe McGinniss, *The Selling of the President 1968* (New York: Trident Press, 1969), p. 20.

27. Ibid., p. 22.

28. Ibid., p. 83 (emphasis in the original).

29. Scammon and Wattenberg, *The Real Majority,* p. 174.

30. Converse et al., "Continuity and Change in American Politics... the 1968 Election," p. 1097.

31. Scammon and Wattenberg, *The Real Majority,* pp. 200–211.

32. Ibid., pp. 35–71.

33. Benjamin I. Page and Richard A. Brody, "Policy Voting and the Electoral Process: The Vietnam War Issue," *American Political Science Review* 66 (1972): 979–95.

34. Converse et al., "Continuity and Change in American Politics... the 1968 Election," p. 1098.

35. Ibid., p. 1099.

36. Diamond and Bates, *The Spot,* p. 187.

37. Crouse, *The Boys on the Bus,* pp. 46–47.

38. Ibid., pp. 46–65.

39. Jeane Kirkpatrick, *The New Presidential Elite* (New York: Russell Sage Foundation, 1976), pp. 305–15; Denis G. Sullivan, Jeffrey L. Pressman, Benjamin I. Page, and John J. Lyons, *The Politics of Representation: The Democratic Convention 1972* (New York: St. Martin's Press, 1974), pp. 330–34; and William Crotty, *Party Reform* (New York: Longman, 1983), pp. 143–51.

40. Crotty, *Party Reform,* pp. 155–202, details the expulsion of the "Daley 59" from the 1072 Democratic convention.

41. Crouse, *The Boys on the Bus,* pp. 339–53.

42. Jamieson, *Packaging the Presidency,* pp. 320–21.

43. Ibid., pp. 322–23.

44. Ibid., p. 304.

45. Everett Carll Ladd, Jr., with Charles D. Hadley, *Transformations of the American Party System* (New York: W. W. Norton, 1975), p. 234. See pp. 181–246 for Ladd and Hadley's larger description of the changed pattern of class alignments in the postindustrial era.

46. Pomper, *The Voter's Choice,* pp. 190–91.

47. Edward G. Carmines and James A. Stimson, "The Two Faces of Issue Voting," *American Political Science Review* 74 (March 1980): 78–91.

48. Warren E. Miller and Teresa E. Levitin, *Leadership and Change: The New Politics and the American Electorate* (Cambridge, MA: Winthrop, 1976), p. 1.

49. Ibid., p. 127.

50. Ibid., pp. 133–39.

51. Arthur H. Miller and Warren E. Miller, "Issues, Candidates, and Partisan Divisions in the 1972 American Presidential Election," *British Journal of Political Science* 5 (1975): 393–431.

52. Arthur H. Miller, Warren E. Miller, Alden S. Raine, and Thad A. Brown, "A Majority Party in Disarray: Policy Polarization in the 1972 Election," *American Political Science Review* 30 (September 1976): 753–78.

53. Samuel Popkin, John W. Gorman, Charles Phillips, and Jeffrey A. Smith, "Comment: What Have You Done for Me Lately? Toward an Investment Theory of Voting," *American Political Science Review* 70 (September 1976): 779–813.

54. Ibid., p. 801.

55. Ibid., p. 794.

Chapter 8. The Politics of Retrospective Rejection: 1976–1980

1. Gerald R. Ford, *A Time to Heal* (New York: Harper & Row, 1979).

2. Edwin Diamond and Stephen Bates, *The Spot: The Rise of Political Advertising on Television* (Cambridge, MA: MIT Press, 1984), p. 235.

3. Larry M. Bartels, *Presidential Primaries and the Dynamics of Public Choice* (Princeton, NJ: Princeton U. Press, 1988), pp. 172–75, 201–3.

4. Jonathon Moore and Janet Fraser, eds., *Campaign for the President: The Managers Look at '76* (Cambridge, MA: Ballinger, 1977), pp. 92–93. Quoted in Bartels, *Presidential Primaries and the Dynamics of Public Choice,* p. 44.

5. For instance, see Diamond and Bates, *The Spot,* pp. 241–44; and Kathleen Hall Jamieson, *Packaging the Presidency* (New York: Oxford U. Press, 1984), pp. 355–56.

6. Bartels, *Presidential Primaries and the Dynamics of Public Choice*, p. 211.

7. Diamond and Bates, *The Spot,* pp. 241–44.

8. Donald R. Kinder and D. Roderick Kiewiet, "Sociotropic Politics: The American Case," *British Journal of Political Science* 11 (1978): 129–61.

9. Arthur H. Miller, "The Majority Party Reunited? A Comparison of the 1972 and 1976 Elections," in *Parties and Elections in an Anti-Party Age,* ed. Jeff Fishel (Bloomington, IN: Indiana U. Press, 1978), p. 130.

10. Robert H. Entman, *Democracy Without Citizens: Media and the Decay of American Politics* (New York: Oxford U. Press, 1989), p. 126.

11. Ibid., pp. 125–26.

12. Thomas E. Patterson, *The Mass Media Election: How Americans Choose Their President* (New York: Praeger, 1980), pp. 120–25. Also see Sidney Kraus, *Televised Presidential Debates and Public Policy* (Hillsdale, NJ: Lawrence Erlbaum Associates, 1988), pp. 73–74.

13. David O. Sears and Steven H. Chaffee, "Uses and Effects of the 1976 Debates: An Overview of the Empirical Studies," in *The Great Debates 1976: Ford vs. Carter,* ed. Sidney Kraus (Bloomington, IN: Indiana U. Press, 1979), pp. 240–58.

14. Warren E. Miller and Teresa E. Levitin, *Leadership and Change: Presidential Elections from 1952 to 1976* (Cambridge, MA: Winthrop, 1976), p. 189.

15. Ibid., p. 211.

16. Everett Carll Ladd, Jr., with Charles D. Hadley, *Transformations of the American Party System,* 2d ed. (New York: W. W. Norton, 1978), pp. 225–39.

17. Miller and Levitin, *Leadership and Change . . . 1952 to 1976,* pp. 199–202; Arthur Miller, "The Majority Party Reunited?" p. 138.

18. J. David Gopoian, "Issue Preference and Candidate Choice in Presidential Primaries," *American Journal of Political Science* 26 (August 1982): 523–46.

19. Bartels, *Presidential Primaries and the Dynamics of Public Choice*, p. 83.

20. David W. Abbott and Edward T. Rogowsky, "Voting Behavior in the 1976 Election: A Preliminary Report," in *Political Parties,* 2d ed., eds. David W. Abbott and Edward T. Rogowsky (Chicago: Rand McNally, 1978), pp. 208–15.

21. Arthur Miller, "The Majority Party Reunited?" pp. 129–30.

22. Abbott and Rogowsky, "Voting Behavior in the 1976 Election," pp. 211–13. Also see Herbert B. Asher, *Presidential Elections and American Politics,* 3d ed. (Homewood, IL: Dorsey, 1984), p. 157.

23. Miller and Levitin, *Leadership and Change . . . 1952 to 1976,* p. 189.

24. Pamela Johnston Conover and Stanley Feldman, "Candidate Perception in an Ambiguous World: Campaigns, Cues, and Inference Processes," *American Journal of Political Science* 33 (November 1989): 912–40. Also see Miller and Levitin, *Leadership and Change . . . 1952 to 1976,* pp. 220–21.

25. Arthur Miller, "The Majority Party Reunited?" pp. 133–34, 138.

26. Morris P. Fiorina, *Retrospective Voting in American National Elections* (New Haven, CT: Yale U. Press, 1981), p. 125.

27. Kristen Renwick Monroe, *Presidential Popularity and the Economy* (New York: Praeger, 1984), p. 140.

28. Ibid., p. 142.

29. Arthur Miller, "The Majority Party Reunited?" p. 132.

30. Bartels, *Presidential Primaries and the Dynamics of Public Choice*, pp. 183–84.

31. Miller and Levitin, *Leadership and Change . . . 1952 to 1976,* pp. 219–20.

32. Fiorina, *Retrospective Voting in American National Politics,* p. 175.

33. Kathleen A. Frankovic, "Public Opinion," in *The Election of 1980,* ed. Gerald Pomper (Chatham, NJ: Chatham House, 1981), pp. 97–102.

34. Diamond and Bates, *The Spot,* pp. 276–79. Also see Jamieson, *Packaging the Presidency,* p. 384.
35. Diamond and Bates, *The Spot,* p. 276; Jamieson, *Packaging the Presidency,* p. 382.
36. Diamond and Bates, *The Spot,* pp. 270–71.
37. Herbert E. Alexander, *Financing Elections,* 3d ed. (Washington, DC: CQ Press, 1984), p. 125; Frank J. Sorauf, *Money in American Elections* (Glenview, IL: Scott, Foresman; Boston: Little, Brown, 1988), pp. 208–9; and Jamieson, *Packaging the Presidency,* pp. 417–28.
38. Quoted by Myles Martel, *Political Campaign Debates: Images, Strategies, and Tactics* (New York: Longman, 1983), p. 20.
39. Michael J. Robinson and Margaret A. Sheehan, *Over the Wire and On TV: CBS and UPI in Campaign '80* (New York: Russell Sage Foundation, 1983), pp. 73–75, 244–47.
40. Frankovic, "Public Opinion," pp. 113–17.
41. Arthur H. Miller and Martin P. Wattenberg, "Throwing the Rascals Out: Policy and Performance Evaluations of Presidential Candidates, 1952–1980," *American Political Science Review* 79 (1985): 359–72; Walter Dean Burnham, "The 1980 Earthquake: Realignment, Reaction, or What?" in *The Hidden Election: Politics and Economics in the 1980 Presidential Campaign,* eds. Thomas Ferguson and Joel Rogers (New York: Pantheon, 1981), pp. 109–10; and Frankovic, "Public Opinion," pp. 113–17.
42. Robert S. Erikson, "Economic Conditions and the Presidential Vote," *American Political Science Review* 83 (June 1989): 567–73.
43. Fred M. Monardi, "Primary Voters as Retrospective Voters," *American Politics Quarterly* 22 (January 1994): 88–103.
44. Gregory B. Markus, ``Political Attitudes During an Election Year: A Report on the 1980 NES Panel Data," *American Political Science Review* 76 (September 1982): 538–60.
45. Jamieson, *Packaging the Presidency,* p. 412.
46. Diamond and Bates, *The Spot,* pp. 258–62.

Chapter 9. The Politics of Retrospective Approval: 1984

1. Gary C. Jacobson and Samuel Kernell, *Strategy and Choice in Congressional Elections,* 2d ed. (New Haven, CT: Yale U. Press, 1983), pp. 94–109. The figures on party assistance to House candidates are cited on p. 105.
2. John C. McAdams and John R. Johannes, "The Voter in the 1982 House Elections," *American Journal of Political Science* 28 (November 1984): 778–81.
3. Paul C. Light and Celinda Lake, "The Election: Candidates, Strategies, and Decisions," in *The Elections of 1984,* ed. Michael Nelson (Washington, DC: CQ Press, 1985), p. 90.
4. Scott Keeter, "Public Opinion in 1984," in *The Election of 1984,* ed. Gerald M. Pomper (Chatham, NJ: Chatham House, 1985), pp. 93–99.
5. Detailed descriptions of Glenn's image-building strategy are provided by Gary R. Orren, "The Nomination Process: Vicissitudes of Candidate Selection," in *The Elections of 1984,* ed. Michael Nelson, pp. 57–59; Edwin Diamond and Stephen Bates, *The Spot: The Rise of Political Advertising on Television* (Cambridge, MA: MIT Press, 1984), pp. 3–32; Richard F. Fenno, *The Presidential Odyssey of John Glenn* (Washington, DC: CQ Press, 1990), pp. 125–210.

6. Benjamin Ginsberg and Martin Shefter, "A Critical Realignment? The New Politics, the Reconstituted Right, and the Election of 1984," in *The Elections of 1984*, ed. Michael Nelson, p. 16; Orren, "The Nomination Process," pp. 58–59; and Diamond and Bates, *The Spot*, pp. 29–32.

7. Orren, "The Nomination Process," pp. 52–53. Also see Larry M. Bartels, *Presidential Primaries and the Dynamics of Public Choice* (Princeton, NJ: Princeton U. Press, 1988), p. 128.

8. Kathleen A. Frankovic, "The Democratic Nomination Campaign: Voter Rationality and Instability in a Changing Campaign Environment," in *Elections in America*, ed. Kay Lehman Schlozman (Boston: Allen & Unwin, 1987), p. 266.

9. Michael J. Robinson, "News Media Myths and Realities: What the Network News Did and Didn't Do in the 1984 General Campaign," in *Elections in America*, ed. Kay Lehman Schlozman, p. 157.

10. Bartels, *Presidential Primaries and the Dynamics of Public Choice*, pp. 103–7, 262.

11. Orren, "The Nomination Process," pp. 40–41.

12. Ginsberg and Shefter, "A Critical Realignment?" pp. 16–17; Orren, "The Nomination Process," pp. 66–67; and Bartels, *Presidential Primaries and the Dynamics of Public Choice*, p. 225.

13. Bartels, *Presidential Primaries and the Dynamics of Public Choice*, pp. 259–61. Frankovic, "The Democratic Nomination Campaign," p. 278, agrees with Bartels that momentum was the key factor in Hart's rise and fall, but disagrees when it comes to an assessment of the role that ideology played in the Democratic race. According to Frankovic, ideology was not related to the vote in the 1984 Democratic primaries.

14. Bartels, *Presidential Primaries*, pp. 263–67. Also see Paul R. Abramson, John H. Aldrich, and David W. Rohde, *Change and Continuity in the 1984 Elections* (Washington, DC: CQ Press, 1986), pp. 41–42. For a more detailed discussion of Jesse Jackson's base of support in the 1984 campaign, see Adolph L. Reed, Jr., *The Jesse Jackson Phenomenon* (New Haven, CT: Yale U. Press, 1986); Lucius J. Barker and Ronald W. Walters, eds., *Jesse Jackson's 1984 Presidential Campaign* (Urbana, IL: U. of Illinois Press, 1989); and Lorenzo Morris, ed., *The Social and Political Implications of the 1984 Jesse Jackson Presidential Campaign* (New York: Praeger, 1990).

15. Gerald M. Pomper, "The Nominations," in *The Election of 1984: Reports and Interpretations*, ed. Gerald M. Pomper (Chatham, NJ: Chatham House, 1985), p. 19. Also see Thomas E. Patterson and Richard Davis, "The Media Campaign: Struggle for the Agenda," in *The Elections of 1984*, ed. Michael Nelson, pp. 116–17.

16. Bartels, *Presidential Primaries*, pp. 84–88.

17. Orren, "The Nomination Process," pp. 69–70.

18. Abramson, *Change and Continuity in the 1984 Elections*, p. 139.

19. Ibid., p. 58. Also see Michael J. Robinson, "Where's the Beef? Media and Media Elites in 1984," in *The American Elections of 1984*, ed. Austin Ranney (Durham, NC: Duke U. Press, American Enterprise Institute, 1985), pp. 196–200.

20. Edwin Diamond and Stephen Bates, "The Ads," in *The Mass Media in Campaign '84*, eds. Michael J. Robinson and Austin Ranney (Washington, DC: American Enterprise Institute, 1985), p. 51.

21. Internal Republican tracking polls.

22. For a discussion of the gender gap in 1984, see Light and Lake, "The Elec-

tion: Candidates, Strategies, and Decisions," p. 105; and Keeter, "Public Opinion in 1984," pp. 101–6. For an analysis of the roots of the gender gap, see Jane J. Mansbridge, "Myth and Reality: The ERA and the Gender Gap in the 1980 Election," *Public Opinion Quarterly* 49 (1985): 164–78.

23. Light and Lake, "The Election: Candidates, Strategies, and Decisions," p. 86.

24. John Kenneth White, *The New Politics of Old Values*, 2d ed. (Hanover, NH: University Press of New England, 1988), pp. 70–73.

25. Light and Lake, "The Election: Candidates, Strategies, and Decisions," p. 107; Abramson et al., *Change and Continuity in the 1984 Elections*, chaps. 6 and 7; Donald R. Kinder, Gordon S. Adams, and Paul W. Gronke, "Economics and Politics in the 1984 American Presidential Election," *American Journal of Political Science* 33 (May 1989): 491–515; Gerald M. Pomper, ``The Presidential Election," in *The Election of 1984*, ed. Gerald Pomper, pp. 142–44.

26. White, *The New Politics of Old Values*, p. 70.

27. Ibid. Also see Abramson et al., *Change and Continuity in the 1984 Elections*, pp. 194–95; and Keeter, "Public Opinion in 1984," pp. 91–92.

28. Light and Lake, "The Election: Candidates, Strategies, and Decisions," p. 74.

29. White, *The New Politics of Old Values*, p. 57.

30. Abramson et al., *Change and Continuity in the 1984 Elections*, p. 175.

31. Martin P. Wattenberg, *The Rise of Candidate-Centered Politics: Presidential Elections of the 1980s* (Cambridge, MA: Harvard U. Press, 1991), pp. 111–13.

32. Abramson et al., *Change and Continuity in the 1984 Elections*, pp. 169–72; and Warren E. Miller, "The Election of 1984 and the Future of American Politics," in *Elections in America*, ed. Kay Lehman Schlozman, pp. 300–301.

33. Abramson et al., *Change and Continuity in the 1984 Elections*, p. 171.

34. Miller, "The Election of 1984 and the Future of American Politics," p. 300.

35. Theodore J. Lowi, "An Aligning Election, A Presidential Plebiscite," in *The Elections of 1984*, ed. Michael Nelson, pp. 281–84.

36. John H. Aldrich, John L. Sullivan, and Eugene Bordiga, "Foreign Affairs and Issue Voting: Do Presidential Candidates 'Waltz Before a Blind Audience'?" *American Political Science Review* 83 (1989): 123–41.

37. Abramson et al., *Change and Continuity in the 1984 Elections*, p. 203.

38. Ibid., p. 175; William Schneider, "The November 6 Vote for President: What Did It Mean?" in *The American Elections of 1984*, ed. Austin Ranney, p. 225.

39. Abramson et al., *Change and Continuity in the 1984 Elections*, p. 203.

Chapter 10. The Triumph of Issue-Based Images: 1988

1. Paul Taylor, *See How They Run: Electing the President in an Age of Mediaocracy* (New York: Knopf, 1990), p. 5.

2. Peter Goldman, Tom Mathews, et al., *The Quest for the Presidency 1988* (New York: Simon & Schuster, 1989), p. 13.

3. Marjorie Randon Hershey, "The Campaign and the Media," in *The Election of 1988: Reports and Interpretations*, ed. Gerald M. Pomper (Chatham, NJ: Chatham House, 1989), p. 96. Also see Thomas E. Patterson, "The Press and Its Missed Assignment," in *The Elections of 1988*, ed. Michael Nelson (Washington, DC: CQ Press, 1989), pp. 63–92.

4. Hershey, "The Campaign and the Media," p. 98.

5. Ibid., p. 100.

6. J. Merrill Shanks and Warren E. Miller, "Partisanship, Policy and Performance: The Reagan Legacy in the 1988 Election," *British Journal of Political Science* 21 (1991): 129–197; J. David Gopoian, "Images and Issues in the 1988 Presidential Election," *Journal of Politics* 55 (February 1993): 151–166.

7. Martin P. Wattenberg, *The Rise of Candidate-Centered Politics: Presidential Elections in the 1980s* (Cambridge, MA: Harvard U. Press, 1991), pp. 134–55.

8. Samuel L. Popkin, *The Reasoning Voter* (Chicago: U. of Chicago Press; 1991), pp. 142–43.

9. Ibid, p. 7.

10. Larry J. Sabato, "Open Season: How the News Media Cover Presidential Campaigns in the Age of Attack Journalism," in *Under the Watchful Eye: Managing Presidential Campaigns in the Television Era.* ed. Mathew D. McCubbins (Washington, DC: CQ Press, 1992), pp. 134–35; Larry J. Sabato, *Feeding Frenzy* (New York: The Free Press, 1991), pp. 66–67 and 148–51. Also see Popkin, *The Reasoning Voter*, p. 142.

11. Charles S. Bullock III and Burdett A. Loomis, "The Changing Congressional Career," *Congress Reconsidered* 3d ed., eds. Lawrence C. Dodd and Bruce I. Oppenheimer (Washington, DC: CQ Press, 1985), pp. 68, 77–78. Gephardt's Washington orientation is evident in his election as House Majority Leader, next-in-line to the Speaker.

12. Taylor, *See How They Run*, p. 15.

13. Goldman, Mathews, et al., *The Quest for the Presidency 1988*, p. 124.

14. Popkin, *The Reasoning Voter*, p. 145.

15. Allen D. Hertzke, *Echoes of Discontent: Jesse Jackson, Pat Robertson, and the Resurgence of Populism* (Washington, DC: CQ Press, 1993), pp. 127–29.

16. Ibid., pp. 129–32.

17. Ibid., p. 134.

18. Goldman, Mathews, et al., *The Quest for the Presidency 1988*, p. 65.

19. Barbara Norrander, *Super Tuesday: Regional Politics and Presidential Primaries* (Lexington, KY: U. of Kentucky Press, 1992), pp. 84–86.

20. Ibid., pp. 187–88 and 191–94.

21. John H. Aldrich and R. Michael Alvarez, "Issues and the Presidential Primary Vote," paper presented at the annual meeting of the American Political Science Association, Chicago, September 1992. Also see Norrander, *Super Tuesday*, pp. 158–59.

22. Paul R. Abramson, John H. Aldrich, Phil Paolino, and David W. Rohde, "'Sophisticated' Voting in the 1988 Presidential Primaries," *American Political Science Review* 25 (March 1992): 55–69.

23. Hertzke, *Echoes of Discontent*, pp. 138–50, esp. p. 144.

24. Ibid., p. 145; and Barbara Norrander, "Nomination Choices: Caucus and Primary Outcomes, 1976–88,"*American Journal of Political Science* 37 (May 1993): 358–61

25. *Newsweek*, October 19, 1987.

26. Taylor, *See How They Run*, p. 201. The behind-the-scenes strategizing in the Bush camp prior to the Dan Rather interview is described in detail by Taylor, pp. 196–201; and Goldman, Mathews, et al., *The Quest for the Presidency, 1988*, pp. 198–201.

27. Roger Simon, *Road Show: In America Anyone Can Become President, It's One of the Risks We Take* (New York: Farrar, Strauss, Giroux, 1990), pp. 3–30, tells

the story of the Straddle ad and the 1988 Republican campaign in New Hampshire.

28. Peggy Noonan, *What I Saw at the Revolution* (New York: Random House, 1990).

29. John Cassidy, "From Wimp to Winner" *(London) Sunday Times,* November 6, 1988. The details of the Paramus focus group are also recounted by Goldman, Mathews, et al., *The Quest for the Presidency 1988,* pp. 299–303; and Simon, *Road Show,* pp. 214–17.

30. Taylor, *See How They Run,* p. 190.

31. Cassidy, "From Wimp to Winner."

32. See Chapter 3 for a review of the role played by "independent expenditure" campaigns in presidential elections as a result of the Supreme Court's *Buckley v. Valeo* decision.

33. Popkin, *The Reasoning Voter,* p. 45.

34. Sabato, *Feeding Frenzy,* p. 159. For a more complete discussion of press coverage of the Quayle affair, see Sabato, pp. 156–71. Of course, Quayle and the Republicans were not the only victims of a media feeding frenzy in 1988. Earlier, Dukakis was hurt when the press pursued the unsubstantiated story that the Democratic nominee was suffering from mental health problems and had undergone psychiatric treatment for depression. Amazingly, these rumors, lacking in substantiation and planted by backers of the extremist candidate Lyndon Larouche, were picked up by the mainstream press. See Sabato, pp. 152–56, for details.

35. When Ronald Reagan first ran for governor of California in 1966, an ad on behalf of incumbent Edmund "Pat" Brown parodied Reagan's lack of credentials for office by showing clips of Reagan in a number of his old television and movie roles—as a cowboy, a salesman, and a down-and-outer. The ad was too sophisticated. Many television viewers saw Reagan's picture so often that they thought it was an ad for Reagan. See Ernest D. Rose and Douglas Fuchs, "Reagan vs. Brown: A TV Image Playback," in *The New Style in Election Campaigns,* ed. Robert Agranoff (Boston: Holbrook Press, 1972), pp. 350–63.

36. Ross K. Baker, "The Congressional Elections," in *The Election of 1988: Reports and Interpretations,* ed. Gerald M. Pomper (Chatham, NJ: Chatham House, 1989), pp. 153–76.

37. Paul R. Abramson, John H. Aldrich, and David W. Rohde, *Change and Continuity in the 1988 Elections* (Washington, DC: CQ Press, 1990), p. 3.

38. Ibid., p. 167.

39. Ibid., p. 173.

40. Wattenberg, *The Rise of Candidate-Centered Politics,* pp. 121–23.

41. Gopoian, "Images and Issues in the 1988 Presidential Campaign," pp. 150 and 158.

42. Shanks and Miller, "Partisanship, Policy and Performance," pp. 130–33, 150–51, 172–80, and 195–97.

43. Ibid., pp. 180–81

44. Ibid., p. 132.

45. Jean Bethke Elshtain, "Issues and Themes in the 1988 Campaign," in *The Elections of 1988,* ed. Michael Nelson (Washington, D.C.: CQ Press, 1989), pp. 117–18.

46. Barbara G. Farah and Ethel Klein, "Public Opinion Trends," in *The Election of 1988: Reports and Interpretations,* ed. Gerald M. Pomper (Chatham, NJ:

Chatham House, 1989), p. 115.

47. Kathleen Hall Jamieson, *Dirty Politics: Deception, Distraction, and Democracy* (New York: Oxford U. Press, 1992), pp. 3–9

48. Hershey, "The Campaign and the Media," p. 99.

49. Taylor, *See How They Run*, p. 223.

50. Ibid., p. 224.

51. John Kenneth White, *The New Politics of Old Values*, 2d ed. (Hanover, NH: University Press of New England, 1988); Farah and Klein, "Public Opinion Trends," p. 118; and Gerald M. Pomper, "The Presidential Election," in *The Election of 1988: Reports and Interpretations*, ed. Gerald M. Pomper (Chatham, NJ: Chatham House, 1989), pp. 137–44.

52. Wattenberg, *The Rise of Candidate-Centered Politics*, p. 146.

53. Kathleen A. Bratton, "Retrospective Voting and Future Expectations: The Case of the Budget Deficit in the 1988 Election," *American Politics Quarterly* 22 (July 1994): 277–96.

54. Wattenberg, *The Rise of Candidate-Centered Politics*, p. 130.

55. Ibid., pp. 151–52. Also see Wattenberg's discussion, *The Rise of Candidate-Centered Politics*, pp. 123–29.

56. Kathleen Hall Jamieson. From her participation in a panel on "The Ethics of Political News Reporting and Advertising on Television," Ripon College, Ripon, Wisconsin, October 20, 1989. For an extended discussion of her criticisms of both the revolving door and Willie Horton ads and how they "sidetracked a broader discussion of crime," see Jamieson, *Dirty Politics*, pp. 15–42. Taylor, *See How They Run*, p. 214, also discusses the false inferences contained in the Revolving Door ad.

57. Taylor, *See How They Run*, p. 191.

58. For a review of the Reagan administration's environmental record, see Jonathon Lash, Katherine Gillman, and David Sheridan, *A Season of Spoils* (New York: Pantheon, 1984); Sheldon Kamieniecki, Robert O'Brien, and Michael Clarke, *Controversies in Environmental Policy* (Albany, NY: State U. of New York Press, 1986); and Norman J. Vig and Michael E. Kraft, *Environmental Policy in the 1980s: Reagan's New Agenda* (Washington, DC: CQ Press, 1984).

59. Goldman, Mathews, et al., *Quest for the Presidency 1988*, pp. 362–63.

Chapter 11: 1992: "It's the Economy, Stupid."

1. Seymour Martin Lipset, "The Significance of the 1992 Election," *PS: Political Science and Politics* (March 1993): 7; Patterson, *Out of Order*, pp. 103–13.

2. Christine F. Ridout, "News Coverage and Talk Shows in the 1992 Presidential Campaign," *PS: Political Science and Politics* (December 1993): 712–16; Philip Meyer, "The Media Reformation: Giving the Agenda Back to the People," in *The Elections of 1992*, edited by William Nelson (Washington, DC: CQ Press, 1993), pp. 98–101; Doris Graber, "Making Campaign News User Friendly: The Lessons of 1992 and Beyond," *American Behavioral Scientist* 37 (November 1993): 328–36. The reference to user-friendly news formats is from Graber, p. 332. For a more critical assessment of televised town hall meetings, see Dan Nimmo, "The Electronic Town Hall in Campaign '92: Interactive Forum or Carnival of Buncombe?" in *The 1992 Presidential Campaign: A Communication Perspective*, ed. Robert E. Denton, Jr. (Westport, CT: Praeger, 1994), pp. 207–26.

3. Ridout, "News Coverage and Talk Shows in the 1992 Presidential Campaign." Also see Thomas E. Patterson, *Out of Order* (New York: Knopf, 1993).

4. According to the Congressional Budget Office, the richest one percent of families gained 60 percent of all the entire after-tax gain of wealth in the country from 1977 to 1989. See Sylvia Nasar, "The 1980's: A Very Good Time for the Very Rich," *The New York Times,* March 5, 1992. The potential for a populist rebellion against the growing inequalities of the Reagan-Bush era is also pointed out in two books by Kevin Phillips: *The Politics of Rich and Poor* (New York: Random House, 1990) and *Boiling Point: Democrats, Republicans, and the Decline of Middle Class Prosperity* (New York: Harper Collins, 1993).

5. Jon F. Hale, "A Different Kind of Democrat: Bill Clinton, the DLC, and the Construction of a New Party Identity," paper presented at the annual meeting of the American Political Science Association, Washington, DC, September 2–5, 1993; Nicol C. Rae, *Southern Democrats* (New York: Oxford U. Press, 1994), pp. 111–127.

6. Lipset, "The Significance of the 1992 Election," pp. 13–14.

7. Clinton media consultant Frank Greer discussed the tactical calculations that went into producing of the "Plan" spot in his appearance before a forum sponsored by *Campaigns and Elections,* Washington, DC, March 13, 1992.

8. Elizabeth Kolbert, "Test-Marketing a President," *The New York Times Magazine,* August 30, 1992, p. 68.

9. For a presentation of the profile of Tsongas and Clinton voters in the Democratic races in various state races, see the exit poll results that accompanied the following stories: Adam Clymer, "Messages of Warning to Bush and of Hope for Democrats," *The New York Times,* March 5, 1992; David E. Rosenbaum, "Surveys Indicate Top Candidates Are Vulnerable," *The New York Times,* March 12, 1992; and "With Clinton Surging, Party Splits on Next Step," *The New York Times,* April 9, 1992.

10. Kolbert, "Test-Marketing a President," p. 68.

11. Ibid., p. 60.

12. Ibid., p. 68; Peter Goldman and Tom Mathews, "America Changes the Guard," *Newsweek,* Special Election Issue *How He Won* (November/December 1992): 56.

13. Goldman and Mathews, "America Changes the Guard," p. 60.

14. CNN News, March 13, 1992.

15. For evidence of the failure of the Tongues Untied ad, see Kathleen Hall Jamieson, *Dirty Politics: Deception, Distraction, and Democracy* (New York: Oxford U. Press, 1992), pp. 262–65.

16. L. Sandy Maisel, "The Platform-Writing Process: Candidate-Centered Platforms in 1992," *Political Science Quarterly* 108, 4 (1993–94): 671–98.

17. James Ceaser and Andrew Busch, *Upside Down and Inside Out: The 1992 Elections and American Politics* (Lanham, MD: Rowman and Littlefield, 1993), pp. 89–104.

18. J. David Gillespie, *Politics at the Periphery: Third Parties in Two-Party America* (Columbia, SC: U. of South Carolina Press, 1993), p. 132.

19. Goldman and Mathews, "America Changes the Guard," p. 87. L. Patrick Devlin, "Contrasts in Presidential Campaign Commercials of 1992. *American Behavioral Scientist* 37 (November 1993), p. 273, reports that in his one month of campaigning, Perot spent slightly under $40 million on television advertising, roughly the amount that Clinton and Bush each spent in

their late-summer and fall campaigns. Nearly half of the Perot budget was spent in the final nine days, possibly helping to account for his late surge.

20. Goldman and Mathews, America Changes the Guard," p. 79.

21. F. Christopher Arterton, "Campaign '92: Strategies and Tactics of the Candidates," in *The Election of 1992,* edited by Gerald M. Pomper (Chatham, NJ: Chatham House, 1993), p. 99.

22. Herbert F. Weisberg, with David C. Kimball, "The 1992 Presidential Election: Party Identification and Beyond," paper presented at the annual meeting of the American Political Science Association, Washington, DC, September 1993. Martin P. Wattenberg, however, interprets the same NES like/dislike responses much differently than does Weisberg. According to Wattenberg, "the open-ended like/dislike responses show that Clinton had the least favorable personal image of any winning candidate since the time series began in 1952." According to Wattenberg, "personal characteristics provided a net advantage for Bush" despite the decline in the rating of the president's competence. See Wattenberg, "How Clinton Won and Dukakis Lost: Candidates as Dynamic Factors in U.S. Presidential Elections," paper presented at the annual meeting of the American Political Science Association, Washington, DC, September 2–3, 1993. Also see Arthur H. Miller, "Economic, Character, and Social Issues in the 1992 Presidential Election," *American Behavioral Scientist* 37 (November 1993): 321–22.

23. Kathleen A. Frankovic, "Public Opinion in the 1992 Campaign," in *The Election of 1992,* edited by Gerald M. Pomper (Chatham, NJ: Chatham House, 1993), pp. 121 and 130.

24. Hart's polling figures were cited by Gregory Markus in his presentation to the Michigan Conference of Political Scientists, Ann Arbor, MI, October 30, 1992.

25. Kathleen A. Frankovic, "Public Opinion in the 1992 Campaign, in *The Election of 1992,* edited by Gerald M. Pomper (Chatham, NJ: Chatham House, 1993), p. 113.

26. Weisberg and Kimball, "The 1992 Presidential Election: Party Identification and Beyond."

27. The statistical breakdown of Clinton's 1992 vote is obtained from William Crotty, "Introduction: A Most Unusual Election," in *America's Choice: The Election of 1992,* edited by William Crotty (Guilford, CT: Dushkin Publishing, 1993), pp. 3 and 14, and Ladd, "The 1992 Vote for Clinton: Another Brittle Mandate?" p. 3. On union family voters, see Paul R. Abramson, John H. Aldrich, and David W. Rohde, *Change and Continuity in the 1992 Election:* (Washington, DC: CQ Press, 1994), pp. 129 and 323.

28. Ladd, "The 1992 Vote for President Clinton: Another Brittle Mandate?" pp. 2–3. For a discussion of the problems that a Clinton-led Democratic party faces in winning the votes of white southerners, see Nicol C. Rae, *Southern Democrats* (New York: Oxford U. Press, 1994), pp. 146–59.

29. Wattenberg, "How Clinton Won and Dukakis Lost."

30. This analysis of younger voters in 1992 is based on Gregory Markus's presentation to the Michigan Conference of Political Scientists, October 30, 1992, and Seymour Martin Lipset, "The Significance of the 1992 Election," *PS: Political Science and Politics* (March 1993): 13.

31. Walter J. Stone, "Asymmetries in the Electoral Bases of Representation, Nomination Politics, and Partisan Change," in *New Perspectives on American*

Politics, edited by Lawrence C. Dodd and Calvin Jillson (Washington, DC: CQ Press, 1994), p. 112.

32. Stephen D. Johnson, Joseph B. Tamney, and Ronald Burton, "Family Values Versus Economy Evaluations in the 1992 Presidential Election," paper presented at the annual meeting of the American Political Science Association, Washington, DC, September 2–5, 1993.

33. Gerald M. Pomper, "The Presidential Election," in *The Election of 1992,* edited by Pomper (Chatham, NJ: Chatham House, 1993), p. 150.

34. Weisberg and Kimball, "The 1992 Presidential Election: Party Identification and Beyond;" Wattenberg, "How Clinton Won and Dukakis Lost." Miller, "Economic, Character, and Social Issues in the 1992 Presidential Election," p. 324, similarly argues that the Republican emphasis on social issues "backfired" as the public came to see the party "as taking unacceptably extreme positions on a number of these issues."

35. Bill Hamilton and Wally Mealiea, "Perotistas: Who Are These People, Anyway?" *Campaigns and Elections* (August 1993): 21–22.

36. Martin P. Wattenberg, *The Decline of American Political Parties, 1952–1992* (Cambridge, MA: Harvard U. Press, 1994), Chapter 10.

37. Ronald B. Rapoport, Walter J. Stone, Lonna Rae Atkeson, James A. McCann, Randall W. Partin, and David W. Ungemah, "Activists and Voters in the 1992 Perot Campaign: A Preliminary Report," paper presented at the annual meeting of the American Political Science Association, Washington, DC, September 2–5, 1993.

38. Ladd, "The 1992 Vote for President Clinton: Another Brittle Mandate?" p. 25.

39. Weisberg and Kimball, "The 1992 Presidential Election: Party Identification and Beyond."

40. Rapoport et al., "Activists and Voters in the 1992 Perot Campaign."

41. Ceaser and Busch, *Upside Down and Inside Out,* p. 122.

42. Ibid., p. 7.

43. Wattenberg, "How Clinton Won and Dukakis Lost."

44. Jo Freeman, "Feminism vs. Family Values: Women at the 1992 Democratic and Republican Conventions," *PS: Political Science and Politics* (March 1993): 21.

45. Maisel, "The Platform-Writing Process: Candidate-Centered Platforms in 1992," pp. 671–98.

46. Freeman, "Feminism vs. Family Values: Women at the 1992 Democratic and Republican Conventions,", p. 22.

47. Ibid.

48. Ibid., p. 23.

49. For further discussion of the figures reported in this and the following paragraph, see Ladd, "The 1992 Vote for President Clinton: Another Brittle Mandate?" pp. 5–7. The patterns that Ladd reports are confirmed by Mary E. Bendyna and Celinda C. Lake, "Gender and Voting in the 1992 Election," in *The Year of the Woman: Myths and Realities,* edited by Elizabeth Adell Cook, Sue Thomas, and Clyde Wilcox (Boulder, CO: Westview, 1994), pp. 243–47. Also see Janet K. Boles, "The Year of the Woman," in *America's Choice: The Election of 1992,* edited by William Crotty (Guilford, CT: Dushkin Publishing, 1993), p. 118.

50. Ladd, "The 1992 Vote for President Clinton: Another Brittle Mandate?" pp. 5–7; Weisberg and Kimball, "The 1992 Presidential Election: Party Iden-

tification and Beyond." For further discussion of the "marital gap," see Herbert F. Weisberg, "The Demographics of a New Voting Gap: Marital Differences in American Voting," *Public Opinion Quarterly* 51 (1987): 335–43.

51. Edward G. Carmines, "Political Issues, Party Alignments, Spatial Models, and the Post–New Deal Party System," in *New Perspectives on American Politics*, edited by Lawrence C. Dodd and Calvin Jillson (Washington, DC: CQ Press, 1994), pp. 93–94.

52. Boles, "The Year of the Woman," p. 118.

53. Ladd, "The 1992 Vote for President Clinton: Another Brittle Mandate?" pp. 5–6.

54. Freeman, "Feminism vs. Family Values: Women at the 1992 Democratic and Republican Conventions," p. 27. Also see the general discussion provided by Linda Witt, Karen M. Paget, and Glenna Matthews, *Running as a Woman: Gender and Power in American Politics* (New York: Free Press, 1994).

55. William Julius Wilson, "The Right Message," *The New York Times*, March 17, 1992.

56. Wattenberg, "How Clinton Won and Dukakis Lost."

57. Miller, "Economic, Character, and Social Issues in the 1992 Presidential Election," pp. 318–21.

58. Abramson, Aldrich, and Rohde, *Change and Continuity in the 1992 Elections* pp. 175–220.

Chapter 12. The Future of American Politics

1. See, for instance Kathleen Hall Jamieson, *Dirty Politics: Deception, Distraction, and Democracy* (New York: Oxford U. Press, 1992), and F. Christopher Arterton, "The Persuasive Art in Politics: The Role of Paid Advertising in Presidential Campaigns," in *Under the Watchful Eye: Managing Presidential Campaigns in the Television Era,* ed. Mathew D. McCubbins (Washington, DC: CQ Press, 1992).

2. Thomas E. Patterson and Robert D. McClure, *The Unseeing Eye: The Myth of Television Power in National Elections* (New York: Paragon Books, 1976), p. 103.

3. Ibid., pp. 102–3

4. Ibid., p. 108

5. Lynda Lee Kaid, "Political Advertising in The 1992 Campaign," in *The 1992 Presidential Campaign: A Communication Perspective,* ed. Robert E. Denton, Jr. (Westport, CT: Praeger, 1994), pp. 113–21.

6. Richard Joslyn, *Mass Media and Elections* (Reading MA: Addison-Wesley, 1984), p. 199.

7. Richard Joslyn, "Political Advertising and the Meaning of Elections," in *New Perspectives on Political Advertising*, eds. Lynda Lee Kaid, Dan Nimmo, and Keith R. Sanders (Carbondale, IL: Southern Illinois U. Press, 1986), pp. 139–83.

8. Ibid., p. 174.

9. Ibid., p. 175.

10. Samuel L. Popkin, *The Reasoning Voter* (Chicago U. of Chicago Press 1991), p. 6.

11. Ibid.

12. Ibid., pp. 30 and 99.

13. Martin P. Wattenberg, *The Rise of Candidate-Centered Politics* (Cambridge, MA: Harvard U. Press, 1991), pp. 121–23.

14. Alexander Heard, *Made in America: Improving the Nomination and Election of Presidents* (New York: HarperCollins, 1991), pp. 59–63; Leslie A. Tucker and David J. Heller, "Putting Ethics Into Practice," *Campaigns and Elections* 7 (March–April 1987): 42–46; and, Karen S. Johnson-Cartee and Gary A. Copeland, *Negative Political Advertising* (Hillsdale, NJ: Lawrence Erlbaum Assoc., 1991), p. 267.

15. Heard, *Made in America,* p. 66.

16. Johnson-Cartee and Copeland, *Negative Political Advertising,* p. 269.

17. See Jamieson, *Dirty Politics,* pp. 262–65, for a more detailed discussion of the press's and public's reaction to this Buchanan ad.

18. Kathleen Hall Jamieson, *Packaging the Presidency* (New York: Oxford U. Press, 1984), p. 449, observes: "The difficulty in relying on news to correct distortions in advertising is, of course, that comparatively few people consume news while many are exposed to ads."

19. Jamieson has done extensive work on the unspoken and often misleading inferences contained in political ads. In *Packaging the Presidency,* p. 449, she complains about "[p]olitical argument by visual association." Her more recent work deals with the manipulation of picture quality (the use of freeze frames, different shadings, etc.) and the audio track (i.e., playing with tonal quality) to affect viewer response. While news reporters are likely to criticize an ad for a misstatement of facts, they are less likely to seize upon these more subtle video and audio distortions.

20. The story of the FCPC, its potential, and limits is told by Tucker and Heller, "Putting Ethics Into Practice," pp. 44–45. See note 14 above.

21. Kathleen Hall Jamieson has made this argument. See David S. Broder, "Who Should Play Cop for Campaign Ads?" *Washington Post National Weekly Edition,* February 13–19, 1989, p. 9.

22. Paul Taylor, *See How They Run: Electing a President in an Age of Mediaocracy* (New York: Knopf, 1990), pp. 268–80.

23. Thomas E. Patterson, *Out of Order* (New York: Knopf, 1993), pp. 234–38.

24. Jamieson, *Dirty Politics,* pp. 260–61.

25. Ibid., p. 261.

26. Johnson-Cartee and Copeland, *Negative Political Advertising,* p. 217.

27. Popkin, *The Reasoning Voter,* p. 40. Also, see p. 235.

28. Ibid., pp. 235–36.

29. Ibid., p. 236.

30. Angus Campbell, "A Classification of Presidential Elections," in *Elections and the Political Order,* eds. Angus Campbell, Philip E. Converse, Warren E. Miller, and Donald E. Stokes (New York: John Wiley & Sons, 1966), pp. 69–79.

31. Everett Carll Ladd, "The 1992 Vote for President Clinton: Another Brittle Mandate?" *Political Science Quarter* 108 (1993): 2.

32. Everett C. Ladd, "Like Waiting for Godot: The Uselessness of Realignment for Understanding Change in Contemporary American Politics," *Polity* 22 (Spring 1990): 520–21. For a more detailed discussion of the changes in voting alignments that resulted from America's transition from industrial to postindustrial society, see Everett Carll Ladd, Jr., with Charles Hadley, *Transformations of the American Party System,* rev. ed. (New York: W.W. Norton, 1978), pp. 181–388. A somewhat different interpretation is presented by Walter Dean Burnham, "Critical Realignment: Dead or Alive?" in *The End*

of Realignment: Interpreting American Electoral Eras, ed. Byron E. Shafer (Madison, WI: U. of Wisconsin Press, 1991), pp. 115–117, who argues that a realignment to a "permanent campaign" took place in 1968–72.

33. Everett Carll Ladd, "On Mandates, Realignments, and the 1984 Presidential Election," *Political Science Quarterly* 100 (Spring 1985): 12–13.
34. Ladd, "The 1992 Vote for President Clinton," pp. 1–2.
35. *Wall Street Journal,* November 27, 1992, cited in Ladd, "The 1992 Vote for President Clinton," p. 3.
36. Ladd, "The 1992 Vote for President Clinton," p. 27; Jerome M. Mileur, "The General Election Campaign: Strategy and Support," in *America's Choice: The Election of 1992,* ed. William Crotty (Guilford, CT: Dushkin Publ. Group, 1993), p. 60; and, Peter F. Nardulli and Jon K. Dalager, "The Presidential Election of 1992 in Historical Perspective," also in *America's Choice: The Election of 1992,* p. 163.
37. Ladd, "The 1992 Vote for President Clinton," pp. 1–2. For a debate over whether or not the concept of "realignment" still provides a useful guide for understanding electoral change in the contemporary era, see Byron E. Shafer, ed., *The End of Realignment? Interpreting American Electoral Eras* (Madison, WI: University of Wisconsin Press, 1991).
38. Ibid., pp. 3–4.
39. Ibid., p. 4.
40. Ibid., pp. 5–7; Janet K. Boles, "The Year of the Woman," in *America's Choice: The Election of 1992,* ed. William Crotty (Guilford, CT: Dushkin Publ. Group, 1993), p. 118.
41. Ladd, "The 1992 Vote for President Clinton," pp. 6–7.
42. The role that a highly educated "intelligentsia" plays in post-industrial society in disrupting the established upper-class/lower-class voting alignment of the New Deal era is described by Everett Carll Ladd, Jr., with Charles D. Hadley, *Transformations of the American Party System,* 2nd ed. (New York: W.W. Norton, 1978), pp. 185–91.
43. Ladd, "The 1992 Vote for President Clinton," pp. 8–11.
44. Mileur, "The General Election Campaign," pp. 51–54.
45. According to Walter Dean Burnham, *Critical Elections and the Mainsprings of American Politics* (New York: W.W. Norton, 1970), pp. 7–8 and 27–31, abnormally high voter intensity, increased voter turnout, and the appearance of third parties are features of an ideal type of realignment sequence.
46. Steve Mitchell, "Should Perot Run for President as a Republican? This Republican Says Yes," *Campaigns and Elections* (August 1993): 26.
47. Frank B. Feigert, "The Ross Perot Candidacy and Its Significance," in *America's Choice: The Election of 1992,* ed. William Crotty (Guilford, CT: Dushkin Publ. Group, 1993), p. 87.
48. Ladd, "The 1992 Vote for President Clinton," pp. 22–23. Also see, Feigert, "The Ross Perot Candidacy and Its Significance," p. 85.
49. Bill Hamilton and Wally Mealiea, "Perotistas: Who Are These People, Anyway?" *Campaigns and Elections* (August 1993), pp. 21–22.
50. Mitchell, "Should Perot Run for President as a Republican?" pp. 25–26.
51. E.J. Dionne, Jr., "Can a Partisan Be Bipartisan? Party Politics in the Bush Administration," in *The Parties Respond: Changes in the American Party System,* ed. L. Sandy Maisel (Boulder, CO: Westview Press, 1990), p. 294.
52. Ibid.
53. William Crotty, "Who Needs Two Republican Parties?" in *The Democrats*

Must Lead, eds. James MacGregor Burns, William Crotty, Lois Lovelace Duke, and Lawrence D. Longley (Boulder, CO: Westview Press, 1992), pp. 29–56. This argument is also forcefully expressed in the volume's articles by Burns, "The Democrats Must Lead—But How?," pp. 3–12, and Jerome M. Mileur, "Dump Dixie—West Is Best: The Geography of a Progressive Democracy," pp. 97–112. Also see Arthur Sanders, *Victory: How a Progressive Democratic Party Can Win and Govern* (Armonk, NY: M.E. Sharpe, 1992).

54. The importance of "inoculation" by a candidate in fending off an attack campaign is detailed by Michael Pfau and Henry C. Kenski, *Attack Politics: Strategy and Defense* (New York: Praeger, 1990).

55. Betty Glad, "What to Say and How to Say It?," pp. 97–112, and Lois Lovelace Duke, "Television, the 1992 Democratic Presidential Hopeful, and Electoral Success," pp. 133–48, both in *The Democrats Must Lead,* eds. James Mac-Gregor Burns et al.

56. Glad, "What to Say and How to Say It?" pp. 115–116; and Duke, "Television, the 1992 Democratic Presidential Hopeful, and Electoral Success," pp. 139–40.

57. Glad, "What to Say and How to Say It?" p. 123.

58. For examples of these arguments, see the following articles in Burns et al., *The Democrats Must Lead:* Charles V. Hamilton, "Minority Politics and 'Political Realities' in American Politics," pp. 149–57; Mary Lou Kendrigan, "Progressive Democrats and Support for Women's Issues," pp. 159–71; and, Richard Santillan and Carlos Munoz, Jr., "Latinos and the Democratic Party," pp. 173–84.

59. William Galston and Elaine Ciulla Kamarck, "The Politics of Evasion: Democrats and the Presidency," in *American Political Parties: A Reader,* ed. Eric M. Uslaner (Itasca, IL: F.E. Peacock Publishers, 1993), pp. 551–52.

60. Ibid., pp. 552–53.

61. Ibid., p. 554; Richard L. Berke, "Defections Among Men to G.O.P. Helped Ensure Rout of Democrats," *The New York Times,* November 11, 1994.

62. Galston and Kamarck, "The Politics of Evasion: Democrats and the Presidency," p. 547.

63. Wattenburg, *The Rise of Candidate-Centered Politics,* pp. 10–11.

64. John G. Stewart, *One Last Chance: The Democratic Party, 1974–76* (New York: Praeger, 1974), pp. 106–12. Also see Wattenberg, *The Rise of Candidate-Centered Politics,* pp. 107–9.

65. Kevin Phillips. *The Politics of Rich and Poor* (New York: Random House, 1990). Especially see the book's "Introduction" and pp. 3–52.

66. Ibid., esp. pp. 57, 78, and 84.

67. Ibid., p. 201. Also see pp. 190–94.

68. Robert Cameron Mitchell, "Public Opinion and the Green Lobby: Poised for the 1990s?" in *Environmental Policy in the 1990s: Toward a New Agenda* (Washington, DC: CQ Press, 1990), pp. 81–99.

69. Poll data from various 1989 and 1990 NBC News/*Wall Street Journal,* CBS News/*New York Times,* Gallup Organization, and Opinion Dynamics Corporation polls, presented by Everett Carll Ladd, *The American Polity: The People and Their Government* (New York: W.W. Norton, 1991), pp. 271–75.

70. C.B. Holman, "Go West, Young Democrat," *Polity* 22 (Winter 1989): 323–39. Also see Dan Carol and Julie Loughran, "The New Urban West," *Campaigns and Elections* (Oct./Nov. 1993): 41–42.

71. Earl Black and Merle Black, *The Vital South: How Presidents Are Elected* (Cambridge, MA: Harvard Univ. Press, 1992), especially Chapter 13.

72. Mileur, "The General Election Campaign: Strategy and Support," pp. 53 and 59.

73. GOP strategists Angela "Bay" Buchanan, Edward A. Goeas III, and Don Sipple discuss their different perspectives as to what path the GOP should take with regard to the party's strategy for the 1990s in "Republican Roundtable: Three GOP Experts Candidly Discuss the Party's Successes, Failings, and Chances," *Campaigns and Elections* (August 1993): 42–46.

74. Warren E. Miller, "The Electorate's View of Parties," in *The Parties Respond: Changes in the American Party System,* ed. L. Sandy Maisel (Boulder, CO: Westview Press, 1990), p. 111.

75. Ibid., pp. 111–114.

NAME INDEX

SUBJECT INDEX

PRESIDENTIAL CAMPAIGNS AND ELECTIONS

Editing and production supervision by John Beasley
Cover design by Willis Proudfoot
Composition by Point West, Inc.
Printed and bound by Braun-Brumfield, Inc.